VISUAL QUICKSTART GUIDE

CorelDRAW 9

FOR WINDOWS

Phyllis Davis

Visual QuickStart Guide
CorelDraw 9 for Windows
Phyllis Davis

Peachpit Press
1249 Eighth Street
Berkeley, CA 94710
510-524-2178
800-283-9444
510-524-2221 (fax)

Find us on the World Wide Web at: http://www.peachpit.com

Peachpit Press is a division of Addison Wesley Longman

Editor: Nancy Davis
Production Coordinator: Kate Reber
Interior design and production: Phyllis Davis
Cover design: The Visual Group

Notice of Rights

Notice of Liability

The information in this book is distributed on an "As Is" basis, without warranty. While every precaution has been take in the preparation of the book, neither the author nor Peachpit Press, shall have any liability to any person or entity with respect to any loss or damage caused or alleged to be caused directly or indirectly by the instructions contained in this book or by the computer software and hardware products described in it.

Trademarks

Visual QuickStart Guide is a registered trademark of Peachpit Press, a division of Addison Wesley Longman. Corel, CorelDRAW, Corel CAPTURE, Corel PHOTO-PAINT, Corel SCRIPT, and Corel SCRIPT Editor, Corel TEXTURE, and CorelTRACE, are registered trademarks of Corel Corporation or Corel Corporation Limited in Canada, the United States and/or other countries. Throughout this book trademarked names are used. Rather than put a trademark symbol in every occurrence of a trademarked name, we state that we are using the names only in an editorial fashion and to the benefit of the trademark owner with no intention of infringement of the trademark.

Disclaimer

The *CorelDRAW 9 for Windows: Visual QuickStart Guide* is not sponsored by or affiliated with Corel Corporation.

ISBN 0-201-35451-9

9 8 7 6 5 4 3

Printed and bound in the United States of America

This book is dedicated to my best friend,

HAROLD

Heartfelt thanks to

Nancy Davis, the best editor in the world
and a sweet friend.

and

Matt Wagner for his continued trust in me.
Without him, this book would have never
happened.

and

Kate Reber whose wise suggestions about
layout and production helped make this book
look so good.

Table of Contents

Table of Contents

Table of Contents

The Basics

Welcome to the amazing and fun world of CorelDraw 9! I am a professional user and big fan of CorelDraw, and have been for many years. This latest version is really great!

My purpose in writing this book is to share my experience as a professional who has worked extensively with CorelDraw. In keeping with the *Visual QuickStart Guide* format, my aim is to present easy, step-by-step directions with illustrations to take the mystery out of graphic design.

CorelDraw 9 offers a complete set of tools for creating many kinds of drawings and multi-page documents, from birthday cards, brochures, newsletters, and logos to garden designs and World Wide Web pages and sites. This program has incredible power and loads of features, all incorporated into a newly-designed interface. As sophisticated as it is, it's also easy to use. You can run with it as far as you please. With CorelDraw 9 and your imagination, the sky's the limit!

If you are new to CorelDraw 9, the program may seem a bit dense at first because it is so rich in features. But, if you take it one step at a time—putting one foot in front of the other down the road of graphic design—you'll be creating beautiful drawings in no time. For those of you who are acquainted with previous versions of CorelDraw, use this book as a guide to new features and techniques, and as a handy reference.

WHAT IS CORELDRAW 9?

CorelDraw 9 is an *object-oriented* drawing program. Objects are created using drawing tools that make shapes defined by mathematical formulas. A CorelDraw object has properties that can be changed without affecting the way it looks close up or far away. You can move an object easily without affecting other objects around it.

Computer imaging programs are either based on *objects* or *bitmap* images. Other terms for object are *vector* or *drawing*; another term for bitmap is *raster*.

As with Windows, each object has properties. Hence, a vector object has properties that define it, such as color, shape, and size. A vector object appears the same on the screen with smooth lines and continuous colors, whether you are looking at it from far away or up close. Vector drawings are *resolution independent*, meaning that the printout quality depends only on the resolution of the printer.

Bitmap images are made up of tiny dots called *pixels* that are arranged and colored to form a pattern. The shape and color of a bitmap image appear smooth from a distance, but if you were to view a bitmap image close up, you would see tiny individual squares. Bitmap images depend on the resolution at which they are saved for printout quality.

In addition to its extensive and powerful vector drawing tools, CorelDraw 9 includes drawing management tools, full-fledged writing tools, expanded bitmap capabilities, a user-friendly help system, and more than 40,000 pieces of clipart, and over 1,400 fonts.

WHAT'S NEW IN CORELDRAW 9?

There are so many new features that a complete list would be huge. Below are some of the new and enhanced features:

- **Rectangle Tool**—With the enhanced rectangle tool, you can now individually round the corners of a rectangle.
- **Interactive Mesh Fill Tool**—with this tool, you can quickly fill an object with a blended rainbow of colors.
- **Interactive Contour Tool**—using this tool, you can quickly add contours inside or outside of an object.
- **Eyedropper and Paintbucket Tools**—the Eyedropper Tool lets you pick up a color from any object. The Paintbucket Tool lets you drop that color onto any object.
- **Digital Camera support**—a new interface for acquiring images from over 120 models of digital cameras lets you bring your pictures into CorelDraw and enhance them
- **Mini Preview**—a new feature of the Print dialog box, the Mini Preview gives you a quick look at the pages to be printed.

How does CorelDraw 9 work?

CorelDraw documents are made up of separate elements called *objects*. An object's edge is called a *path*. Paths can be *closed* or *open*. An object with a closed path can be filled with color, whereas an object with an open path cannot. The path of an object passes through *nodes* that shape the path.

Some CorelDraw tools automatically create closed path objects. For instance, the Ellipse Tool makes various sized ovals and circles, the Rectangle Tool makes rectangles and squares, and the Polygon Tool makes polygons with any number of sides.

Other tools create closed or open path objects, depending on how they are used. The Freehand Tool can be used to draw a line (an open path) or a squiggly circle (a closed path). The Bézier Tool can be used to draw smooth curving lines, or closed, curvy shapes.

If you want to modify an object, you must first tell the program which object to modify by *selecting* it. When an object is selected, *handles* appear in a rectangular formation around the object.

Objects can be modified using a variety of features including menu commands, dialog boxes, *dockers*, and tools. For instance, an object's path can be shaped by moving its nodes and *control points* with the Shape Tool. An object can be *uniformly filled* with a *spot* or *process* color with one click using the Color Palette. Objects can also be filled with *patterns, textures*, and *fountain fills* with the Interactive Fill Tool. Objects can be *rotated*, *skewed*, *scaled*, and *mirrored* using their handles and the Pick Tool. With the Interactive Blend Tool you can blend one object into another, creating a morph.

CorelDraw lets you be creative with text. Text can be either *artistic* or *paragraph* and can float free on the page as a *text object*, follow the path of an object, or use an object as a container to shape it. Text can also be *converted to curves*, changing it to a graphical object whose outline can be modified like any other object's outline.

You can change the view of a drawing to make editing easier. You can *zoom in* to get a close up look and work with small details and *zoom out* to see the drawing as a whole. You can also use the Pan Tool to move the drawing in the drawing window.

To speed up screen redraw and help with editing, a document can be viewed in *simple wireframe, wireframe*, or *draft* mode. The drawing can also be seen in *enhanced* mode or *Full-Screen Preview*.

You can use precision tools such as *guidelines*, *grids*, *rulers*, and the *Align and Distribute* dialog box to make your drawings exact.

When you finish a drawing, your file can be *printed* or *saved to file* for *high resolution output* or as *separations*. You can see what the printed document will look like in *Print Preview mode*.

THE CORELDRAW 9 SCREEN (FIGURE 1)

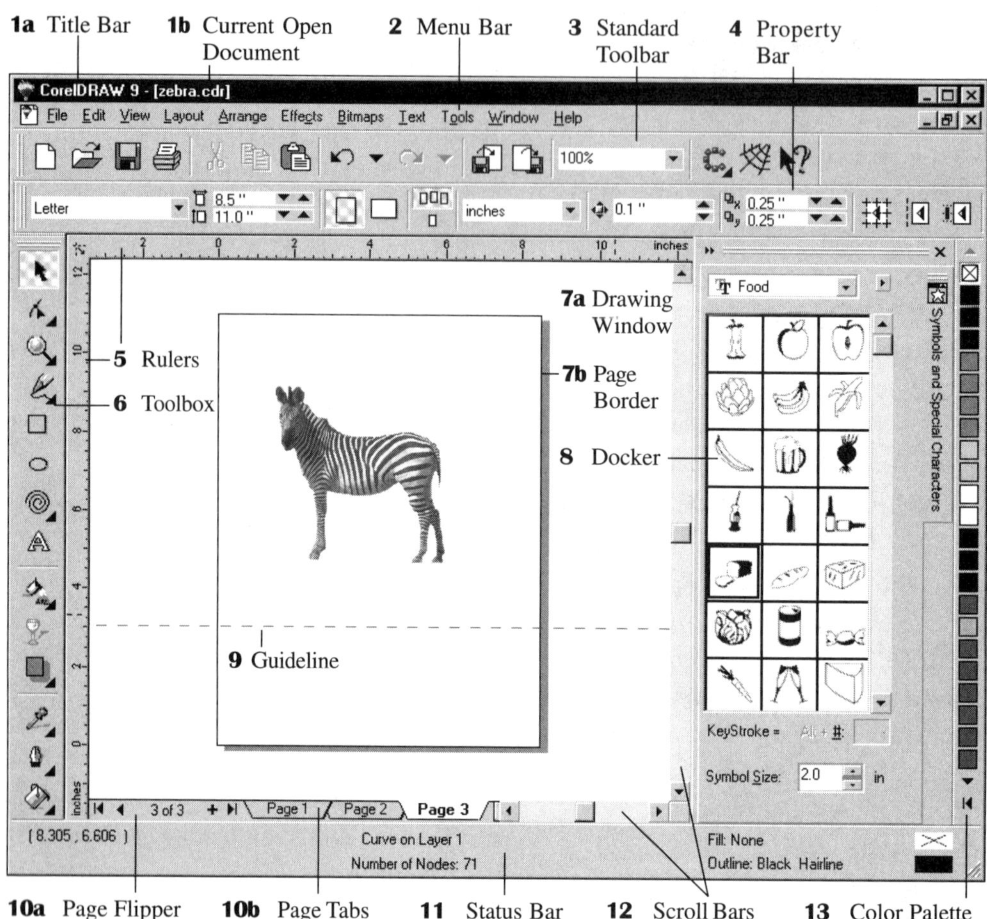

KEY TO THE CORELDRAW 9 SCREEN

1a, b *Title Bar*
Displays the program name and current document name.

2 *Menu Bar*
Click any menu title to access commands, fly-outs, and dialog boxes.

3 *Standard Toolbar*
One of ten toolbars, the Standard Toolbar buttons give you quick access to standard Windows commands such as New, Open, Save, Cut, Copy, Paste, and Print. It also includes several CorelDraw 9 commands, including Redo, Import, Export, and Zoom.

4 *Property Bar*
The Property Bar is a is a *context-sensitive* toolbar. Buttons and drop-down lists change dynamically, depending upon what is selected. This gives you easy access to the most important commands associated with the selected tool or item.

5 *Rulers*
The mouse pointer's current position is indicated with marks on the vertical and horizontal rulers. Rulers can be moved to where you need them and used to accurately size objects. The measurement unit they display can be changed to virtually any system.

6 *Toolbox*
One of the ten toolbars, the Toolbox contains forty-two drawing and editing tools. As with every toolbar, you can drag it out onto the drawing window, making it float, or dock it along any edge of the screen, as shown here.

7a, b *Drawing Window* and *Page Border*
You can draw anywhere you want in the drawing window, but anything outside the page border will not be printed.

8 *Dockers*
Dockers are like power tools on your desktop. There are 25 dockers, each geared to a specific command or purpose, such as extruding, scaling, contouring, managing objects, and checking for HTML conflicts.

9 *Guidelines*
A non-printing guide that comes in three flavors—horizontal, vertical, and angled. Guidelines are used for aligning objects. Press and drag from either ruler to create guidelines.

10a, b *Page Flipper* and *Page Tabs*
The page flipper is used to add pages to a document, and to move to another page, or to the beginning or end of a document. The page tabs give quick access to nearby pages.

11 *Status Bar*
Displays the position of the mouse pointer, and detailed object information, such as size, fill color, outline width, and position. Click the right mouse button on the Status Bar to access a pop-up menu you can use to select other information options.

12 *Scroll Bars*
Scroll Bars are used to navigate around the drawing window. If you click the down arrow on the vertical scroll bar, the drawing page will move up. If you click the right arrow on the horizontal scroll bar, the page will move left.

13 *Color Palette*
The Color Palette is used to fill and outline your objects with color. There are many defined color systems that can be loaded into the Color Palette, including Pantone and Trumatch, and two palettes designed especially for World Wide Web browsers.

CORELDRAW 9 CONTROLS

Figures 2a–g show the controls you will use when working with CorelDraw 9 dialog boxes.

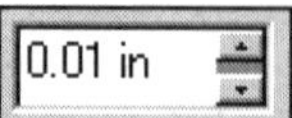

Figure 2a. *Text boxes and spin buttons. You can enter text or numbers in text boxes. Spin buttons are used to increase or decrease numbers. To increase a number, click the up arrow. To decrease a number, click the down arrow.*

Figure 2b. *Tab pages. Found in dialog boxes, tab pages give access to commands and are organized by category. Click a tab to move from one tab page to another.*

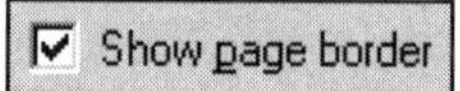

Figure 2c. *Check boxes. Click a check box to turn an option on or off. A check in the box indicates that the option is on.*

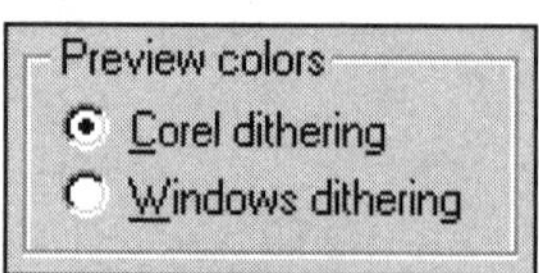

Figure 2d. *Option buttons. Option buttons are usually contained in an* area, *and you can select only one item from two or more options. Click the small circle to select an option. The selected option button has a black dot in it.*

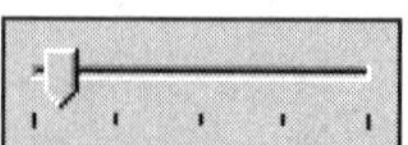

Figure 2e. *Sliders. Sliders let you increase or decrease a setting. To move the slider, position the mouse over the slider bar, press the left mouse button, and drag right to increase or left to decrease.*

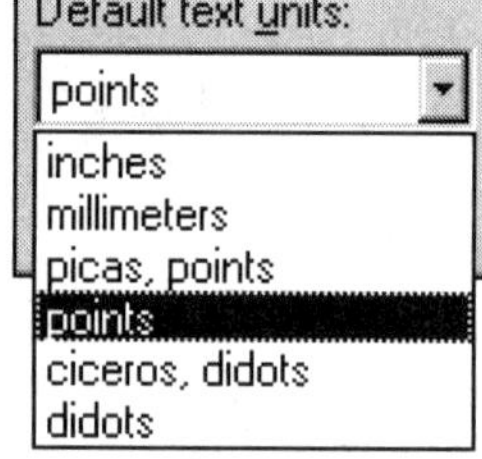

Figure 2f. *Drop-down lists. Drop-down lists present a selection of items from which to choose. To open the list, click the little arrow to the right of the list box. Some drop-down lists allow you to enter your text.*

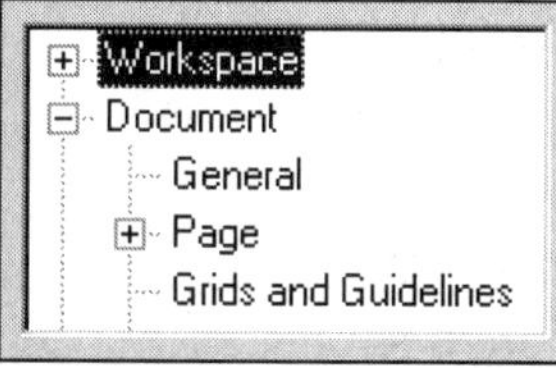

Figure 2g. *Tree view windows. Tree view windows present items in a hierarchical list. Click the plus sign to expand the list, then click the item to select and highlight it.*

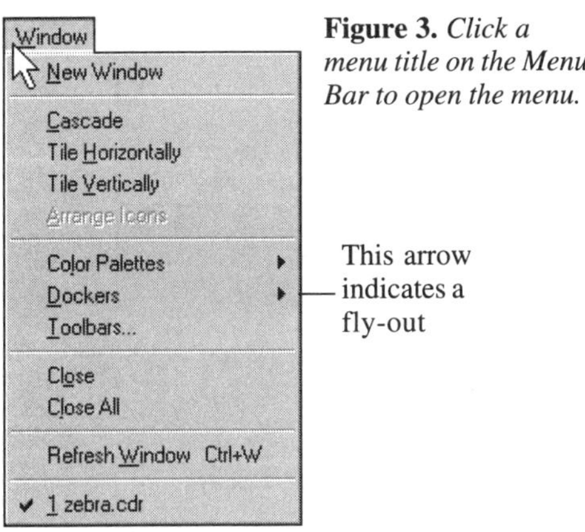

Figure 3. *Click a menu title on the Menu Bar to open the menu.*

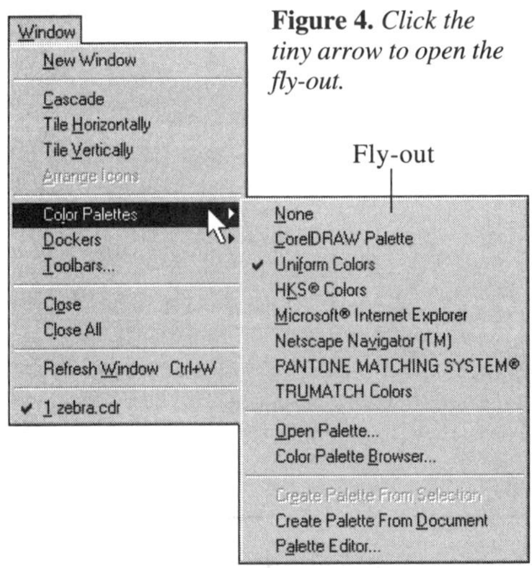

Figure 4. *Click the tiny arrow to open the fly-out.*

Menus

There are 11 menus available on the Menu Bar. These menus give access to commands, fly-outs (sub-menus that open off of main menus), and dialog boxes.

To open a menu and select an item:

1. Position the mouse pointer over a menu title and click. The menu will open (**Figure 3**). If you see a tiny arrow to the right of a menu item, it means that there is an available fly-out. To open the fly-out, click the tiny arrow (**Figure 4**).
2. Move the mouse down to highlight the item you want.
3. Click to select the item.

Tip:

- A menu item with an ellipsis (...) after it means that this item will open a dialog box.

Terms Used in This Book

- *Click* means to quickly press and release the left mouse button.
- *Double-click* means to quickly press and release the left mouse button twice.
- *Right click* means to quickly press and release the right mouse button.
- *Select* or *choose* means to use the mouse pointer to highlight a menu item and click.

Large Menus and Dialog Boxes

CorelDraw 9 menus and dialog boxes contain many commands and items to select. Consequently, some of them are quite large. Several of the figures in this *Visual QuickStart Guide* are too big to display in their entirety or become very small when sized to fit the page. In order to fit these large items, some menus have been shortened using a jagged edge (**Figure 5**). The menu item being selected is shown, but lower or middle menu items are removed to conserve space. In a large dialog box, a circle is drawn around the area under discussion (**Figure 6**).

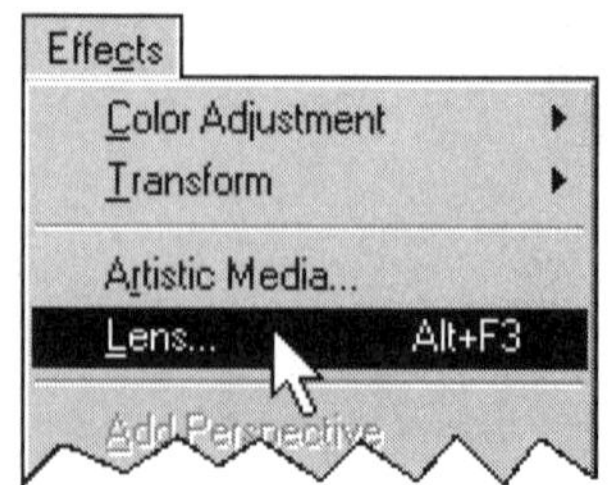

Figure 5. *Menus in some figures have been cropped using a jagged edge.*

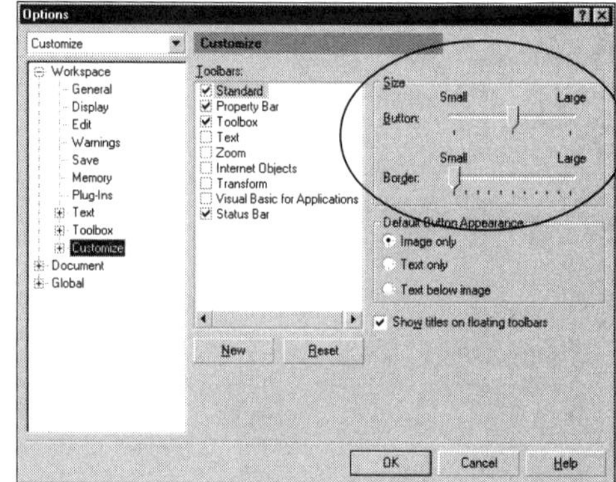

Figure 6. *A circle appears around the area under discussion in a large dialog box.*

Keyboard Shortcuts

Many menu commands have keyboard equivalents. Keyboard shortcuts (also called *hot keys*) always use the Ctrl, Shift, or Alt keys (or a combination of them) plus a letter or number key. Many times the letter is a mnemonic. For instance, the Print command uses the letter P.

As an example, the keyboard shortcut for the Save command is Ctrl+S.

To use the keyboard shortcut for the Save command:

1. Press and hold down the Ctrl key.
2. Press and release the S key.
3. Release the Ctrl key.

Tip:

- Many keyboard shortcuts are listed next to their corresponding commands on the menus.

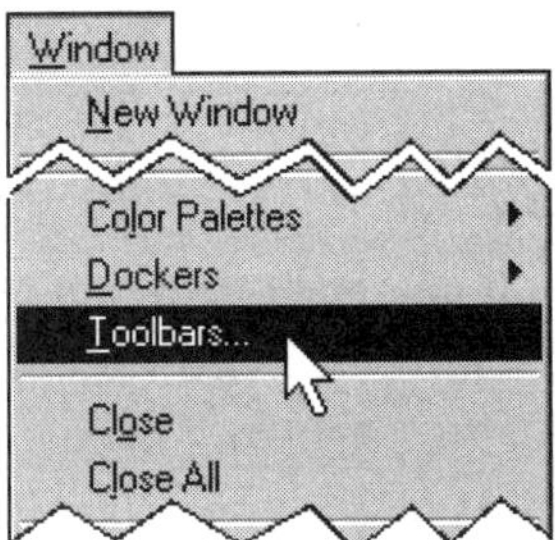

Figure 7. *Choose Toolbars from the Window menu.*

TOOLBARS

There are nine toolbars available in CorelDraw 9. They give access to commands and dialog boxes with just the click of a button. Three toolbars are available, by default, when you launch CorelDraw 9 for the first time. They are the Standard Toolbar, the Property Bar, and the Toolbox.

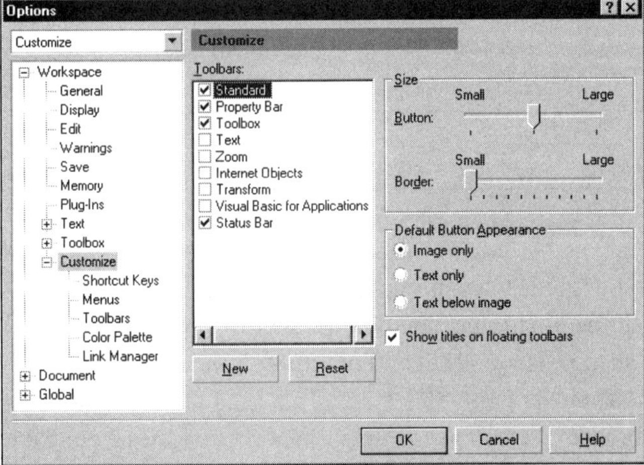

Figure 8. *Put checks in the check boxes next to the toolbars you want to have displayed, then click OK.*

To access the toolbars:

1. Choose Toolbars from the Window menu (**Figure 7**). The Options dialog box will open with Customize selected in the tree view window (**Figure 8**).
2. In the Toolbars list box, click the check boxes next to the toolbars you want to display.
3. Click OK. The toolbars you selected will appear.

Toolbars

TOOLBARS ON THE DESKTOP

All toolbars can be used *floating* or *docked*. An example of a docked toolbar is the Toolbox. In Figure 1 on page 4, the Toolbox is docked on the left side of the screen. To undock the Toolbox and make it float, position the mouse pointer over the double gray lines at the top of the Toolbox. Press the left mouse button and drag the Toolbox into the drawing window. To dock any toolbar, drag it to any edge of the screen—top, bottom, left, or right.

THE PROPERTY BAR

The Property Bar (**Figure 9**), located by default near the top of the screen below the Standard Toolbar, is a context-sensitive command bar. It displays different buttons and options depending on which tool or object is selected. For instance, when the Zoom Tool is selected, the Property Bar contains only zoom-related commands.

Figure 9. *The Property Bar is context-sensitive. If nothing is selected, it displays tools that pertain to the overall document such as page size and orientation.*

THE STATUS BAR

The Status Bar (**Figure 10**) is your guide to what's happening in the drawing window. It gives you information about the position of the pointer and the properties of the selected object, including its shape, size, and fill and outline colors. The Status Bar can be one or two lines high. You can change its size by clicking the right mouse button on the bar and selecting Size, then choosing One Line or Two Lines from the fly-out (**Figure 11**). For a complete discussion about customizing the Status Bar, turn to pages 130–131.

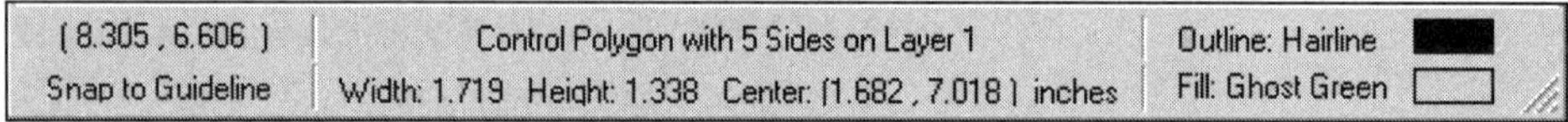

Figure 10. *The Status Bar shows you what's happening and gives information about what's selected.*

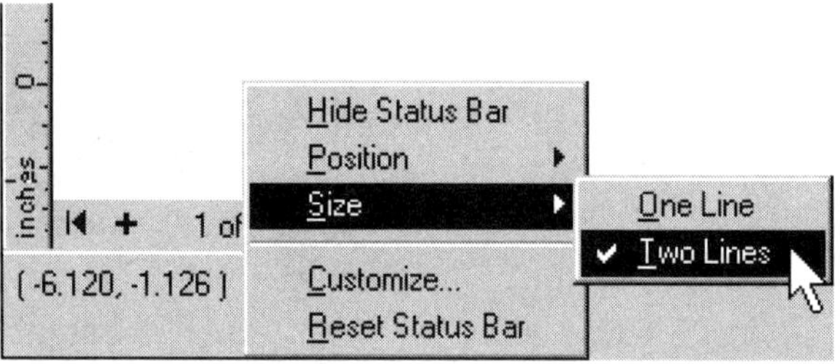

Figure 11. *If you right mouse click on the Status Bar, you can change the information that is being shown.*

THE TOOLBOX

The Toolbox (**Figure 12**) contains 46 tools used for creating and editing objects. Many of the tools are located on fly-outs, accessed by clicking the tiny black arrow at the lower-right corner of the tool button. The letters to the right of the Toolbox in Figure 12 indicate the corresponding fly-out (**Figures 13a–i**).

Figure 12. *The CorelDraw 9 Toolbox.*

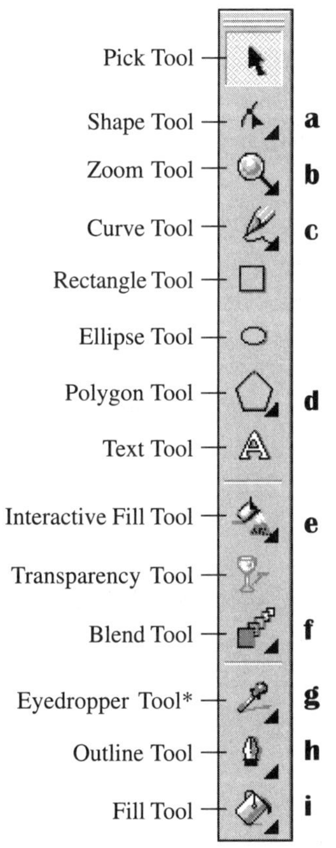

* New CorelDraw 9 tools.

Figures 13a–g. *Toolbox fly-out menus.*

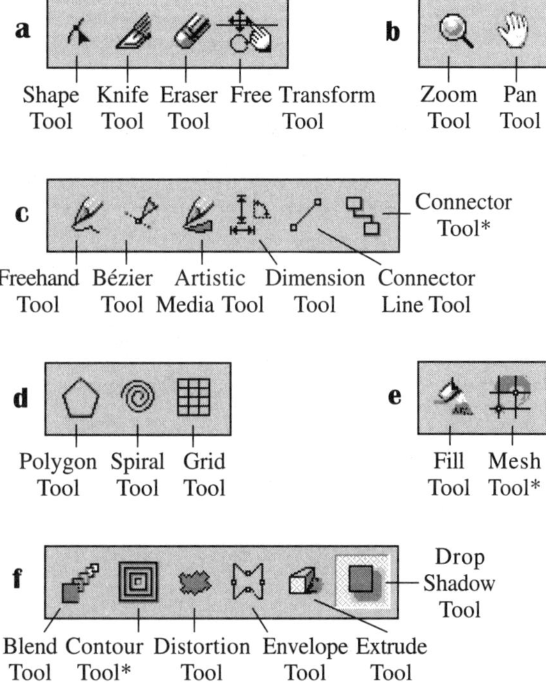

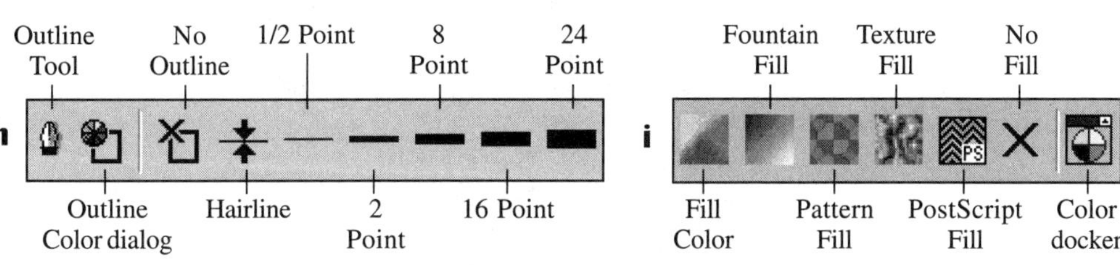

The Toolbox

THE ZOOM TOOL

The Zoom Tool is used for magnifying or reducing the view of a drawing. You can zoom in to see detail or zoom out to view an entire drawing. The Property Bar works in concert with the Zoom Tool (**Figure 14**). When the Zoom Tool is selected the Property Bar displays zoom-specific buttons. You can use it to toggle between the Zoom and Pan Tools.

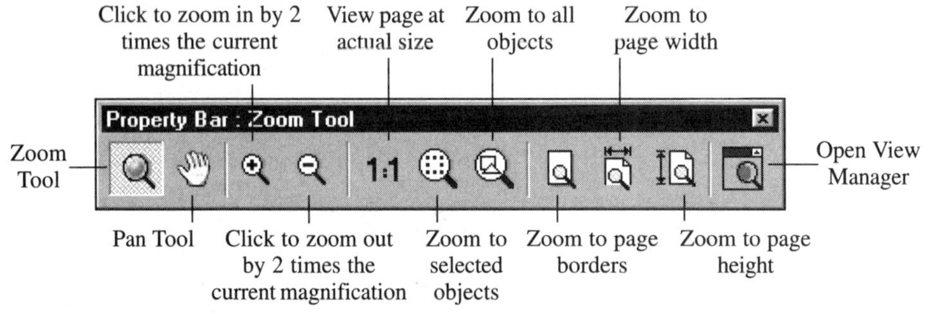

Figure 14. *The Property Bar shows zoom-related buttons when the Zoom Tool is selected.*

To zoom in using the Zoom Tool:

1. Select the Zoom Tool from the Toolbox (**Figure 15**).
2. Position the mouse over the area you want to zoom in on.
3. Click the left mouse button. The view will zoom in 2 times the magnification.

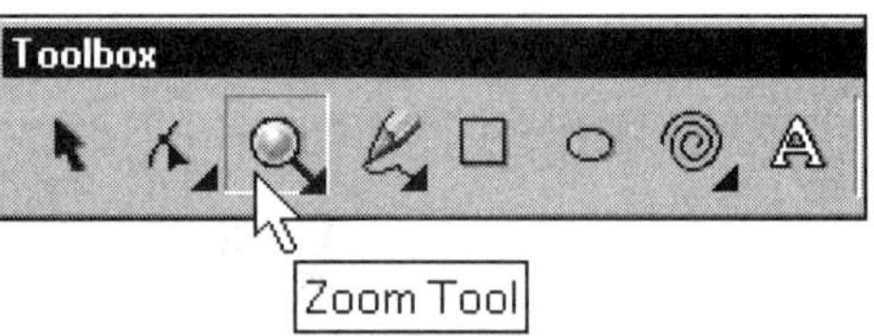

Figure 15. *Click the Zoom Tool in the Toolbox to select it. The mouse pointer will change to a magnifying glass with a plus on the lens.*

Tip:

- Zooming has no effect on the drawing, only your view of it.

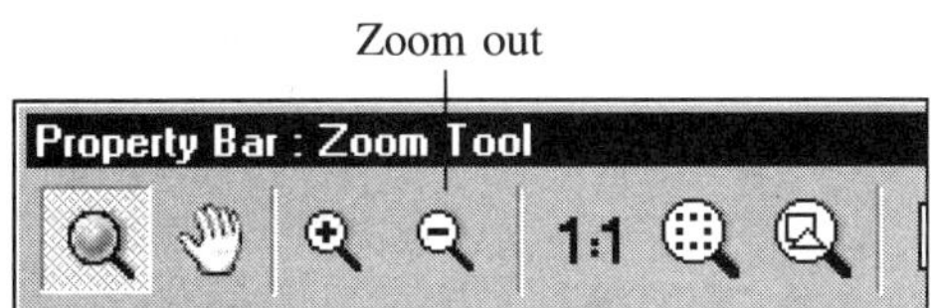

Figure 16. *Click the Zoom Out button on the Property Bar.*

To zoom out using the Zoom Tool:

1. Select the Zoom Tool from the Toolbox (**Figure 15**).
2. Position the mouse over the area you want to zoom out on.
3. Right click. The view will zoom out.

or

1. Select the Zoom Tool from the Toolbox (**Figure 15**).
2. Click the Zoom Out button on the Property Bar (**Figure 16**).

Tips:

- To zoom to a selected object, press Shift+F2 on the keyboard.
- To zoom out to half the magnification, press F3 on the keyboard.

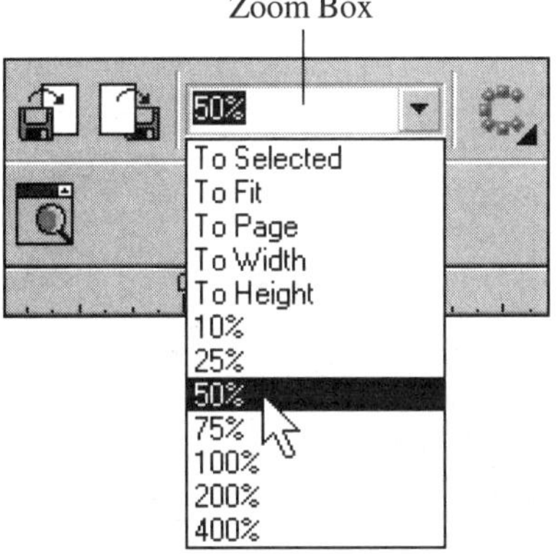

Figure 17. *Use the Zoom Box on the Standard Toolbar to zoom to preset magnifications.*

To zoom using the Standard Toolbar:

1. On the Standard Toolbar near the top of the screen, click the arrow on the Zoom Box to see all the preset magnifications (**Figure 17**).
2. Select a magnification. The view will zoom to that magnification.

Tip:

- To zoom to a specific magnification, type a number in the drop-down list box (**Figure 18**), then press Enter on the keyboard.

Figure 18. *Type a number in the Zoom Box, then press Enter on the keyboard to zoom to a specific magnification.*

Zoom Out; The Zoom Box

THE PAN TOOL

The Pan Tool is used to move a drawing within the drawing window.

To use the Pan Tool:

1. Click the small arrow at the bottom right of the Zoom Tool to access the fly-out (**Figure 19**).
2. Click the Pan Tool to select it. Notice that the Pan Tool takes the place of the Zoom Tool in the Toolbox when it is selected (**Figure 20**). The mouse pointer will change to a hand.
3. Position the Pan Tool over the drawing window (**Figure 21**).
4. Press the left mouse button and drag. The drawing will move within the drawing window (**Figure 22**).

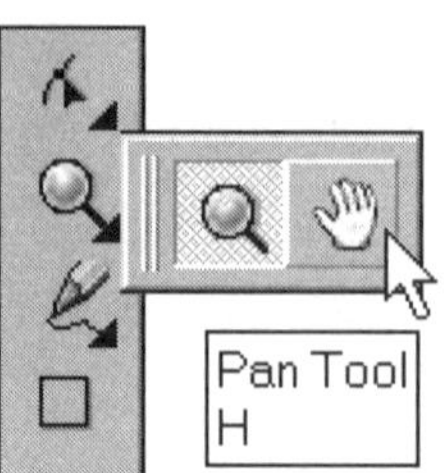

Figure 19. *To select the Pan Tool, click the small arrow at the bottom right of the Zoom Tool, then select it from the fly-out or press H on the keyboard.*

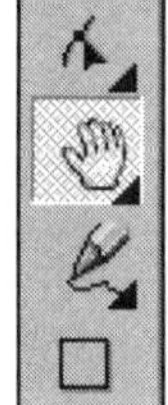

Figure 20. *Once you've selected the Pan Tool, it appears in the Toolbox. To get the Zoom Tool back in that position, just select it from the fly-out.*

Figure 21. *Position the Pan Tool over the drawing window.*

Figure 22. *Press the left mouse button and drag the Pan Tool hand to move the image.*

WHAT ARE *Special Projects?*

Throughout this book, you will see sections called "Special Projects." Special Projects take the techniques already covered in the book and show you how to put them together to create real-world projects. These projects—such as creating a heart, setting up a newsletter, and giving your drawings the illusion of motion—can easily be adapted for your own needs.

Viewing a Document

The View menu gives you commands for changing the *view quality*. View quality is the way a drawing is displayed in the drawing window. The five view qualities range from displaying only simple outlines to all outlines, complex fills, and bitmap images. They are as follows:

- **Simple Wireframe**—this view hides fills, extrusions, contours, and intermediate blend objects. It shows only simple outlines and monochromatic bitmaps.
- **Wireframe**—this view hides fills and displays monochromatic bitmaps, extrusions, contours, and intermediate blend objects.
- **Draft**—this view quality shows some fills and only low-resolution bitmaps.
- **Normal**—this is the default view. This view quality shows all fills, objects, and high-resolution bitmaps.
- **Enhanced**—this view uses *oversampling* to enhance the view quality.

In addition, you can view a drawing in Full-Screen Preview mode by pressing F9 on the keyboard.

Figure 23a. *Simple wireframe view.*

Figure 23a. *Wireframe view.*

Figure 23a. *Draft view.*

Figure 23a. *Normal view.*

Figure 23a. *Enhanced view.*

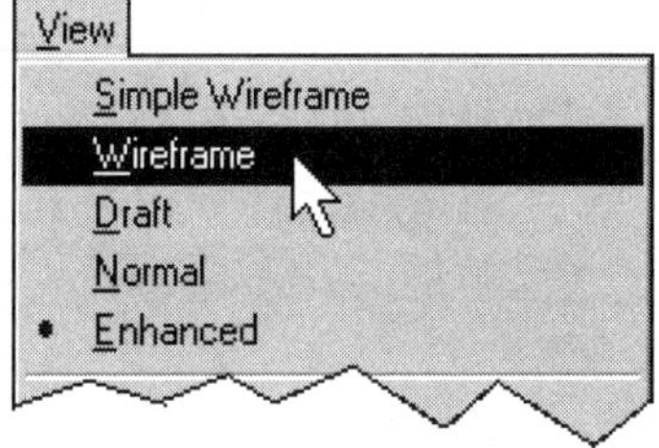

Figure 24. *Select the view quality that you want to use from the View menu.*

To change the view quality:

1. Open the View menu by clicking the menu title (**Figure 23**).
2. Select the view quality you want to use from the menu items.

DESKTOP POWER TOOLS: DOCKERS

Unlike most dialog boxes, dockers stay on the screen after changes are applied, letting you continue to make changes without having to open the docker again. When not using a docker, you can minimize it, leaving only the name tab visible. You can also undock them and work with them floating on the screen.

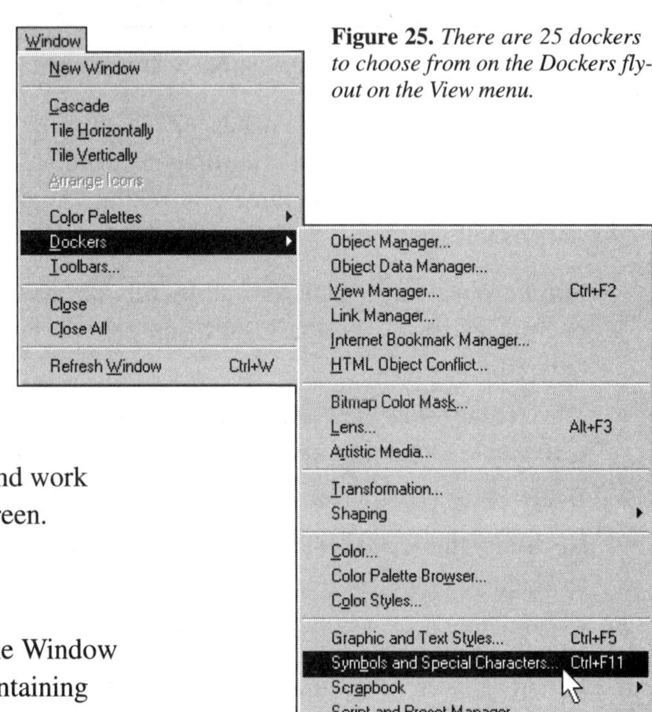

Figure 25. *There are 25 dockers to choose from on the Dockers fly-out on the View menu.*

To view a docker:

1. Choose Dockers from the Window menu. A large fly-out containing all the docker names appears (**Figure 25**).
2. Choose a name from the fly-out list. The docker will open (**Figure 26**).

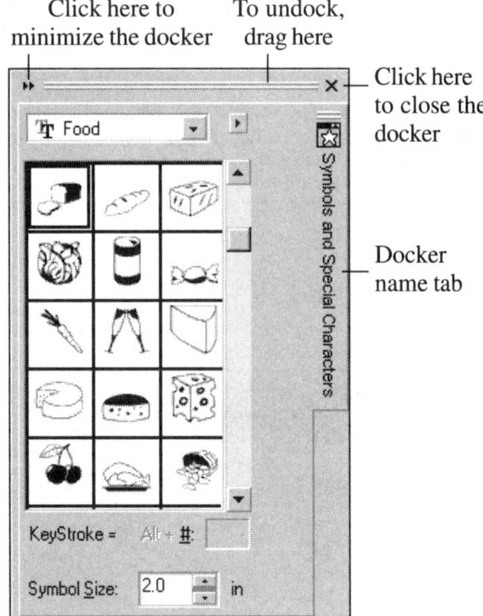

Figure 26. *A docker.*

Tips:

- You can have more than one docker open at one time. To switch from docker to docker, just click the name tab of the docker with which you want to work.
- Dockers can be docked at the right, left, top, or bottom of the drawing window.

Figure 27. *You can roll a docker up to get it out of the way. Just click the tiny arrow.*

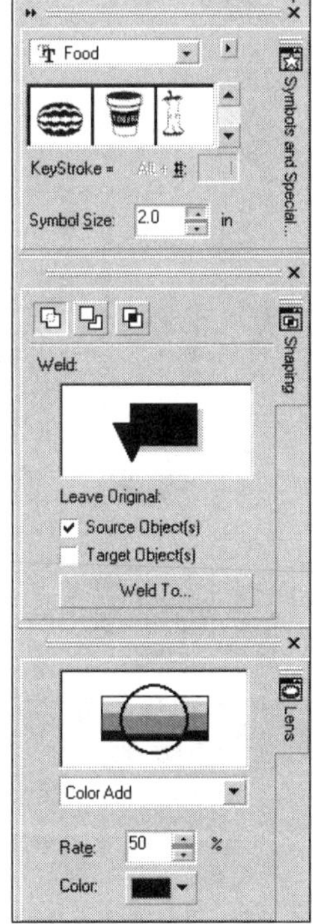

Figure 28. *To close a docker when several dockers are open, click the Close button at the upper-right corner of the docker window. Sometimes the Close button won't be visible, so you can close the docker instead by right clicking on the docker name tab and choosing Close from the pop-up menu.*

To undock a docker:

1. Position the mouse pointer over the two horizontal lines at the top of the docker.
2. Press the left mouse button and drag the docker onto the desktop.

Tip:

- When a docker is undocked, you can roll it up to get it out of the way. Just click the little up arrow at the top-right corner of the docker window. To unroll the docker, click the arrow again (**Figure 27**).

To close a docker when several dockers are open:

Click the Close button at the upper-right corner of the docker (**Figure 28**).

or

Right click on the name tab of the docker that you want to close, then choose Close from the pop-up menu.

GETTING HELP

CorelDraw 9 comes with a comprehensive help system that has been developed with users' requests in mind. There are seven parts in the help system:

- **The User's Guide**—this is the paper manual that ships with CorelDraw. You can read it at your leisure, even away from your computer.
- **Online Help**—built in the standard Windows style, Online Help has three tab pages, set up like a book with Contents, Index, and Find (**Figure 29**).
- **Technical Support**—if you are having any problems getting CorelDraw to work, check here.
- **Hints**—this helper displays information about the task that you are performing. When you click a tool or object, the Hints window changes to show you information pertaining to the selected item (**Figure 30**).
- **CorelTutor**—the Tutor gives you step-by-step instruction on how to complete specific tasks (**Figure 31**). You can even get the Tutor to demonstrate how to do something.
- **What's This?**—this helper gives you an on-demand description of the tools you are using (**Figure 32**).
- **ToolTips**—these are the balloons that appear when the mouse passes over a button or drop-down list on a toolbar (**Figure 33**).

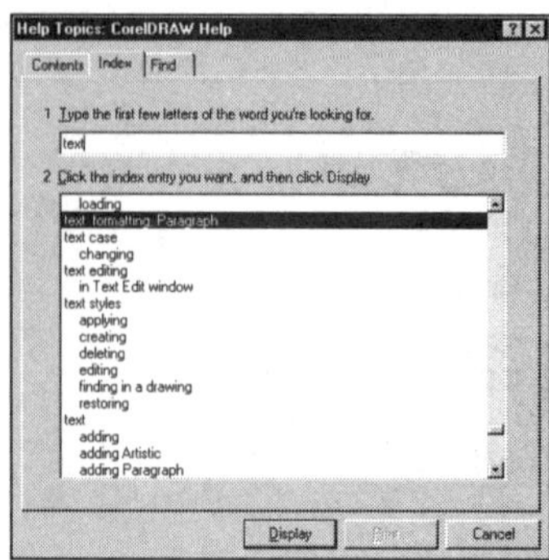

Figure 29. *Online Help is easy to use. Just type what you're looking for in the text box at the top of the Index tab page.*

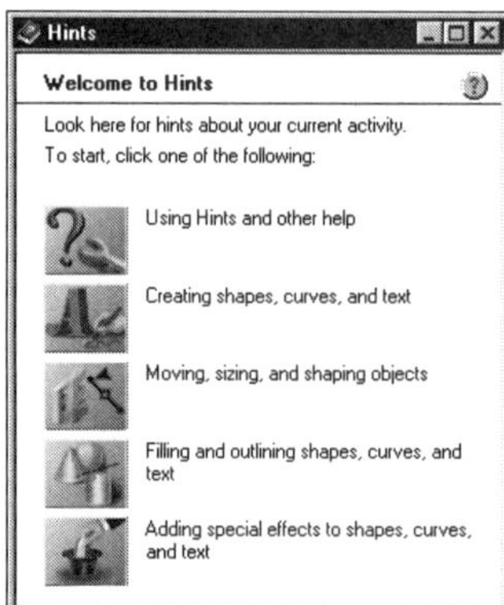

Figure 30. *Hints.*

Figure 31. *Corel Tutor.*

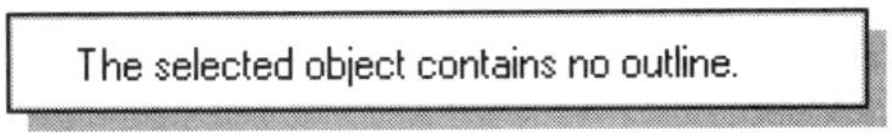

The selected object contains no outline.

Figure 32. *What's This? help.*

Figure 33. *A ToolTip.*

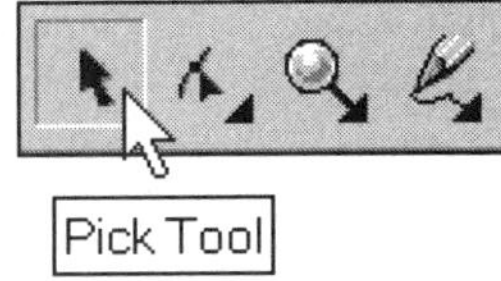

Figure 34. *Select any type of help from the Help menu.*

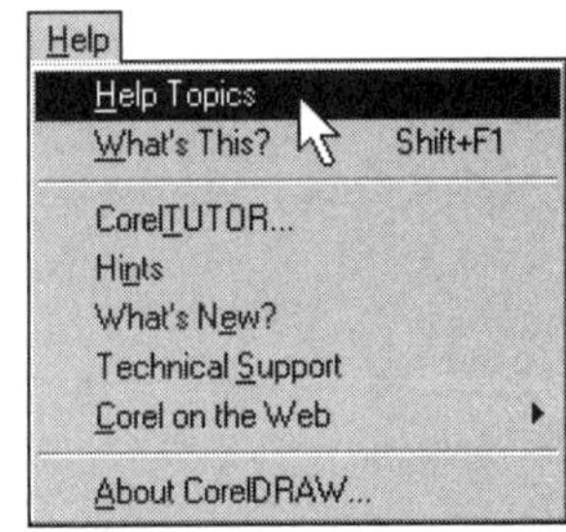

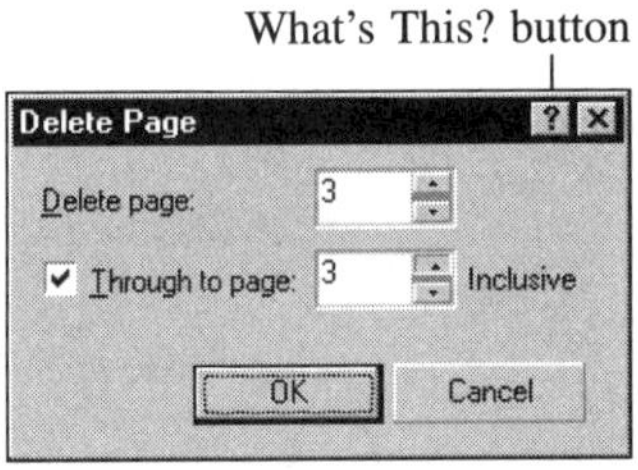

What's This? button

Delete Page
Delete page: 3
Through to page: 3 Inclusive
OK Cancel

Figure 35. *A What's This? help button.*

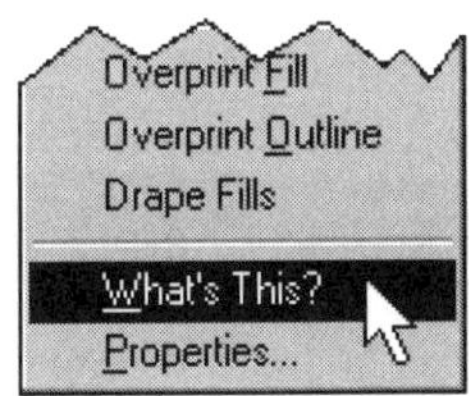

Figure 36. *You can select What's This? from virtually any pop-up menu.*

To open Online Help, Technical Support, Hints, or CorelTutor:

1. Click the Help menu title on the Menu Bar (**Figure 34**).
2. Select the type of help you want.

Tip:

- To reach Corel technical support on the Web, enter the following URL: http://www.corel.com/support/technical/

To use What's This? help:

1. Click the button with the question mark in it, found at the top right of any dialog box (**Figure 35**).
2. Move the mouse pointer over the object you want to know about and click. A help window will appear (**Figure 29**).

or

Right mouse click on an item you are curious about, then select What's This? from the pop-up menu (**Figure 36**).

To see ToolTips:

Slowly move the mouse pointer over any button. A balloon help window will appear, telling you what the button does.

SOME TERMS YOU SHOULD KNOW

Object

Everything you create in CorelDraw is an object.

Path

The outside perimeter of an object. A path can be either open or closed. Paths pass through nodes.

Properties

The attributes of objects, such as fill color, size, and shape.

Objects

Closed path

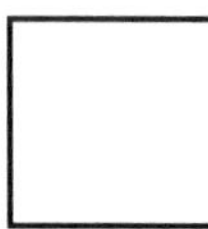
Open path

Handles

A set of eight black squares that appear in a rectangular formation around a selected object.

Nodes

The squares that paths pass through. They can be used to shape paths with the Shape Tool.

Control Points

The handle that shapes a line segment. Control points are attached to nodes with levers.

Line Segment

The portion of path between two nodes.

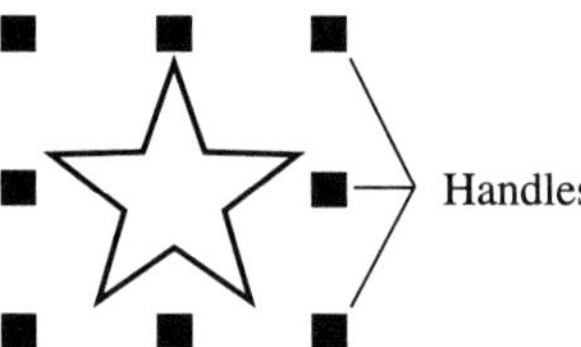

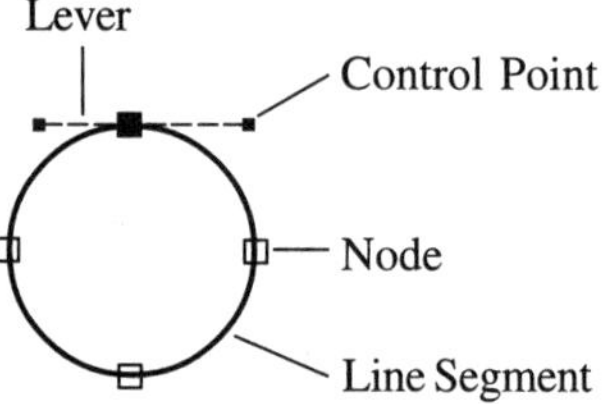

Select

Click with the Pick Tool to select objects and the Shape Tool to select nodes.

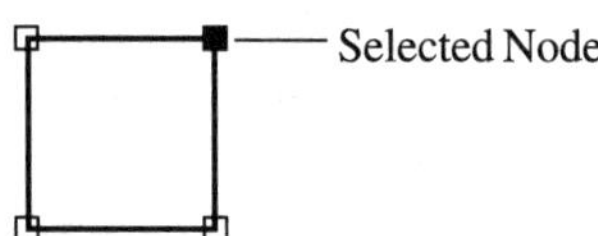

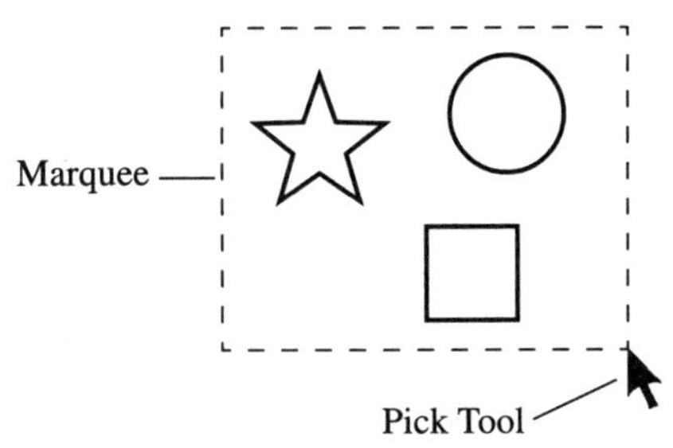

Multiple Select

Press the Shift key while clicking to select several objects or nodes at once.

Marquee Select

Using the Pick or Shape Tool, press the left mouse button and drag to create a dashed rectangle that encloses objects or nodes.

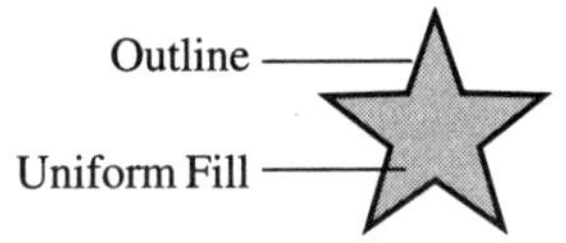

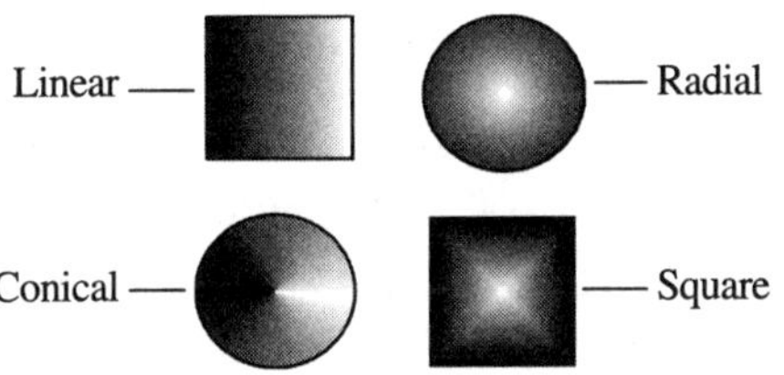

Outline

The line representing the path that can be colored or invisible.

Fill

A uniform color, pattern, texture, or fountain fill, added to the inside of an object.

Fountain Fill

A gradual blend from one color to another or a cascade of different colors.

Stacking Order

Guidelines

Non-printing lines that can be used to align objects.

Layer

A transparent plane on which objects are placed when drawing.

Stacking Order

The sequence in which objects are drawn in the drawing window. The first object drawn appears at the bottom of the stack, while the last object drawn is on top.

Group

A set of objects that are combined so they can be moved or modified as a single object.

Nested Group

A grouping of two or more groups that behave as a single object.

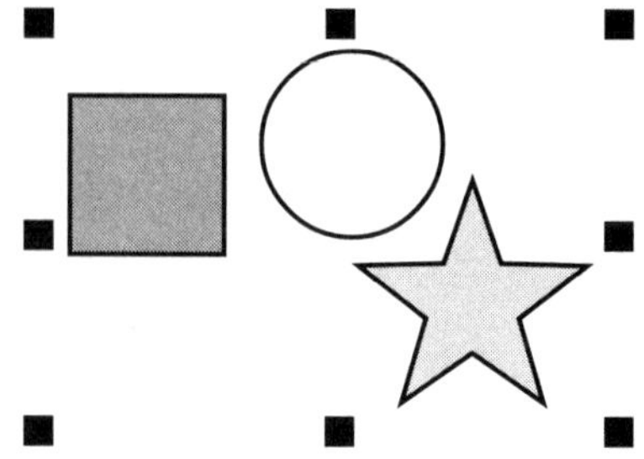

Grouped objects, selected

HARDWARE CONSIDERATIONS

Corel Corporation recommends the following as the minimum system requirements for running CorelDraw 9 on your Windows 95/98/NT machine:

- 133 MHz Pentium with 32 MB RAM and an SVGA graphics card.

However, for best performance they recommend:

- 133 MHz Pentium with 64 MB RAM and an SVGA graphics card.

This book was created using a 450 MHz Pentium with 256 MB RAM and an SVGA graphics card with 16 MB RAM. It was also tested on a 100 MHz Pentium with 64 MB RAM and an SVGA graphics card with 8 MB RAM. When testing CorelDraw 9, the 450 Pentium was hardly pushed to its limits. The 100 MHz Pentium was fine for creating complex vector graphics, though it was pushed to the limit when working with complex extrusions and blends, bitmaps, and bitmap filters.

SUMMARY

In this chapter you learned:

- What CorelDraw 9 is
- How CorelDraw works
- About toolbars
- What's in the Toolbox
- About dockers and how they work

You also learned how to:

- Use a menu
- Use keyboard shortcuts
- Zoom in and out
- Use the Pan Tool
- View a drawing
- Get help

Startup

2

It's time to get started! First, you will launch CorelDraw 9, then add a shortcut for the CorelDraw 9 program to your Windows desktop. From there you will create a new document, open an existing one, and save a document. Then you will discover how to import and export graphics and text, close a document, and exit CorelDraw 9. Finally, you will learn how to restore a damaged CorelDraw file using a backup file that is created automatically for you by CorelDraw.

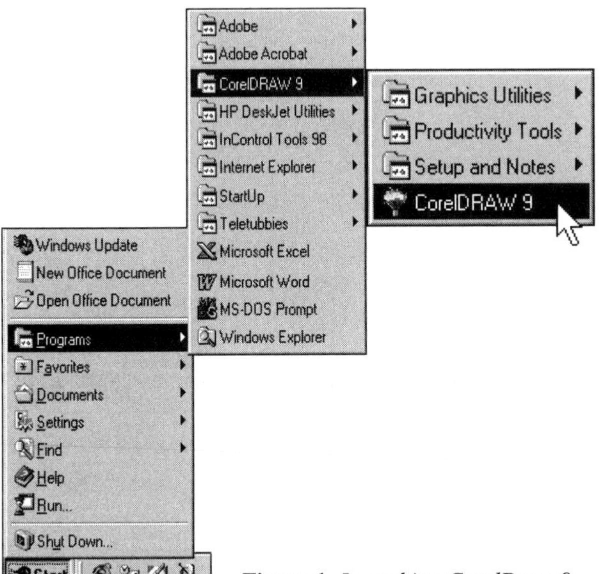

Figure 1. *Launching CorelDraw 9.*

To launch CorelDraw 9:

1. On the Windows desktop, click the Start button on the Status Bar, move up to the Programs item, and select it.
2. On the Programs fly-out select the CorelDraw 9 program folder. (This is the default location where the CorelDraw 9 installation program places the program group.)
3. On the fly-out, click CorelDraw 9 (**Figure 1**).

To put a shortcut to the CorelDraw 9 program on the Windows desktop:

1. *Right* mouse click on the Start button and select Explore from the pop-up menu (**Figure 2**). This will open the Windows Explorer with the Start Menu folder near the bottom of the left pane.
2. Click on the plus sign (+) next to the Programs folder which resides under the Start Menu folder (**Figure 3**). This will expand the Programs folder.
3. Under the expanded Programs folder, select the CorelDraw 9 folder (**Figure 4**). The right pane of Explorer will display several folders and a CorelDraw 9 shortcut.
4. Move to the right pane of Explorer and, using the right mouse button, click and drag the CorelDraw 9 shortcut from the Explorer window onto the Windows desktop (**Figure 5**).
5. Release the mouse button. A pop-up menu will appear on the desktop (**Figure 6**).
6. Click Create Shortcut(s) Here. The CorelDraw 9 shortcut will appear on the desktop (**Figure 7**).

Figure 2. *Right mouse click on the Start button and select Explore.*

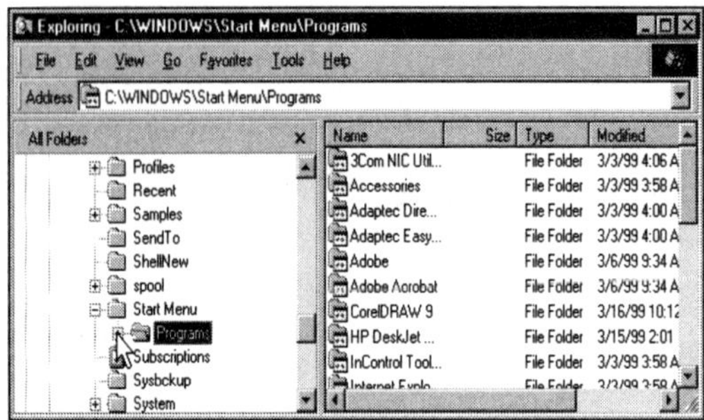

Figure 3. *Click on the plus sign next to Programs under the Start Menu folder.*

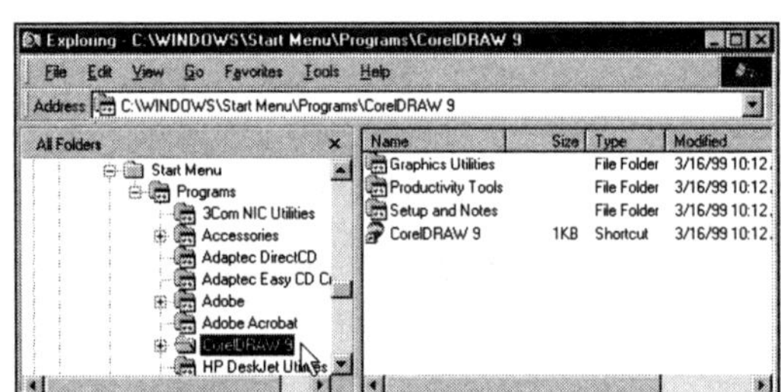

Figure 4. *Under the Programs folder, select CorelDraw 9.*

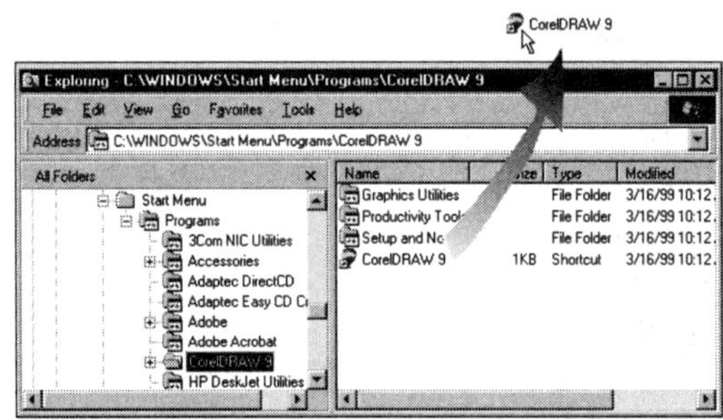

Figure 5. *Press the right mouse button and drag the CorelDraw 9 shortcut from the Explorer window to your Windows desktop.*

Figure 6. *Click Create Shortcut(s) Here.*

Figure 7. *The CorelDraw 9 shortcut appears on the Windows desktop.*

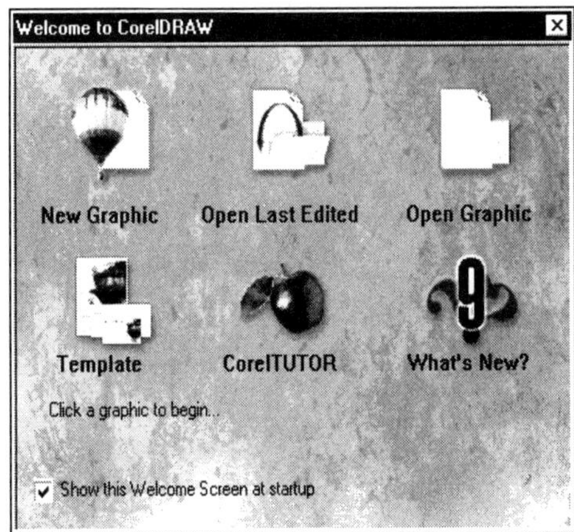

Figure 8. *The CorelDraw 9 Welcome Screen.*

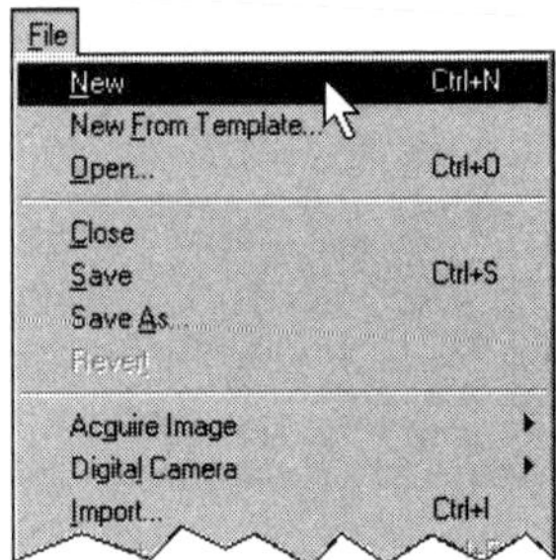

Figure 9. *To start a new document, select New on the File menu.*

When you launch CorelDraw 9 for the very first time, you will see the Welcome Screen (**Figure 8**). This window displays six options that you can select:

- Start a new graphic
- Open the last file you worked on
- Open an existing CorelDraw file
- Use a template as the basis for a new document
- Start CorelTutor
- Find out what's new

To choose any one of these options, click the desired item.

If you do not want to see the Welcome Screen every time you launch the program, be sure to remove the check from the check box at the bottom of the screen. If you do uncheck the box, CorelDraw will automatically open a new document for you every time you launch the program (this is the same as the "New Graphic" option on the Welcome Screen).

To start a new document:

If you decide to remove the Welcome Screen as described above, CorelDraw will automatically start a new document for you every time you launch the program.

If you are already working in CorelDraw and want to start a new document, choose New from the File menu (**Figure 9**) or press Ctrl+N on the keyboard.

Documents can be based on a CorelDraw *template*. Templates are special, predesigned files that help you quickly create professional-looking documents such as greeting cards, business cards, and brochures. You will need to put CorelDraw CD-ROM Disk #1 into your CD-ROM drive to access the templates.

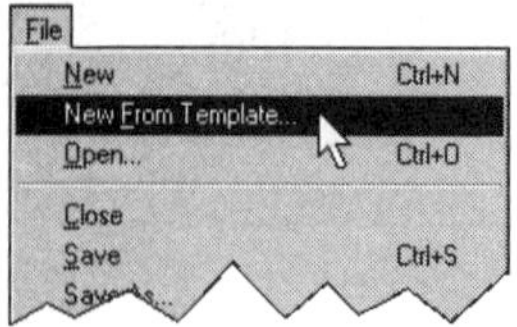

Figure 10. *Select New From Template from the File menu.*

To start a new document using a template:

1. Choose New From Template from the File menu (**Figure 10**). The Template Wizard will open (**Figure 11**).
2. Select what type of template you would like to use. CorelDraw 9 ships with over 450 templates, many of which are designed for PaperDirect pre-printed papers.
3. When you have selected the template type you want to use, click Next to move to the next Wizard panel (**Figure 12**). If you have not loaded CorelDraw Disk #2 into your CD-ROM drive, a dialog box will appear asking you to do so (**Figure 13**).
4. On the second panel, select the type of document you would like to create—brochure, label, postcard, etc.

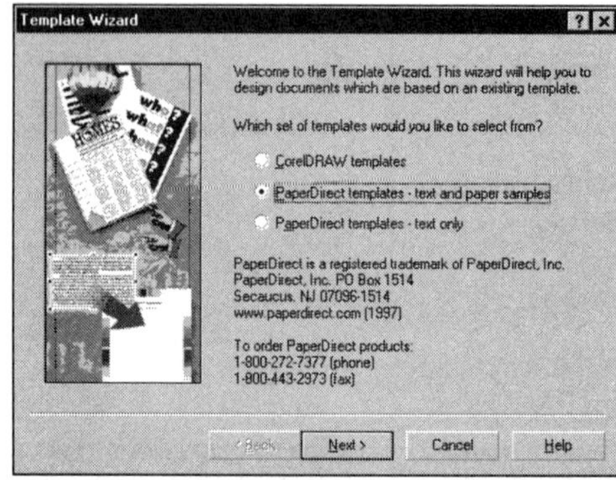

Figure 11. *Select the type of template you want to use to create the new document.*

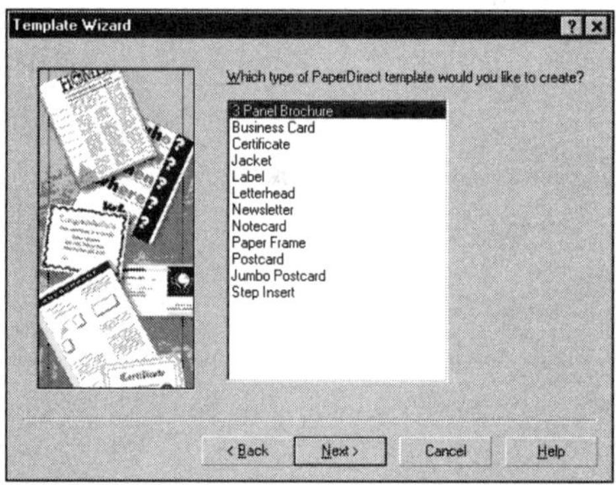

Figure 12. *Select the type of document you want to create.*

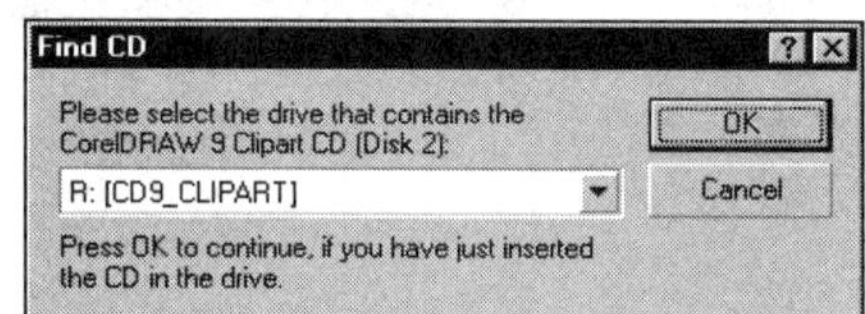

Figure 13. *Insert CD-ROM Disk 2 into your CD-ROM drive, then click OK.*

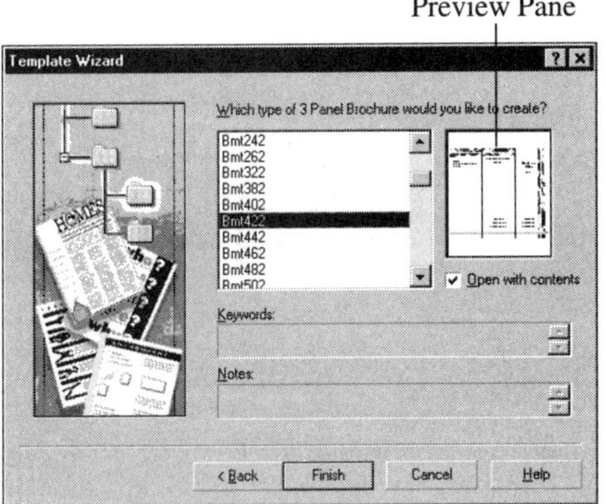

Figure 14. *Select the template design that fits your project best.*

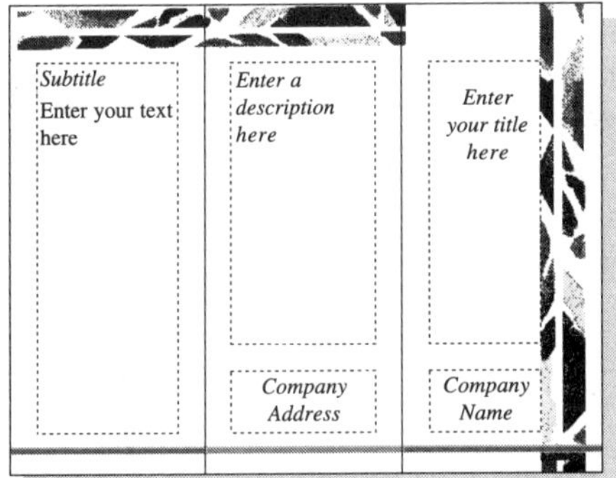

Figure 15. *When the Wizard is finished, a new document is created using the template you selected as a guide.*

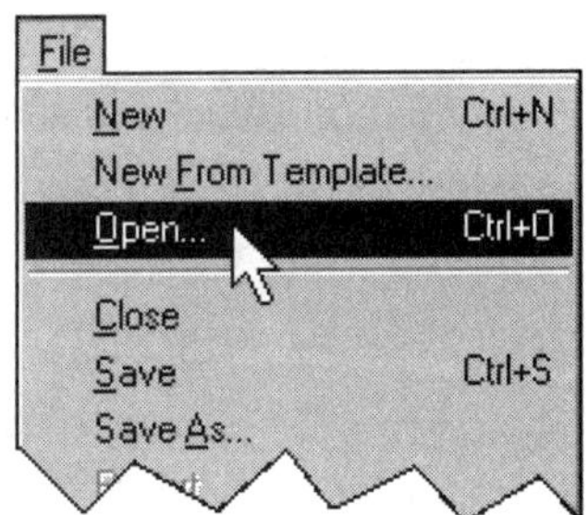

Figure 16. *Choose Open from the File menu.*

5. Click Next to move to the third panel.
6. Select a design from the template list, using the preview pane to see what it looks like (**Figure 14**).
7. Put a check mark in the Open with contents check box to have the document created with the template design.
8. Click Finish. The Wizard will close and a new document will be created from the template, ready for your modifications (**Figure 15**).

To open an existing document:

1. Choose Open from the File menu (**Figure 16**) or press Ctrl+O on your keyboard. The Open Drawing dialog box will appear (**Figure 17**).
2. Move to the folder where the document is stored, then choose the CorelDraw file you want to access and click Open.

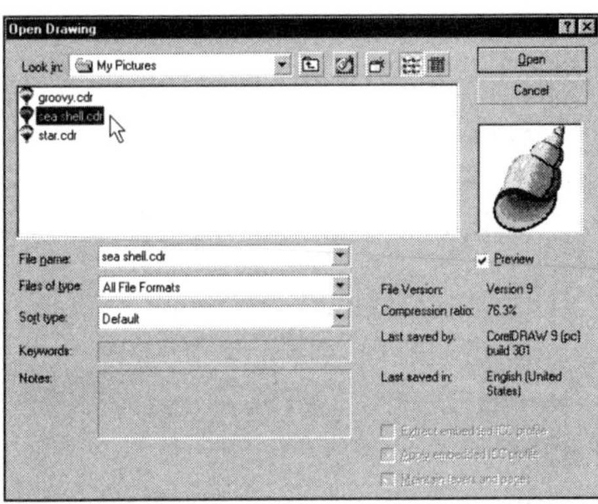

Figure 17. *Select the file you want to open, then click the Open button.*

To save your work:

1. Choose Save from the File menu (**Figure 18**) or press Ctrl+S on the keyboard. The Save Drawing dialog box will appear (**Figure 19**).
2. Move to the folder where you want to save the drawing, then type a name in the File name text box.
3. Click the Save button.

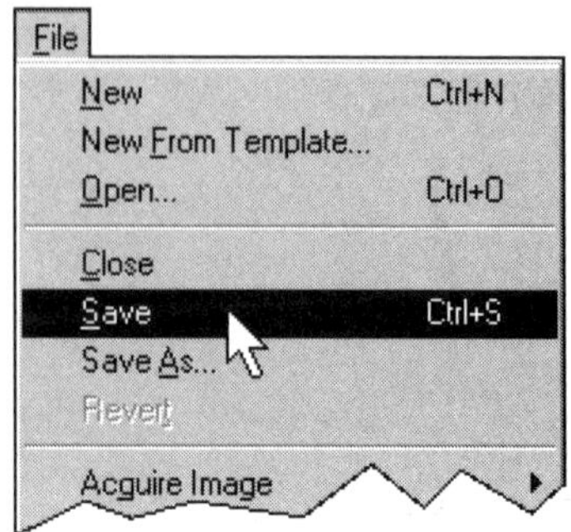

Figure 18. *Choose Save from the File menu.*

To save a copy of a file:

1. Open the file you want to copy.
2. Choose Save As from the File menu (**Figure 20**). The Save Drawing dialog box will open (**Figure 19**).
3. Move to the folder where you want to save the copy and modify the file name in the File name text box or type in a new name.
4. Click the Save button.

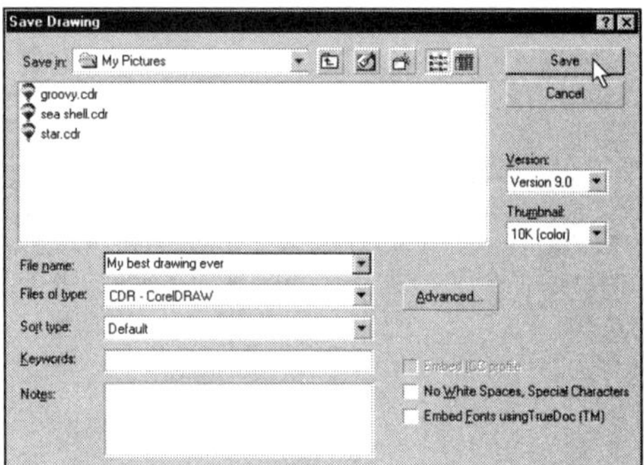

Figure 19. *Use the Save Drawing dialog box to name your file and save your work.*

Tip:

- To help you find a file in the future, you can add a few keywords and notes in those text boxes on the Save Drawing dialog box.

> **THERE'S ALWAYS A WAY OUT!**
>
> If you find yourself in a window that you did not mean to use, don't panic! Remember that you can always press the Cancel button. The dialog box will close and you will return to the drawing window with nothing changed.

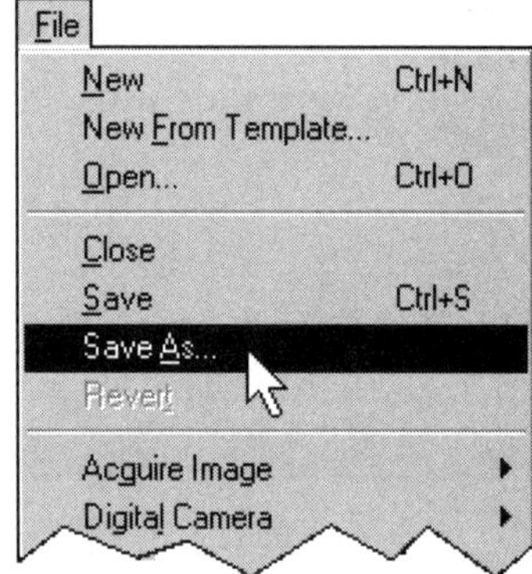

Figure 20. *To save a copy of a drawing, use Save As on the File menu.*

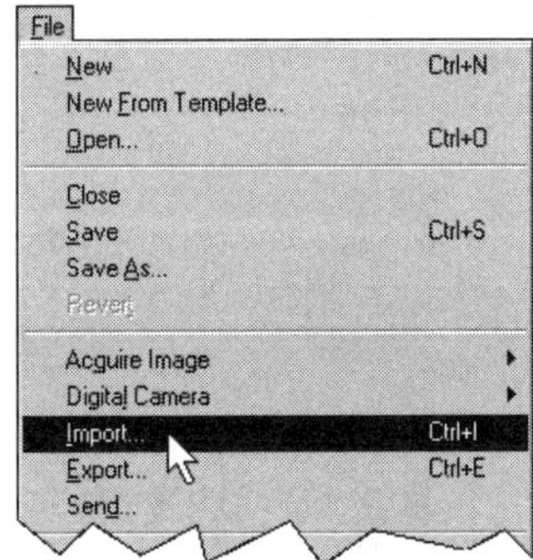

Figure 21. *To import a graphic, choose Import from the File menu.*

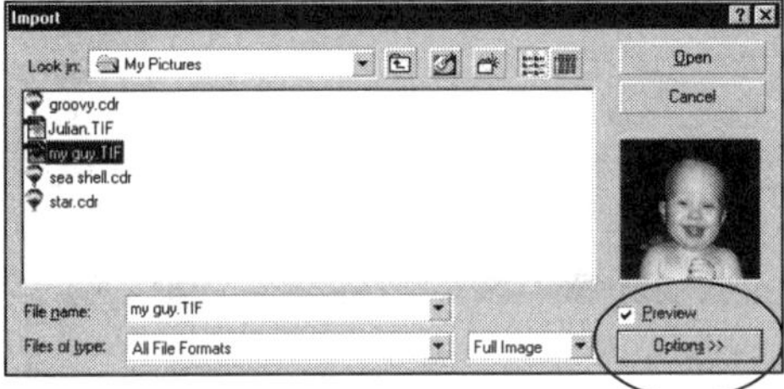

Figure 22. *The Import dialog box.*

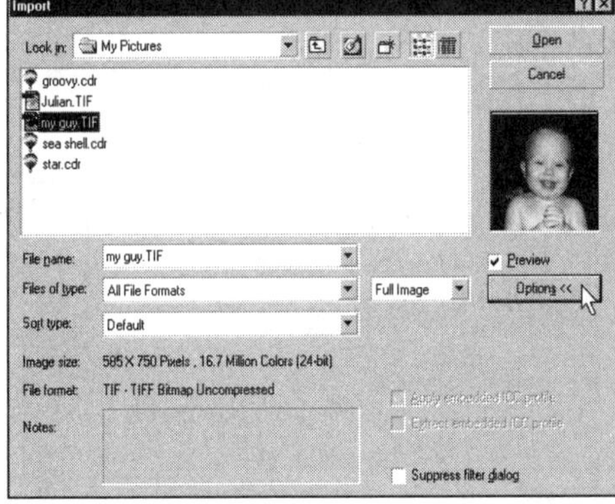

Figure 23. *Press the Options button to learn more about the graphic you are going to import.*

You can import many types of files—CorelDraw clipart, text, graphics CAD drawings, etc.—into your projects. (For an easy way to import CorelDraw graphics using the Clipart docker, see Chapter 16.)

To import a file:

1. Choose Import from the File menu (**Figure 21**) or press Ctrl+I on the keyboard. The Import dialog box will open.
2. Move to the folder where the file is stored and highlight the file you want to import. To see a preview of the image, make sure a check appears in the box next to Preview on the right side of the window (**Figure 22**).
3. To see more information about the file you are about to import, press the Options button at the lower rightof the window (**Figure 22**). The bottom of the window will expand to give you information about the the file's format and size, any notes accompanying the file, etc. (**Figure 23**).
4. Click the Open button. The file will appear, selected, in your document.

Every image you see in *CorelDraw 9 for Windows: Visual QuickStart Guide*, has either been designed by me or is a piece of clipart from the CorelDraw CD-ROM disks. If you see a clipart image you want to use for your own drawing, look in Appendix A to find the exact location of the image.

Exporting graphics in almost any file format for import into another program or use on a Web site is easy with CorelDraw. Just create the professional drawing you need, then export it using the appropriate file format, such as .tif, .pct, .ai, or .gif.

To export a drawing:

1. Select the drawing that you want to export.
2. Open the Export dialog box by choosing Export from the File menu (**Figure 24**) or press Ctrl+E on the keyboard.
3. Move to the folder where you would like to store the graphic, then type a name in the File name text box (**Figure 25**).
4. Select the file type you want to save the graphic as by clicking the down arrow next to the Files of type drop-down list and selecting a file type (**Figure 26**).
5. If the graphic that you are exporting is part of a larger graphic (in other words, you selected a portion of a drawing before you opened the Export window), make sure that the Selected only check box in the lower-right corner is checked (**Figure 27**).
6. Click the Export button. Depending upon the file type you selected, a Bitmap Export dialog box will open, displaying the possible settings for that file type (**Figure 28**). In this dialog box you can set:

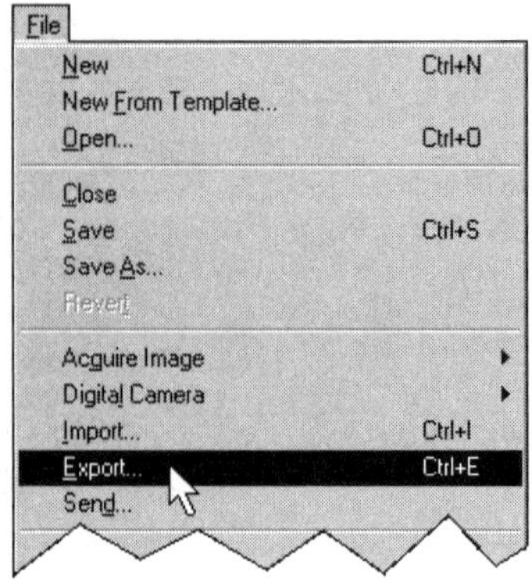

Figure 24. *To export a drawing, choose Export from the File menu.*

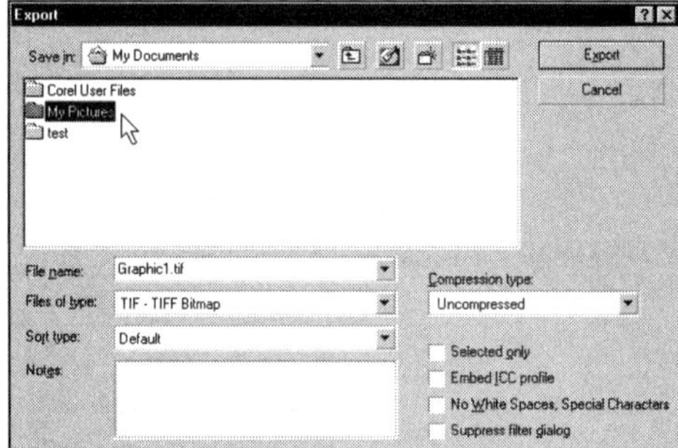

Figure 25. *Use the Export dialog box to select the location where you want to put the file and the type of file that you want to export.*

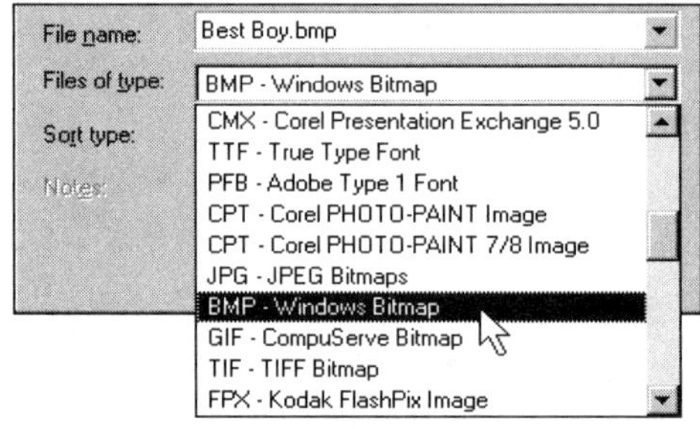

Figure 26. *Press the down arrow next to the Files of type list box to select a file format.*

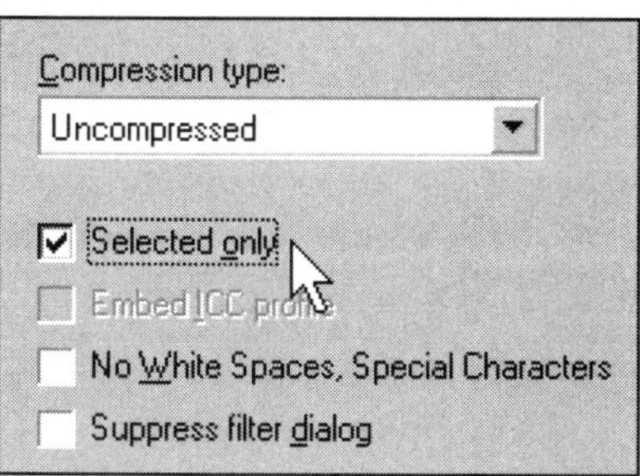

Figure 27. *If you are exporting a portion of a drawing, make sure the Selected only box in the Export window is checked.*

Make sure this padlock appears locked

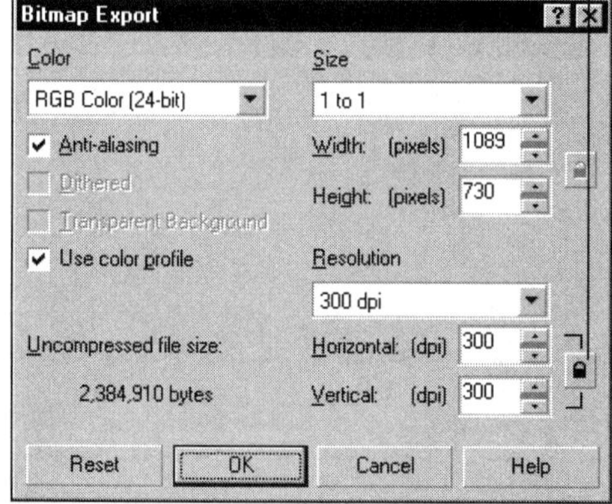

Figure 28. *The Bitmap Export dialog box lets you set the number of colors, size, and resolution of the drawing you are exporting. If you change the resolution settings, make sure the tiny padlock appears locked. This will make sure that the horizontal and vertical resolution settings are the same. Many printers cannot handle different horizontal and vertical settings. Also, the result could be pretty ugly.*

- The number of colors with which the graphic will be exported
- The image size
- The image resolution in *dots per inch* (dpi)

Remember that the higher any of these settings are—more colors, a larger image size, higher image resolution—the larger the file. Using larger sized files means that display time on your computer will increase and printing the files will take much longer (sometimes hours!).

7. When you are happy with the settings, click OK.

Tips:

- Before you export a graphic that is made up of more than one object, be sure you *group* the objects together, otherwise your graphic will not export correctly. (Grouping objects together is discussed on page 214.)
- Always try to get away with using the least amount of colors and the lowest resolution you can. You might have to export the image a few times until you get the desired effect, but smaller images mean time saved for you when you load or print the graphic.

WHAT YOU NEED TO KNOW ABOUT FILE EXTENSIONS

File extensions are the three letters that come after the period in a file name. For instance, the file MyFile.Cdr has a file extension of .Cdr. These file extensions tell the computer (and the human!) what kind of file it is and how to interpret it.

CorelDraw uses several file extensions:

- .Cdr–this is the native CorelDraw file extension that will automatically be attached to your documents when you save them.
- .Cdt–CorelDraw Template
- .Cmx–Corel Presentation Exchange

Other file extensions that you may see in your journey as a CorelDraw graphics artist:

- .Cpt–Corel Photo-Paint
- .Bmp–Windows bitmap
- .Eps–Encapsulated PostScript file
- .Tif–Tag Image File Format (Tiff) bitmap

If you surf the World Wide Web, you will probably see these formats used:

- .Gif–CompuServe bitmap
- .Jpg–Joint Photographic Experts Group (Jpeg) bitmap

For more information about the .Gif and .Jpg file formats, take a look at Chapter 17, *CorelDraw 9 and the Web*.

HOW TO VIEW FILE EXTENSIONS IN WINDOWS

To see all file extensions, open any Windows window—for instance, double click on My Computer to open that window—and select Folder Options from the View menu. In the Options dialog box, click the View tab to bring that tab page to the front. For Windows 95, make sure that the check box next to "Hide MS-DOS file extensions for file types that are registered" is unchecked. For Windows 98/NT, make sure that the check box next to "Hide file extensions for known file types" is unchecked.

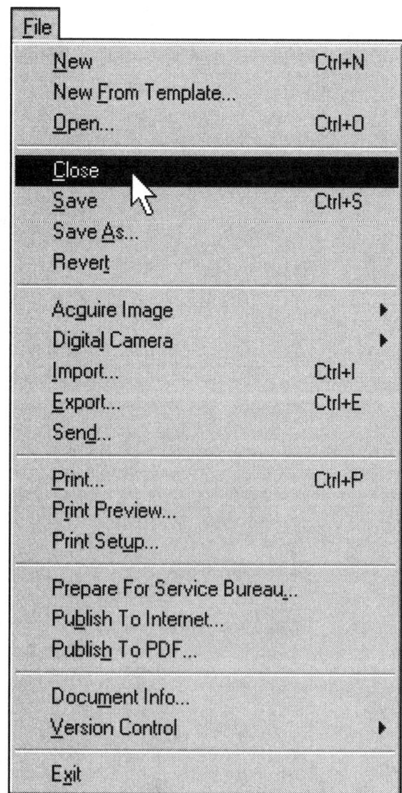

Figure 29. *To close a document choose Close from the File menu.*

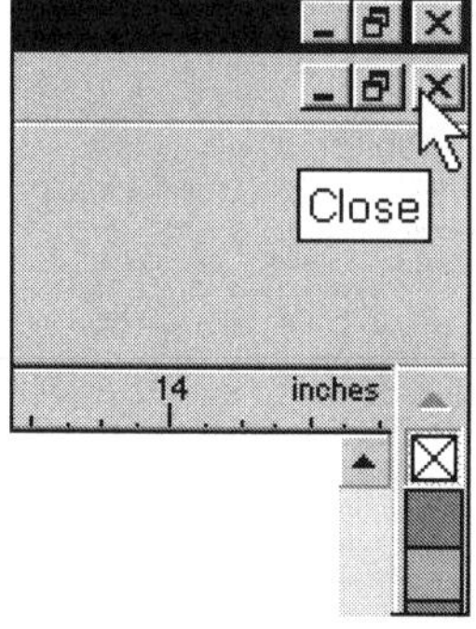

Figure 30. *To close a document, press the Close button at the upper right-hand corner of the document window.*

To close a document:

Choose Close from the File menu (**Figure 29**).

or

Press Ctrl+F4 on the keyboard.

or

Click on the Close button (**Figure 30**) at the upper right-hand corner of the document window.

Tip:

- If the document you are closing has not been saved recently, CorelDraw will automatically ask whether you want to save it.

How Many Documents Can I Have Open at Once?

The number of CorelDraw documents you can have open at one time is only limited by the amount of RAM you have in your computer.

Sometimes files become corrupted. If you try to open a CorelDraw file and it does not function properly, don't panic! CorelDraw is set to automatically make backups of all your drawings. You can use these backup files to restore a corrupted file.

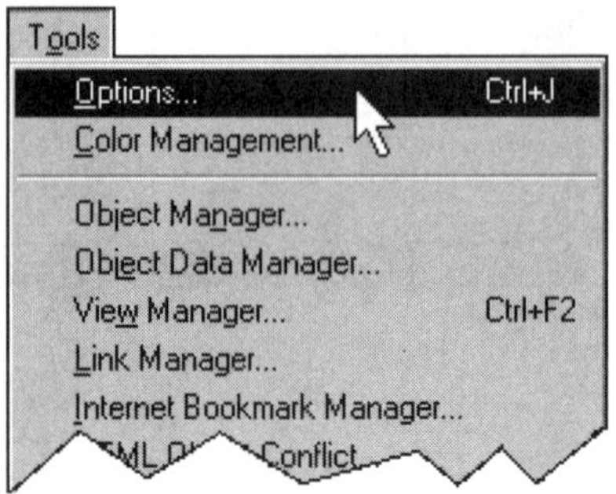

Figure 31. *Choose Options from the Tools menu.*

To set backup options:

1. Choose Options from the Tools menu (**Figure 31**) or press Ctrl+J on the keyboard. The Options dialog box will open with Workspace selected in the tree view window (**Figure 32**).
2. Click on Save in the tree view window (**Figure 33**).
3. On the Save panel of the Options dialog box, make sure there is a check mark in the Auto-backup every _ minutes check box (**Figure 34**). By default, a backup will be made every 10 minutes. You can change this number to suit your needs.
4. Set the place where the backup file will be stored using the options buttons below the check box (**Figure 34**). By default the backup is placed in the same folder as the file that it backs up. You can change this to a specific folder, if you desire.

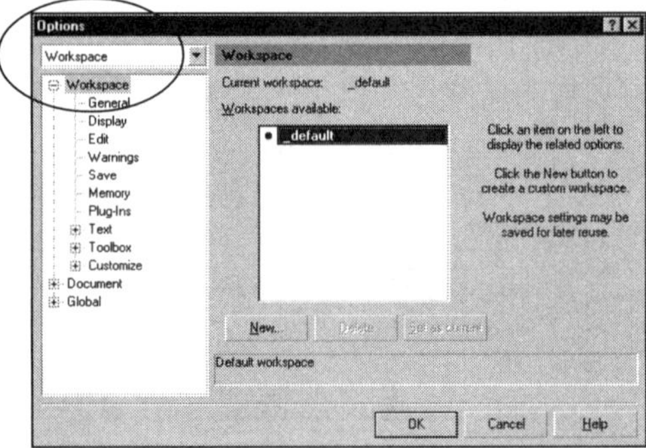

Figure 32. *The Options dialog box will open with Workspace selected in the tree view window.*

Figure 33. *Click Save in the tree view window.*

Tip:

- Don't set the auto-backup time to less than 5 minutes. If you are working on a large file, saving it can slow your computer down and interrupt your work.

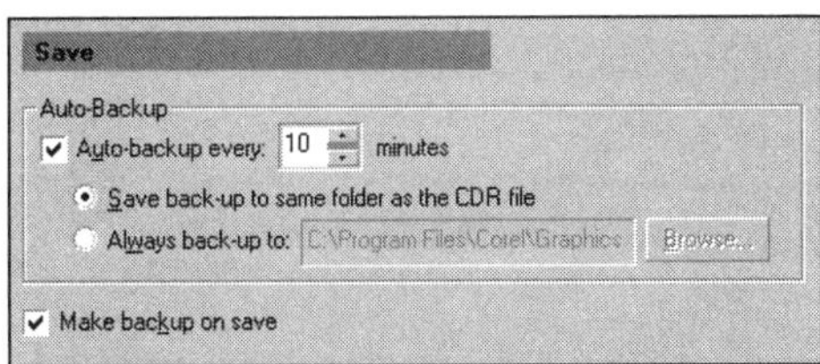

Figure 34. *Use the Auto-Backup area on the Save panel on the right side of the dialog box to change auto-backup settings.*

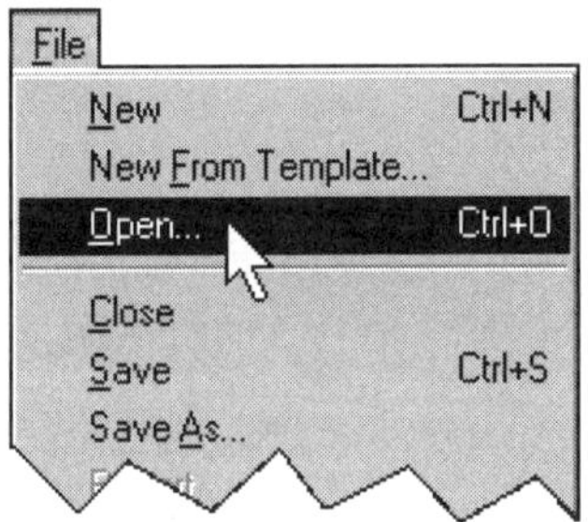

Figure 35. *To restore a file using a backup, choose Open from the File menu.*

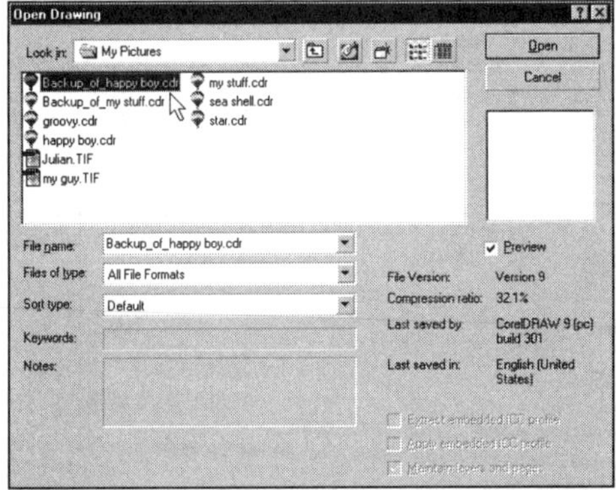

Figure 36. *The backup file will have "Backup_of_" added before the original file name. Select the backup file name that matches the original.*

To restore a corrupted file:

1. Choose Open from the File menu (**Figure 35**) or press Ctrl+O on the keyboard. The Open Drawing dialog box will appear (**Figure 36**).
2. Move to the folder where the backup is stored. By default, this is the same folder where the original file lives.
3. Auto-backup files have "Backup_of_" added before the original file name. Select the backup file name that matches the corrupted original file name. For example, if the original corrupted file is named Train.Cdr, select Backup_of_Train.Cdr.
4. Click Open. The backup will open.
5. Save the backup using Save As on the File menu to rename the file without the "Backup_of_" prefix.

Tip:

- Remember that a backup file is generated only periodically, so the backup may not be "up to the minute." It may have been made five or eight minutes before the original file was corrupted. But, an older backup file is better than no file at all!

To exit CorelDraw:

Choose Exit from the File Menu (**Figure 37**).

or

Press Alt+F4 on the keyboard.

or

Click the Close button in the extreme upper right-hand corner of the screen (**Figure 38**).

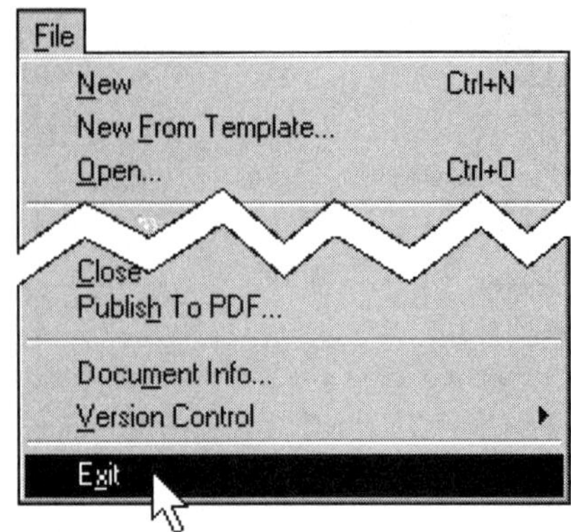

Figure 37. *To exit CorelDraw 9, choose Exit from the File menu.*

Tip:

- When you exit CorelDraw, all open files will close. If changes have been made to an open file since it was last saved, CorelDraw will automatically ask whether you want to save it.

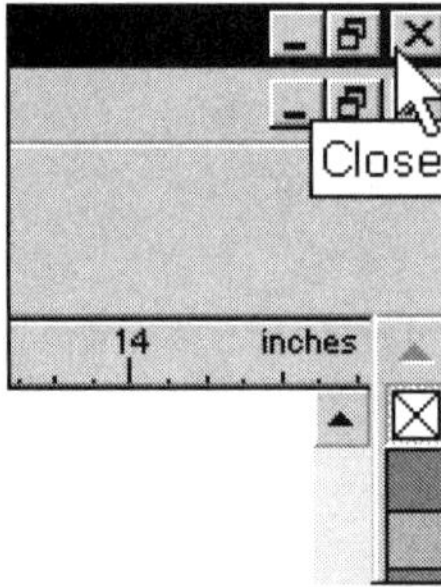

Figure 38. *Another way to exit CorelDraw is to click the Close button in the extreme upper-right corner of the screen.*

SUMMARY

In this chapter you learned how to:

- Launch CorelDraw 9
- Start a new document
- Open an existing document
- Save your work
- Import and export a graphic
- Close a document
- Restore a file using a backup
- Exit CorelDraw 9

Rectangles and Ellipses

This chapter will get you started on the road to creating fantastic graphics with CorelDraw 9. The simple shapes you create here are the basis for every drawing, no matter how complex. (Check out the train on this page. It's mostly simple rectangles and circles, but the complete drawing is rather complex—more than 150 objects!)

In this chapter you will draw rectangles and squares, and round their corners. Next, you will create ellipses and circles, then manipulate one of their *properties* to create pie shapes and arcs. Finally, you will learn how to set the default drawing settings for the Ellipse Tool.

Everything you create using the tools in CorelDraw 9, whether it's a line, a triangle, or a circle, has a *path.* Paths can be either *open* or *closed.* The beginning and end of an open path do not connect. For instance, a line is an open path. A closed path has no distinct beginning or end, just as a circle or rectangle has no beginning or end. In other words, a closed path is a *shape*.

In CorelDraw, a line or shape is also known as an *object*. The outside perimeter of an object is a path. In addition, every object has *properties* that can be set. These properties include such items as the object's size, shape, position, and color.

To draw a rectangle:

1. Choose the Rectangle Tool from the Toolbar (**Figure 1**) or press F6 on the keyboard. Your mouse pointer will change to a cross-hair with a little rectangle connected to it.
2. Press the left mouse button down and drag it diagonally (**Figure 2**). As you drag, the rectangle will appear. When you release the mouse, the rectangle will be selected, showing four *nodes*, one at each corner (**Figure 3**). (Nodes are discussed in Chapter 6, *Nodes and Paths*.)

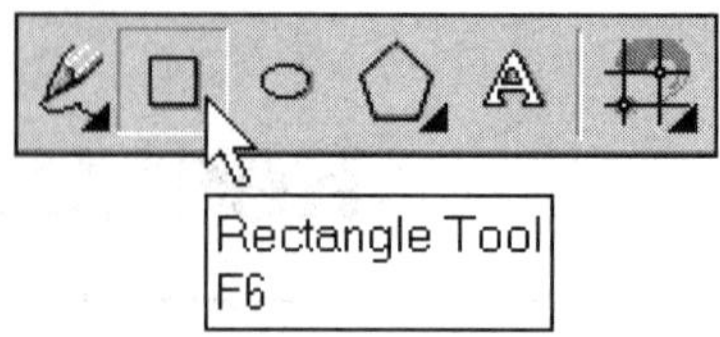

Figure 1. *The Rectangle Tool.*

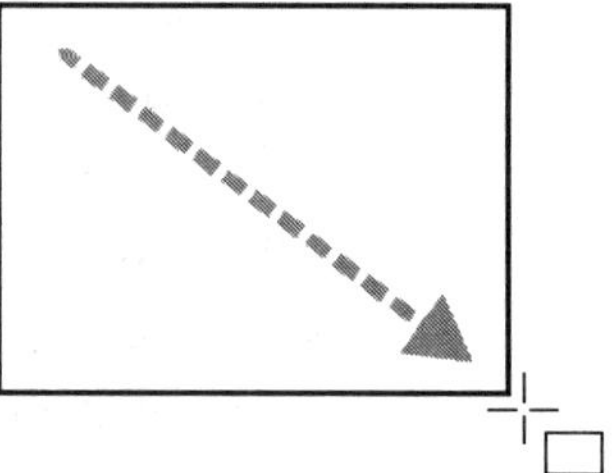

Figure 2. *Drag the mouse diagonally to draw the rectangle.*

Tips:

- To draw a perfect square, hold down the Ctrl key while you drag the mouse. Make sure you release the mouse button first, otherwise the object will spring back to a non-symmetrical shape.
- Remember that you can change the outline color or fill of any closed path object that you create (fills and outlines are discussed in Chapter 10, *Color and Fills*).

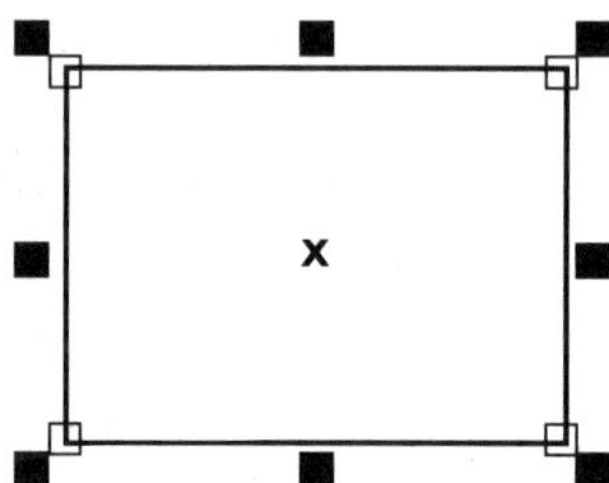

Figure 3. *When you release the mouse button, the rectangle will be selected, showing four nodes.*

How to Draw an Object from the Center

Hold down the Shift key while dragging the mouse to draw a rectangle or ellipse from the center. When your object is the desired size, release the mouse button first, otherwise, the object will spring closer to the mouse pointer and be created from its edge.

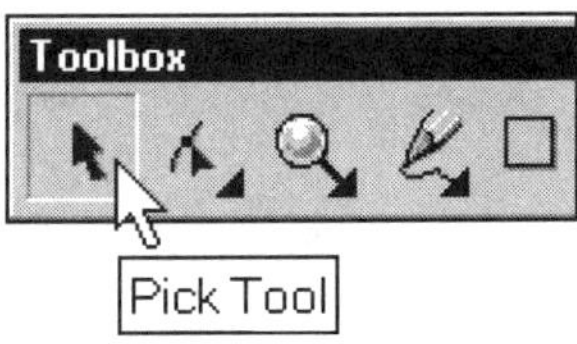

Figure 4. *Select the Pick Tool from the Toolbox.*

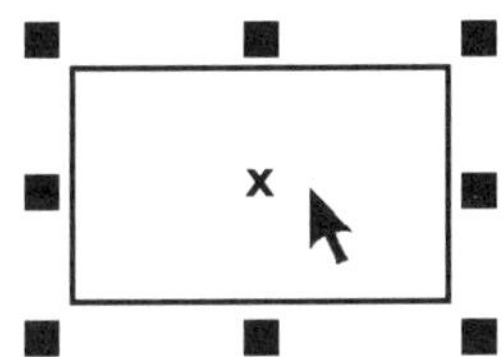

Figure 5. *Click on the rectangle with the Pick Tool to select it.*

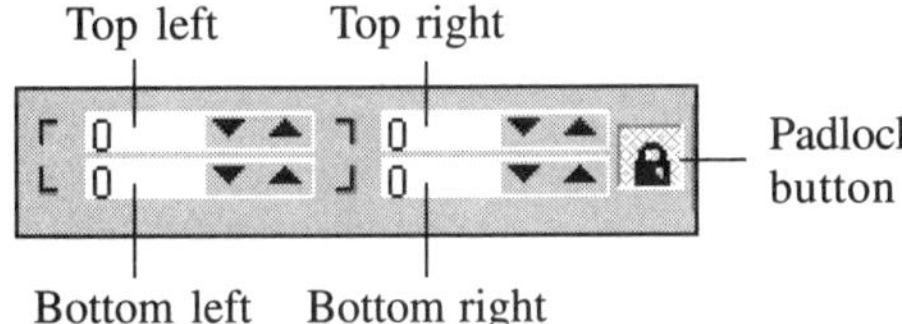

Figure 6. *Type a setting in one of the rectangle corner roundness text boxes or click the up or down arrows to increase or decrease corner roundness.*

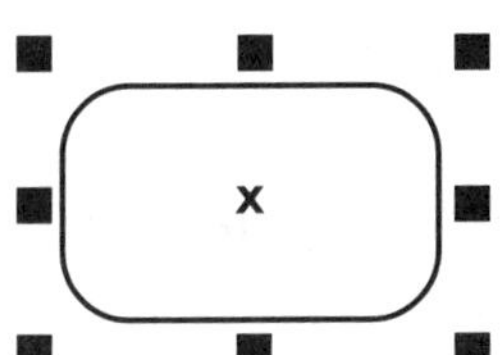

Figure 7. *The rounded rectangle.*

With CorelDraw 9, you can round all corners of a rectangle at once or round them one at a time. The corners of a rectangle can be slightly rounded to create a softening effect or very rounded, almost changing the rectangle shape to a circle.

To round the corners of a rectangle:

1. Select the Pick Tool from the Toolbox (**Figure 4**).
2. Click on the rectangle to select it. Eight black squares, *handles*, will appear around the rectangle (**Figure 5**).
3. On the Property Bar near the top of the screen, enter a number in one of the corner roundness text boxes or click the up or down arrows to the right of the text boxes (**Figure 6**). The corners of the rectangle will become rounded (**Figure 7**).

Tips:

- The larger the number is, the rounder the corners will be.
- If the Property Bar is not displayed, turn to page 9 for directions on how to open it.
- If the small padlock button on the Property Bar is depressed, the corners will all round at the same time. If the button is not pressed, you can round the corners of the rectangle individually.

Round the Corners of a Rectangle

To create an ellipse:

1. Select the Ellipse Tool from the Toolbox (**Figure 8**) or press F7 on the keyboard. Your mouse pointer will change to a cross-hair with an attached ellipse.
2. Press the left mouse button down and drag it diagonally (**Figure 9**). As you drag, the ellipse will appear. When you release the mouse, the ellipse will be selected, displaying one node at the top (**Figure 10**).

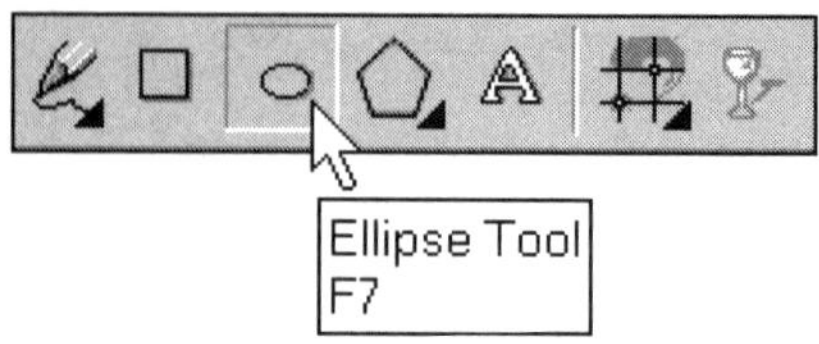

Figure 8. *The Ellipse Tool.*

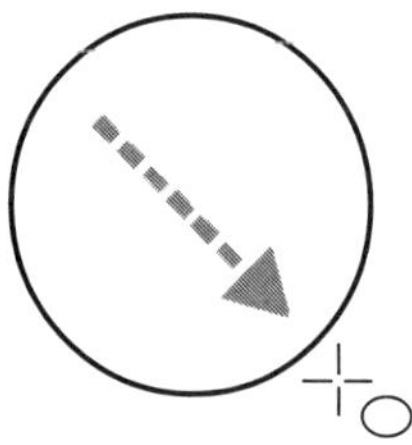

Figure 9. *Drag the mouse diagonally to create the ellipse.*

Tip:

- To draw a perfect circle, press down the Ctrl key while you drag the mouse. Release the mouse button first when you are finished dragging or the circle will spring to an elliptical shape.

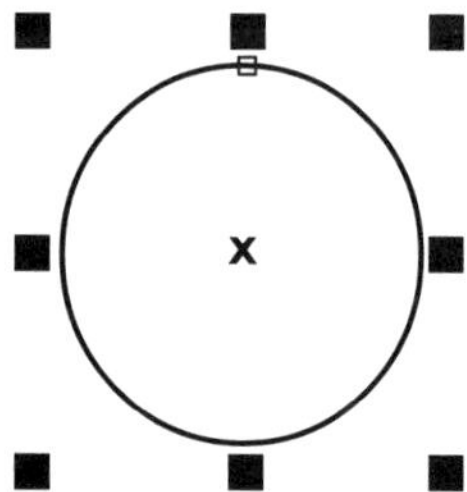

Figure 10. *When you release the mouse button, the ellipse will be selected, displaying one node at the top.*

There's an X in my Object!

Everytime you draw a new object, an X will appear inside it. This X is there to make it easier for you to move the object using the mouse. For details on moving objects, turn to page 45.

Drawing Symmetrical Objects from the Center

To create a perfectly symmetrical object such as a circle or square from the center, hold down both the Ctrl and Shift keys while dragging the mouse. When your object is the desired size, release the mouse button first, otherwise, the object will spring closer to the mouse pointer and be created from its edge.

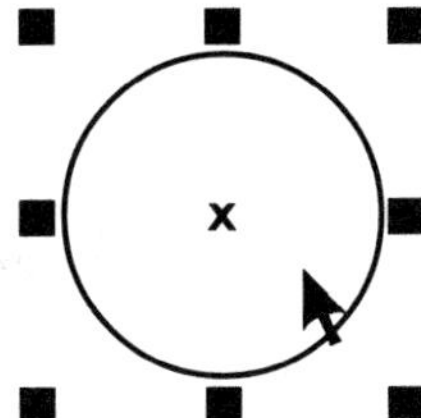

Figure 11. *Click on the ellipse with the Pick Tool to select it.*

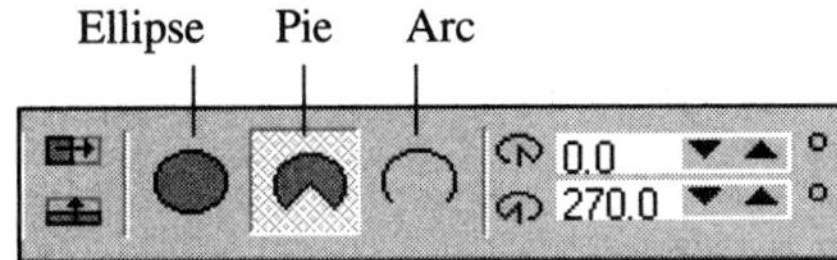

Figure 12. *Click the Pie or Arc button on the Property Bar to change the ellipse to one of those shapes.*

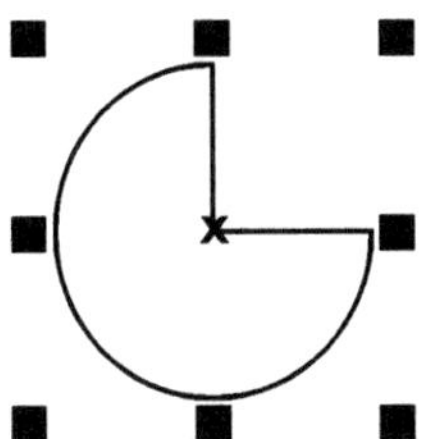

Figure 13. *When you click the Pie button, the ellipse changes to a pie shape.*

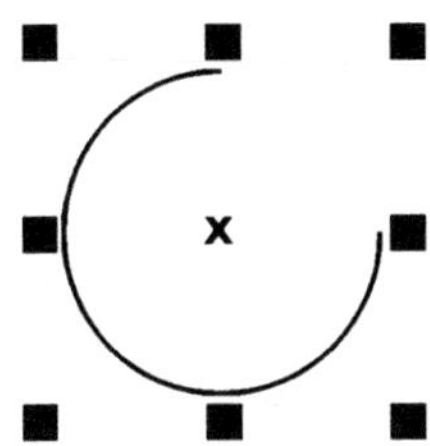

Figure 14. *When you click the Arc button on the Property Bar, the ellipse changes to an arc.*

To change an ellipse into a pie shape or arc:

1. Select the Pick Tool from the Toolbox (**Figure 4**).
2. Click on the ellipse to select it (**Figure 11**). Eight black handles will appear around the ellipse.
3. To change the ellipse to a pie shape, click the Pie button on the Property Bar (**Figure 12**). The ellipse will change to a pie shape (**Figure 13**).

   or

   To change the ellipse to an arc, click the Arc button on the Property Bar. The ellipse will change to an arc (**Figure 14**).

Tip:

■ You can use the Property Bar to set the starting and ending angles for pie shapes and arcs, as well as their direction of rotation—clockwise or counterclockwise (**Figure 15**).

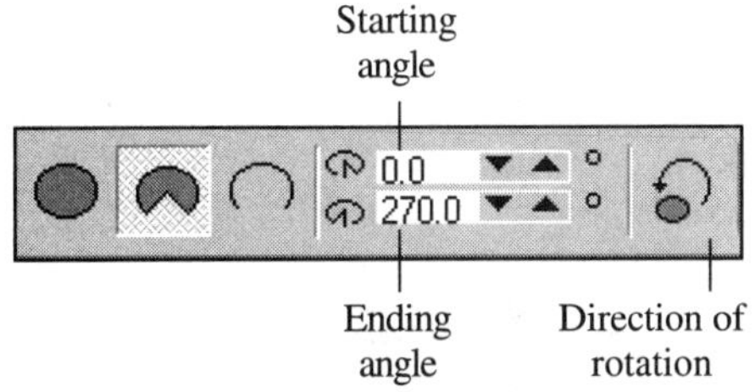

Figure 15. *You can use the Property Bar to change the starting and ending angles and rotation direction of pie shapes and arcs.*

You can change the default properties of the Ellipse Tool to make it always draw pie shapes or arcs.

Figure 16. *When you right mouse click on the Ellipse Tool a pop-up menu appears. Select Properties.*

To change the Ellipse Tool defaults:

1. Right mouse click on the Ellipse Tool in the Toolbar. A pop-up menu will appear (**Figure 16**).
2. Select Properties from the pop-up menu. The Options dialog box will appear with the Ellipse Tool selected in the list box at the left (**Figure 17**).
3. In the Ellipse Tool settings area on the right side of the dialog box, select the type of shape you would like to draw, Pie or Arc, using the option buttons. Then set the starting and ending angles and rotation direction.
4. Click OK. Every time you use the Ellipse Tool from now on, the tool will draw the shape you specified (**Figure 18**).

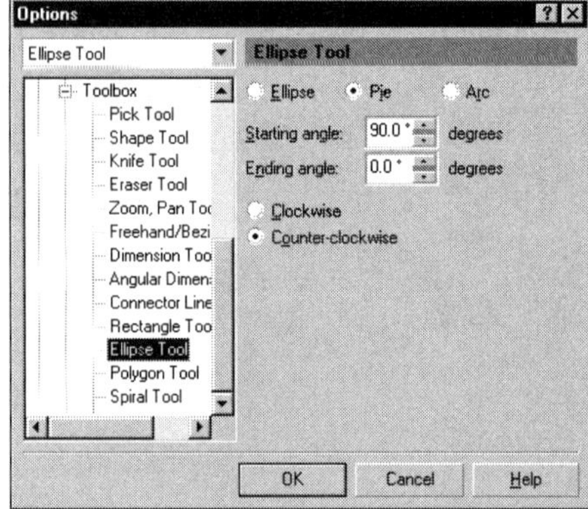

Figure 17. *Use the Options dialog box to set new Ellipse tool defaults.*

Tip:

- You can always change the tool back to its original default by using the steps outlined above and selecting the Ellipse option button.

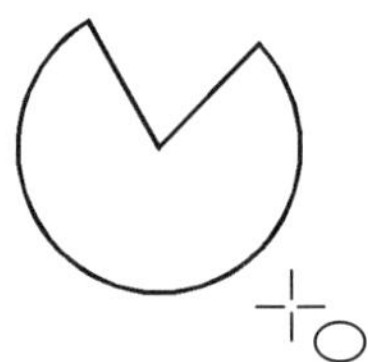

Figure 18. *After you change the defaults, the Ellipse Tool draws what you selected.*

SUMMARY

In this chapter you learned how to:

- Draw rectangles
- Round a rectangle's corners
- Draw ellipses
- Make an ellipse into a pie shape or an arc
- Set the Ellipse Tool's defaults

Change Ellipse Tool Defaults

Select, Move, and Size

In Chapter 3 you learned how to draw simple shapes such as squares and circles. Now it's time to learn how to select, move, copy, clone, and resize them. The tool you will use to do all this is one you've already used, the *Pick Tool* (**Figure 1**).

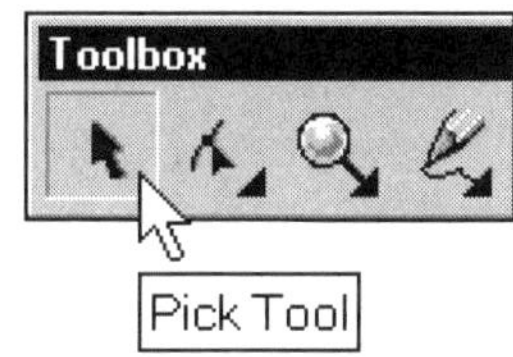

Figure 1. *The Pick Tool.*

The Pick Tool is used to select objects and also manipulate an object's *handles*. Handles are the large black squares that appear in a rectangular formation around an object when it is selected by the Pick Tool (**Figure 2**). They are used to change the overall shape of an object.

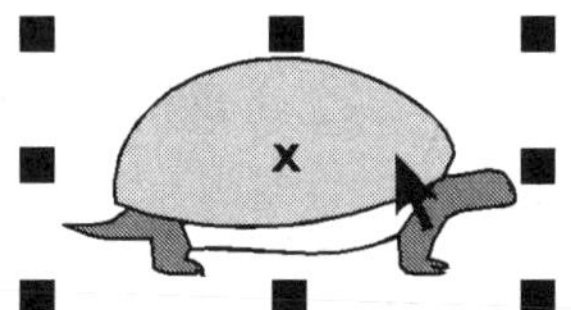

Figure 2. *Handles appear around an object when it is selected with the Pick Tool. Use handles to horizontally and vertically size an object.*

To select an object:

1. Select the Pick Tool from the Toolbox.
2. Click on the object. Eight black handles will appear around the object (**Figure 3**).

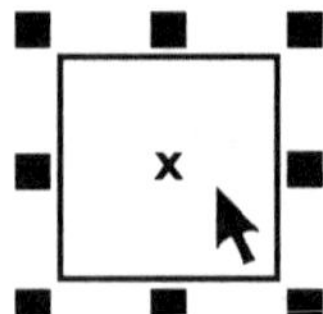

Figure 3. *Handles appear around an object when it is selected.*

To select multiple objects by clicking:

1. Select the Pick Tool from the Toolbox.
2. Hold down the Shift key while clicking on the objects you want to select. As you select objects, the handles' rectangular formation will expand to include the objects (**Figure 4**).

Figure 4. *The handles' rectangular formation expands to include each object as it is selected. In this case, the bunny and flowers are selected, whereas the t-rex and crown are not.*

To select multiple objects by dragging (marquee select):

1. Make sure the Pick Tool is selected, then place the pointer arrow to the left of the objects you want to select.
2. Press the left mouse button down and drag it to select the objects. As you drag, a dashed blue rectangle, or *marquee*, will appear, indicating the selected area (**Figure 5**).
3. Release the mouse button when the marquee encompasses the objects you want to select. The items will be selected as a group with the eight handles appearing in a rectangular formation around the objects (**Figure 6**).

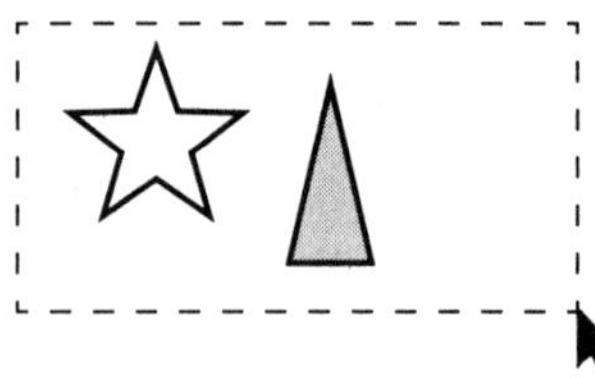

Figure 5. *As you drag the mouse to select multiple objects, a dashed rectangle, or marquee, appears around the selected area.*

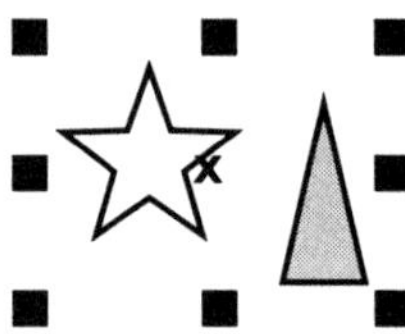

Figure 6. *When the mouse is released, handles appear around the selected objects.*

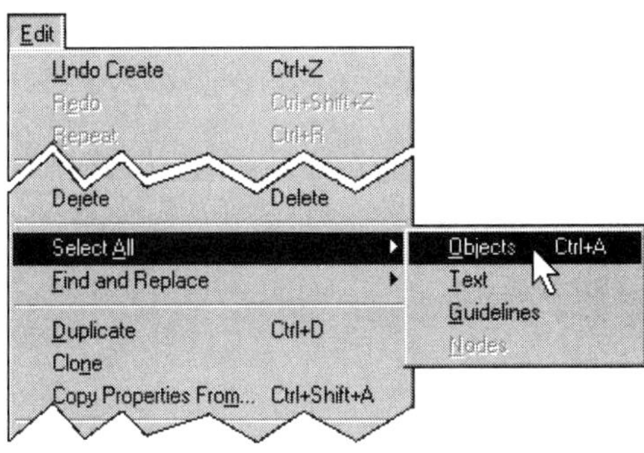

Figure 7. *To select all objects on a page, choose Objects from the Select All fly-out on the Edit menu.*

Figure 8. *As you move an object, a wireframe representation of the object appears on the screen. The object itself remains stationary until you release the mouse.*

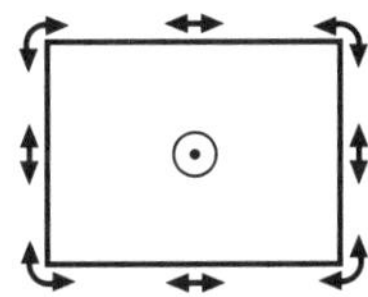

Figure 9. *Double-headed arrows appear around an object when you double-click on it or click once with the object already selected.*

To select all objects on a page:

Choose Objects from the Select All fly-out on the Edit menu (**Figure 7**), or press Ctrl+A on the keyboard, or double-click on the Pick Tool in the Toolbox.

To deselect an object:

1. Select the Pick Tool.
2. Click outside the selected object.

or

Press the Esc key on the keyboard.

Tip:

- To deselect one object within a multiple selection, hold down the Shift key and click on that object.

To move an object:

1. Position the Pick Tool over the object.
2. Press the left mouse button and drag the object to its new location. As you drag, a marquee and wireframe representation of the object will follow along with your pointer until you release the mouse button (**Figure 8**).

Select All; Deselect; Move

WHAT ARE THOSE FUNNY DOUBLE-HEADED ARROWS AROUND MY OBJECT?

If you click on a selected object—one whose handles are already visible—the handles will change to double-headed arrows (**Figure 9**). These arrows are used to skew and rotate an object and will be discussed in Chapter 12 and Chapter 14. To get the big black handles back again, click once on the object.

There are two ways to copy an object: by copying the object to the Windows Clipboard and then pasting it into the document, or by duplicating the object. The end result of these two procedures is the same, but the amount of computing power they use is very different.

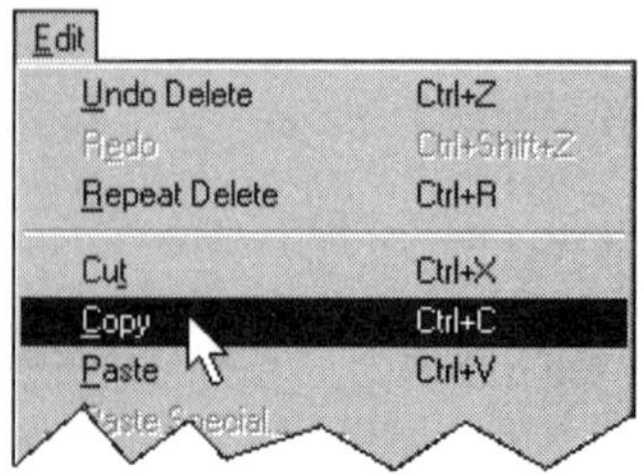

Figure 10. *Choose Copy from the Edit Menu.*

To copy an object using the Windows Clipboard:

1. Use the Pick Tool to select the object you want to copy.
2. Choose Copy from the Edit menu (**Figure 10**) or press Ctrl+C on the keyboard to copy the object to the Windows Clipboard.
3. Choose Paste from the Edit menu (**Figure 11**) or press Ctrl+V on the keyboard. A copy of the object will appear, selected, directly on top of the original. To move the copy, place the the Pick Tool over the copy (not on the object's black handles), press the left mouse button, and drag the object to another position (**Figure 12**).

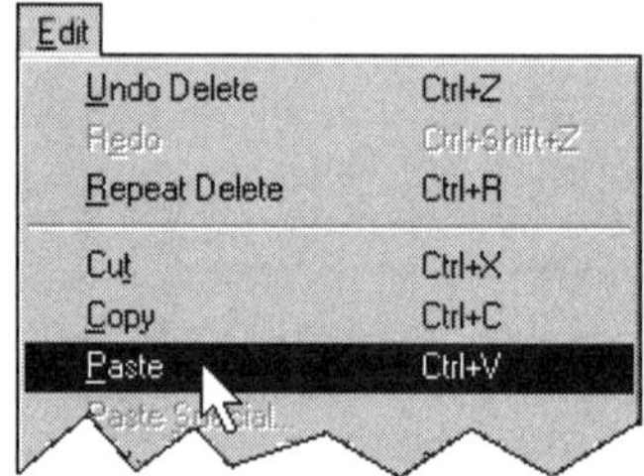

Figure 11. *Choose Paste from the Edit menu.*

Figure 12. *As you drag the copy to a new position, a wireframe representation of the object appears on the screen.*

COPYING USING THE CLIPBOARD VS. DUPLICATING

If you copy an object to the Clipboard, you can then paste it to other pages in your CorelDraw document. It will also be available to other Windows programs. For instance, you could paste a rectangle copied from CorelDraw into Microsoft Word. However, copying and pasting an object, especially a complex one, will put your computer to work for a long time.

CorelDraw's duplicate command bypasses the Clipboard, making it a fast operation. In addition, you can specify exactly where a duplicate will appear in relation to the original (see page 50), whereas a copy will always appear on top of the original.

To copy an object by dragging:

1. Position the Pick Tool over the object you want to copy.
2. Press the *right* mouse button and drag the mouse. As you drag, a wireframe version of the object will appear on the screen (**Figure 13**).
3. Release the mouse button. A pop-up menu will appear. Click on Copy Here (**Figure 14**).

Figure 13. *As you drag with the right mouse button depressed, a wireframe copy of the original appears on the screen.*

Figure 14. *Select Copy Here from the pop-up menu.*

To duplicate an object:

1. Select the object to be duplicated using the Pick Tool.
2. Choose Duplicate from the Edit menu (**Figure 15**) or press Ctrl+D on the keyboard. The duplicate will appear, selected, to the right and slightly above the original by default (**Figure 16**).

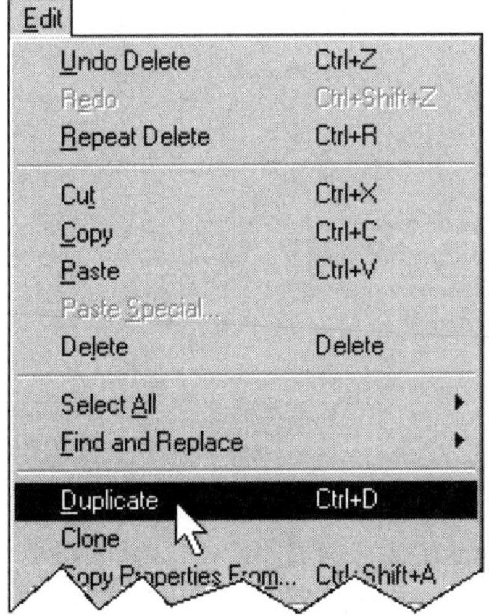

Figure 15. *Choose Duplicate from the Edit menu.*

Tip:

- Another quick way to duplicate an object is to press the [+] key on your keypad. This duplicates the object, and places it directly on top of the original.

Figure 16. *The duplicate appears slightly above and to the right of the original.*

Copy by Dragging; Duplicate an Object

Smart duplication is a CorelDraw 9 feature that helps you quickly create evenly spaced duplicate objects.

Figure 17. *Use the Pick Tool to select the object you want to duplicate.*

To create a series of objects using smart duplication:

1. Use the Pick Tool to select the object you want to duplicate (**Figure 17**).
2. Choose Duplicate from the Edit menu or press Ctrl+D on the keyboard. A duplicate of the original will appear selected (**Figure 18**).
3. Using the Pick Tool, move the duplicate object to its position in the series (**Figure 19**). Be sure to leave the duplicate object selected.
4. Choose Duplicate from the Edit menu or press Ctrl+D on the keyboard to duplicate the repositioned duplicate object. A second duplicate will appear selected, positioned the same distance from the first duplicate as the first duplicate is from the original object (**Figure 20**).
5. Continue pressing Ctrl+D on the keyboard or choosing Duplicate from the Edit menu until there are as many evenly spaced duplicate objects as you need (**Figure 21**).

Figure 18. *A duplicate of the original object appears selected.*

Figure 19. *Reposition the duplicate object.*

Figure 20. *When you create a second duplicate, it appears selected the same distance from the first duplicate as the first duplicate is from the original object.*

Figure 21. *Continue creating as many evenly spaced duplicates as you need.*

Figure 22. *Use the Pick Tool to select the object you want to clone.*

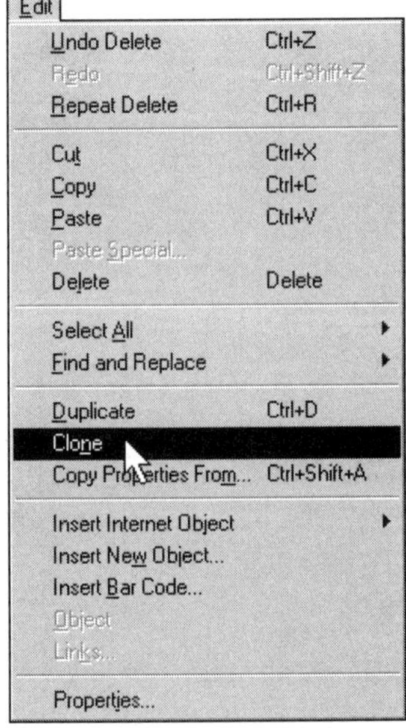

Figure 23. *Select Clone from the Edit menu.*

Figure 24. *A clone of the original appears, by default, above and to the right of the original.*

Like duplication, *cloning* bypasses the Windows Clipboard to quickly create a copy of the original. However, unlike duplication—where the two objects only look alike and are not connected in any other way—cloning creates a link between original and copy. Any changes made to the original also effect the clone. This would be handy, for instance, if you had 100 cloned circles in a drawing and wanted to change their fill color from red to blue. All you would need to do is select the original circle and fill it with blue. All the clones would automatically fill with blue.

To clone an object:

1. Select the object with the Pick Tool (**Figure 22**).
2. Choose Clone from the Edit menu (**Figure 23**). A clone of the original will appear selected (**Figure 24**).

Tips:

- The link between a clone and the original only goes one way. If you alter the original, the clone is changed also. But, if you alter the clone, the original is unaffected.
- You can keep an eye on whether you've selected a clone by watching the Status Bar. If a clone is selected, it will state something such as "Clone Curve on Layer 1." If the original is selected, the Status Bar will read something such as "Control Curve on Layer 1."

The Options dialog box lets you set the properties for all the tools in the Toolbox, as well as customize your work environment. Using the Options dialog box, you can set precisely where a clone or duplicate will appear in relationship to the original.

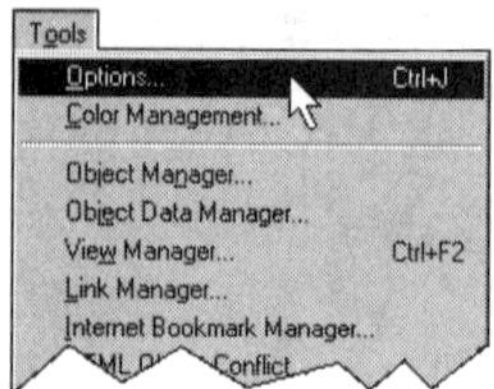

Figure 25. *To access the Options dialog box, choose Options on the Tools menu.*

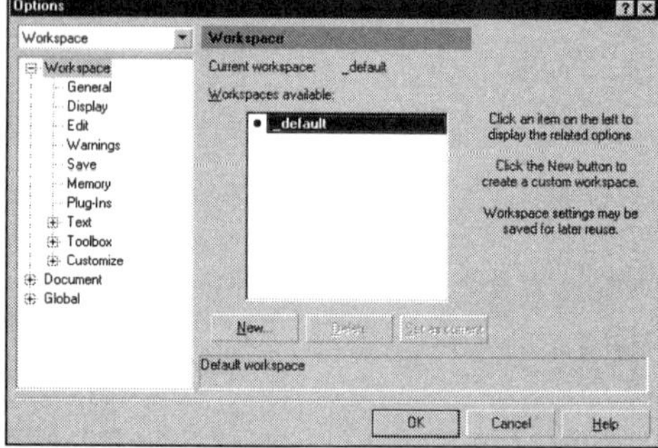

Figure 26. *The Options dialog box is used to set the properties for CorelDraw's tools and workspace.*

To set precisely where a clone or duplicate will appear:

1. Choose Options from the Tools menu (**Figure 25**) or press Ctrl+J on the keyboard. The Options dialog box will open (**Figure 26**).
2. In the tree view box at the left of the Options dialog box, click Edit (**Figure 27**). The right side of the dialog box will change to display the Edit settings (**Figure 28**).
3. In the Duplicate placement area on the Edit panel, enter the distance you want cloned or duplicated objects to appear from the original by typing numbers in the Horizontal and Vertical text boxes. If you want the copy to appear exactly on top of the original, enter 0 in both text boxes.
4. Place a check mark in the box next to Save with document only if you want to save these changes only with this document.
5. Click OK. The Options dialog box will close.

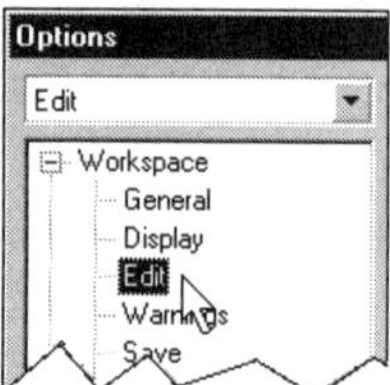

Figure 27. *Click Edit to display the Edit panel on the right side of the dialog box.*

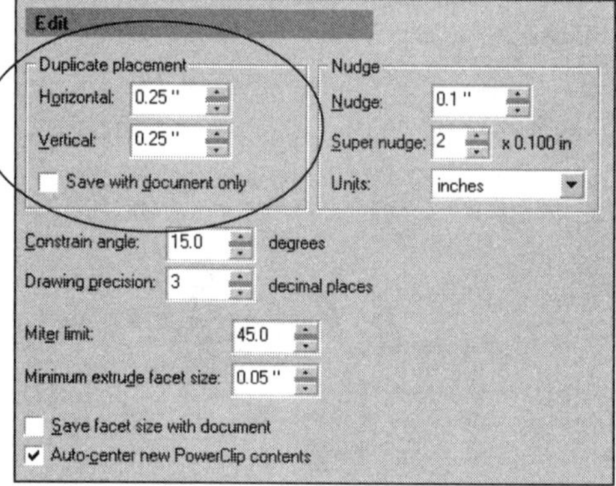

Figure 28. *After clicking Edit, use the Duplicate placement area to set where clones and duplicates will appear.*

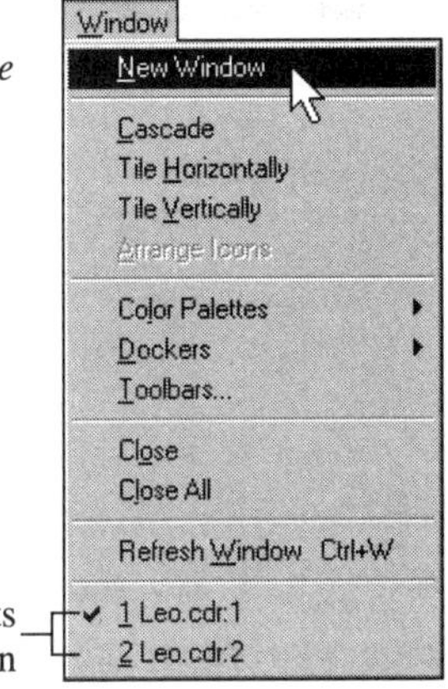

Figure 29. *Choose New Window from the Window menu.*

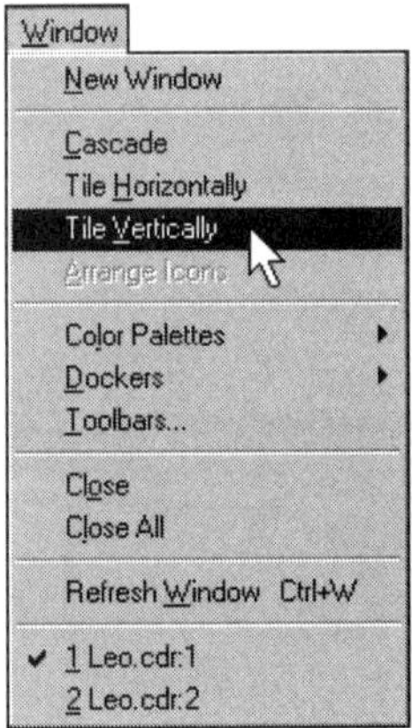

Figure 30. *Choose Tile Vertically to tile the two windows side-by-side.*

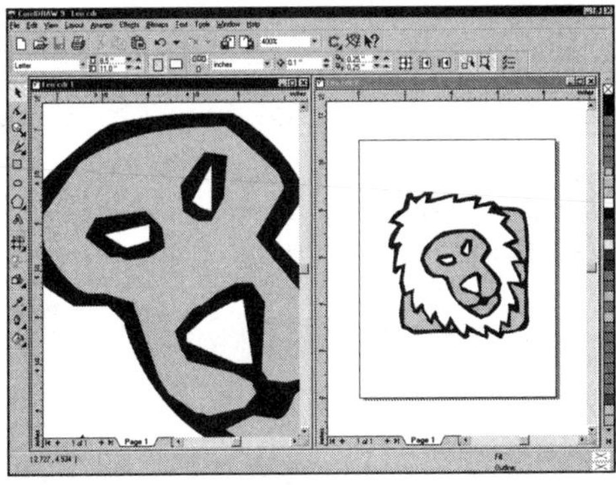

Figure 31. *The same drawing in two windows shown in different display sizes.*

It's important to consider how your drawings are set up on the screen. For instance, when you are working on a complex drawing with many small details, it can be very helpful to view the drawing in two windows. The window on the left would be in a large display size—perhaps 400%—to edit the detail, while the other window would be in a smaller view size so you could see the changes made to the entire drawing.

To view the same drawing in two windows:

1. Open a drawing or get one started in a new document.
2. Choose New Window from the Window menu (**Figure 29**). A new window will appear on top of the original (you won't be able to see the first one). If you look up at the title bar, you will notice the graphic's name has a :2 appended to it.
3. Tile the windows by choosing Tile Vertically from the Window menu (**Figure 30**). The two windows will appear side-by-side (**Figure 31**).

To view two different documents at the same time:

1. Open the two drawings.
2. Choose Tile Vertically from the Window menu. The two windows will appear side-by-side.

As you probably know, it's easy to copy files or move files between windows in Windows using drag-and-drop. CorelDraw 9 allows you to do the same thing with your drawings. You can copy an object in one window and paste it into another. In addition, you can move an object from one document to another with a simple drag-and-drop operation.

Figure 32. *Open two documents and tile them vertically.*

To copy an object from one document to another:

1. Open two documents.
2. Tile the documents by choosing Tile Vertically from the Window menu.
3. Use the Pick Tool to select the object you want to copy and choose Copy from the Edit menu or press Ctrl+C on the keyboard.
4. Click the title bar of the other document's window, the one in which you want to paste the object (**Figure 32**). This will make that window active.
5. Choose Paste from the Edit menu or press Ctrl+V on the keyboard. The object will appear in the second document (**Figure 33**).

Figure 33. *Click the title bar of the second window to make it active, and then choose Paste from the Edit menu. The copied object appears in the second window.*

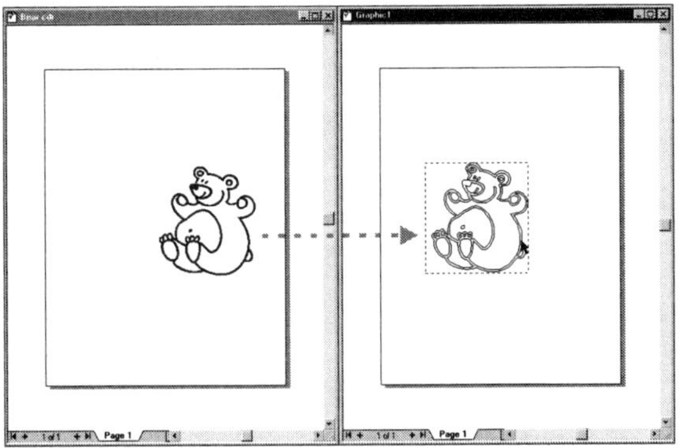

Figure 34. *Use the Pick Tool to drag the object from one document window to another. As you drag the object, a wireframe version of the object appears.*

To move an object from one document to another:

1. Open two documents.
2. Choose Tile Vertically from the Window menu to tile the documents.
3. Place the point of the Pick Tool on the outline of the object you want to move. Press the left mouse button and drag it to the other document (**Figure 34**).
4. Release the mouse button when you are happy with the object's new position. The object will move to the other document (**Figure 35**).

Figure 35. *When you release the mouse button, the object moves to the other document window.*

Tip:

- You can also move or copy an object from one document to another by dragging the object with the right mouse button. When you release the button, a pop-up menu will appear, asking whether you wish to move or copy the object there.

Handles appear in a rectangular formation around an object when it is selected with the Pick Tool. These handles have various functions:

- The handles that appear to the right center and left center of the object affect the object's *horizontal scale*—they make an object wider or narrower (**Figure 36**).
- The handles that appear at the top center and bottom center of an object affect the object's *vertical scale* and make an object taller or shorter (**Figure 37**).
- The handles that appear at the corners affect the object's *proportional scale*. These handles let you change the horizontal and vertical size of an object equally (**Figure 38**).

Figure 36. *The handles at the left center and right center of a selected object affect the object's width.*

Figure 37. *The handles at the top center and bottom center of a selected object affect the object's height.*

Figure 38. *The handles at the corners of a selected object affect the object's height and width equally.*

The Property Bar can be Used to Exactly Size and Position an Object

To use the Property Bar to size and position an object, select the object with the Pick Tool. Enter measurements in the text boxes at the left of the bar, then press Enter on the keyboard.

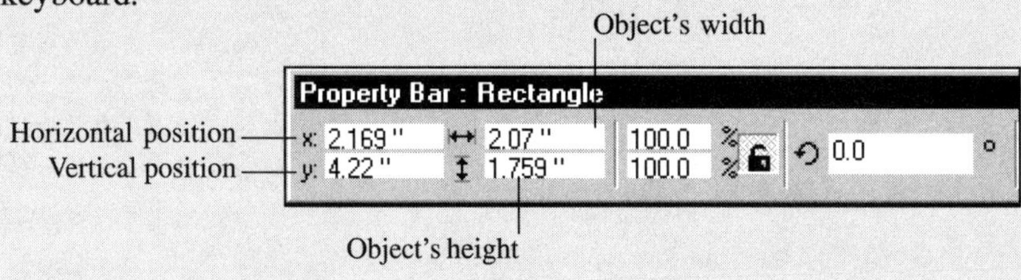

Handles and Scaling

Figure 39. *Drag either the left or right handle to make an object wider or narrower.*

Figure 40. *As you drag inward, a wire-frame version of the resized object appears on the screen. The original remains stationary until the mouse is released.*

Figure 41. *As you drag outward, a wire-frame version of the resized object appears. The original remains stationary until the mouse is released.*

To change an object's width:

1. Select the object using the Pick Tool.
2. Position the pointer over either the left center or right center handle (**Figure 39**). Press the left mouse button and horizontally drag the handle. As you drag, a wireframe representation of the resized object appears. In addition, the mouse pointer will change to a double-headed horizontal arrow. If you drag the handle toward the object, it will become narrower (**Figure 40**). If you drag the handle away from the object, it will become wider (**Figure 41**).
3. Release the mouse button when you are happy with the width.

Tip:

- You can keep an eye on the object's new width by watching the horizontal ruler bar at the top of the screen.

To change an object's height:

1. Select the object using the Pick Tool.
2. Position the pointer over either the top center or bottom center handle (**Figure 42**). Press the left mouse button and vertically drag the handle. As you drag, a wireframe representation of the resized object appears. Also, the mouse pointer will change to a double-headed vertical arrow. If you drag the handle toward the object, it will become shorter (**Figure 43**). If you drag the handle away from the object, it will become taller (**Figure 44**).
3. Release the mouse button when the object is the desired height.

Tip:

- You can keep an eye on the object's new height by watching the vertical ruler bar at the left of the screen.

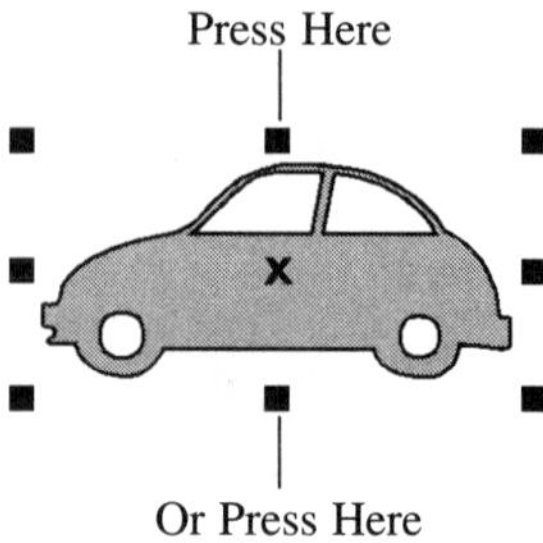

Figure 42. *To change an object's height use either the top center or bottom center handle.*

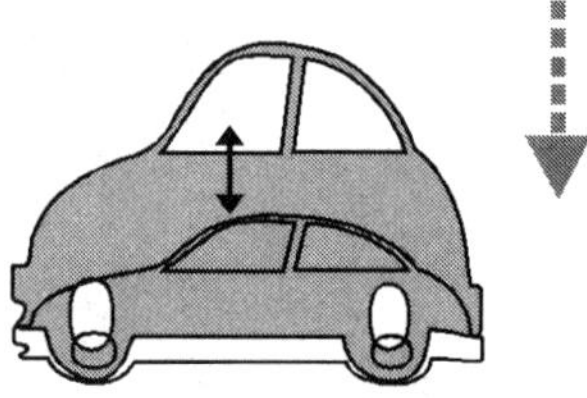

Figure 43. *As you drag the handle toward the object, a wireframe version of the shorter object appears. The object itself remains stationary until the mouse is released.*

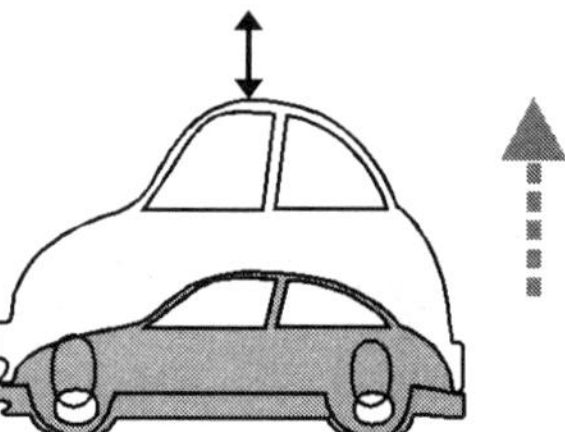

Figure 44. *As you drag the handle away from the object, a wireframe version of the taller object appears. The object itself stays stationary until you release the mouse button.*

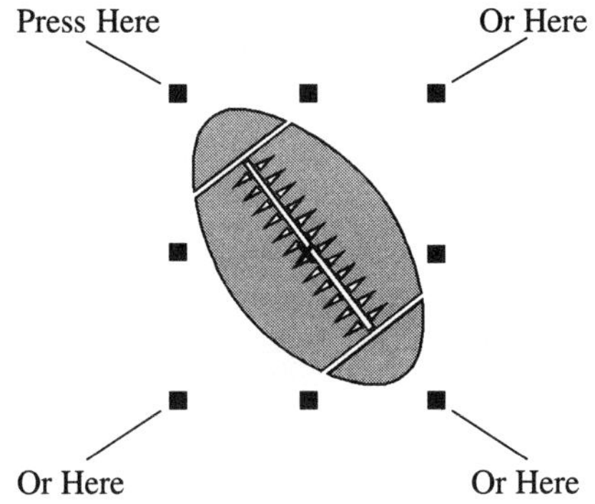

Figure 45. *The handles at the corners of an object are used to proportionally resize the object's height and width.*

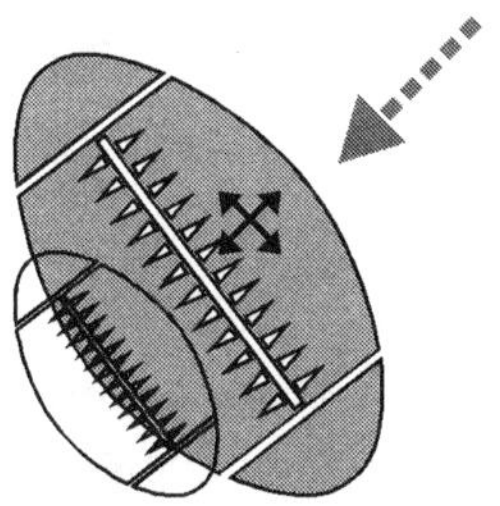

Figure 46. *As you drag a corner handle toward an object, it becomes proportionally smaller.*

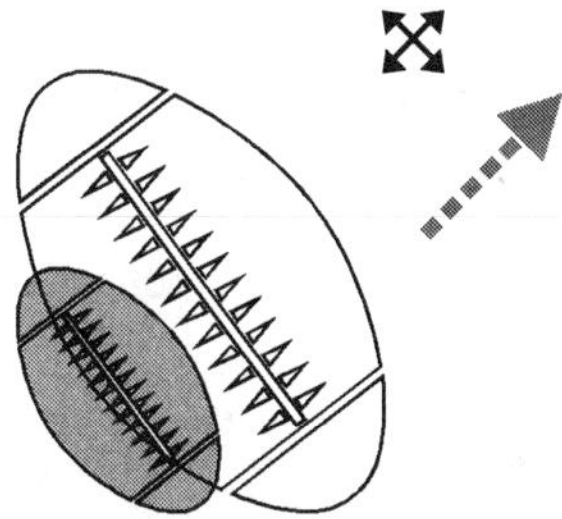

Figure 47. *As you diagonally drag a corner handle away from an object, it becomes proportionally larger.*

To proportionally change an object's width and height:

1. Select the object with the Pick Tool.
2. Press the left mouse button and diagonally drag any one of the corner handles (**Figure 45**). As you drag a wireframe representation of the resized image appears. In addition, the mouse pointer will change to a four-headed arrow shaped like an X. If you drag toward the object, it will become smaller (**Figure 46**). If you drag away from the object, it will become larger (**Figure 47**).
3. Release the mouse button when you are happy with the object's new size.

MORE ABOUT DRAGGING HANDLES

- To scale an object from its center, hold down the Shift key while dragging a handle.
- Press the Ctrl key while dragging a handle to resize the object in 100 percent increments. The size of your object can be as big or small as you'd like. Just change the ruler scale to match what you need, for instance, miles, kilometers, pixels, or millimeters.

To delete an object:

1. Select the object using the Pick Tool.
2. Choose Delete from the Edit menu (**Figure 48**) or press the Delete key on the keyboard.

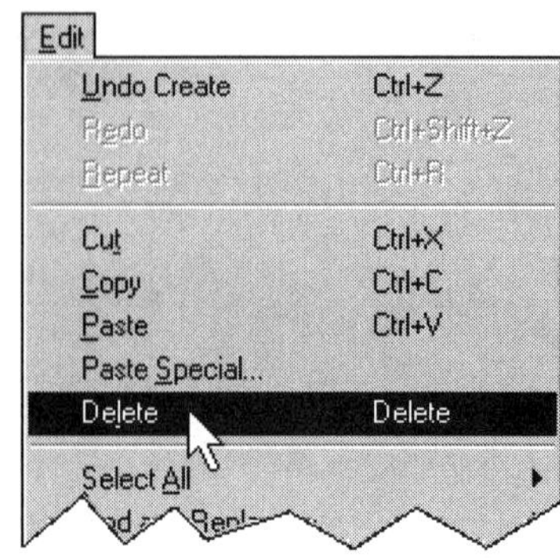

Figure 48. *To delete an object, select it, and then choose Delete from the Edit menu.*

Tip:

- If you press the Backspace key instead of the Delete key, nothing will happen.

THE TAB KEY AND SELECTING

When working with several objects that are close together or on top of each other, it can be difficult to click on the object you want to select.

You can use the keyboard to select the correct object by clicking on an object in your drawing with the Pick Tool, then successively pressing the Tab key until the correct object is selected. As you press the Tab key, watch the Status Bar. It will give you information about which object is currently selected.

SUMMARY

In this chapter you learned how to:

- Select and move an object
- Select all objects on a page
- Marquee select objects
- Copy and duplicate objects
- Clone objects
- View two documents
- Copy and move objects between documents
- Resize objects horizontally and vertically
- Proportionally resize an object
- Delete an object

Polygons, Stars, and Spirals

5

CorelDraw makes it easier than ever to create complex objects with just a simple click and drag of the mouse. Using the Polygon and Spiral tools found on the Shape fly-out, shown in **Figure 1**, you can quickly draw polygons, stars, and spirals. The techniques you learn in this chapter will enable you to add dynamic, professional-quality effects to your documents and presentations.

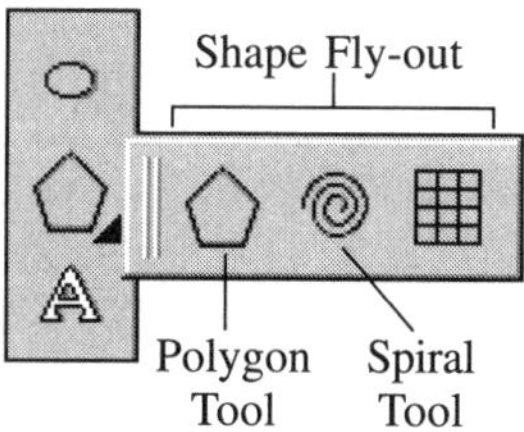

Figure 1. *The Shape fly-out.*

In this chapter you will learn how to create multi-sided polygons using the Polygon Tool. Then you will discover how to access the Toolbox tab page of the Options dialog box to specify the number of sides a polygon will have. From there, you will use the same Toolbox tab page to create several different types of stars and specify how many points each star has and the depth of each star's interior angles. Finally, you will use the Spiral Tool to create fantastic spirals with just a click and drag of the mouse.

To create a polygon:

1. Choose the Polygon Tool from the CorelDraw Toolbox (**Figure 2**) or press Y on the keyboard. Your mouse pointer will change to a cross-hair with a little polygon attached to it.
2. Press the left mouse button and drag it diagonally (**Figure 3**). The polygon will appear as you drag the mouse, becoming larger as you pull diagonally. When you release the mouse button, small nodes will appear around the polygon's perimeter and the polygon will be selected.

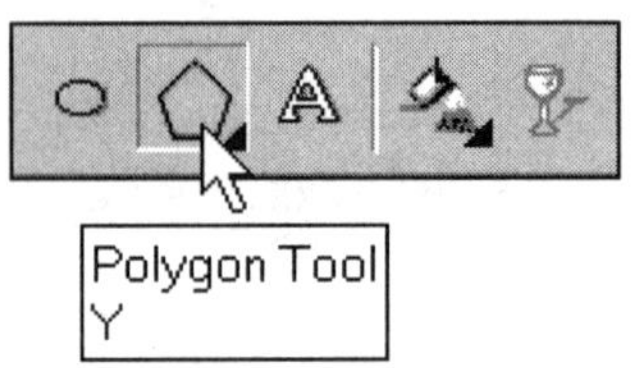

Figure 2. *Choose the Polygon Tool from the Toolbox.*

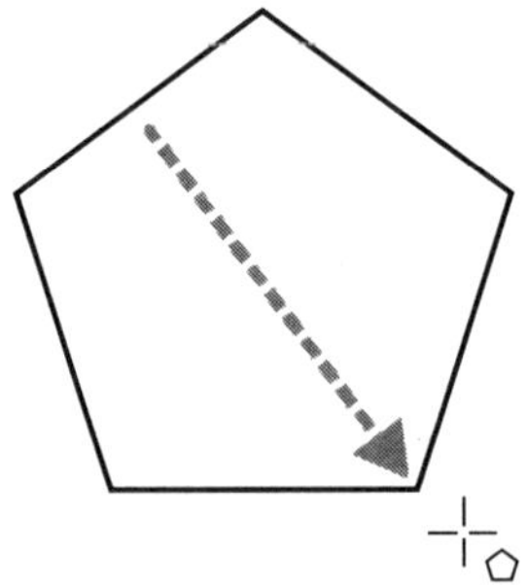

Figure 3. *Drag the mouse diagonally to create the polygon.*

Tip:

- Remember that you can change the outline color or fill of any closed path object that you create (see page 37 for a discussion of closed path objects).

How to Draw an Object from the Center

Hold down the Shift key while dragging the mouse to draw a polygon from the center. When your object is the desired size, release the mouse button first, otherwise the object will spring closer to your mouse pointer and be created from its edge.

Drawing Perfectly Symmetrical Objects

If you want to create a perfectly symmetrical object, hold down the Ctrl key while dragging the mouse. Be sure to release the mouse button before you let go of the Ctrl key, otherwise your object will spring to a non-symmetrical shape.

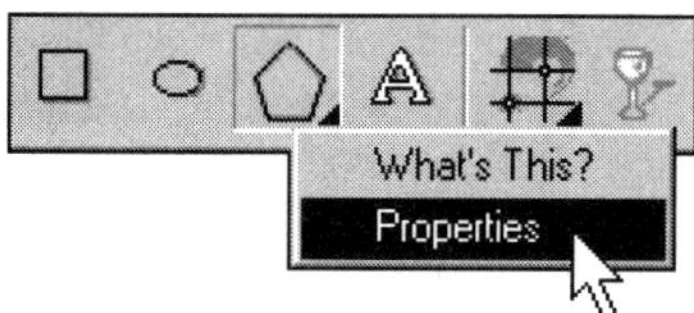

Figure 4. *Click with the right mouse button on the Polygon Tool to access Properties from the pop-up menu.*

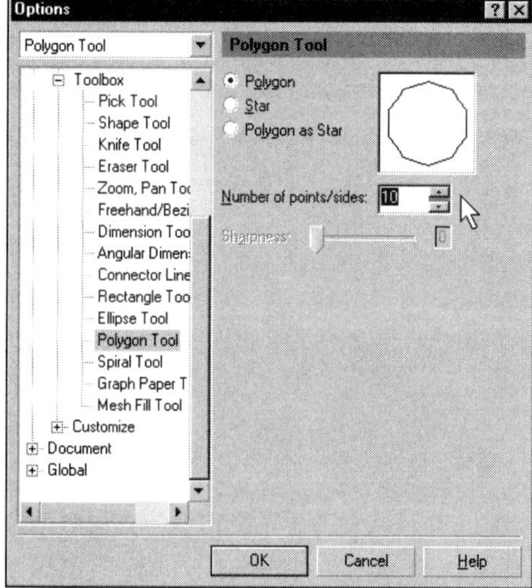

Figure 5. *Use the Options dialog box to set the number of sides a polygon will have.*

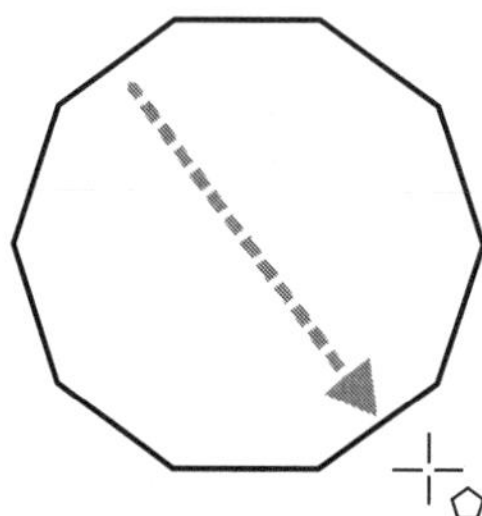

Figure 6. *Drag the mouse diagonally to create a custom polygon.*

To set the number of sides a polygon will have:

1. Double-click on the Polygon Tool in the Toolbox or right mouse click on the Polygon Tool and select Properties from the pop-up menu (**Figure 4**). The Options dialog box will open with the Polygon Tool selected (**Figure 5**).
2. Use the spin buttons to the right of the Number of points/sides text box to change the number in the text box or type the desired number in the text box. A preview of the polygon will appear in the window's preview pane. When you are happy with the polygon's shape, click OK. (To learn more about spin buttons, turn to page 6.)
3. With the Polygon Tool selected, press the left mouse button and drag it diagonally to draw a polygon with the number of sides you just specified (**Figure 6**).

Tips:

- When you change the Polygon Tool's *Number of points/sides* setting, the new setting will only affect polygons drawn after you changed the setting. Any polygons previously created will remain as they were.
- You can set a polygon to have as few as 3 sides (a triangle) or as many as 500 sides!

Stars are an extension of the simple polygon shape. The Polygon Tool is used to create stars. You may have already noticed that the Polygon Tool area of the Options dialog box (**Figure 7**) includes the choice of two star types: *Star* and *Polygon as Star*.

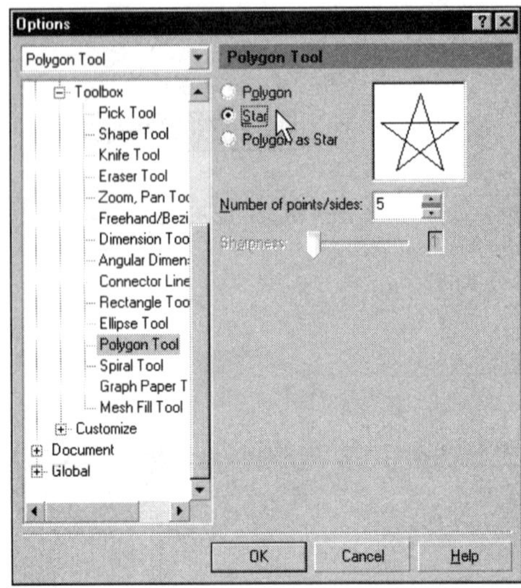

Figure 7. *Select Star as the default Polygon Tool shape in the Options dialog box.*

To draw a star:

1. Double-click on the Polygon Tool found in the Toolbox or right mouse click on the Polygon Tool and select Properties from the pop-up menu. The Options dialog box will open with the Polygon Tool selected.
2. Select the Star option button (**Figure 7**).
3. Set the number of points you want the star to have using the text box and spin buttons. If the number of points is 7 or more, the Sharpness slider bar and text box will become enabled. A higher sharpness setting will make each of the star's angles sharper (**Figures 8a–b**).
4. Click OK.
5. Using the Polygon Tool, hold down the left mouse button and drag it diagonally (**Figure 9**). The star will appear as you drag the mouse, becoming larger as you pull diagonally. When you release the mouse button the star will be selected.

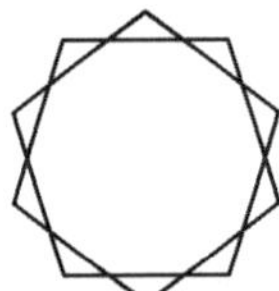

Figure 8a. *This is a 10-sided star with a Sharpness setting of 1.*

Figure 8b. *This is also a 10-sided star with a Sharpness setting of 3.*

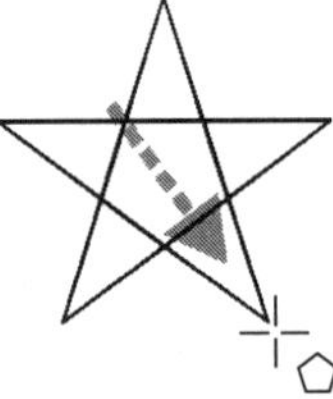

Figure 9. *Drag the mouse diagonally to create the star.*

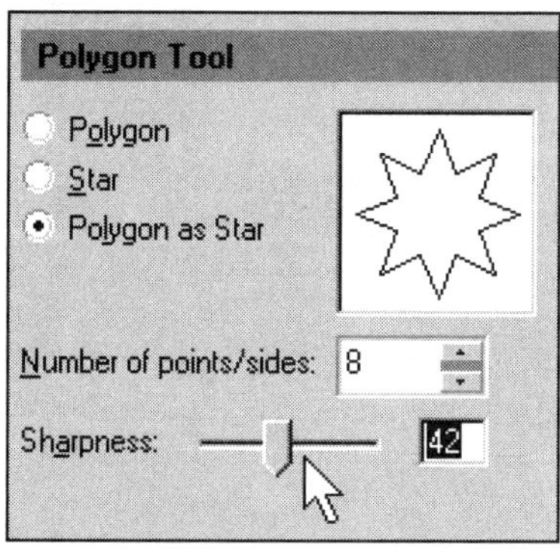

Figure 10. *The Polygon as Star setting creates stars with only an outline. You can use the Sharpness slider bar to change the star's angles.*

Figure 11. *Drag the Polygon Tool diagonally to create a polygon as star.*

Figures 12a–c.

To create a polygon as star:

1. Double-click on the Polygon Tool found in the Toolbox or right mouse click on the Polygon Tool and select Properties from the pop-up menu. The Options dialog box will open with the Polygon Tool selected (**Figure 7**).
2. Select the Polygon as Star option button. The star that appears in the preview pane is different from the star in the preceding section in that its lines don't cross (**Figure 10**). Only a star outline is visible.
3. Set the number of points you want the star to have, and then turn your attention to the Sharpness slider bar and text box (**Figure 10**). Play with the slider bar by moving the slider from right to left. Notice the change that sharpness has on the star in the preview pane.
4. When you are happy with the shape of the star, click OK.
5. With the Polygon Tool selected, press the left mouse button and drag it diagonally. The star will appear as you drag the mouse, becoming larger as you pull diagonally (**Figure 11**). Stars can be used for many types of drawings and borders (**Figures 12a–c**).

With CorelDraw 9 you can create two types of spirals: symmetrical and logarithmic. The space between each revolution of a symmetrical spiral is the same, whereas the space between each revolution of a logarithmic spiral constantly increases.

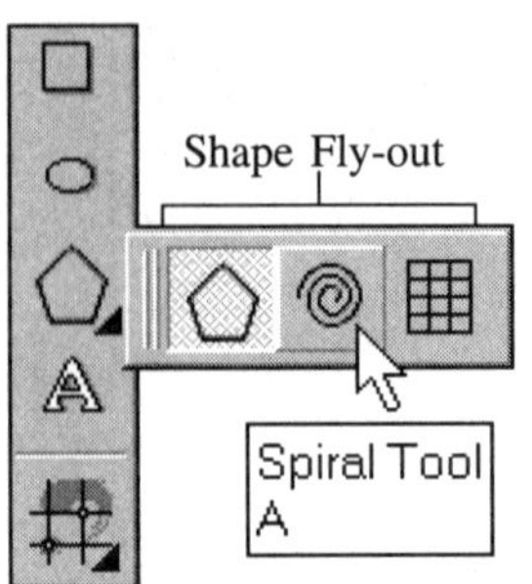

Figure 13. *The Spiral Tool is located on the Shape fly-out.*

To create a symmetrical spiral:

1. To select the Spiral Tool:
   a. Click the little arrow on the Polygon Tool to open the Shape fly-out.
   b. Select the Spiral Tool from the Shape fly-out (**Figure 13**). The fly-out will close.

   or

   Press A on the keyboard.

   The mouse pointer will change to a cross-hair with a tiny spiral attached to it. The Spiral Tool button will replace the Polygon Tool button in the Toolbox (**Figure 14**).
2. Double-click on the Spiral Tool or right mouse click on the Spiral Tool and select Properties from the pop-up menu. The Options dialog box will open with the Spiral Tool selected (**Figure 15**).
3. Select the Symmetrical option button as the Spiral Tool default, and use the spin buttons to set the Number of revolutions (you can also type a number in the text box).
4. Click OK. The dialog box will close.

Figure 14. *When the Spiral Tool is selected, its Toolbox button takes the place of the Polygon Tool button. To get the Polygon Tool button back, just select it from the Shape fly-out.*

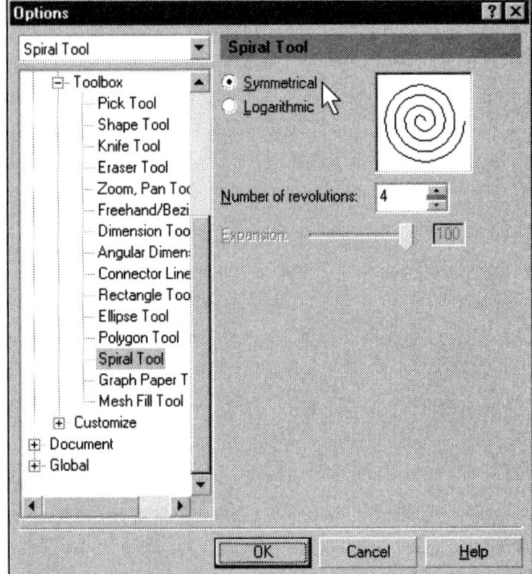

Figure 15. *Use the Spiral Tool panel in the Options dialog box to change spiral default settings.*

Draw a Symmetrical Spiral

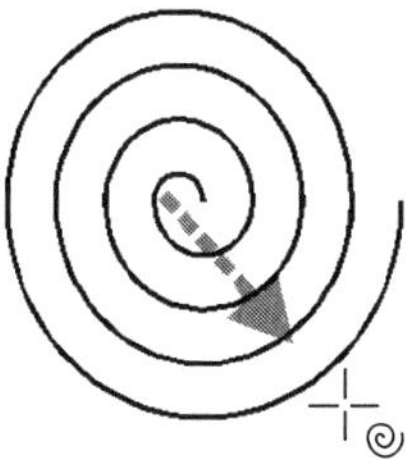

Figure 16. *Drag the Spiral Tool diagonally to create a symmetrical spiral.*

5. With the Spiral Tool selected, press the left mouse button and drag it diagonally to create the symmetrical spiral (**Figure 16**). Release the mouse button when the spiral is the desired size.

To draw a logarithmic spiral:

1. Select the Spiral Tool from the Toolbox (**Figure 13**) or press A on the keyboard.
2. Double-click on the Spiral Tool to open the Options dialog box with the Spiral Tool selected (**Figure 15**).
3. In the Spiral Tool area, click the Logarithmic option button, set the Number of revolutions, and use the Expansion slider bar to set the expansion rate for each revolution of the spiral (**Figure 17**). As you move the slider, watch how the spiral expands in the preview pane.
4. Click OK when you are happy with the settings.
5. With the Spiral Tool selected, press the left mouse button and diagonally drag the tool to draw a logarithmic spiral (**Figure 18**).
6. Release the mouse button when the spiral is the right size.

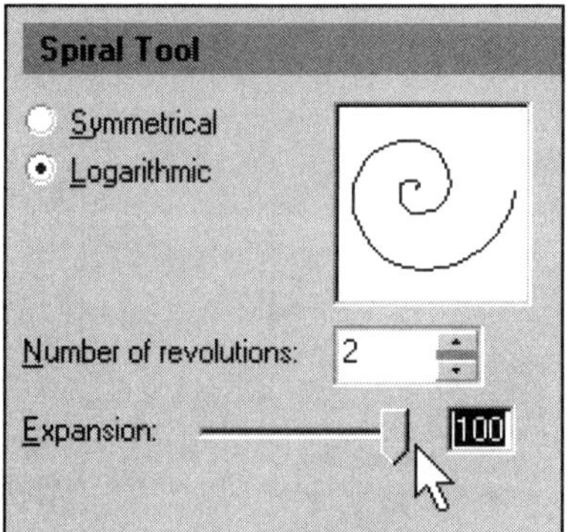

Figure 17. *Use the Spiral Tool area of the Options dialog box to select Logarithmic spiral, Number of revolutions, and Expansion rate.*

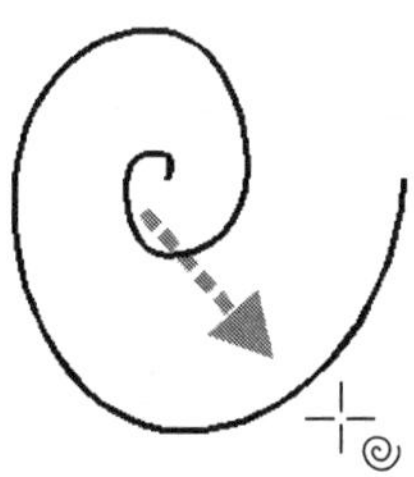

Figure 18. *Drag the Spiral Tool diagonally to create a logarithmic spiral.*

More about spirals:

- You can draw spirals that rotate in a clockwise or counterclockwise direction, depending on which way you drag the mouse. If you drag the Spiral Tool diagonally up to the right, the spiral will rotate clockwise (**Figure 19**). If you drag the Spiral Tool diagonally down to the right, the spiral will rotate counterclockwise (**Figure 20**).
- You can add just a few lines to transform a spiral into something familiar (**Figure 21**).

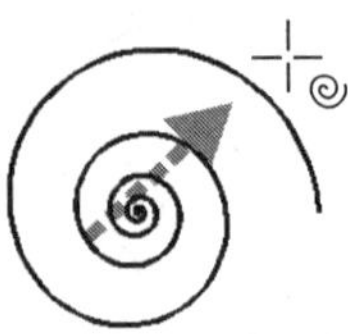

Figure 19. *If you drag the Spiral Tool diagonally up to the right, the spiral will rotate clockwise.*

Figure 20. *If you drag the Spiral Tool diagonally down to the right, the spiral will rotate counterclockwise.*

Figure 21. *Adding a few lines to a spiral transforms it into something familiar.*

SUMMARY

In this chapter you learned how to:

- Draw polygons
- Change the number of sides of a polygon
- Draw stars and polygons as stars
- Adjust a star's sharpness
- Change Spiral Tool default settings
- Draw symmetrical and logarithmic spirals

Nodes and Paths

6

The *Shape Tool* (**Figure 1**) is used to manipulate an object's *nodes*. Nodes are the small, hollow squares that appear on an object's path right after the object is drawn or when it has been selected with the Shape Tool (**Figure 2**).

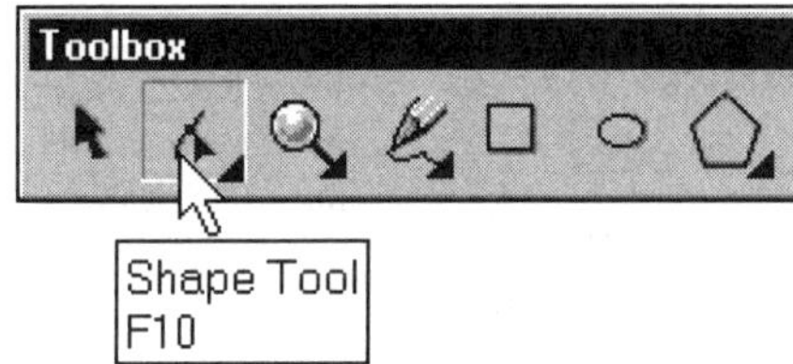

Figure 1. *The Shape Tool.*

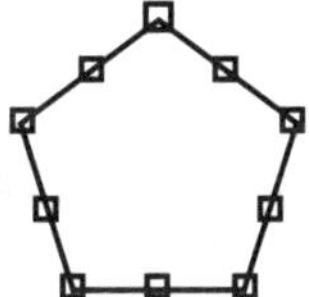

Figure 2. *Nodes appear on an object's path when it is selected.*

Figure 3. *The mouse pointer changes to a large black arrowhead.*

These nodes may appear to be tiny squares of no consequence, but, in fact, they are very powerful. Nodes are used to manipulate specific line segments of an object's path. When you select the Shape Tool, the mouse pointer changes to a triangular, black arrowhead (**Figure 3**).

When you select an individual node with the Shape Tool, several things will happen: the node will change from hollow to black, and one or two *control points* attached to the node with *levers* will become visible (**Figure 4**). Control points determine the curvature of segments of a path. The levers are just a visual representation of which control point goes with which node. (You may have to zoom in to see this since these items are very small. For information on zooming in, see pages 12–13.)

There are three kinds of nodes:

- A *smooth* node is used to create a seamless curve. The control points of a smooth node are always directly opposite each other. If you were to move a control point, the opposite control point, which is locked into alignment with that control point, would move also. The distances between control points can vary (**Figure 5**). This means that the path on one side of a node can be curved differently than the path on the other side of the node.
- A *symmetrical* node is very similar to a smooth node, in that its control points are always opposite each other and if you were to move a control point, the opposite control point would move also. What's different about a symmetrical node is that the control points are always the same distance from each other (**Figure 6**). This makes for a completely even shape on both sides of the node.

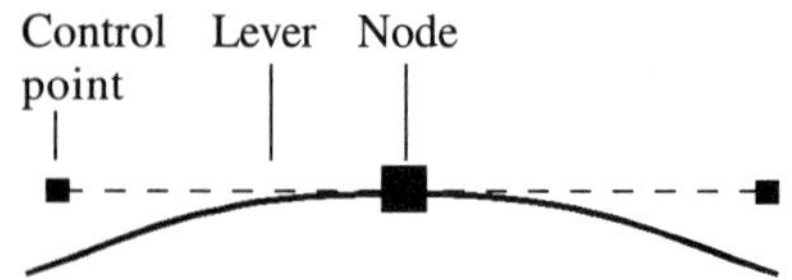

Figure 4. *When a node is selected with the Shape Tool, the node's control points become visible.*

Figure 5. *A smooth node's control points are locked into alignment, and the distances between the control points can vary.*

Figure 6. *A symmetrical node's control points are locked into alignment, and the control points are always the same distance apart.*

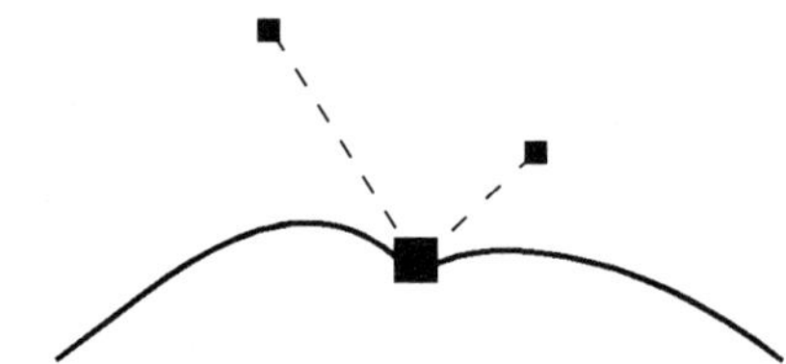

Figure 7. *A cusp node's control points move independently.*

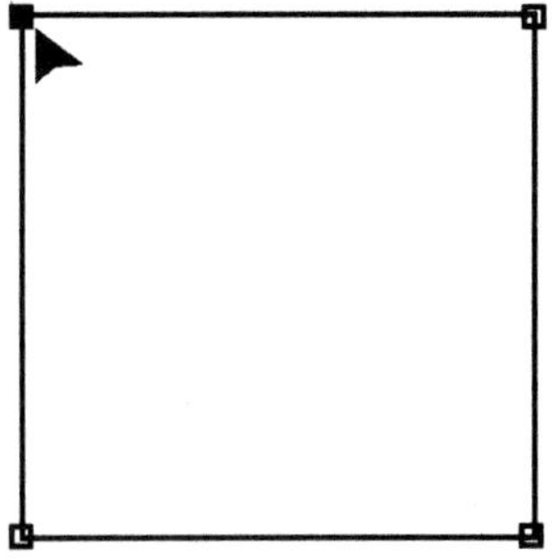

Figure 8. *The selected node has no control points, therefore, the line that passes through it is straight.*

- A *cusp* node is used to create sharp corners on a path. The cusp node's control points move independently of each other; thus, a curve that passes through a cusp node can bend at a sharp angle (**Figure 7**).

In order for a path segment to be bent, it must have control points. If a path segment is not bordered on either side by a control point, that path segment will be straight (**Figure 8**). A node can have from 0 to 2 control points.

A RULE OF THUMB FOR NODES

When you make changes to a node, the changes will affect the line segment located in a *counterclockwise* position from the node.

For instance, in the circle below (**Figure 9a**), the upper node is selected. When the Property Bar is used to add a new node, the new node is added to the line segment located in a counterclockwise position from the selected node (**Figure 9b**).

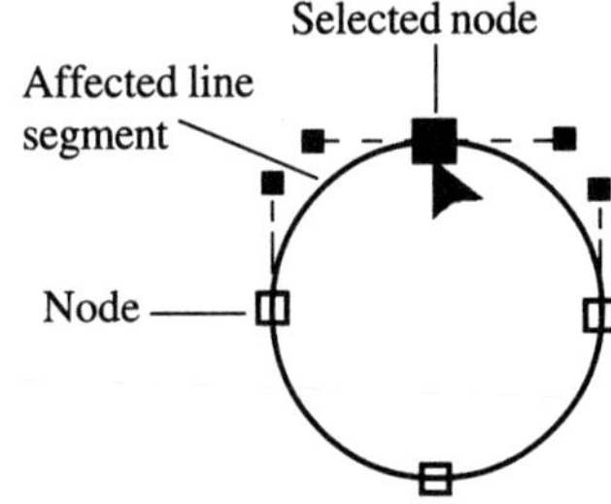

Figure 9a. *The circle's upper node is selected. Any changes will affect the line segment located in the counterclockwise position.*

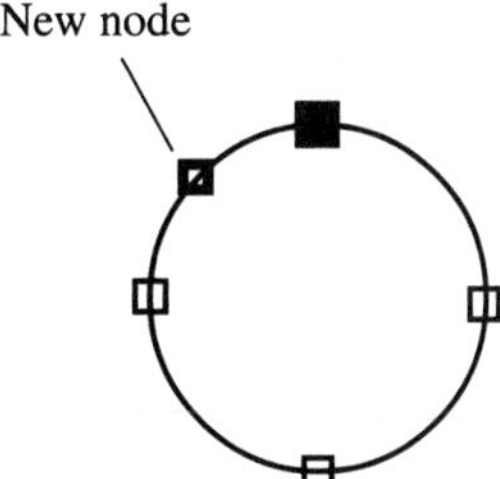

Figure 9b. *The new node is added to the counterclockwise line segment.*

If you draw a shape such as a circle or rectangle, you will not be able to edit its nodes until you *convert the object to curves.*

To convert an object to curves:

1. Select the object using the Pick Tool.
2. Choose Convert To Curves from the Arrange menu (**Figure 10**) or press Ctrl+Q on the keyboard.

Tip:

- Check the Status Bar to see if an object is already made up of curves or if it is a defined shape. If an object is a specific shape, the Status Bar will say something such as "Ellipse on Layer 1" or "Symmetrical Polygon with 10 sides on Layer 1" (**Figure 11**). If an object has been converted to curves, the Status Bar will display something such as "Curve on Layer 1" and will tell you how many nodes the object has (**Figure 12**).

Figure 10. *Choose Convert To Curves from the Arrange menu to change a specific shape to an object comprised of curves.*

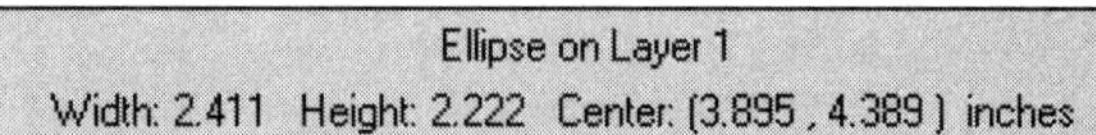

Figure 11. *The Status Bar will tell you whether you need to convert an object to curves. In this case, an elliptical shape is selected and the Status Bar states that this object is an "Ellipse on Layer 1."*

Figure 12. *After converting the elliptical shape to curves, the Status Bar states that the object is a "Curve on Layer 1."*

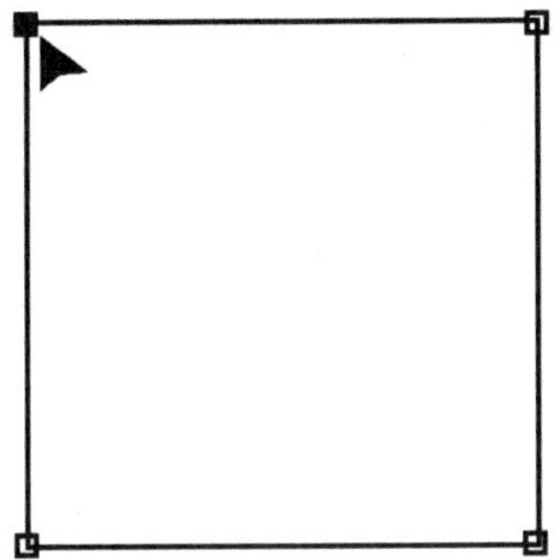

Figure 13. *Use the Shape Tool to click on the node you want to select.*

To select a node:

1. Select the object using the Shape Tool. The object's nodes will appear on the shape's path. (Check the Status Bar to make sure it says that the object is a curve. If it says the object is a rectangle or ellipse, for instance, you will have to *convert the object to curves*. See the previous page for more on how to do this.)
2. Select a node with the Shape Tool. The node will change from hollow to black (**Figure 13**).

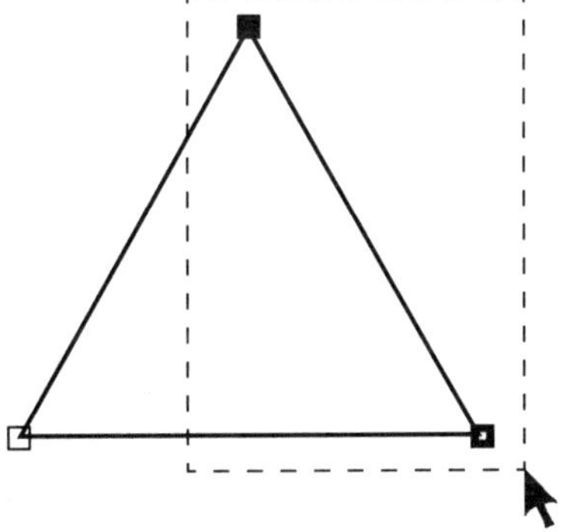

Figure 14. *You can marquee select several nodes at once.*

To select multiple nodes:

1. Select the object with the Shape Tool.
2. Hold down the Shift key while clicking on the nodes you wish to select.

or

Press the left mouse button and drag the mouse. A dashed rectangle, or marquee, will appear as you drag. Release the mouse when the marquee encompasses the nodes you wish to select (**Figure 14**).

REMEMBER TO USE THE STATUS BAR

The Status Bar provides all sorts of useful information. If you want to know what kind of object or node you are looking at, select the item and take a look at the Status Bar.

The Property Bar (**Figure 15**) is used to edit the properties of nodes and paths. In previous versions of CorelDraw, the Node Edit roll-up was used for this purpose. This roll-up no longer exists.

When a node is changed, it alters the shape of the path passing through the node. For instance, suppose there were two lines you wanted to connect. You would use the Property Bar to join the nodes at the end of each line.

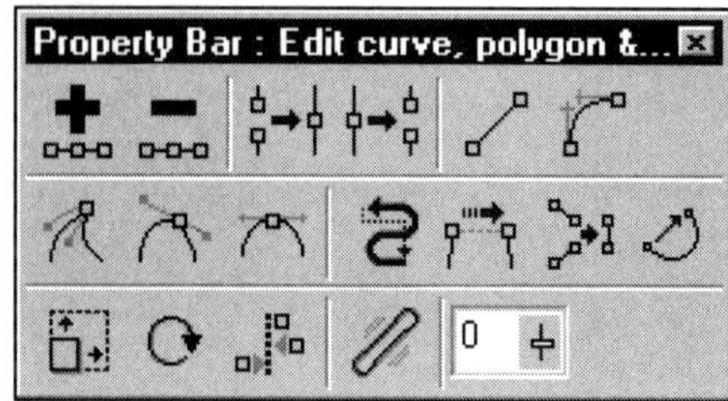

Figure 15. *You can use the Property Bar to change node properties.*

Sometimes you will encounter a node with no control points (**Figure 16**). This is because the path that is passing through the node is a perfectly straight line segment. To add control points to such a node, you will need to *convert the line to curves.*

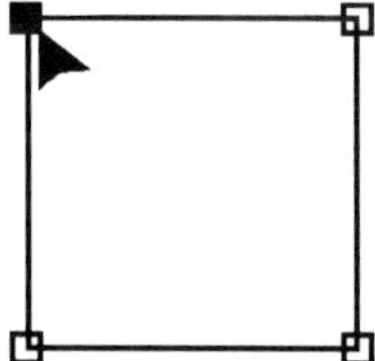

Figure 16. *The selected node has no control points, therefore the line is perfectly straight.*

To add control points to a node or make a straight line curved:

1. Use the Shape Tool to click the node with no control points. This will select the node. The Property Bar will dynamically change to display the node edit buttons.
2. Click the Convert Line To Curve button (**Figure 17**). Control points will appear, bordering each side of the line segment (**Figure 18**), one on the selected node and the other on the node located in a counter-clockwise position from the selected node.

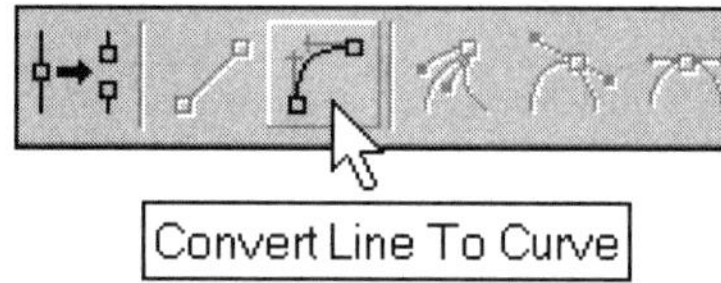

Figure 17. *Click the Convert Line To Curve button to add a control point to a node.*

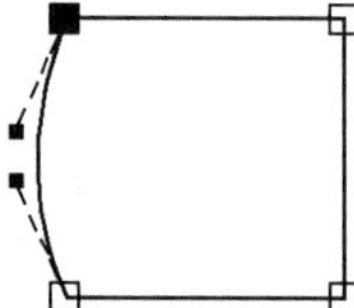

Figure 18. *After pressing the Convert Line To Curve button, control points appear bordering the line segment.*

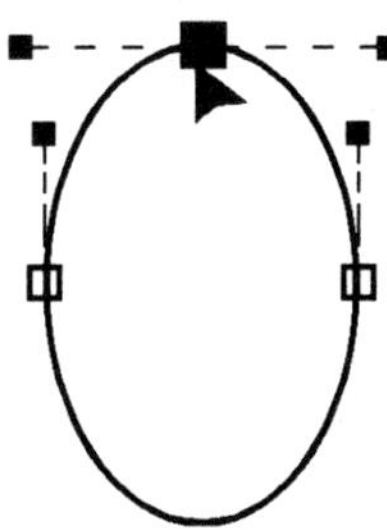

Figure 19. *Use the Shape Tool to select the node you want to convert.*

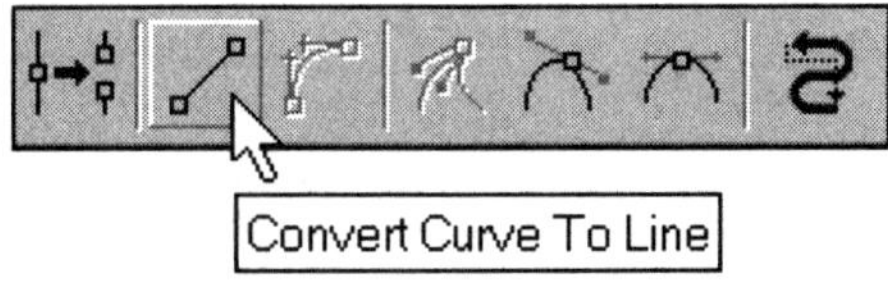

Figure 20. *Click the Convert Curve To Line button to make a curved line straight.*

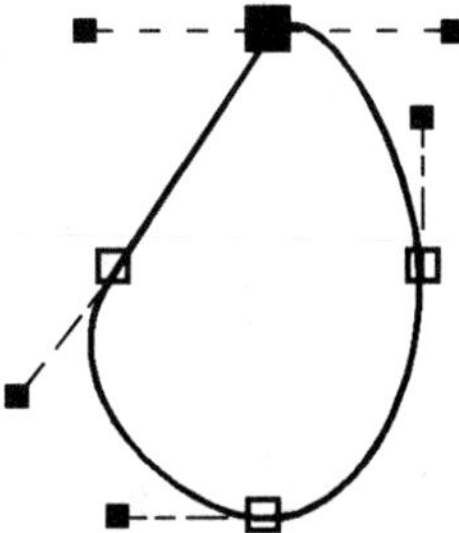

Figure 21. *When the curved line is converted to a straight one, the control points bordering each side of the line disappear.*

To make a curved line segment perfectly straight, you will have to do the opposite of converting a line to curves—you will need to *convert a curve to a line.*

To make a curved line straight:

1. Use the Shape Tool to click on the node you want to convert to select the node (**Figure 19**). The Property Bar will change dynamically to display node editing buttons.
2. Click the Convert Curve To Line button (**Figure 20**).
3. The control points will disappear and the line will become straight (**Figure 21**).

> **SWITCH BETWEEN TOOLS**
>
> To quickly switch between the tool you are using and the Pick Tool, press the space bar on your keyboard. To return to the other tool, press the space bar again.

Special Project:

Create a Heart

Changing a circle into a heart is easy to do. Follow the steps to discover how to create a heart by converting nodes from one type to another, moving control points to achieve the desired curve, and moving the nodes themselves to stretch path segments.

To start the heart:

1. Draw a perfect circle using the Ellipse Tool while holding down the Ctrl key (**Figure 22**).
2. Convert the circle to curves by either pressing Ctrl+Q on the keyboard or choosing Convert To Curves on the Arrange menu.
3. Select the object with the Shape Tool to display its nodes (**Figure 23**).
4. Use the Shape Tool to select the node at the bottom of the circle. When you do, several control points appear (**Figure 24**) at the bottom and sides. If you look at the Status Bar, you will see that the node you have selected is a "Curve Symmetrical"—meaning, a symmetrical node. The bottom of a heart is pointed, so you are going to have to convert the symmetrical node to a cusp node to achieve the point.

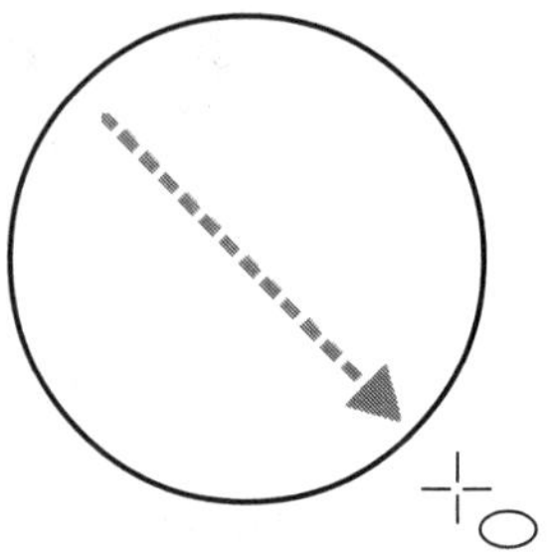

Figure 22. *Hold down the Ctrl key while using the Ellipse Tool to draw a perfect circle.*

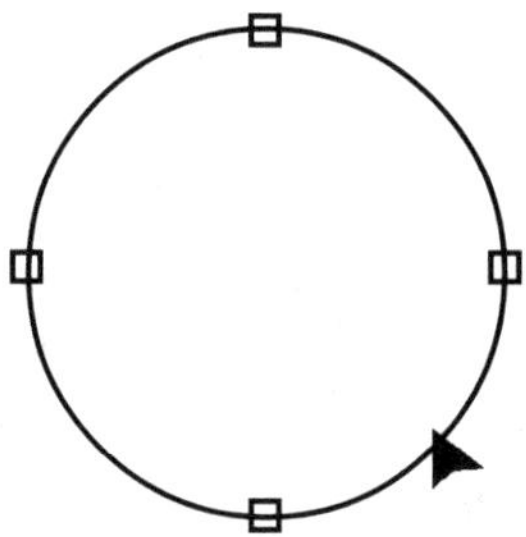

Figure 23. *Use the Shape Tool to select the object and display its nodes.*

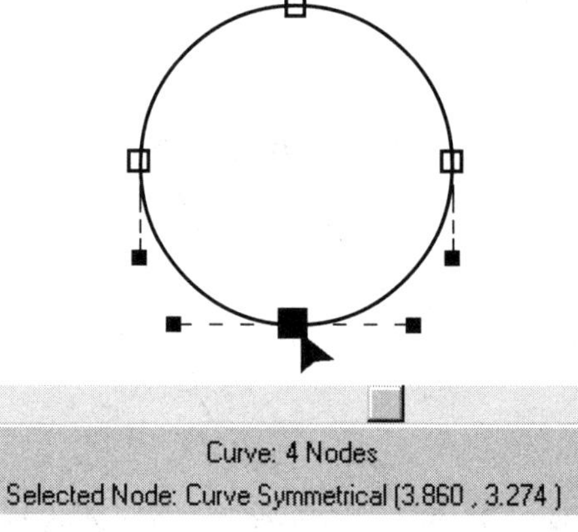

Figure 24. *When you select the bottom node, the Status Bar tells you what type of node it is.*

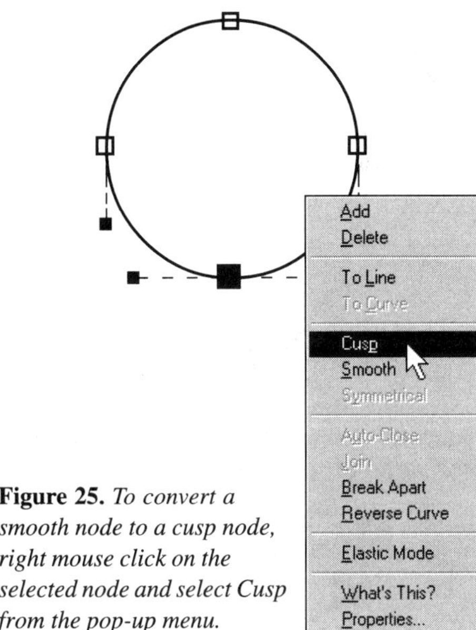

Figure 25. *To convert a smooth node to a cusp node, right mouse click on the selected node and select Cusp from the pop-up menu.*

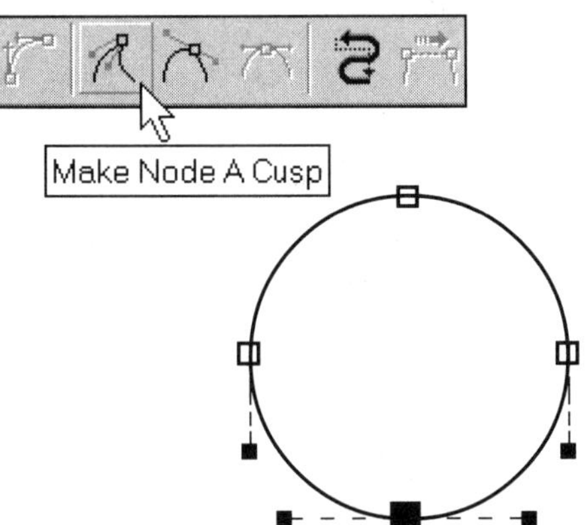

Figure 26. *Click the Make Node A Cusp button on the Property Bar to convert the node.*

To convert a smooth node to a cusp node:

1. Use the Shape Tool to select the node you want to convert.
2. Position the pointer on the selected node and right mouse click to open the pop-up menu and select Cusp (**Figure 25**).

or

1. Select the node with the Shape Tool.
2. Click the Make Node A Cusp button near the center of the Property Bar to convert the symmetrical node to a cusp node (**Figure 26**). (Thankfully, ToolTips help will display to tell you which button is the Make Node A Cusp button!)

Tip:

- Use either of the procedures above to convert any type of node to another type—for instance, you could convert a smooth node to a symmetrical node.

DISPLAYING THE PROPERTY BAR

If the Property Bar is not displayed on the CorelDraw screen, then you will need to open it. Turn to page 9 for directions on how to do this.

Next, to make the circle look more like a heart, you will need to move the bottom node down a little to elongate the sides of the circle.

To move a node:

1. Select the node with the Shape Tool.
2. Press the left mouse button and drag until you are satisfied with the shape (**Figure 27**).
3. Release the mouse button.

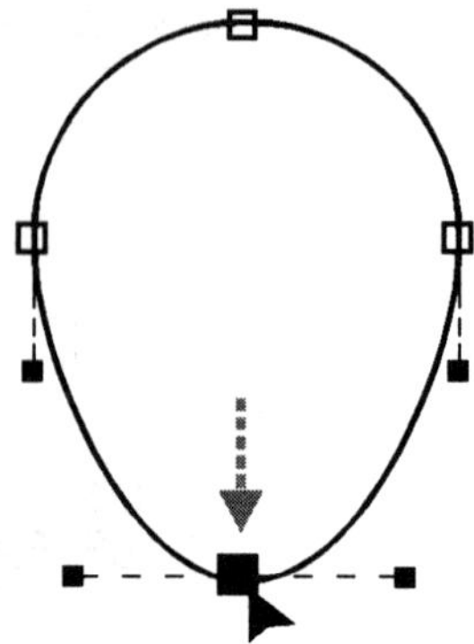

Figure 27. *Press the left mouse button and drag the node to the desired position.*

The next step is to move the node's control points upward to create the heart's point at the bottom of the circle.

To move a control point:

1. Select the node you want to edit with the Shape Tool.
2. Move the tip of the Shape Tool arrow to the control point you want to move.
3. Press the left mouse button and drag the control point until you have achieved the desired curve (**Figure 28**).

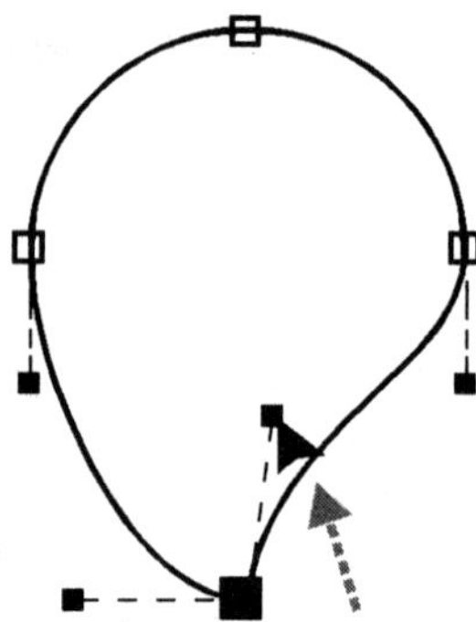

Figure 28. *Drag the control point until you have achieved the desired curve.*

To create the heart's point, both the right and left control points at the bottom of the circle should be stretched up to create the point (**Figure 29**).

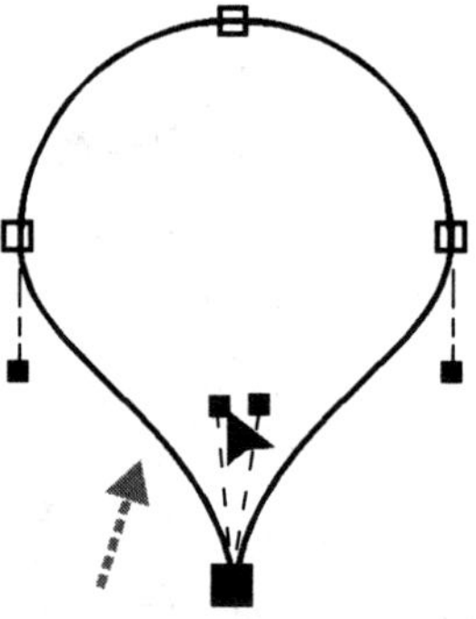

Figure 29. *To create the heart's bottom point, drag the control points upward.*

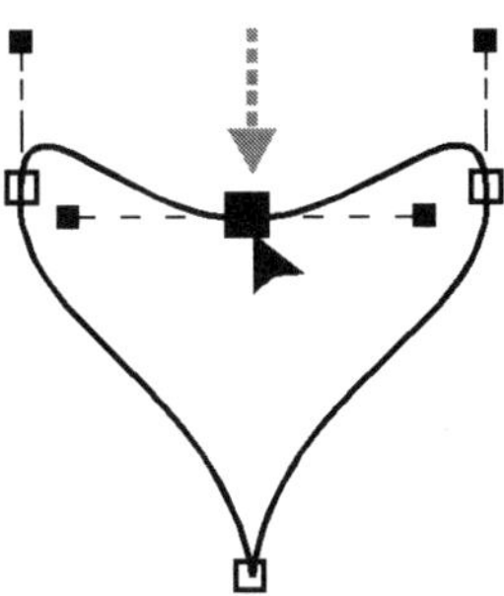

Figure 30. *Drag the cusp node down to shape the top of the heart.*

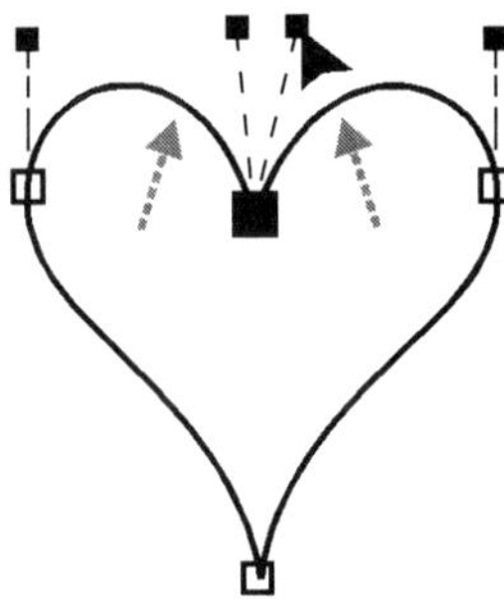

Figure 31. *Drag the control points up to create the heart's sharp angle.*

Finishing the heart is easy. All you have to do is apply what you have learned to the node at the top of the circle. Look at the shape of the top of the circle. What shape do you need there to create a heart? The top of a heart has a sharp dimple—an angle—so you are going to need a cusp node.

To create the top of the heart:

1. Convert the symmetrical node at the top of the circle to a cusp node.
2. Move the cusp node down, using the Shape Tool, to begin shaping the top of the heart (**Figure 30**).
3. Next, drag and stretch the cusp node's control points up to create the sharp angle and rounded tops of the heart (**Figure 31**). *Voilà!* Hearts can be used in many kinds of drawings (**Figures 32a–d**).

Figures 32a–d.

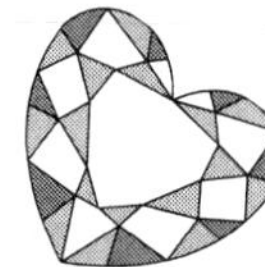

To manually add a node to a path:

1. Select the object using the Shape Tool.
2. Click on the path where you want to add the node. A circular, temporary node will appear on the line segment (**Figure 33**).
3. With the Shape Tool's pointer positioned over the temporary node, right mouse click and select Add from the pop-up menu (**Figure 34**) or press the [+] key on your keypad.

or

1. Click with the Shape Tool on the path where you want to add the node. A circular, temporary node will appear on the path. The Property Bar will dynamically change to display the node edit buttons.
2. Click the Add Node(s) button on the Property Bar (**Figure 35**).

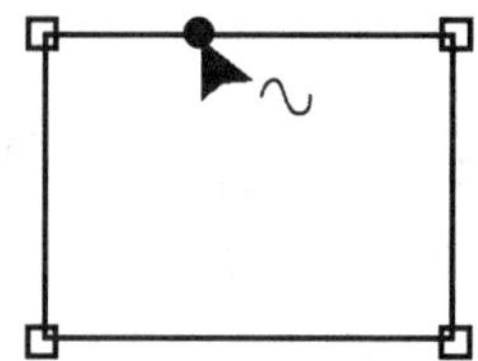

Figure 33. *Use the Shape Tool to click on the path where you want to add a node.*

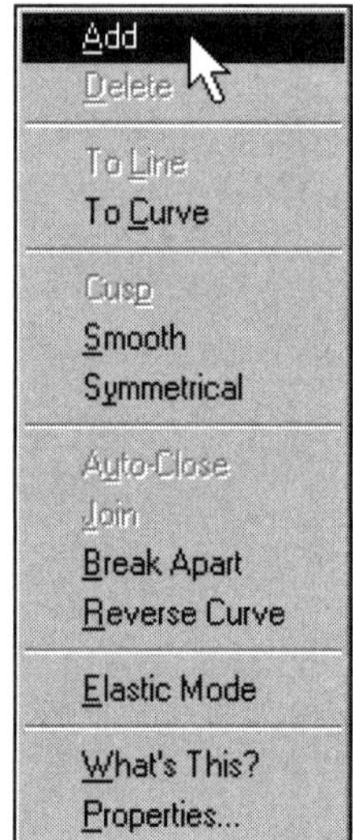

Figure 34. *Select Add from the pop-up menu.*

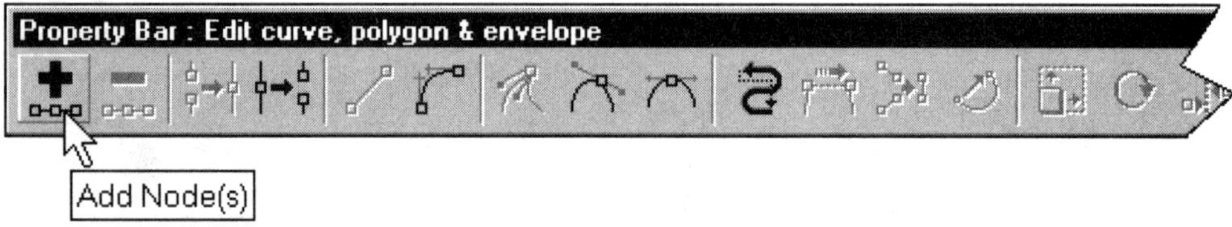

Figure 35. *Click the Add Node(s) button on the Property Bar.*

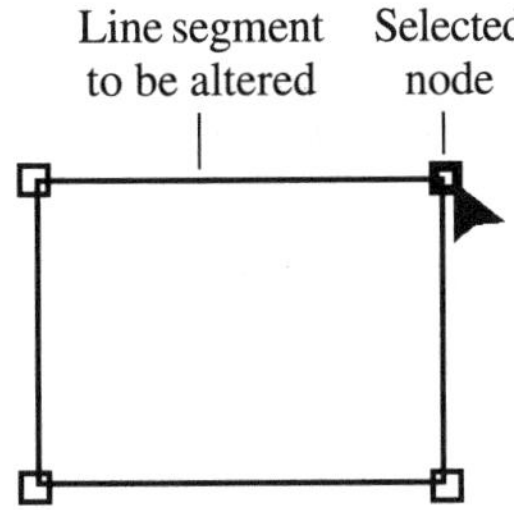

Figure 36. *Select the node that is positioned clockwise to the line segment that you want to alter.*

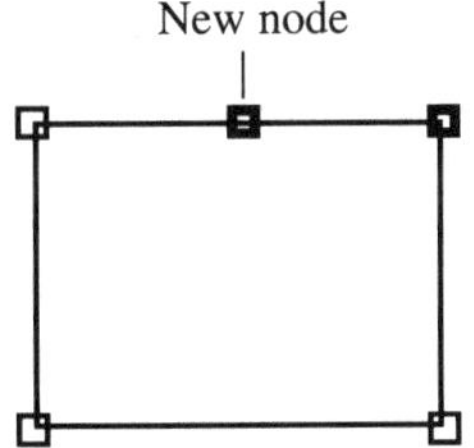

Figure 37. *The new node appears at the center of the line segment.*

To automatically add a node to a line segment:

1. Select the node whose position is clockwise to the line segment you want to edit (**Figure 36**). The Property Bar will dynamically change to display the node editing buttons.
2. Click the Add Node(s) button on the Property Bar (**Figure 35**). A new node will appear, selected, that evenly divides the path into two segments (**Figure 37**).

Tip:

- The type of node you select before pressing the Add Node(s) button determines what type of node will be added. For instance, if you select a cusp node and then press the Add Node(s) button, a new cusp node will be added to the path.

ToolTips and the Property Bar

There are so many buttons on the Property Bar that it can look rather confusing. Remember that ToolTips help is always available. As you slowly pass the mouse pointer over the different buttons, small balloons will appear, describing what each button does. **Figure 35** shows the ToolTip that appears when the mouse is passed over the Add Node(s) button.

To delete a node from a path:

1. Select the node you want to delete using the Shape Tool.
2. With the Shape Tool's pointer positioned over the selected node, right mouse click and choose Delete from the pop-up menu (**Figure 38**) or press the Delete key on your keyboard.

or

Double-click on the node you want to delete. The node will disappear.

or

1. Select the node you want to delete using the Shape Tool. The Property Bar will change dynamically to display the node editing buttons.
2. Click the Delete Node(s) button on the Property Bar (**Figure 39**).

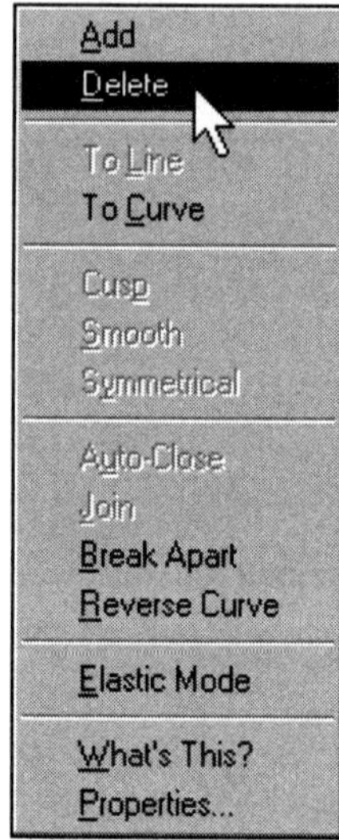

Figure 38. *After selecting the node you want to delete, click the right mouse button and choose Delete from the pop-up menu.*

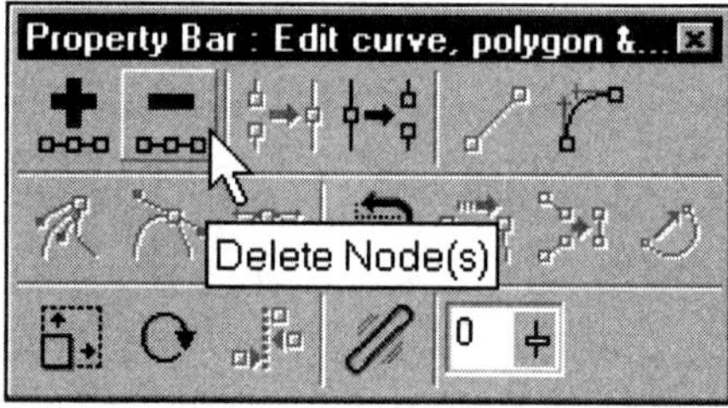

Figure 39. *You can also use the Property Bar to delete nodes.*

Tips:

- Several nodes can be deleted at once by selecting multiple nodes and using either of the above methods.
- You can also delete a node by selecting it and then pressing the [-] key on your keypad.
- If you try to delete a node by selecting it and then pressing the Backspace key, your computer will beep and nothing will happen.

Delete a Node From a Path

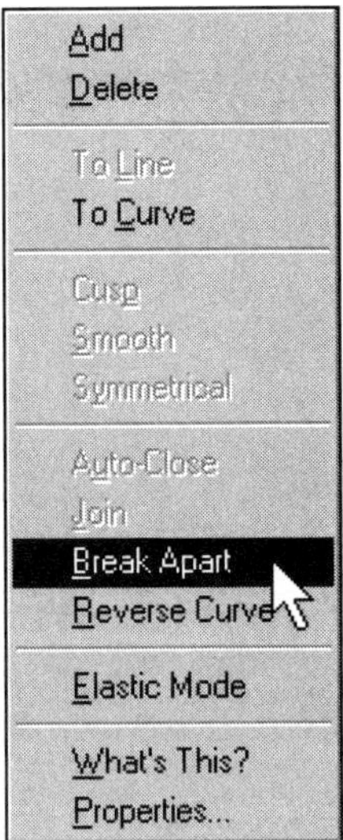

Figure 40. *After selecting the node you want to break into two, right mouse click and choose Break Apart from the pop-up menu.*

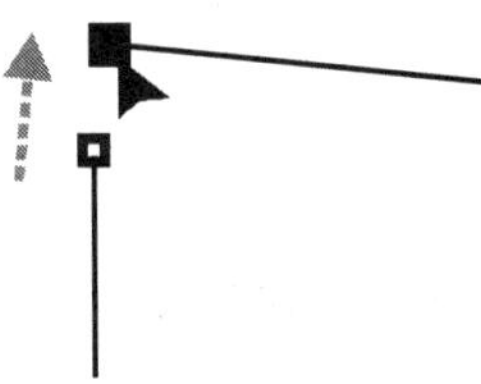

Figure 41. *A broken curve contains two nodes, one on top of the other. Move one of the nodes away using the Shape Tool.*

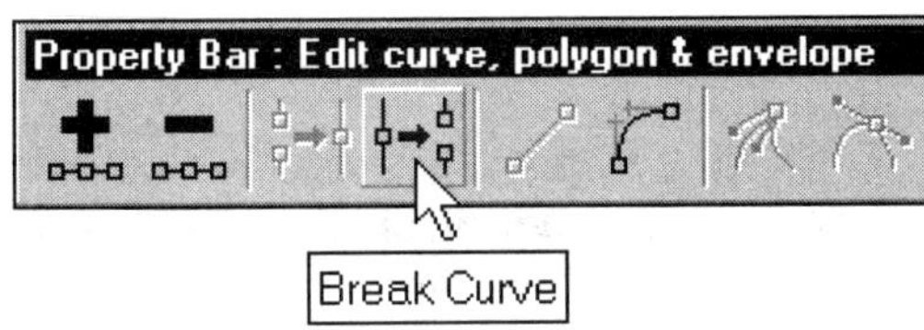

Figure 42. *You can also use the Property Bar to break apart a curve or node.*

To break a curve or break apart a node:

1. With the Shape Tool, select the node where you want to break the curve.
2. Position the Shape Tool's pointer over the selected node and right mouse click. Choose Break Apart from the pop-up menu (**Figure 40**). There are now two nodes where there was one.
3. Use the Shape Tool to move one of the nodes off the other (**Figure 41**).

or

1. Select the node where you want to break the curve with the Shape Tool. The Property Bar will change dynamically to display the node editing buttons.
2. Click the Break Curve button on the Property Bar (**Figure 42**).

Tip:

- If you break apart the path of a closed object that is filled with color—a circle, for instance—the color will disappear because the path is now open.

To join two nodes into one:

1. Select one node with the Shape Tool. The Property Bar will change dynamically to display the node editing buttons.
2. Press Shift and then click and select the second node that you want to join to the first (**Figure 43**).
3. Click the Join Two Nodes button on the Property Bar (**Figure 44a**). The two nodes will move together and become one (**Figure 44b**).

To join two nodes with a straight line:

1. Select the two nodes you want to join with a line (**Figure 43**). The Property Bar will change dynamically to display the node editing buttons.
2. Click the Extend Curve to Close button on the Property Bar (**Figure 45a**). A straight line will appear, joining the two nodes (**Figure 45b**).

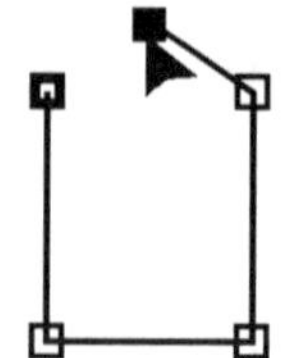

Figure 43. *Use the Shape Tool to select the two nodes you want to join together.*

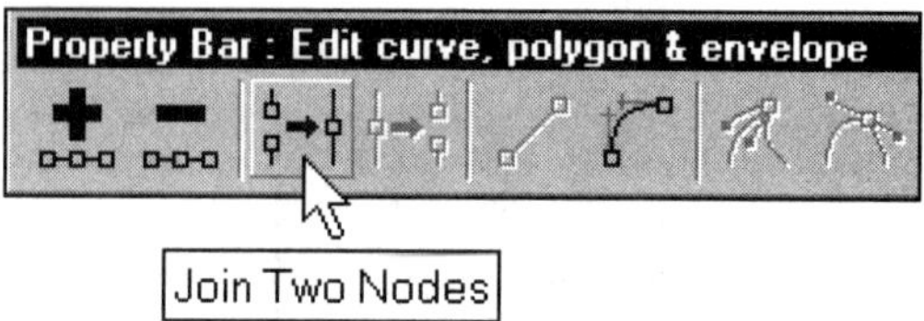

Figure 44a. *Click the Join Two Nodes button to join the two selected nodes into one.*

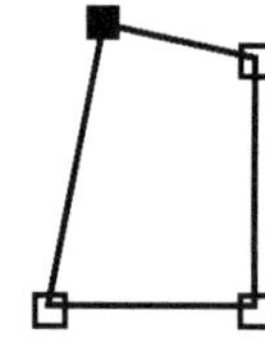

Figure 44b. *When the Join Two Nodes button is pressed, the line segments attached to those nodes move together.*

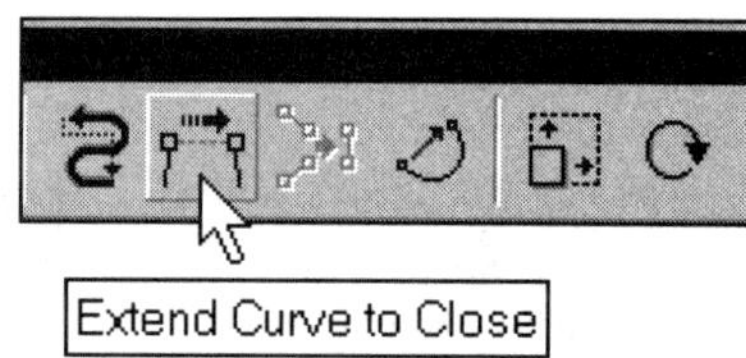

Figure 45a. *Click the Extend Curve to Close button on the Property Bar to add a line that joins the two nodes.*

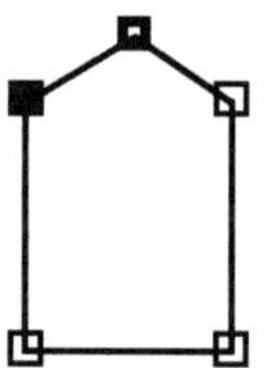

Figure 45b. *After the Extend Curve to Close button is pressed, a straight line appears, joining the two selected nodes.*

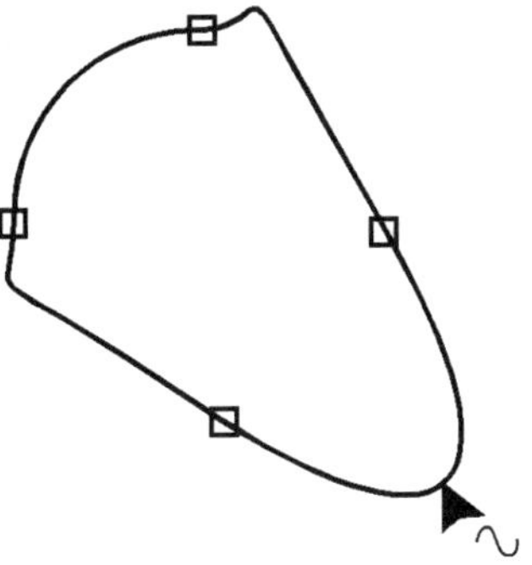

Figure 46. *Use the Shape Tool to drag a path and change its shape.*

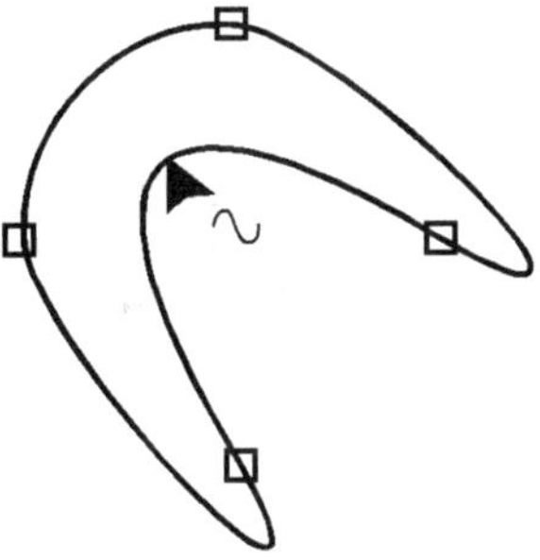

Figure 47. *As you drag a path, the object's nodes will remain stationary. The shape of each path segment will change, depending upon the node type that it passes through.*

An object's path can also be manipulated without using nodes.

To directly manipulate an object's path:

1. Select the object using the Shape Tool. (If the Status Bar says that the object is a specific shape, not a curve with nodes, you will have to convert the object to curves.)
2. Place the pointer of the Shape Tool on the object's path. When you do, a small squiggle will appear attached to the Shape Tool's triangle pointer (**Figure 46**).
3. Press the left mouse button, and drag the mouse (**Figure 46**). As you drag, notice that stretching the line segment also affects the rest of the object—the nodes stay stationary while the line segments stretch and curve according to the node type they pass through (**Figure 47**).
4. When you are happy with the shape, release the mouse button (**Figure 48**). A simple dot and curved line brings the shape to life (**Figure 49**).

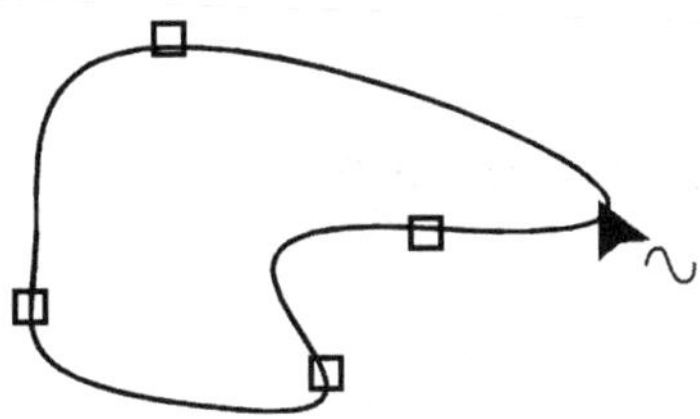

Figure 48. *The object's new shape.*

Figure 49. *A dot and curved line adds personality.*

Special Project:

Make Waves

It's time to take what you have learned and create something fun. The wave shape is easy to make and can be used in many drawings, including seagulls and house roofs (check out the town scene on page 67).

To create waves:

1. Draw a perfect circle using the Ellipse Tool while holding down the Ctrl key (**Figure 50**).
2. Convert the circle to curves by either choosing Convert To Curves from the Arrange menu or pressing Ctrl+Q on the keyboard.
3. Select the circle using the Shape Tool. Four nodes will become visible around the circle (**Figure 51**).
4. Marquee select the nodes on the right and left sides of the circle (**Figure 52**).
5. With the Shape Tool's pointer positioned over one of the selected nodes, right mouse click and select Break Apart from the pop-up menu (**Figure 53**). This will break the selected nodes apart. Next, you will need to break the entire object apart.

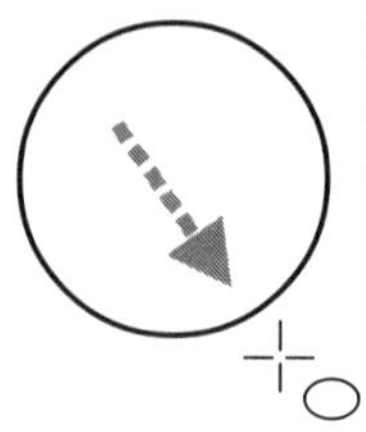

Figure 50. *Draw a perfect circle by holding down the Ctrl key while dragging the Ellipse Tool.*

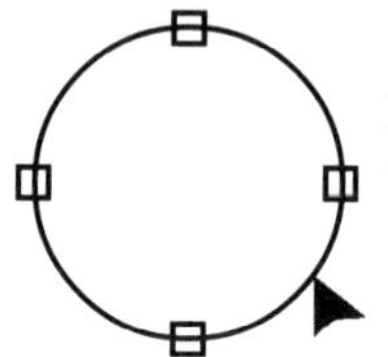

Figure 51. *Select the converted circle with the Shape Tool.*

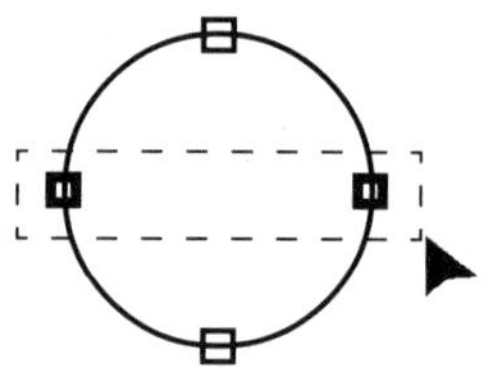

Figure 52. *Use the Shape Tool to marquee select the left and right nodes.*

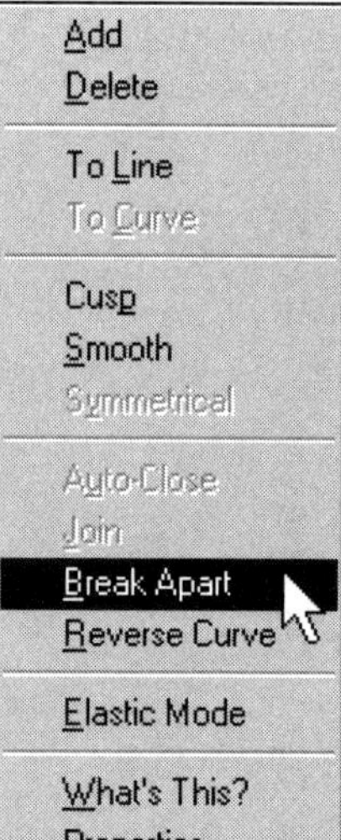

Figure 53. *Place the Shape Tool pointer on one of the selected nodes and right click. Choose Break Apart from the pop-up menu to break the selected nodes apart.*

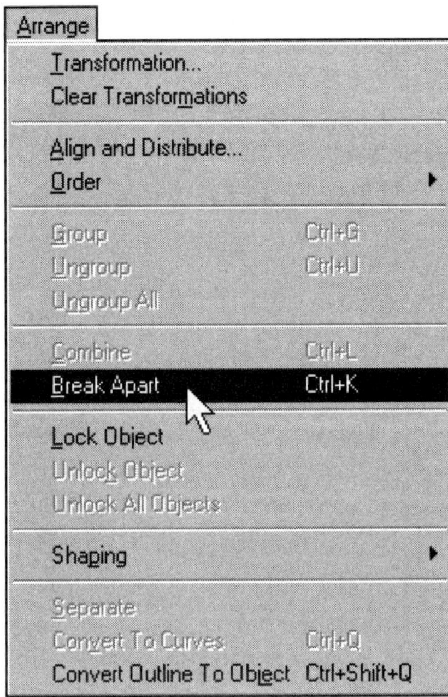

Figure 54. *Select Break Apart from the Arrange menu.*

6. Choose Break Apart from the Arrange menu (**Figure 54**) or press Ctrl+K on the keyboard. This will break the selected object—the circle—into two halves—an upper and a lower.
7. Switch to the Pick Tool and position the pointer on the path at the top of the broken circle. Press the left mouse button and drag it up. When you release the mouse, the upper arc will be selected (**Figure 55**).
8. Press the Delete key on the keyboard to delete the top half of the circle. You will be left with the bottom half—the left side of a wave (**Figure 56**).
9. Select the bottom arc with the Pick Tool.
10. Press Ctrl+D on the keyboard or choose Duplicate from the Edit menu. A duplicate of the arc will appear (**Figure 57**).

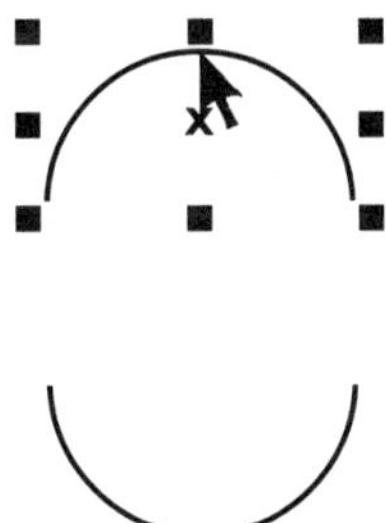

Figure 55. *Select the upper arc and drag it up and away from the lower arc.*

Figure 56. *After you delete the top arc, the bottom arc remains.*

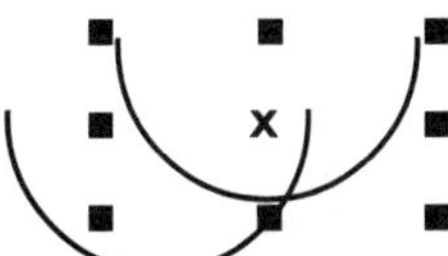

Figure 57. *A duplicate arc appears above and to the right of the original arc.*

11. Move the duplicate arc over to the right, positioning the left tip of the duplicate on top of the right tip of the original (**Figure 58**). You've made your first wave! Be sure to leave the duplicate selected because you're going to use smart duplication to create a series of arcs.

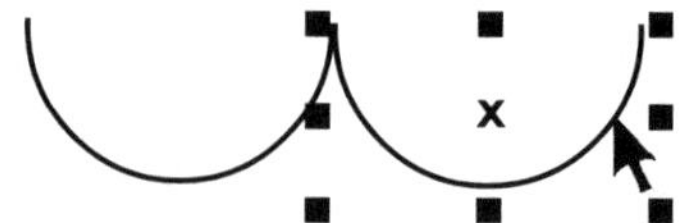

Figure 58. *Use the Pick Tool to drag the selected duplicate to its new position.*

12. Press Ctrl+D or choose Duplicate from the Edit menu. A third arc appears to the right of the second arc (**Figure 59**). Continue creating duplicates until you have as many waves as you want (**Figure 60**).

Figure 59. *When you duplicate the second, repositioned arc, the next duplicate appears to the right of that second arc.*

Figure 60. *It's easy to make an ocean of waves.*

SUMMARY

In this chapter you learned how to:

- Convert an object to curves
- Convert a line to curves
- Convert a curve to a line
- Select nodes
- Convert node types
- Move, add, and delete nodes
- Break a node into two
- Join two nodes together
- Make waves

Lines and Curves

CorelDraw 9 offers three tools for drawing lines and curves: the Freehand, Bézier, and Artistic Media Tools. You can find them on the Curve fly-out (**Figure 1**).

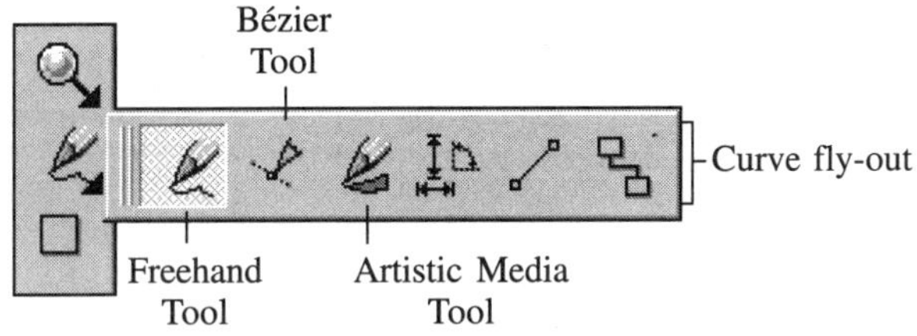

Figure 1. *The Curve fly-out.*

Of the three, the Freehand Tool is the most straightforward because it works like a pencil on paper. As you drag the Freehand Tool, it creates curves and lines, mirroring the motions of the mouse.

The Bézier Tool draws on a node-by-node basis. As you learned in the last chapter, nodes control the curve of the line segment that passes through them. With the Bézier Tool you can draw smooth, accurate curves node-by-node. With each click of the mouse a node is created and each node is connected to the previous node by a line segment.

With the Artistic Media Tool you can draw lines of varying thicknesses and shapes, paint with a brush or sprayer, and draw calligraphic lines. It works just like the Freehand Tool because you drag it to draw. However, instead of creating a single, thick outline, it actually creates an object made up of a closed path.

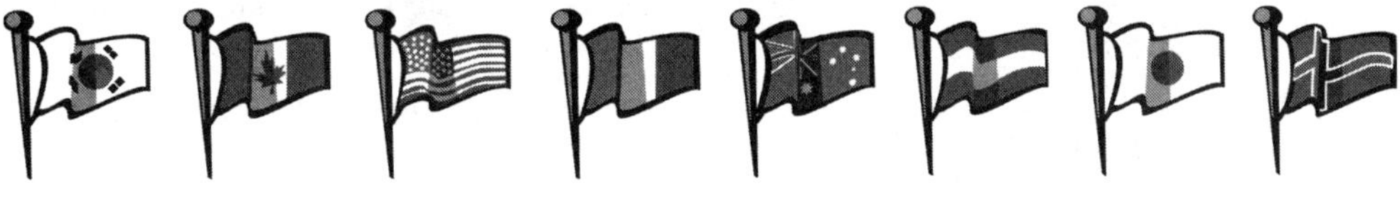

The Freehand Tool is easy to use and will probably feel familiar to you right from the start. At first, your lines may appear rough, but you can always refine them using their nodes and the Shape Tool. As you continue to practice with the Freehand Tool, drawing will come quite naturally.

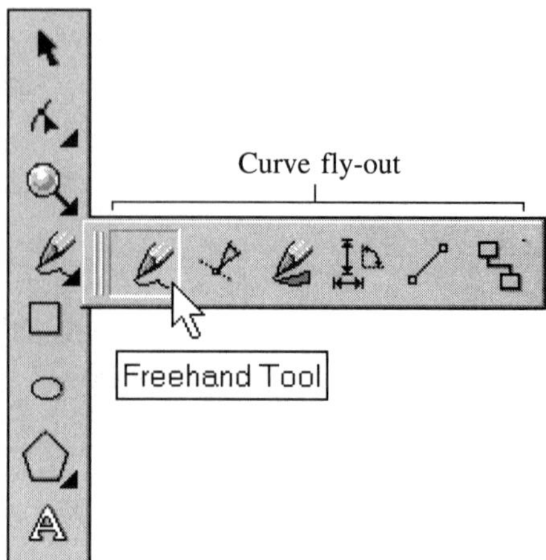

Figure 2. *Select the Freehand Tool from the Curve fly-out.*

To draw a straight line:

1. Select the Freehand Tool (**Figure 2**). The mouse pointer will change to a cross-hair with a little squiggle attached to it.
2. Click on the place where you want the line to begin.
3. Click on the place where you want the line to end (**Figure 3**). The tool will stop drawing.

Figure 3. *Click where you want the line to begin, then click where you want the line to end.*

To constrain (force) a straight line to an angle:

1. Select the Freehand Tool, click on the place where you want the line to start, and hold down the Ctrl key.
2. Move the mouse to where you want the line to end. Notice that as you move the mouse around, the line moves in 15° increments (**Figure 4**).
3. Click on the place where you want the line to end, then release the Ctrl key.

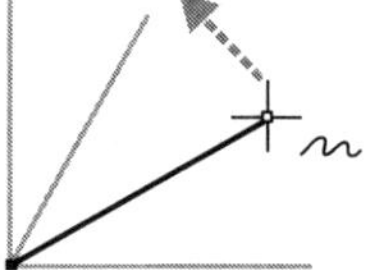

Figure 4. *Hold the Ctrl key down to constrain the line to 15° increments.*

Tip:

- Keep an eye on the Status Bar as you draw the line. It will tell you what angle the line is at.

Figure 5. *Drag the mouse to draw a curve.*

Figure 6. *When you are finished drawing, release the mouse. Several nodes will appear along the length of the curve.*

WHY ARE THERE MORE NODES AT ONE END OF THE CURVE THAN THE OTHER?

As you draw a curve with the Freehand Tool, CorelDraw automatically places nodes along the curve. The faster you move the mouse, the fewer nodes will appear along the path. If you slow down while drawing, CorelDraw is programmed to add extra nodes. It assumes that you are trying to emphasize that part of the curve. Remember that if there are too many nodes on a curve section, you can delete them using the Shape Tool.

To draw a curved line:

1. Select the Freehand Tool from the Toolbox.
2. Position the Freehand Tool to where you want the curve to start.
3. Press the left mouse button and drag it, like you would a pencil on paper, to create the curve (**Figure 5**).
4. Release the mouse when you are finished. CorelDraw will smooth the curve shape and several nodes will appear along the path (**Figure 6**).

To erase part of a line as you draw:

1. Without releasing the mouse button and discontinuing the line you are drawing, hold down the Shift key.
2. Drag the Freehand Tool backwards along the line that you've already drawn.
3. Release the Shift key when you have finished erasing (but don't release the mouse button) and resume drawing the line.

Tip:

- This may seem tricky at first, but it will become easier with practice!

To create a closed object:

Use the Freehand Tool to create the shape you desire, making sure that the line segments begin and end at the same point.

With the Bézier Tool, you can draw smooth curves very precisely, node-by-node. As each node is created, you can control how curvy a line is by manipulating the node's control points.

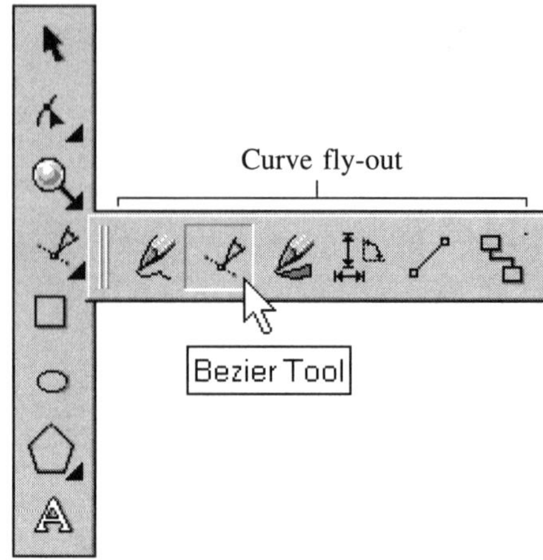

Figure 7. *Select the Bézier Tool from the Curve fly-out.*

To draw a straight line:

1. Select the Bézier Tool from the Curve fly-out (**Figure 7**). The mouse pointer will change to a cross-hair with a tiny curve connected to it.
2. Click on the place where you want to position the first node.
3. Click where you want to place the second node. A straight line segment will appear between the two nodes (**Figure 8**).

Figure 8. *Click where you want the line to begin, then click again where you want the line to end.*

Tip:

- Press the Spacebar twice, or select another tool, to stop drawing with the Bézier Tool.

To create a closed object:

Select the Bézier Tool and click to add nodes and create the shape you desire. To close the object, make sure the last click of the mouse is positioned directly on top of the first node you placed.

WHO WAS BÉZIER ANYHOW?

The Bézier curve—the curve representation used most frequently in computer graphics—is named after Pierre Bézier, a French engineer who worked for the car manufacturer Renault. In the 1960s, in an attempt to draw car parts, he developed the mathematical equations that represent a curve geometrically.

Figure 9. *After selecting the Bézier Tool, press the left mouse button and drag to create a node with two control points.*

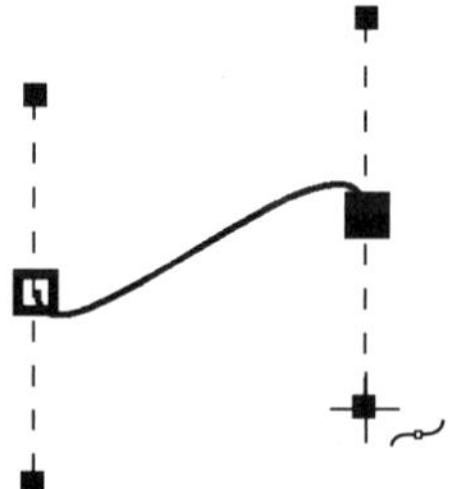

Figure 10. *Press and drag the mouse again to add a second node and create a curve.*

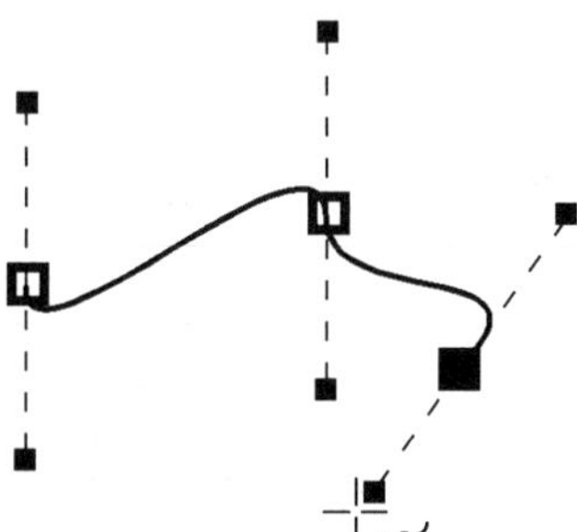

Figure 11. *Press and drag the mouse a third time to add another node and curve.*

To create a curve:

1. Select the Bézier Tool from the Curve fly-out.
2. Position the Bézier Tool where you want to start the curve, press the left mouse button, and drag the mouse. A node will appear with two control points that stretch in opposite positions as you drag the mouse (**Figure 9**).
3. Release the mouse when the control points are the desired distance from the node.
4. Move the mouse to the place where you want to position the next node. Press and drag the mouse to create another node with two control points. A curved line segment will appear between the two nodes (**Figure 10**). If you want to add another node to continue the curve, repeat this step again (**Figure 11**). If you want to stop adding nodes to this curve, press the Spacebar twice.

Tips:

- To create a node with one control point, click to create the node, then position the mouse over the node, press the left mouse button and drag.
- To create a node with no control points, just click (don't drag).
- The distance between a node and its control points determines how curved the line segment will be. The further away the control points are from the node, the deeper the curve will be.

Special Project:

Draw a Flag

It's time to take the skills you have learned and use them to create an object. Check out the flags on page 87. They use Bézier curves to create the look of flags flying in the breeze.

To draw a flag:

1. Use the Zoom Box on the Standard Toolbar to zoom in to 200% and then select the Bézier Tool.
2. Position the pointer where you want the top left corner of the flag to be. Press the mouse button and drag it up diagonally to the left (**Figure 12**). Release the mouse.
3. Move the pointer to the right about 1 inch (2.5 centimeters) and press and drag the mouse down diagonally to the left (**Figure 13**).
4. Continue pressing the mouse while you drag that new control point up to the right (**Figure 14**). This will press the curve down, making it dip. Release the mouse.
5. Position the mouse pointer again to the right about 1 inch. This node will create the upper-right corner of the flag. Press the mouse and drag it up diagonally to the right (**Figure 15**), then release the mouse.

Figure 12. *Select the Bézier Tool, then press and drag the mouse diagonally up to the left.*

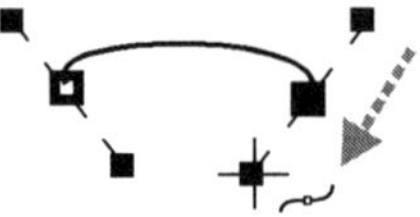

Figure 13. *Press the mouse again and drag the control point down and to the left.*

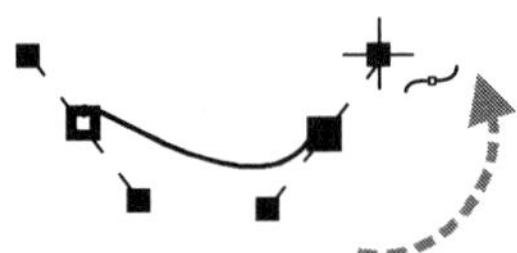

Figure 14. *Continue pressing the mouse and swing the control point around up to the right.*

Figure 15. *Create another node by pressing the mouse and dragging diagonally up to the right.*

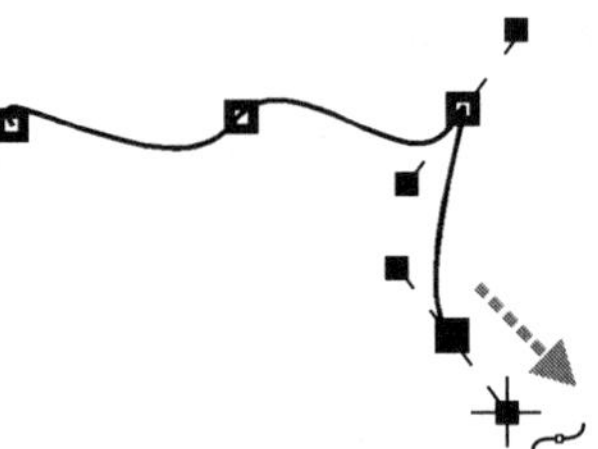

Figure 16. *Create a fourth node about an inch below the third node by pressing the mouse and dragging diagonally down to the right.*

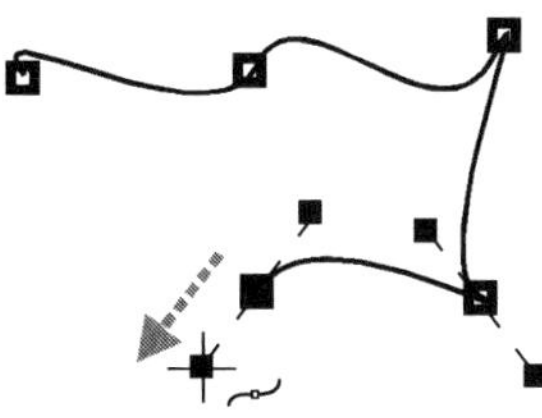

Figure 17. *Press and drag the mouse down and to the left.*

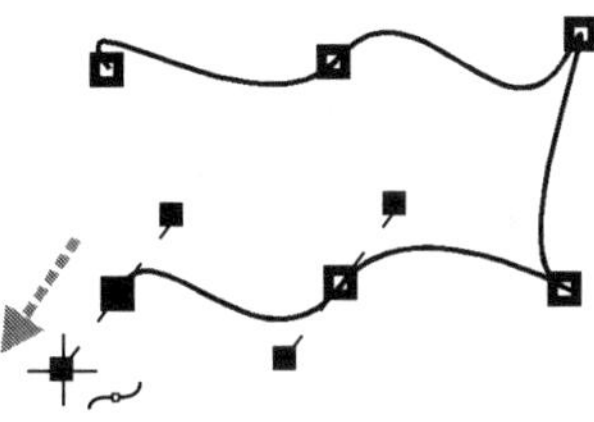

Figure 18. *Create the next node by pressing and dragging the mouse down to the left again.*

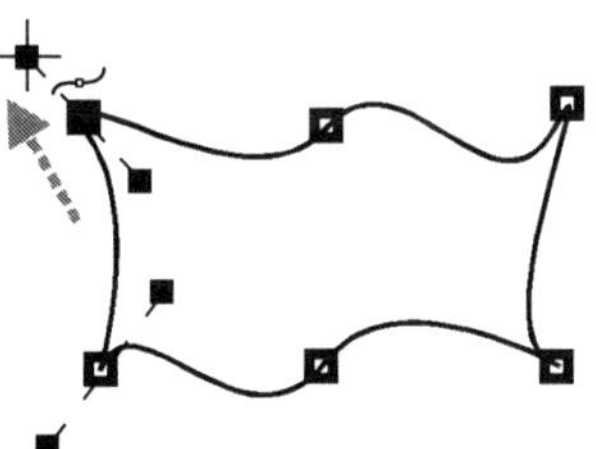

Figure 19. *Close the object by positioning the mouse over the first node and pressing and dragging the mouse up to the left.*

Figure 20. *It's easy to make a waving flag.*

6. Move the mouse pointer down about an inch below the node you just created. Press the mouse button and drag it diagonally down to the right (**Figure 16**) and release the mouse. You've just created the right side of the flag.
7. Position the mouse about an inch to the left of that node and press and drag the mouse down diagonally to the left (**Figure 17**), then release the mouse. This will make the curve mirror the one above it.
8. Move the mouse again one inch to the left and press and drag it diagonally down to the left (**Figure 18**) to mirror the curve that is above it. Release the mouse.
9. Position the cursor on top of the first node you created, then press and drag the mouse up diagonally to the left (**Figure 19**) to close the object. Release the mouse and press the Spacebar twice to stop drawing with the Bézier Tool.
10. Add stars and lines as you desire (see Chapter 5 for more about drawing stars). You could even use the Rectangle and Ellipse Tools to create a flag pole (**Figure 20**).

Creating lines and curves is just the beginning! Using the Outline fly-out (**Figure 21**) and the Outline Pen dialog box (**Figure 22**), you can make your lines thicker, change their style from solid to dashed or dotted, add arrowheads, and give them a calligraphic look.

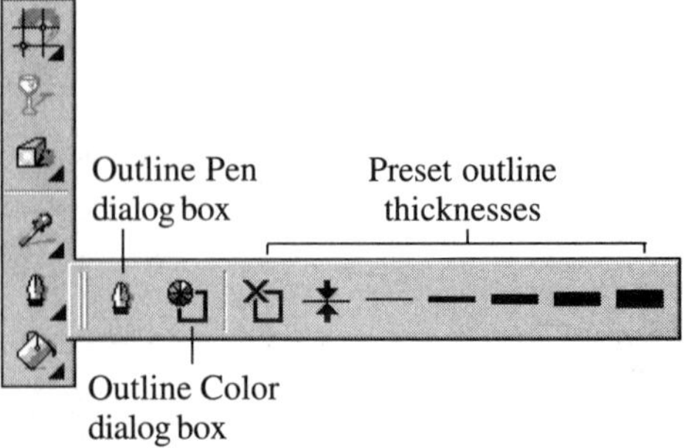

Figure 21. *The Outline fly-out.*

The Outline fly-out

As you may have already noticed, the last three buttons on the CorelDraw 9 toolbar are separated from the rest by a line.This is because these three buttons which include the Eyedropper and Paintbucket Tools, the Outline Tool, and the Fill Tool, work differently from their neighbors. Instead of being tools that are used for drawing, such as the Rectangle Tool, these three buttons access fly-outs that change the appearance of a drawing.This chapter will make full use of the Outline Tool and its fly-out (**Figure 21**). The Fill Tool, and Eyedropper and Paintbucket Tools will be discussed later in Chapter 10, *Color and Fills*. To access the Outline fly-out, just click the Outline Tool button on the Toolbar.

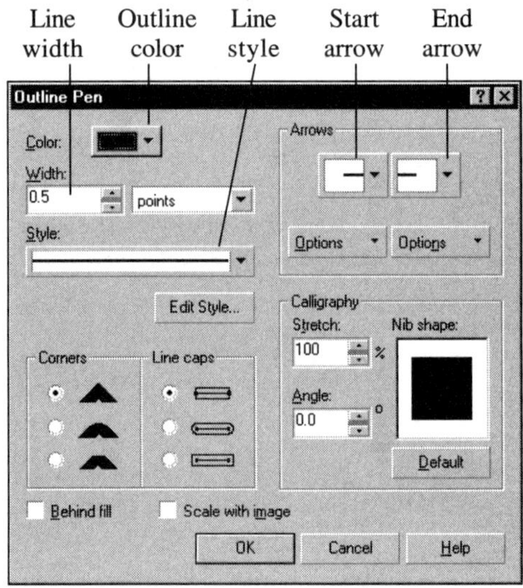

Figure 22. *The Outline Pen dialog box is used to change the properties of the lines that you draw.*

The Outline Pen dialog box

The Outline Pen dialog box (**Figure 22**) is used to change the properties of the lines that you draw with the Freehand, Bézier, and Artistic Media Tools and the outlines of the objects you draw with the Rectangle, Ellipse, and Polygon Tools.

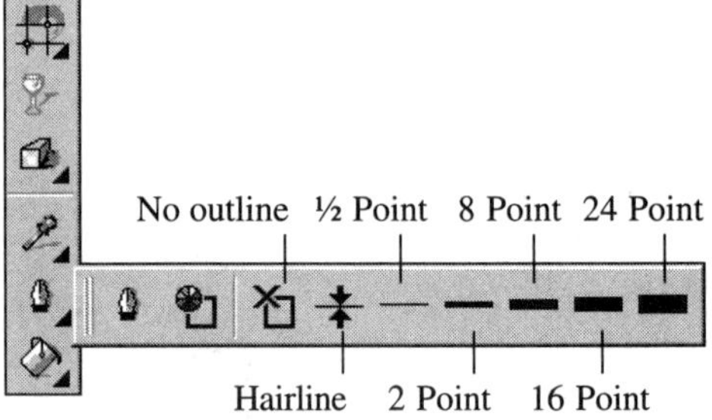

Figure 23. *The Outline fly-out contains several preset line widths.*

To change line thickness:

1. Use the Pick Tool to select the object whose line you want to change.
2. Click the Outline Tool to open the fly-out.
3. Click one of the preset outline width buttons (**Figure 23**).

or

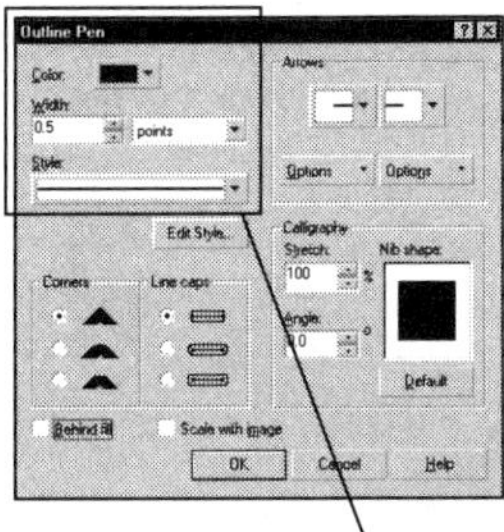

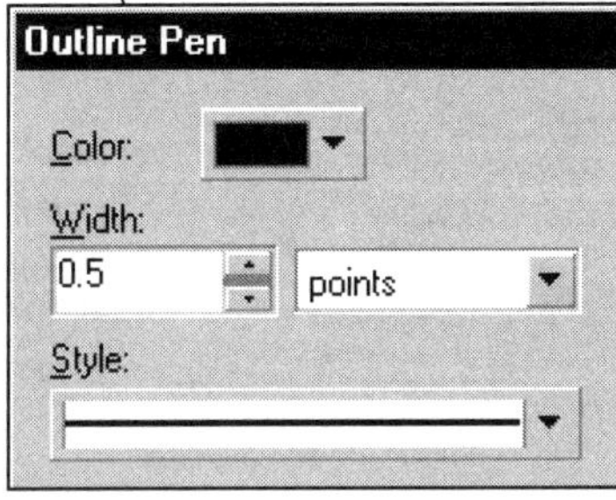

Figure 24. *Use the Width text box and spin buttons to change a line's thickness.*

1. Use the Pick Tool to select the object you want to change.
2. Click the Outline Tool to open the fly-out.
3. Click the Outline Pen dialog box button (**Figure 21**). The Outline Pen dialog box will open.
4. Use the Width text box or spin buttons to enter a new line thickness (**Figure 24**).
5. Click OK. The dialog box will close and the line will assume the new width.

or

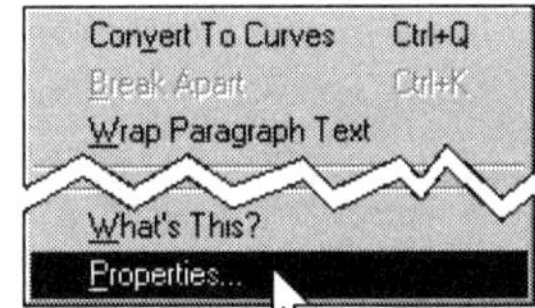

Figure 25. *Choose Properties from the bottom of the pop-up menu.*

1. Use the Pick Tool to right click on the line you want to change. A pop-up menu will appear (**Figure 25**).
2. Choose Properties from the bottom of the menu. The Outline Properties dialog box will open (**Figure 26**).
3. With the Outline tab page in front, use the Width text box or spin buttons to enter a new width.
4. Click Apply. The line will assume its new width.

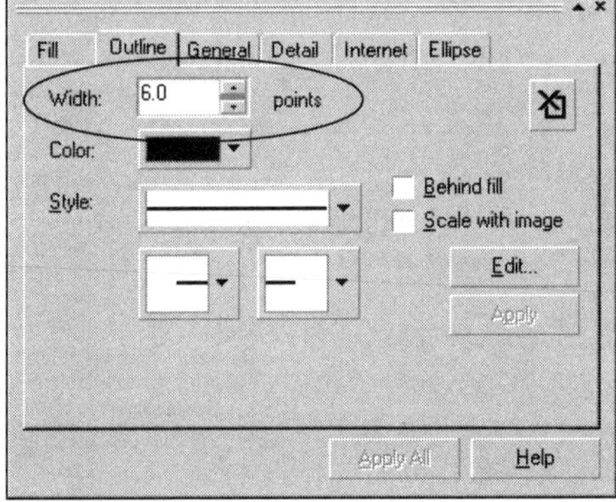

Figure 26. *On the Outline tab page, use the Width text box and spin buttons to change a line's thickness.*

To change the line style:

1. Select the object you want to change with the Pick Tool.
2. Click the Outline Tool button to open the fly-out and then click the Outline Pen dialog box button (**Figure 21**) to open the dialog box.
3. Click the down arrow in the Style box (**Figure 27**).
4. Move your mouse down the list that appears until you find the line style you want, then click that one (**Figure 28**). The drop-down list will close and the line style you selected will appear in the line style box.
5. Click OK. The dialog box will close.

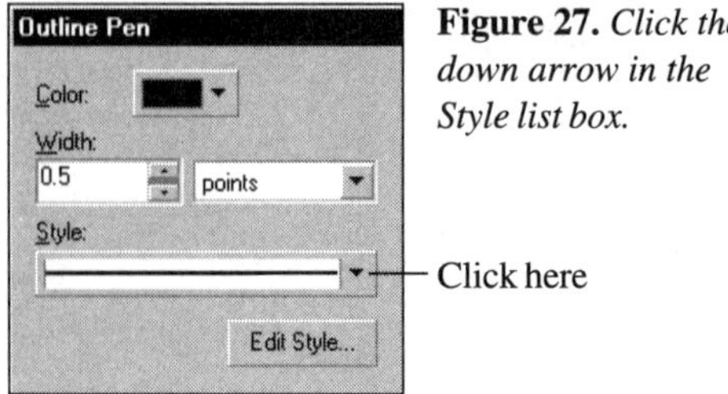

Figure 27. *Click the down arrow in the Style list box.*

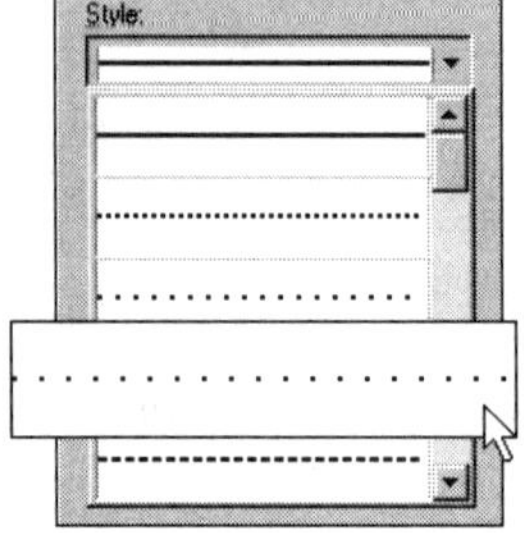

Figure 28. *Choose the line style you want from the list that appears.*

To add arrowheads to a line:

1. Select the line with the Pick Tool.
2. Open the Outline Pen dialog box by clicking the Outline Tool button to open the fly-out and then clicking the Outline Pen dialog box button.
3. In the Arrows area, use the Start Arrow and End Arrow drop-down lists to select arrow styles (**Figure 29**).
4. Click OK when you have selected both a start arrow and an end arrow.

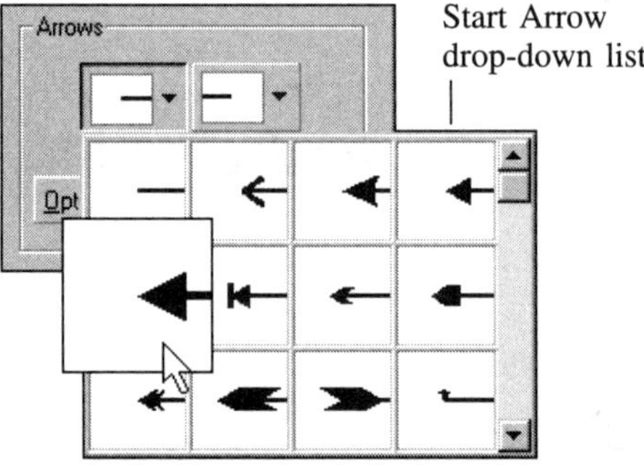

Figure 29. *Use the Start Arrow drop-down list to select an arrow style. Do the same with the End Arrow drop-down list.*

Tip:

- Check out the options available on the Start Arrow and End Arrow drop-down lists. You'll be surprised at what you find there (**Figures 30a–c**).

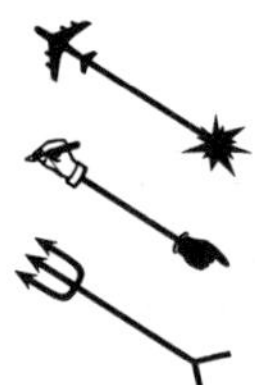

Figures 30a–c. *There are many arrowheads from which to choose.*

Figure 31. *Use the Pick Tool to select the object that will become an arrowhead.*

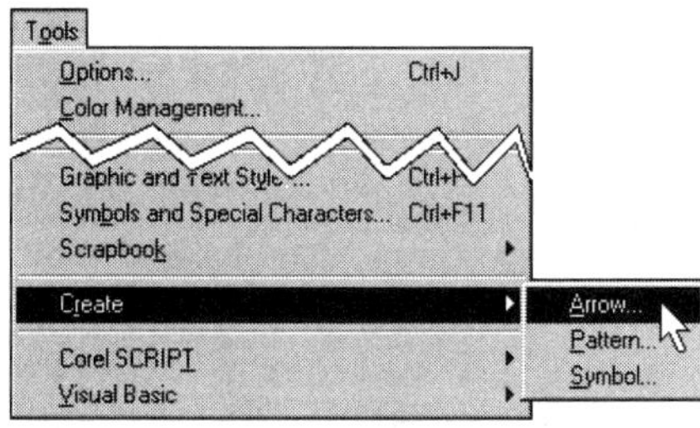

Figure 32. *Choose Arrow from the Create fly-out found on the Tools menu.*

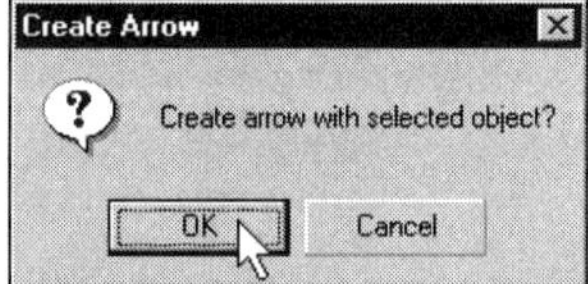

Figure 33. *Click OK in the Create Arrow dialog box.*

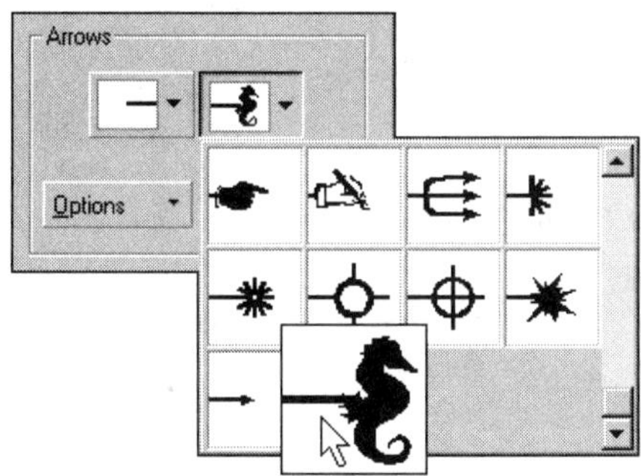

Figure 34. *The custom arrowhead appears at the end of the Start Arrow and End Arrow drop-down lists.*

Figure 35. *A custom arrowhead applied to a curvy line.*

With CorelDraw 9, you can create custom arrowheads using any shape, letter, or symbol.

To create a custom arrowhead:

1. Select the letter, symbol, or shape with the Pick Tool that will become an arrowhead (**Figure 31**).
2. Choose Arrow from the Create fly-out found on the Tools menu (**Figure 32**). The Create Arrow dialog box will appear asking whether you want to create an arrowhead with the selected object (**Figure 33**).
3. Click OK.
4. Use the Pick Tool to select the line to which you want to add the arrowhead.
5. Open the Outline Pen dialog box by clicking the Outline Tool to open the fly-out and then clicking the Outline Pen dialog box button.
6. Use the Start Arrow or End Arrow drop-down list to select your custom arrowhead (**Figure 34**).
7. Click OK when you are finished making a selection. The custom arrowhead will appear attached to the selected line (**Figure 35**).

Tip:

- If your custom arrowhead is too small, use the directions on the next page to make it bigger.

It's easy to change the shape and size of existing arrowheads. Also, if you create a custom arrowhead following the directions on the previous page, many times the arrowhead will be very small. To make the custom arrowhead bigger, use the Edit Arrowhead dialog box, as described below.

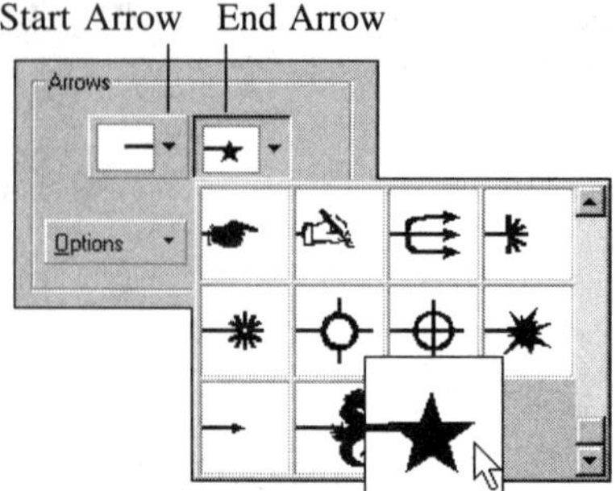

Figure 36. *Select an arrowhead using the Start Arrow or End Arrow drop-down lists.*

To change the shape or size of an arrowhead:

1. Open the Outline Tool fly-out and click the Outline Pen dialog box button (**Figure 21**) or press F12 on the keyboard. The Outline Pen dialog box will open.
2. In the Arrows area, use the Start Arrow or End Arrow drop-down lists to select the arrowhead you want to edit (**Figure 36**).
3. Choose Edit from the Options drop-down list below the arrowhead you have selected (**Figure 37**). The Edit Arrowhead dialog box will appear (**Figure 38**).
4. Drag the handles found around the arrowhead to change its size (**Figure 39**).
5. Click OK when you are finished editing the arrowhead to close the Edit Arrowhead dialog box.
6. In the Outline Pen dialog box, click OK to close the dialog box. The next time you add that arrowhead to a line, it will appear in its edited form (**Figure 40**).

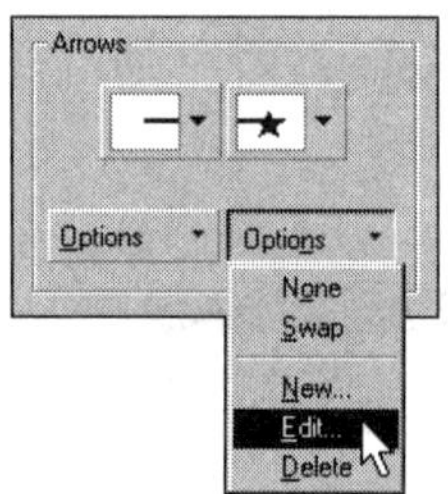

Figure 37. *Choose Edit from the Options drop-down list below the arrowhead you selected.*

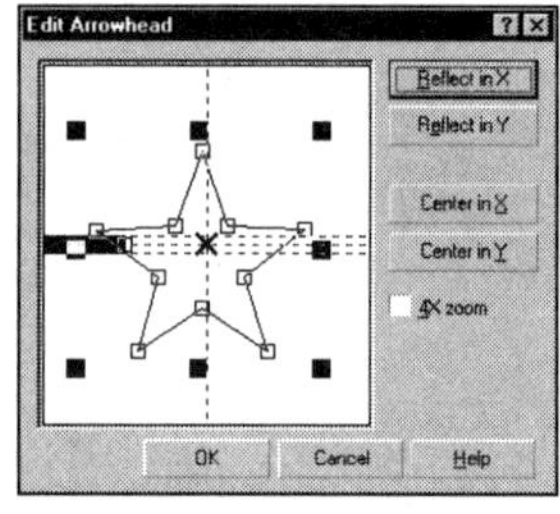

Figure 38. *Use the Edit Arrowhead dialog box to change the size of an arrowhead.*

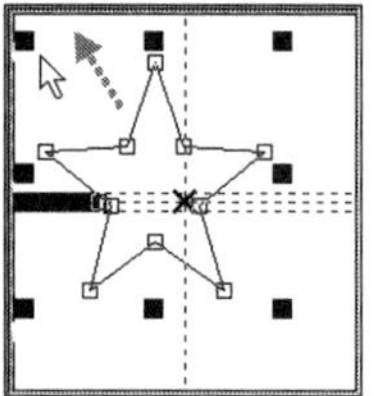

Figure 39. *Drag the handles to resize the arrowhead.*

Figure 40. *The resized arrowhead applied to a line.*

Change an Arrowhead's Shape or Size

Figure 41. *Select the line you want to alter with the Pick Tool.*

Figure 42. *Open the Outline Pen dialog box by clicking the Outline Pen button.*

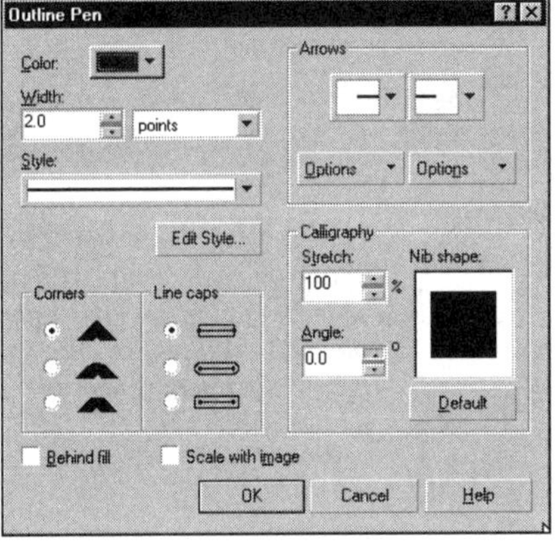

Figure 43. *The Outline Pen dialog box.*

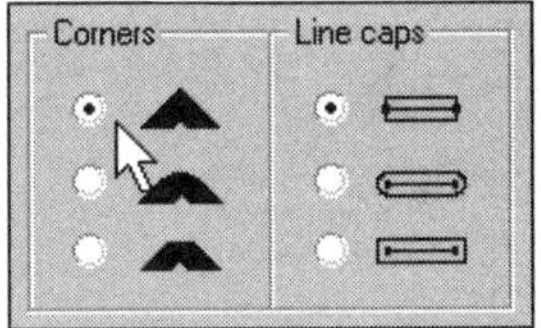

Figure 44. *Select a nib shape by choosing one of the corner styles in the Corners area.*

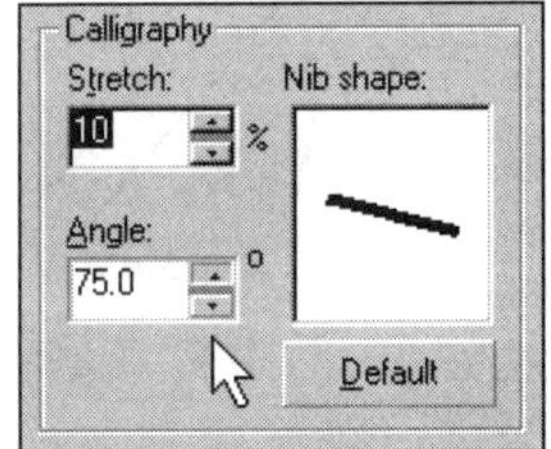

Figure 45. *Set the Stretch and Angle of the nib in the Calligraphy area.*

To give a line the appearance of calligraphy:

1. Select the line you want to alter with the Pick Tool (**Figure 41**).
2. Open the Outline Tool fly-out and click the Outline Pen button (**Figure 42**) or press F12 on the keyboard. The Outline Pen dialog box will open (**Figure 43**).
3. Select a corner style (**Figure 44**). The top and bottom styles, Miter and Bevel, respectively, will create a square *nib* shape. (A nib is the point of a calligraphy pen.) The middle style, Rounded, will create a round nib shape.
4. In the Calligraphy area, set the nib's Stretch and Angle using the available text boxes (**Figure 45**). The Stretch setting determines how square or round the nib will be. The lower the setting, the thinner the nib and the more variation there will be in drawn line thickness.
5. Click OK. The line will be reshaped and look like it was drawn with a calligraphy pen (**Figure 46**). Notice the variation in the line thickness.

Figure 46. *When you click OK the line is transformed.*

Cutting the path of any object is easy using the Knife Tool found on the Shape Tool fly-out (**Figure 47**). What the Knife Tool actually does is cut away a portion of an object's path while adding new paths. In addition to the obvious functionality of a "knife"—splitting an object in two—it lets you completely reshape an object by redrawing its path. The Knife Tool works like the Freehand Tool—you can cut an object with either straight or freehand lines.

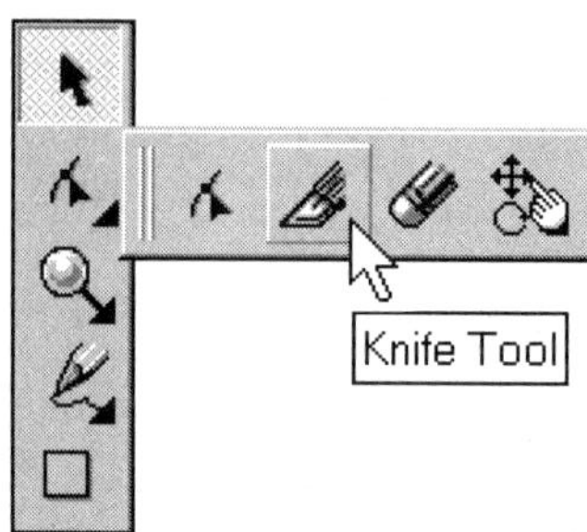

Figure 47. *Select the Knife Tool from the Shape Tool fly-out.*

To cut an object with a straight line:

1. Open the Shape Tool fly-out and click the Knife Tool button (**Figure 47**). The mouse cursor will change to an angled knife (**Figure 48**).
2. Position the knife cursor over the object where you want to start cutting. When the cursor is directly over the object's path it will snap upright, indicating that it's ready to cut (**Figure 49**).
3. Click the left mouse button.
4. Move the knife cursor to where you want to stop cutting.
5. Click the left mouse button. A new line appears, splitting the object in two (**Figure 50**). If you change to the Pick Tool, you'll see that you can drag the split pieces apart (**Figure 51**).

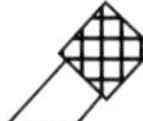

Figure 48. *The mouse cursor changes to an angled knife.*

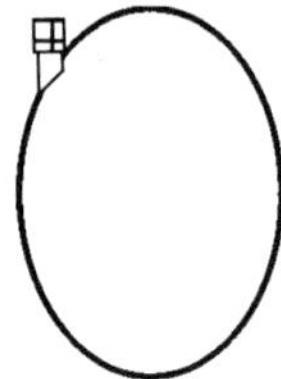

Figure 49. *When you position the knife cursor over the path you want to cut, it will snap upright, indicating it's ready to cut.*

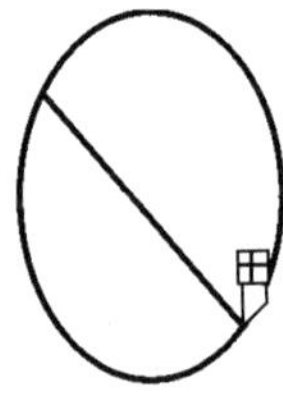

Figure 50. *When you complete the cut, a straight line appears, splitting the object in two.*

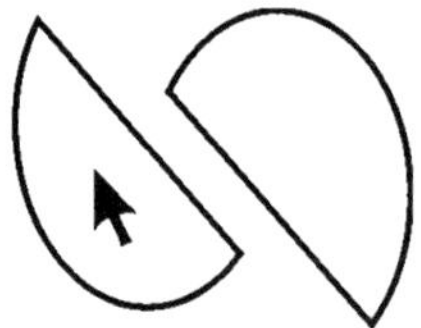

Figure 51. *Use the Pick Tool to drag the two sections apart.*

Figure 52. *When you position the knife cursor where you want to start cutting, it will snap upright to indicate it's ready.*

To cut an object with a freehand line:

1. Open the Shape Tool fly-out and click the Knife Tool button (**Figure 47**). The mouse cursor will change to an angled knife (**Figure 48**).
2. Move the knife cursor over the object's path where you want to start cutting (**Figure 52**). The knife cursor will snap upright when it is in position over the path, indicating that it is ready to cut.
3. Press the left mouse button and drag the mouse as if you were drawing a line with the Freehand Tool (**Figure 53**).
4. Release the mouse button when the knife cursor reaches the place on the object's path where you want to stop cutting. The new freehand line splits the object in two (**Figure 54**). If you change to the Pick Tool, you'll see that you can drag the split pieces apart (**Figure 55**).

Figure 53. *Press the left mouse button and drag to create a freehand cut.*

Figure 54. *When you are finished cutting the new freehand cut splits the object in two.*

Tips:

- When you use the Knife Tool to split an object, that object is automatically converted to curves.
- If you cut a complex object and cannot drag the pieces apart, choose Break Apart from the Arrange menu or press Ctrl+K on the keyboard. This will break the object apart at the cut and let you handle the pieces separately.

Figure 55. *You can use the Pick Tool to drag the pieces apart.*

One way to remove part of an object would be to use the Shape Tool to cut or delete nodes. Another way to remove object parts is with the Eraser Tool. With a simple click and swipe, paths disappear!

To erase part of an object:

1. Select the object that you want to erase part of with the Pick Tool.
2. Open the Shape Tool fly-out and click the Eraser Tool button (**Figure 56**). The mouse cursor will change to a pencil eraser with a circle attached to it (**Figure 57**). The circle indicates the area that will be erased when the Eraser Tool is used.
3. Position the eraser cursor over the object part you want to erase.
4. Double-click the mouse button to erase the area circumscribed by the circle (**Figure 58**).

   or

   Press the mouse button and drag the mouse to remove a larger portion of the object (**Figure 59**).

Tip:

- If you erase too much, you can always undo what you've done by choosing Undo from the Edit menu or pressing Ctrl+Z on the keyboard.

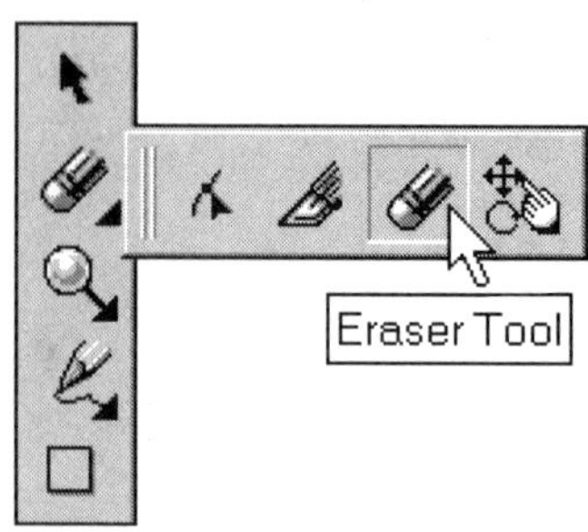

Figure 56. *Click the Eraser Tool on the Shape Tool fly-out to select it.*

Figure 57. *When you select the Eraser Tool, the mouse cursor changes to an eraser with a circle around it. The circle shows the area that will be erased.*

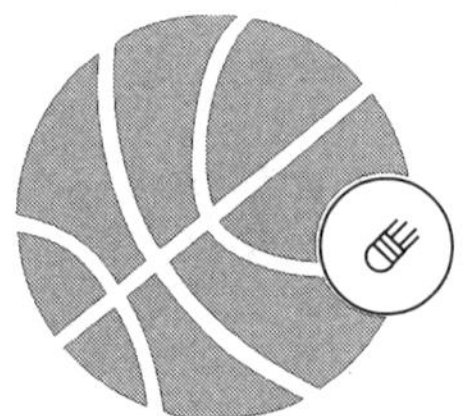

Figure 58. *Position the eraser cursor over the area you want to erase and click the left mouse button.*

Figure 59. *Drag the eraser cursor to remove a larger area of an object.*

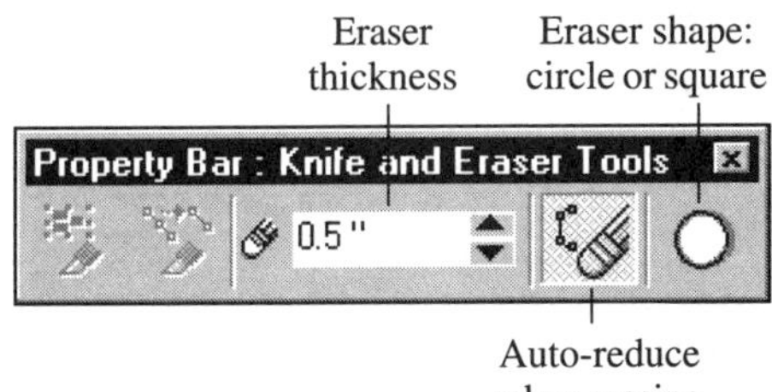

Figure 60. *The Property Bar dynamically changes to display the Eraser Tool editing buttons.*

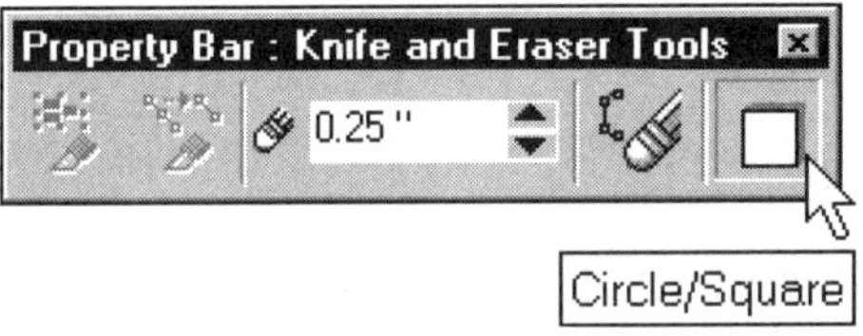

Figure 61. *Click the Circle/Square button to toggle between the two eraser shapes.*

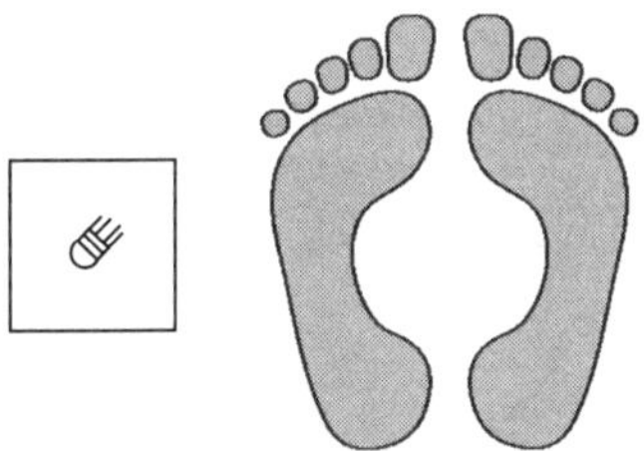

Figure 62. *The mouse cursor changes to an eraser with a square around it when the square-shaped eraser is selected.*

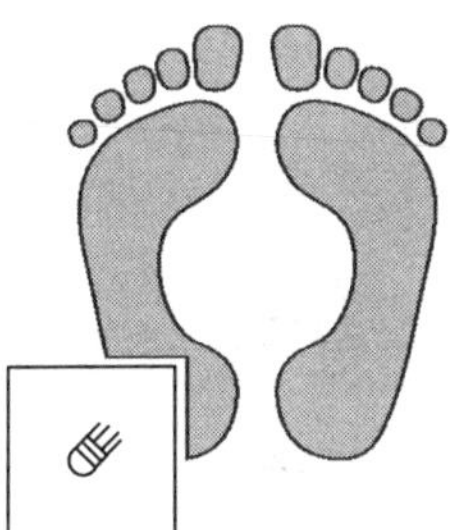

Figure 63. *Use the thickness text box to set the area that will be erased.*

To change the size or shape of the area that is erased:

1. Use the Shape Tool fly-out to click the Eraser Tool. This will make the Eraser Tool appear on the Toolbar (**Figure 56**). The Property Bar will dynamically change to display the Eraser Tool editing buttons (**Figure 60**).
2. To change the shape of the area being erased, click the Circle/ Square button to select either a circular or square shape (**Figure 61**). If you select the square-shaped eraser, the mouse cursor will change to an eraser with a square around it (**Figure 62**). The square shows the area that will be erased.
3. To set the size of the area being erased use the Eraser Thickness text box and spin buttons. The default size is .25". The circle or square around the eraser cursor will change to the dimension that you select.
4. Double-click the mouse button to erase the area circumscribed by the Eraser Tool. **Figure 63** shows the square-shaped eraser being used.

   or

   Press the mouse button and drag the mouse to remove a larger portion of the object.

With the Artistic Media Tool you can draw lines of varying thicknesses and shapes, paint with a brush or sprayer, or draw calligraphic lines. This tool offers several interesting drawing modes: Preset, Brush, Sprayer, Calligraphic, and Pressure.

The Artistic Media Tool can be used in two ways. You can:

- Draw with the tool just as you would with the Freehand Tool, by pressing the left mouse button and dragging to create a line.
- Select an object that has already been created, such as a line or circle, and apply one of the Artistic Media Tool strokes to it.

At first, your drawings may appear rough, but with practice they will quickly become smooth, professional, and nothing short of amazing!

To access the different modes of the Artistic Media Tool:

1. Select the Artistic Media Tool from the Curve fly-out (**Figure 64**) or press I on the keyboard.
2. Click one of the five buttons on the Property Bar near the top of the screen (**Figure 65**). Each Artistic Media mode produces different effects (**Figure 66**).

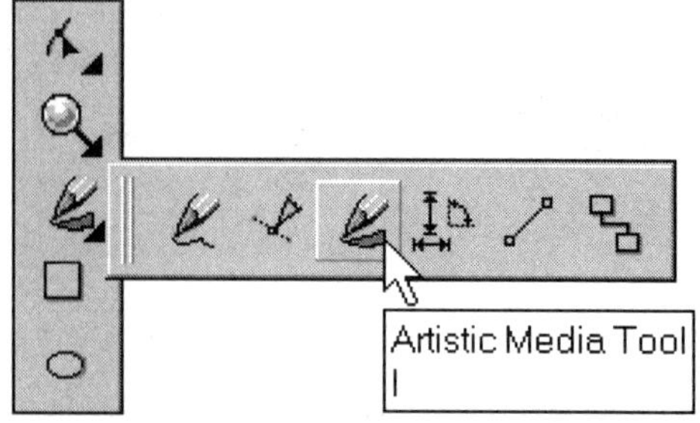

Figure 64. *Click the Artistic Media Tool on the Curve fly-out.*

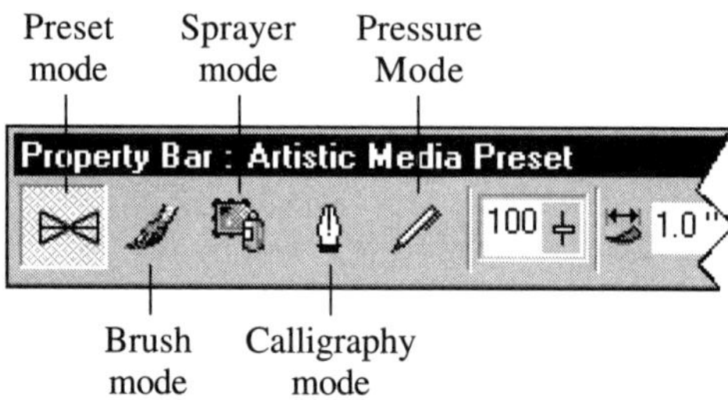

Figure 65. *There are five Artistic Media Tool drawing modes. You can access them by clicking the appropriate button on the Property Bar.*

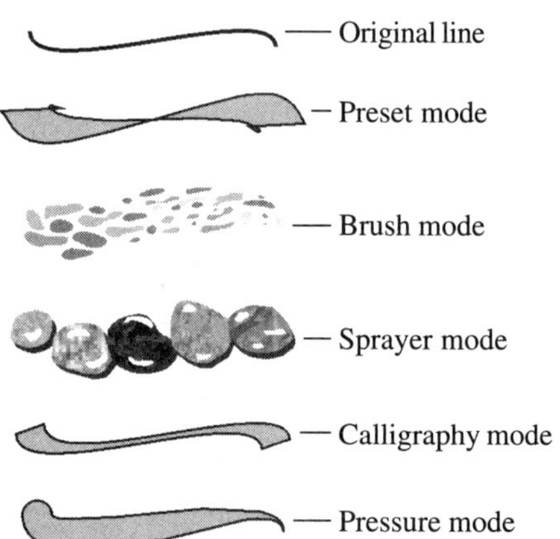

Figure 66. *The five different modes of the Artistic Media Tool applied to the same line.*

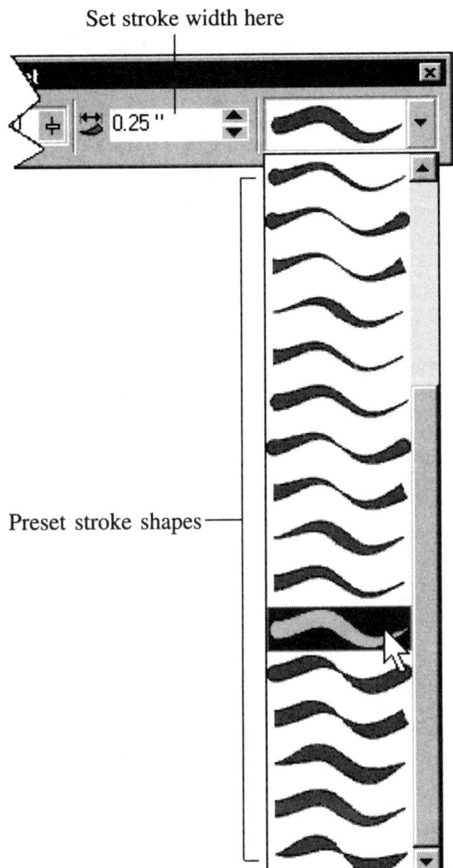

Figure 67. *Use the right side of the Property Bar to set the stroke's width and shape.*

The Preset mode of the Artistic Media Tool will draw curves using preset strokes that you select using the Property Bar.

To draw a Preset curve:

1. Select the Artistic Media Tool from the Curve fly-out (**Figure 64**). The mouse pointer will change to a small paintbrush.
2. Use the Property Bar to select the Preset mode button (**Figure 65**).
3. Set the width of the curve using the text box and spin buttons to the right of the Artistic Media mode buttons (**Figure 67**).
4. Select a stroke shape from the drop-down list of preset strokes.
5. Press the left mouse button and drag (**Figure 68**). When you release the mouse button, the curve will redraw, displaying only an outline and the stroke shape you selected (**Figure 69**).

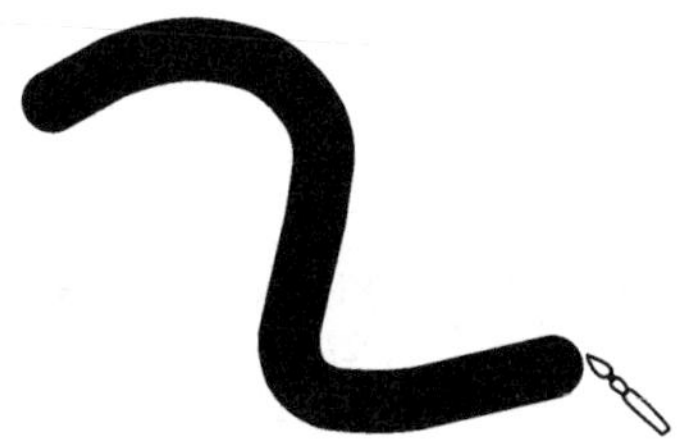

Figure 68. *As you drag the mouse, the curve appears.*

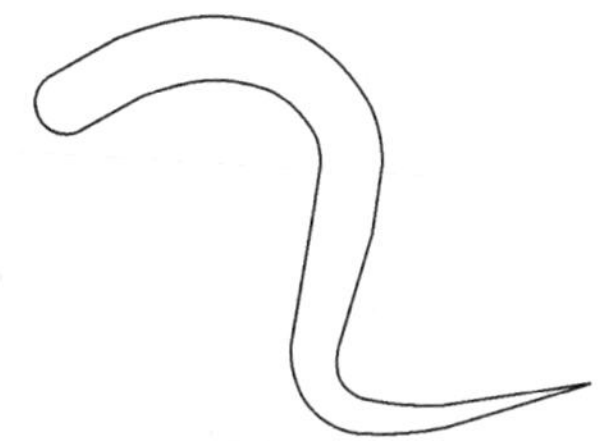

Figure 69. *When you release the mouse button, the curve redraws as an outline and assumes the stroke shape you selected.*

The Brush mode lets you apply pre-defined brush strokes to curves. It works just like the Preset mode. All you have to do is select a brush stroke, then click and drag!

To draw a Brush curve:

1. Select the Artistic Media Tool from the Curve fly-out (**Figure 64**). The mouse pointer will change to a small paintbrush.
2. Click the Brush mode button on the Property Bar (**Figure 65**).
3. Set the width of the curve using the text box and spin buttons to the left of the Brush Stroke drop-down list (**Figure 70**).
4. Use the Brush Stroke drop-down list to select the type of stroke you want to use.
5. Press the left mouse button and drag (**Figure 71**). When you release the mouse button, the curve will redraw, displaying the brush stroke you selected (**Figure 72**).

Tip:

- To change the shape of a curve that has already been drawn, select the Shape Tool, then select the curve, and manipulate the curve's nodes and handles. For more information about nodes and handles, turn to Chapter 6, *Nodes and Paths*.

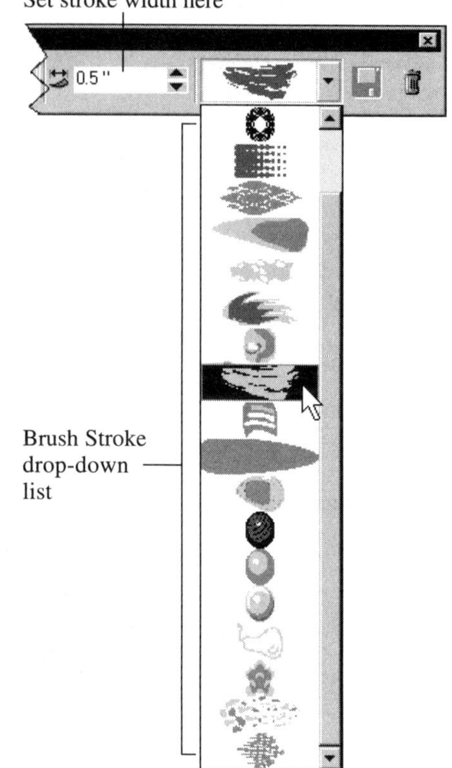

Figure 70. *Use the right side of the Property Bar to set the type of stroke and its width.*

Figure 71. *As you drag the mouse, the curve appears.*

Figure 72. *When you release the mouse button, the curve redraws, using the brush stroke you selected.*

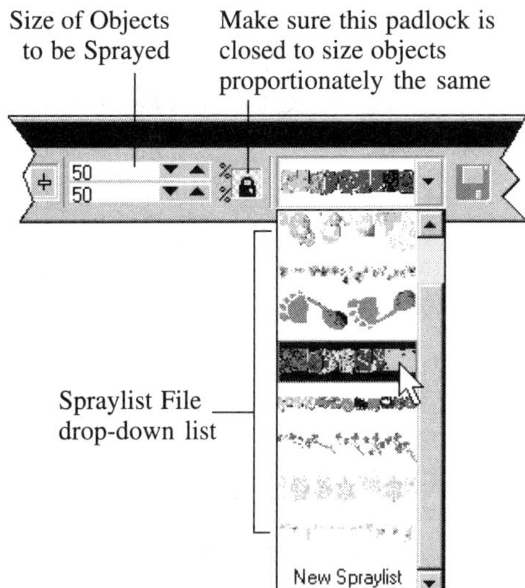

Figure 73. *Use the Spraylist File drop-down list to select a sprayer stroke. The Size of Objects to be Sprayed text box lets you change the size of the objects applied to the curve.*

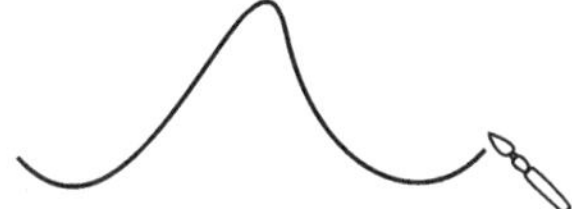

Figure 74. *Drag the mouse to draw the curve.*

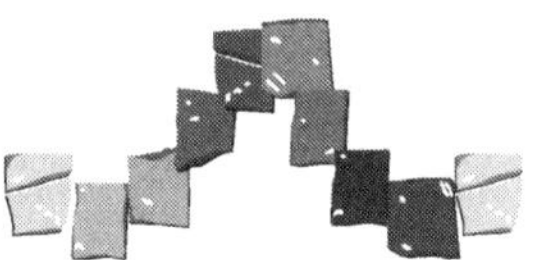

Figure 75. *When you release the mouse button, the curve redraws, using the sprayer objects you selected.*

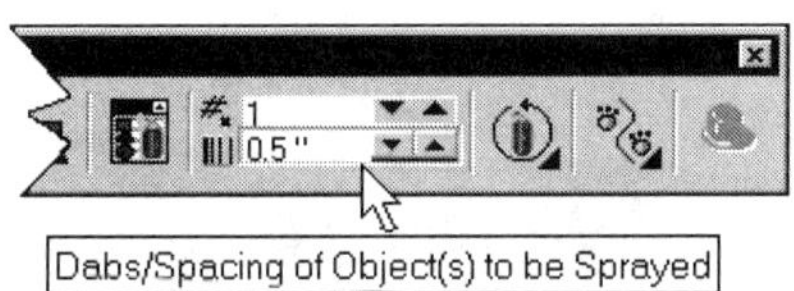

Figure 76. *Use the Dabs/Spacing of Object(s) to be Sprayed text boxes to set how far apart the objects are.*

The Sprayer mode lets you add a series of objects to the curves you draw—from ghosts and bats to flowers and pebbles.

To draw a Sprayer curve:

1. Select the Artistic Media Tool from the Curve fly-out (**Figure 64**). The mouse pointer will change to a small paintbrush.
2. Click the Sprayer mode button on the Property Bar (**Figure 65**).
3. Use the Spraylist File drop-down list to select the type of stroke you want to use (**Figure 73**).
5. Press the left mouse button and drag (**Figure 74**). When you release the mouse button, the curve will redraw, displaying the sprayer objects you selected (**Figure 75**).

Tips:

- To make the objects that are applied to the curve smaller or larger, use the Size of Objects to be Sprayed text box and spin buttons on the Property Bar (**Figure 73**). If you want the sizing of the objects to remain proportionately the same, make sure the tiny padlock to the right of the text box is closed.
- To make the objects applied to the curve closer together or further apart, use the Dabs/Spacing of Object(s) to be Sprayed text boxes on the Property Bar (**Figure 76**).

The Calligraphy mode is easy to use. All you have to do is set the width of the curve you are going to draw and the *nib* angle. A nib is the point of a calligraphy pen.

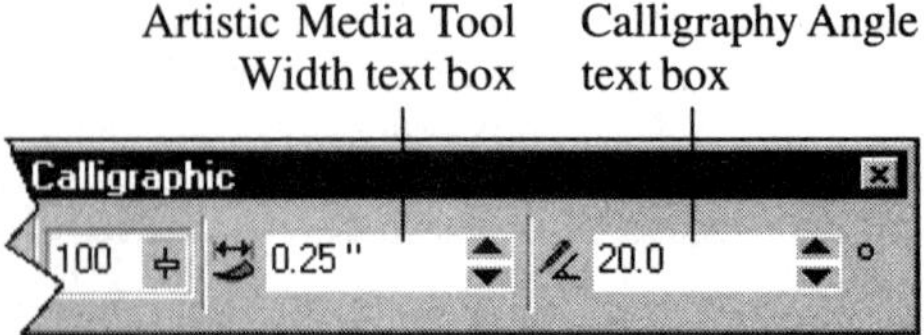

Figure 77. *After clicking the Calligraphy mode button, set the tool's width and nib angle using the two text boxes at the right of the Property Bar.*

To draw a Calligraphy curve:

1. Select the Artistic Media Tool from the Curve fly-out (**Figure 64**). The mouse pointer will change to a small paintbrush.
2. Click the Calligraphy mode button on the Property Bar (**Figure 65**).
3. Set the width of the curve using the Artistic Media Tool Width text box and spin buttons (**Figure 77**).
4. Use the Calligraphy Angle text box and spin buttons to set the angle of the tool's nib.
5. Press the left mouse button and drag (**Figure 78**). When you release the mouse button, the curve will redraw, displaying the outline of the calligraphy curve. (**Figure 79**). Turn to Chapter 10, *Colors and Fills*, to find out how to fill the calligraphy curve with colors and textures (**Figure 80**).

Figure 78. *With the mouse button pressed, drag to create the calligraphy curve.*

Figure 79. *When you release the mouse button, an outline of the calligraphy curve remains.*

Tip:

- You can use the Shape Tool to manipulate the curve's nodes and handles, changing the shape of the calligraphy curve. For details about how to do this, turn to Chapter 6, *Nodes and Paths*.

Figure 80. *You can fill the calligraphy curve with a variety of interesting colors and textures.*

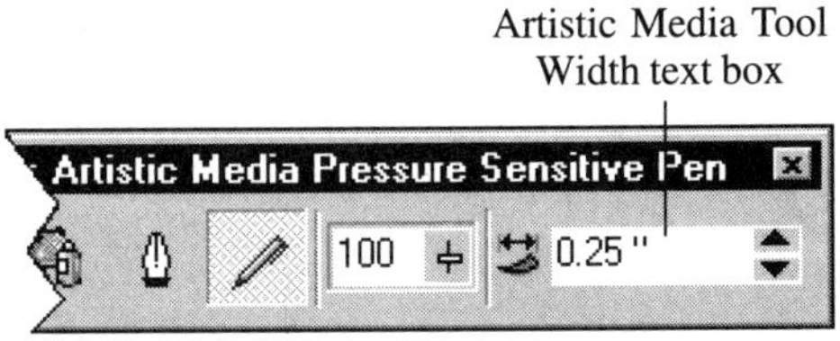

Artistic Media Tool
Width text box

Artistic Media Pressure Sensitive Pen 100 0.25 "

Figure 81. *Use the text box and spin buttons at the right end of the Property Bar to set the pressure curve's width.*

Figure 82. *As you drag the mouse, press the up and down arrow keys on the keyboard to make the curve thicker and thinner.*

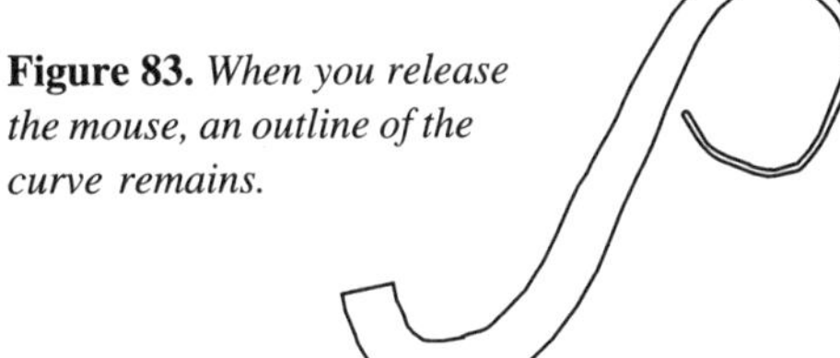

Figure 83. *When you release the mouse, an outline of the curve remains.*

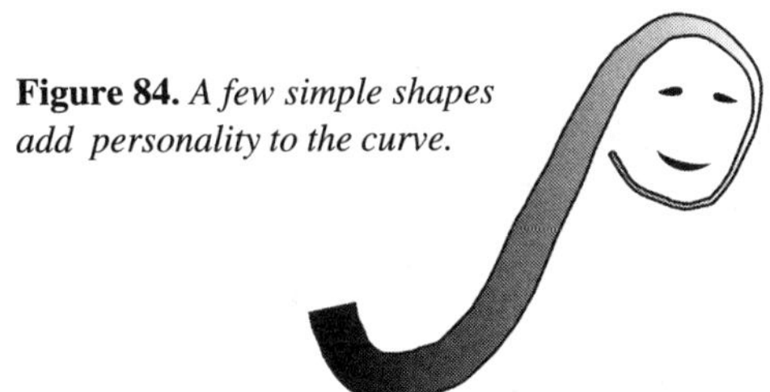

Figure 84. *A few simple shapes add personality to the curve.*

The Pressure drawing mode works with either a pressure-sensitive pen or the up or down arrows on the keyboard.

To draw using the Pressure mode:

1. Select the Artistic Media Tool from the Curve fly-out (**Figure 64**). The mouse pointer will change to a small paintbrush.
2. Click the Pressure mode button on the Property Bar (**Figure 65**).
3. Set the width of the curve using the Artistic Media Tool Width text box and spin buttons (**Figure 81**).
4. Press the left mouse button and drag. Use the up arrow on the keyboard to apply more pressure and make the line thicker (**Figure 82**). Use the down arrow to make the line thinner. If you are using a pressure pen or stylus, the line will get thicker when you press harder and thinner when you press less hard.
5. When you release the mouse button, the curve will redraw, displaying the outline of the pressure curve. (**Figure 83**). A few shapes and some color add personality (**Figure 84**).

It's also possible to apply the Preset, Brush, or Sprayer modes to a curve that has already been drawn.

To apply an Artistic Media Tool mode to an existing curve:

1. Select the Artistic Media Tool from the Curve fly-out (**Figure 64**). The mouse pointer will change to a small paintbrush.
2. Using the Property Bar, select one of the three modes—Preset, Brush, or Sprayer (**Figure 65**).
3. Use the mouse to select the existing curve you want to change (**Figure 85**). When the curve is selected, tiny nodes will appear around it.
4. Select a stroke using the drop-down list on the Property Bar (**Figures 67, 70, and 73**). The curve will assume the selected stroke (**Figure 86a–c**).

Tip:

- To change to a different stroke, choose Undo from the Edit menu or press Ctrl+Z on the keyboard, then select the new stroke.

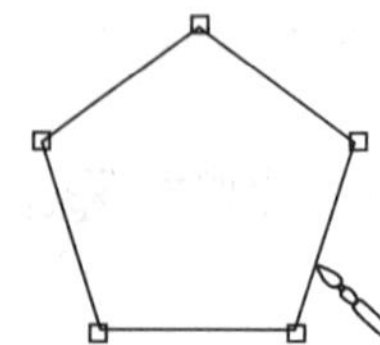

Figure 85. *When you select the existing object with the mouse, tiny nodes appear around its perimeter.*

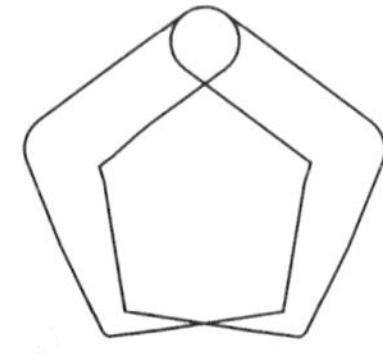

Figure 86a. *Preset mode.*

Figure 86b. *Brush mode.*

Figure 86c. *Sprayer mode.*

Figures 86a–c. *The three different modes applied to the same object.*

SUMMARY

In this chapter you learned how to:

- Draw lines and curves
- Create closed objects
- Erase part of a line
- Create a flag
- Change line thickness
- Create arrowheads
- Cut objects using the Knife Tool
- Use the Eraser Tool
- Draw with the Artistic Media Tool

Page and Document Setup

Besides being a versatile drawing tool, CorelDraw 9 includes expanded desktop publishing capabilities. This means that you can use CorelDraw 9 to create many types of multiple-page publications such as brochures, flyers, and catalogs. (Formerly, this required separate desktop publishing software.) In addition, you can create documents for any paper size that is used anywhere in the world.

In this chapter you will learn how to set page size and orientation. Then you will set a document's default unit of measure. From there you will add and remove pages from a document and find out how to quickly move between pages. Finally, you discover how to view a document's information.

Desktop Publishing Folding Styles

Printers use special terms for the way paper is folded. Below are a few standard folding styles:

Full Page	Booklet	Tent Fold	Side Fold	Top Fold
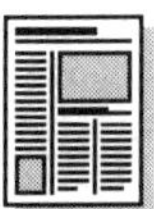	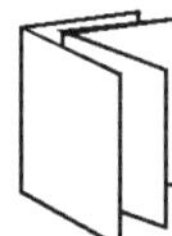	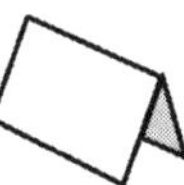	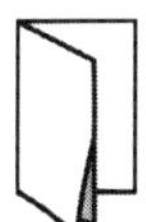	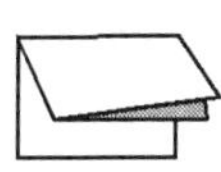

To select a page size and orientation:

1. Without anything selected on the drawing page, at the left end of the Property Bar click the down arrow next to the Paper Type/Size drop-down list (**Figure 1**). (Notice that the Property Bar's title bar reads "Property Bar: No Selection.")
2. Select the paper size that you want (**Figure 2**). If you don't remember how large a particular predefined page size is, just select it. Its dimensions will be displayed automatically in the width and height text boxes to the right of the drop-down list.
3. Use the Portrait and Landscape buttons on the Property Bar to select a page orientation.

or

1. From the Layout menu, choose Page Setup (**Figure 3**). This will open the Options dialog box with Size selected (**Figure 4**).
2. Click the arrow next to the Paper list box to display the predefined paper sizes (**Figure 5**). Select the paper size that you want. If you don't remember how large a particular predefined page size is, just select it. Its dimensions will be displayed automatically in the Width and Height text boxes.

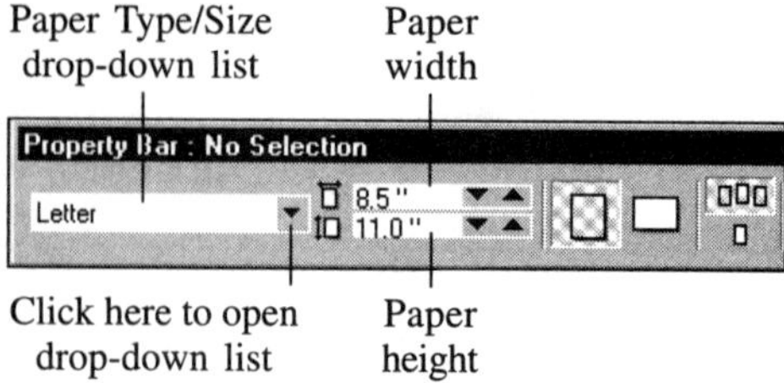

Figure 1. *Use the Property Bar to select page size and orientation.*

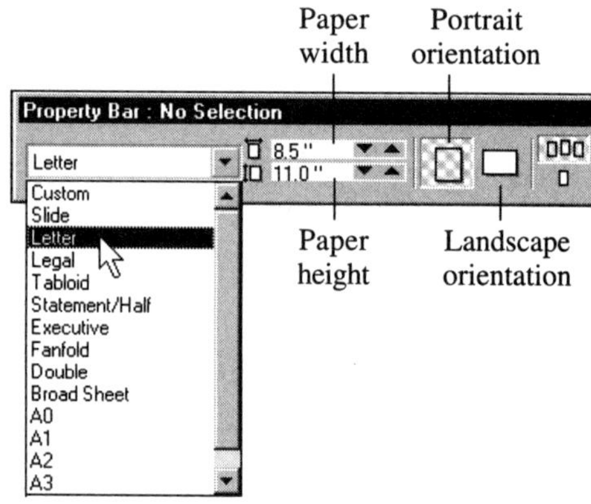

Figure 2. *Use the drop-down list to select a paper size. You can also create a custom paper size by typing the paper dimensions you need in the paper width and height text boxes.*

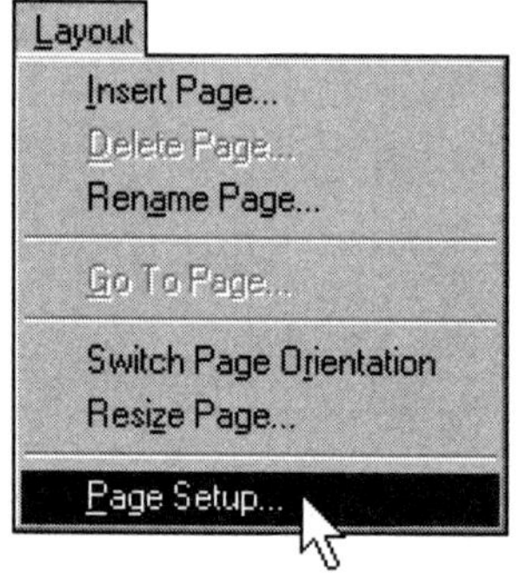

Figure 3. *Choose Page Setup from the bottom of the Layout menu.*

Set Page Size and Orientation

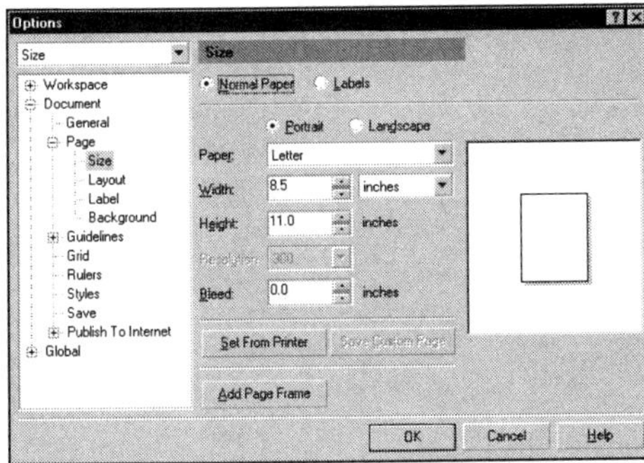

Figure 4. *The Size panel of the Options dialog box is used to select page size and orientation.*

3. Use the option buttons next to Portrait and Landscape to select a page orientation, then click OK. The dialog box will close and the page will assume the new size and orientation.

Tip:

- Check out the "Labels" item in the Paper list box. There are hundreds of predefined labels, categorized by manufacturer—Ace, Avery, Nashua, and Nebs, to name a few—and manufacturer's stock number.

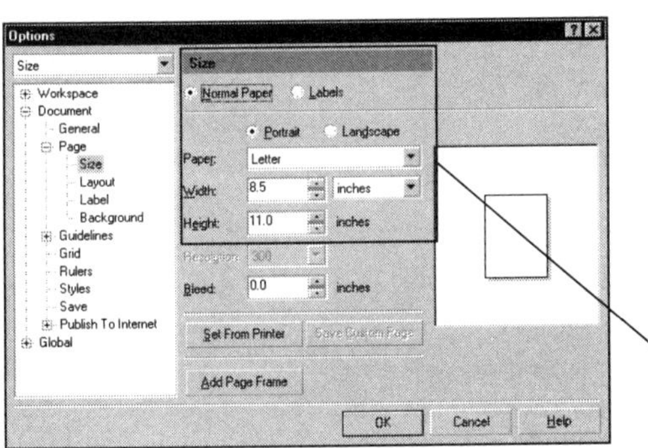

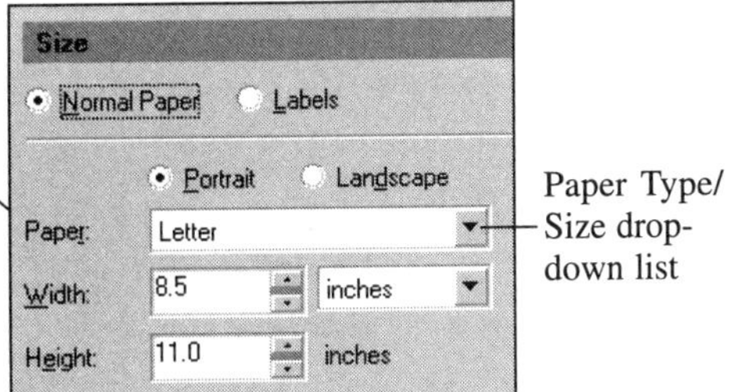

Paper Type/ Size drop-down list

Figure 5. *On the Size panel in the Options dialog box, use the Paper Type/Size drop-down list to select the paper size you need. Click the Portrait or Landscape radio button to select a page orientation.*

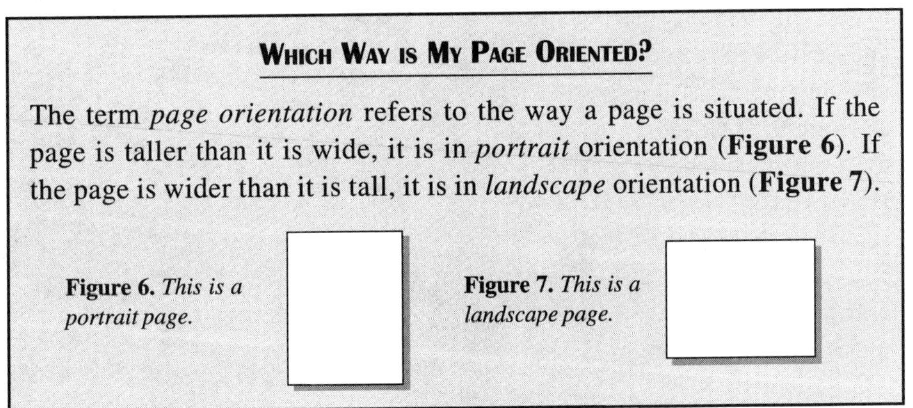

WHICH WAY IS MY PAGE ORIENTED?

The term *page orientation* refers to the way a page is situated. If the page is taller than it is wide, it is in *portrait* orientation (**Figure 6**). If the page is wider than it is tall, it is in *landscape* orientation (**Figure 7**).

Figure 6. *This is a portrait page.*

Figure 7. *This is a landscape page.*

To change the unit of measure for the current document:

On the Property Bar, use the Drawing Units drop-down list to select a new measurement system (**Figure 8**).

or

1. Open the Options dialog box by choosing Page Setup from the Layout menu (**Figure 3**).
2. Use the list box next to the Width text box to select a new measurement system (**Figure 9**).
3. Click OK.

or

1. Right click on a ruler. A pop-up menu will appear (**Figure 10**).
2. Choose Ruler Setup from the pop-up menu. The Options dialog box will open with Rulers selected (**Figure 11**).
3. In the Units area near the top of the dialog box, use the list boxes found to the right of Horizontal and Vertical to select a new measurement unit. (Be sure the box next to "Same units for Horizontal and Vertical rulers" is checked, otherwise the rulers will display different measurement units.)
4. Click OK.

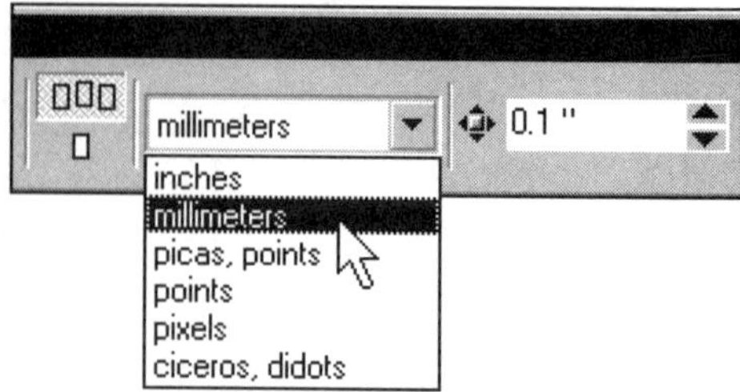

Figure 8. *Use the Drawing Units drop-down list to select a new measurement system.*

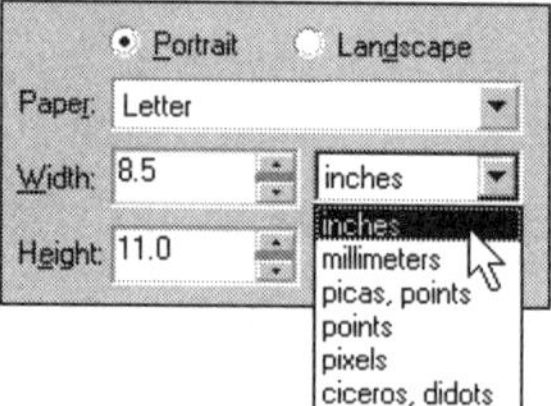

Figure 9. *You can use the list box next to the Width text box to select the unit of measure.*

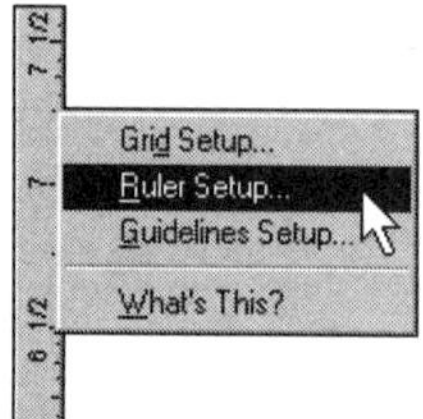

Figure 10. *Choose Ruler Setup from the pop-up menu.*

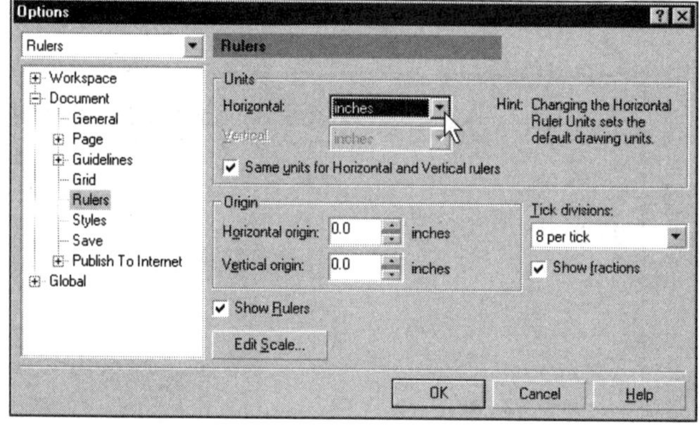

Figure 11. *Use the Horizontal and Vertical drop-down lists to set a measurement system.*

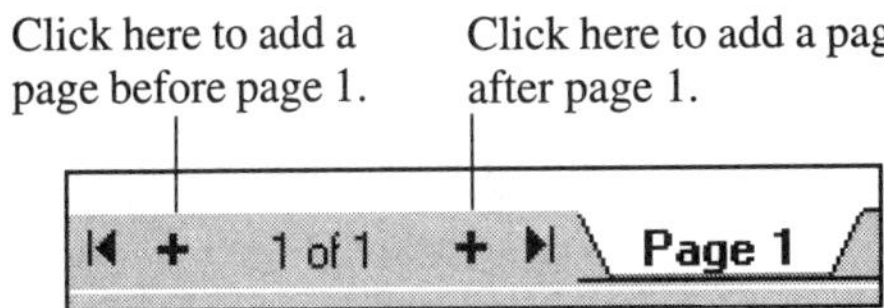

Figure 12. *The Navigator.*

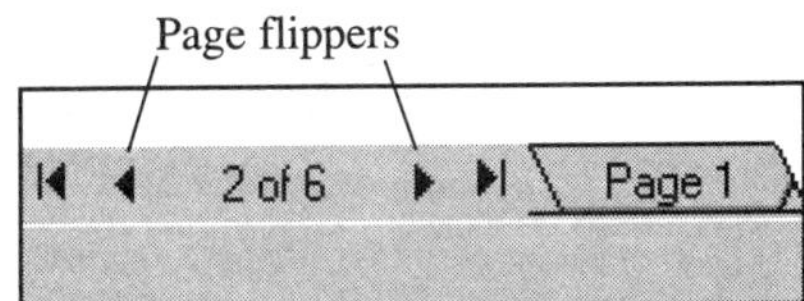

Figure 13. *Use the page flippers to move to the next or previous page.*

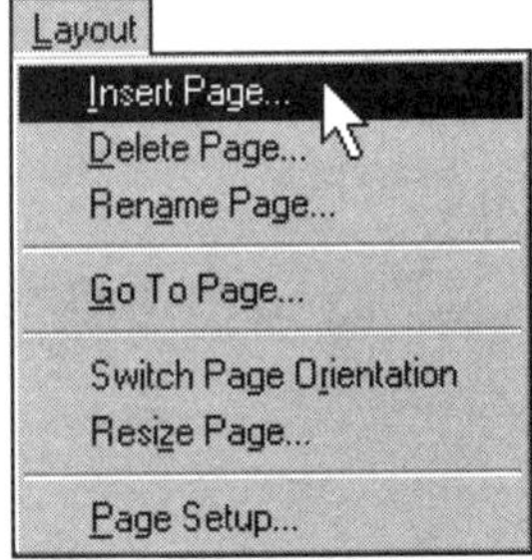

Figure 14. *Choose Insert Page from the Layout menu.*

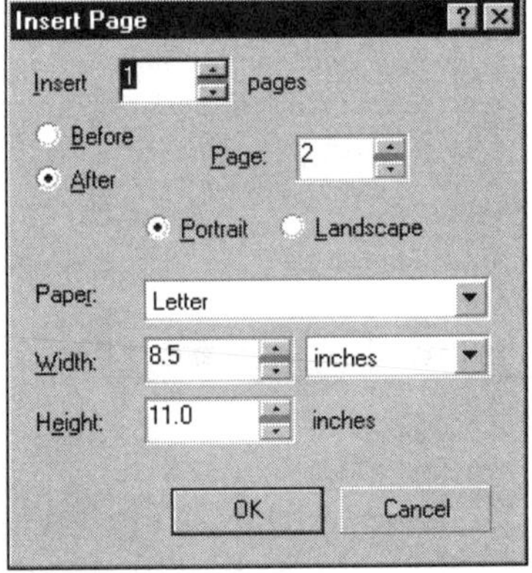

Figure 15. *Enter the number of pages you want to insert and then click OK. You can also set page size and orientation for the new pages that are different from the existing pages.*

To add pages to a document:

1. Look at the bottom-left corner of your screen. You will see several plus signs, and the page you are currently working on (**Figure 12**). This bar is called the *Navigator*.
2. To insert a new page after the current page, click the plus sign to the right of the page counter. Several things will happen:
   - A new page will be added.
   - One or both of the plus signs will change to arrows (**Figure 13**). These arrows are called *page flippers*.
   - Page tabs will appear. You can click any one of the tabs to move to that page.

or

1. Choose Insert Page from the Layout menu (**Figure 14**) or press the Page Up key on the keyboard. The Insert Page dialog box will appear (**Figure 15**).
2. Enter the number of pages you want to add and whether the new pages should be inserted before or after the specified page, then click OK.

Tip:

- The maximum number of pages you can have in one document is 999.

Add Pages to a Document

To delete a page from a document:

1. Right click on the page tab of the page you want to delete. A pop-up menu will appear (**Figure 16**).
2. Choose Delete Page from the pop-up menu.

or

1. Choose Delete Page from the Layout menu (**Figure 17**). The Delete Page dialog box will open (**Figure 18**), showing the currently selected page. If you want to delete a different page, type that number in the Delete page text box.
2. Click OK.

To delete a range of pages:

1. Open the Delete Page dialog box by choosing Delete Page from the Layout menu (**Figure 17**).
2. Type the number of the first page you want to delete.
3. Click on the box to the left of Through to page to add a check mark to that box and then type the number of the last page you want to delete (**Figure 19**).
4. Click OK.

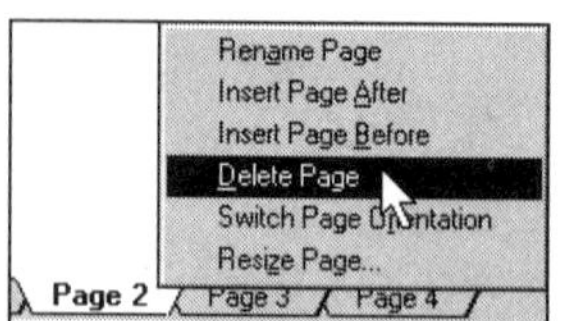

Figure 16. *Right click on the page tab and choose Delete Page from the pop-up menu.*

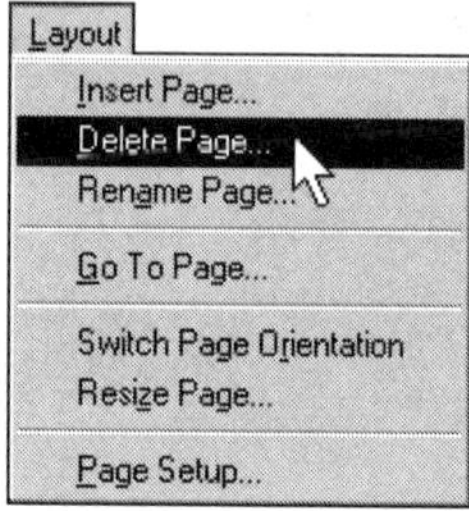

Figure 17. *Choose Delete Page from the Layout menu.*

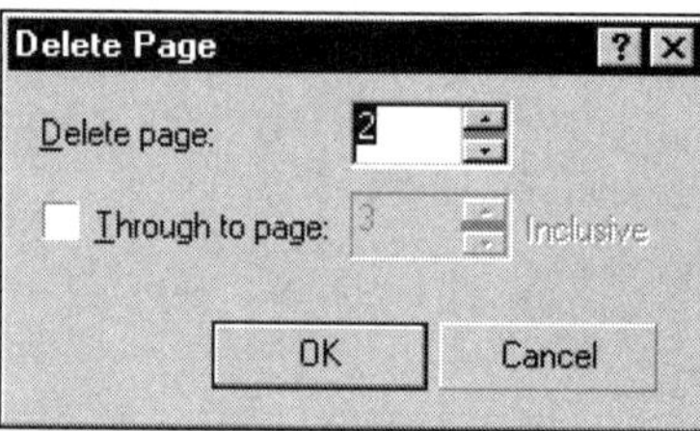

Figure 18. *Type in the page number that you want to delete and then click OK.*

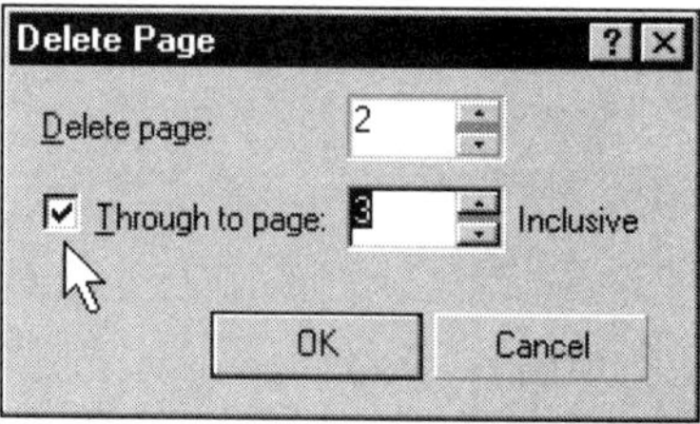

Figure 19. *Check the Through to page box and then enter the last page you want to delete.*

Figure 20. *To move to another page, click the appropriate page tab.*

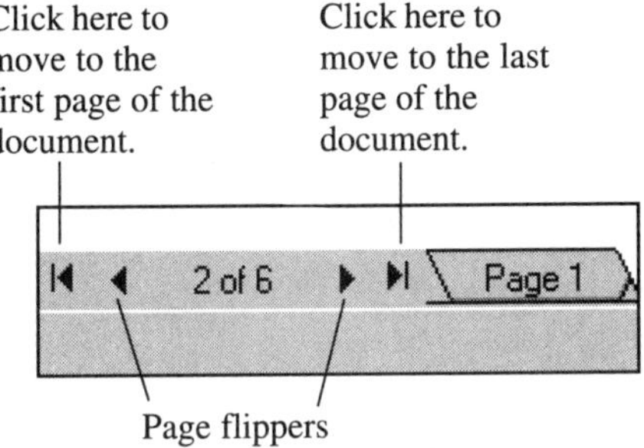

Figure 21. *You can use the page flippers to move to another page.*

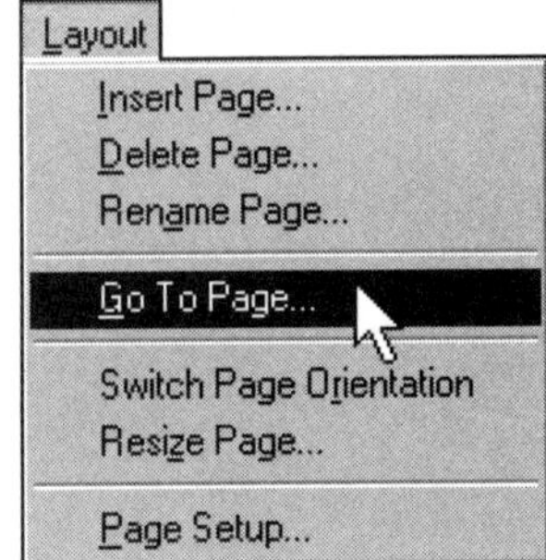

Figure 22. *Choose Go To Page from the Layout menu.*

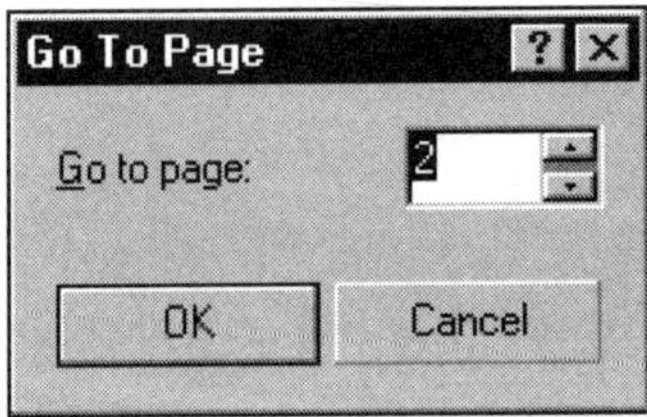

Figure 23. *Use the Go To Page dialog box to move between pages.*

To move between pages:

Click on the appropriate page tab at the bottom left of the screen (**Figure 20**).

or

Click on the right or left pointing arrows—page flippers—that appear on either side of the page counter (**Figure 21**).

or

1. Choose Go To Page from the Layout menu (**Figure 22**). The Go To Page dialog box will open (**Figure 23**).
2. Type in the page number you want to move to and click OK.

Tip:

- The Go To Page dialog box is handy when you are working with a large document. It lets you quickly move from one page to another.

If you Delete the Wrong Page, Don't Panic!

If you remove a page that you did not mean to delete, you can always bring it back by selecting Undo from the Edit menu or by pressing Ctrl+Z on the keyboard.

Move Between Pages

With CorelDraw 9 it's easy to check out a document's statistics. Using the Document Info item on the File menu, you can find out many useful things, including how many objects are in the document, what fonts have been used, the page size and orientation, when the document was created and last modified, and where the document is saved.

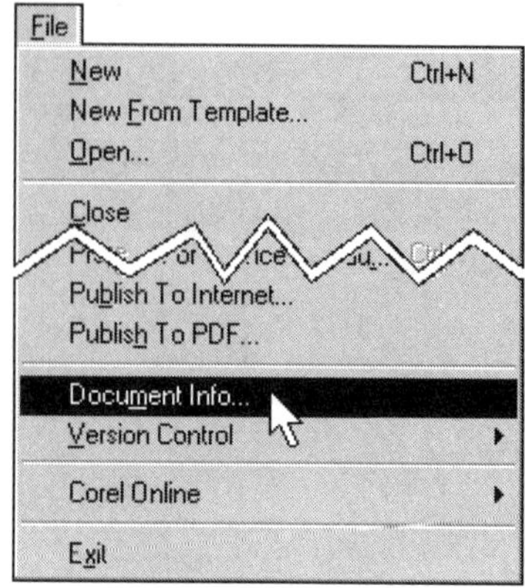

Figure 24. *Choose Document Info from the File menu.*

To view document information:

Choose Document Info from the File menu (**Figure 24**). The Document Information dialog box will open (**Figure 25**). Use the scroll bar to move down through the document's statistics.

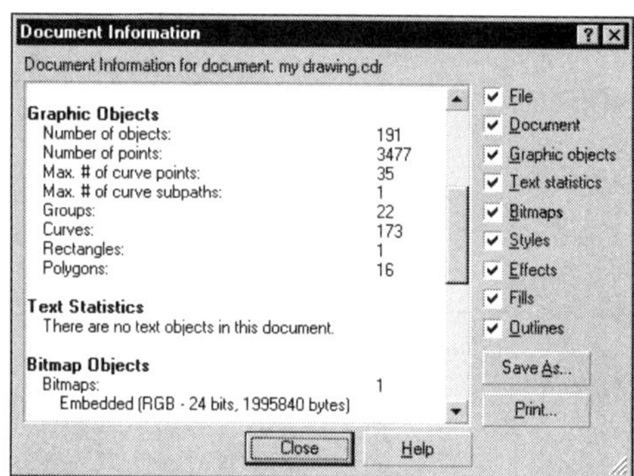

Figure 25. *The Document Information dialog box shows a document's statistics.*

Tip:

- You can use the check boxes to the right of the dialog box to select the document information that you want to see.

Summary

In this chapter you learned how to:

- Change page size and orientation
- Change the unit of measure
- Add and delete pages
- Move between pages
- View document information

Tools for Precision

CorelDraw 9 includes several tools to help you make your drawings more precise. In this chapter, you will learn how to use the horizontal and vertical rulers, how to change the rulers' *zero point*, and how to change the default unit of measure. Next, you will discover *guidelines*—dashed blue lines that do not print—and find out how they can help you shape and align the objects you draw. From there, you will learn about *grids*—regularly spaced dots that also do not print—and how to effectively use the Status Bar. Finally, you will discover how to *align* your objects by lining them up to a common edge.

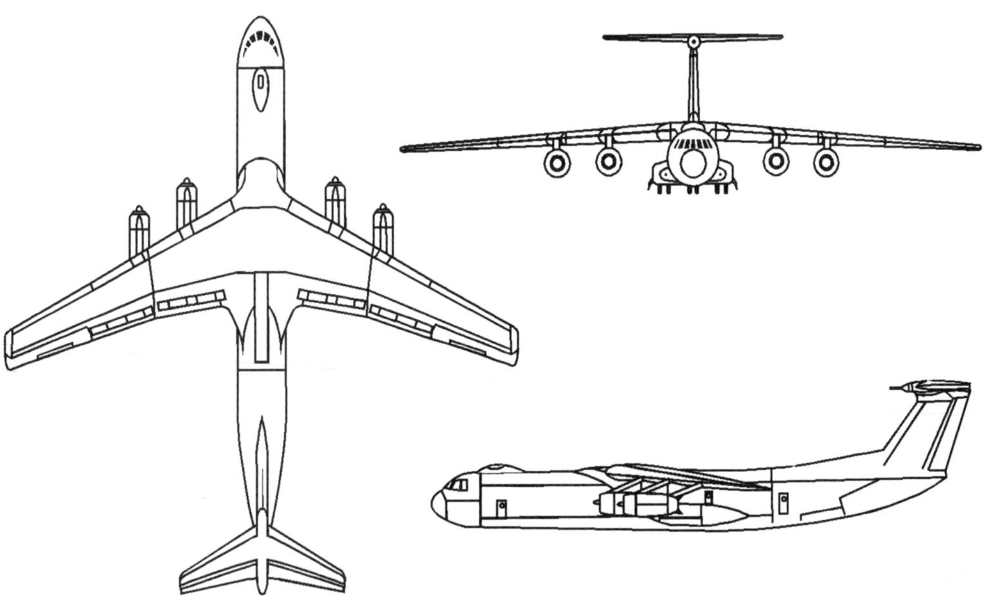

The horizontal ruler is located below the Property Bar and the vertical ruler is on the left side of the screen next to the Toolbox (**Figure 1**). The two rulers meet at a small square on the upper-left side of the screen called the *ruler intersection point*. The rulers monitor the location of the mouse using horizontal and vertical *tracking lines*.

All measurements are made from the *zero point*. This is the point where both the vertical and horizontal rulers show a value of 0. By default, the zero point is located at the bottom-left corner of the page. This is the standard way the printing industry measures a page. However, you might find it easier to measure a page from the top down.

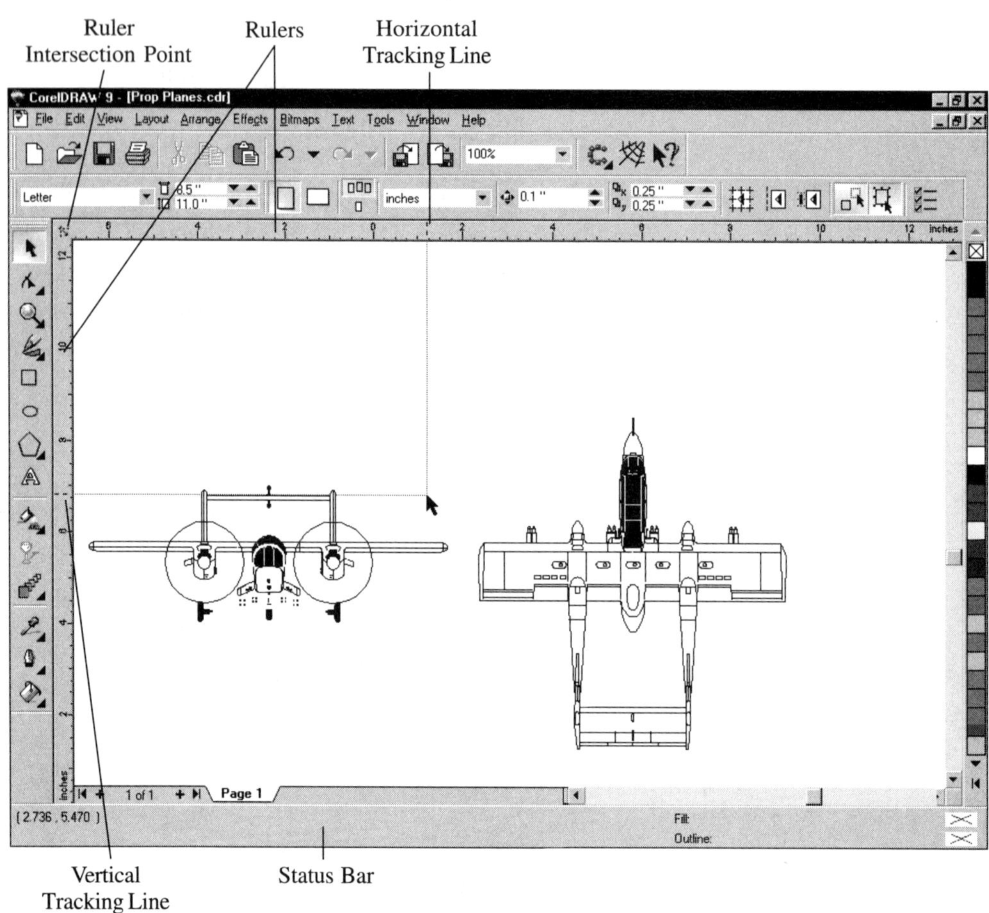

Figure 1. *The rulers, tracking lines, and Status Bar help make your drawings more precise.*

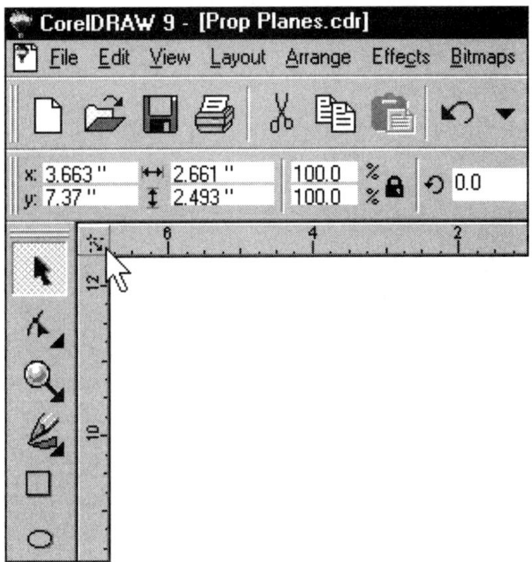

Figure 2. *Place the mouse pointer on the ruler intersection point and then press the left mouse button and drag.*

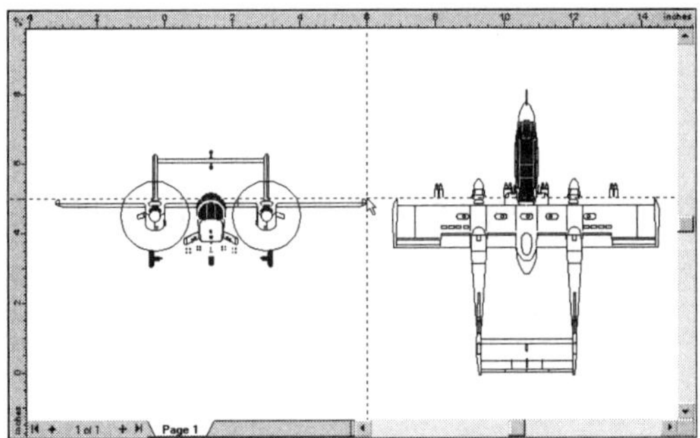

Figure 3. *Drag the dashed lines until they are positioned where you want the new zero point.*

To move the zero point:

1. Move the mouse pointer to the ruler intersection point (**Figure 2**).
2. Press the left mouse button and drag (**Figure 3**). As you do so, two intersecting dashed lines will appear under the mouse cursor.
3. Drag these lines to the position where you would like the zero point to be. For instance, if you want the horizontal and vertical rulers to read 0 at the top-left corner of the page, align these dashed lines to the top-left corner of the page.
4. When you are happy with the dashed lines' position, release the mouse button. The rulers will redraw and show the new zero point.

Tip:

- To move the zero point back to the bottom-left corner of the page—the default—double-click on the ruler intersection point.

To change the default unit of measure:

1. Open the Options dialog box by selecting Page Setup from the Layout menu (**Figure 4**).
2. Use the list box next to the Width text box to select a new measurement system (**Figure 5**).
3. Click Document in the tree view window to the left of the Options dialog box (**Figure 6**). The Document panel will appear at the right of the dialog box. Most of the check boxes on the Document panel will be grayed out.
4. Put a check mark in the box next to Save options as defaults for new documents (**Figure 7**). The rest of the check boxes on the panel will become available.
5. Make sure the box next to Grid and ruler options is checked.

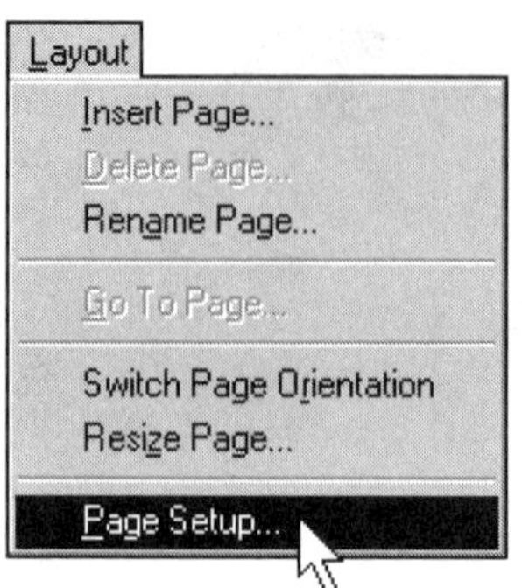

Figure 4. *Choose Page Setup from the Layout menu.*

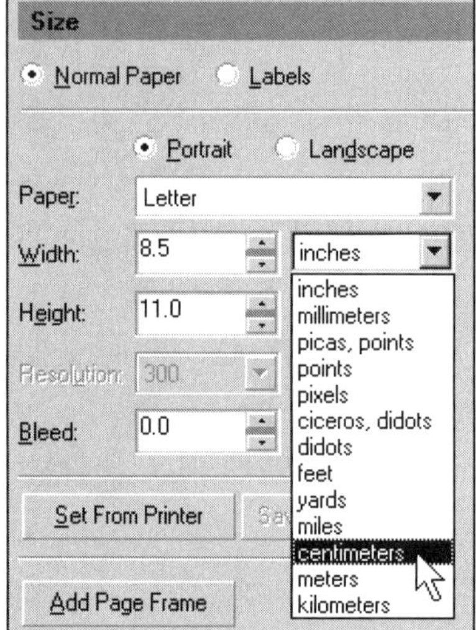

Figure 5. *Use the list box next to the Width text box to select the unit of measure.*

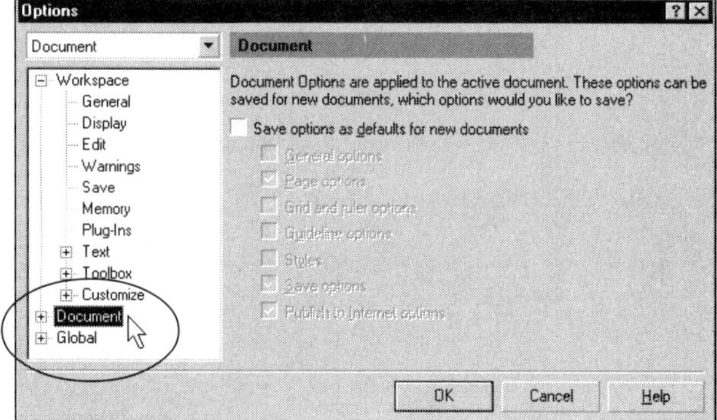

Figure 6. *Click Document in the tree view window to make the Document options appear at the right of the dialog box.*

Set a New Unit of Measure

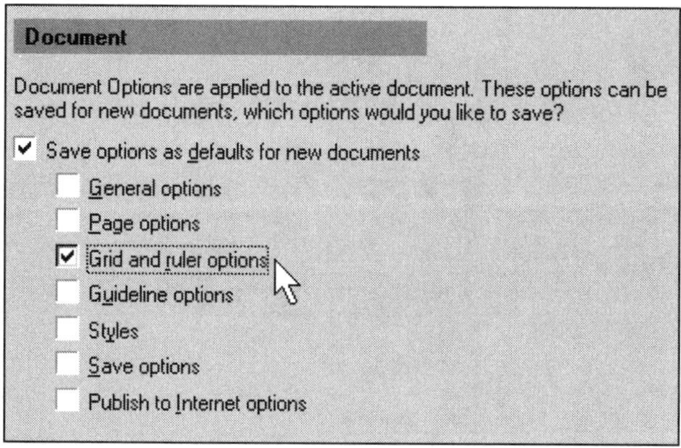
Document Options are applied to the active document. These options can be saved for new documents, which options would you like to save?
Save options as defaults for new documents
General options
Page options
Grid and ruler options
Guideline options
Styles
Save options
Publish to Internet options

Figure 7. *Make sure the box next to Grid and ruler options is checked, and then click OK.*

6. Click OK. The dialog box will close and the new measurement system will appear on the rulers, Property Bar, and Status Bar. The next time you start a new document, the measurement system you chose will appear in the document.

Saving Changes as Defaults for New Documents

There are many things you can save as defaults for new documents on the Document panel in the Options dialog box (**Figure 7**). These include:

- **General options**—any changes made using the General panel, such as the display view (Normal, Draft, Enhanced, etc.) and the resolution at which bitmap extrusions and drop shadows are rendered.
- **Page options**—any changes made using the Page panel, including showing page border, printable area, and bleed area.
- **Guideline options**—any changes made using the Guidelines and Preset panels, including snap to guidelines, guideline color, and preset guideline positioning.
- **Styles**—any changes made using the Styles panel, including text size, font, and color.
- **Save options**—any changes made using the Save panel, including saving textures and blends with files.
- **Publish to Internet options**—any changes made using the Publish to Internet panel, such as the way Web pages are laid out and saved.

Each of the panels discussed above can be displayed by clicking on the appropriate word (General, Page, Save, etc.) in the Options dialog box tree view window (**Figure 6**). Take a look around the Options dialog box. There are many things you can customize to make working in CorelDraw 9 easier for you.

To make the rulers disappear from the screen:

Choose Rulers from the View menu (**Figure 8**). This removes the check mark that is before Rulers on the View menu and hides the rulers from sight.

View
Simple Wireframe
Wireframe
Draft
Normal
• Enhanced
Full-Screen Preview F9
Preview Selected Only
✔ Rulers
Grid
✔ Guidelines
Bleed
Printable Area
Overprinted Objects
✔ Text Frames
Snap To Grid Ctrl+Y
Snap To Guidelines
Snap To Objects
Grid and Ruler Setup...
Guidelines Setup...

Figure 8. *Choose Rulers from the View menu.*

Tip:

- To bring the rulers back again, choose Rulers from the View menu.

In some cases, you might actually want to move the ruler to the area where you are drawing. This makes it easier to watch the vertical and horizontal tracking lines while you draw.

To move a ruler to a new position:

Position the mouse pointer over a ruler, hold down the Shift key, press the left mouse button, and drag the ruler to a new position (**Figure 9**).

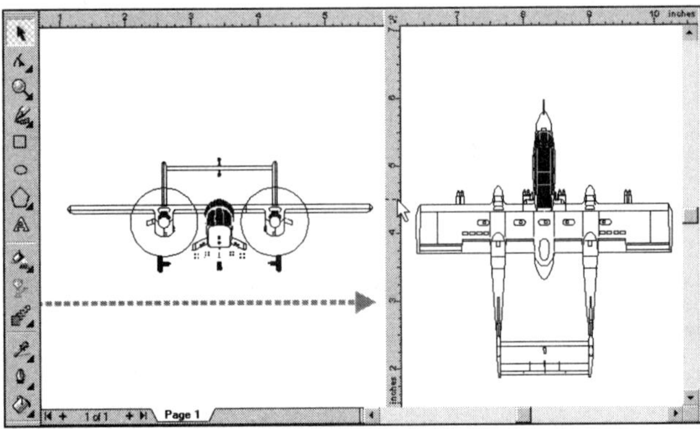

Figure 9. *While pressing the Shift key and the left mouse button, drag the ruler to its new position.*

Tip:

- To move a ruler back to its default position near the edge of the screen, hold down the Shift key and double-click on the ruler.

Guidelines are an extension of rulers that can be positioned anywhere in the drawing window (**Figure 10**). They are very useful for setting up exact areas where you are going to draw and for helping align objects. By default, guidelines do not appear on the printed page, they come in the same flavors as rulers—vertical and horizontal—and they can even be rotated, making them angled. A guideline consists of a dashed blue line. When a guideline is selected, it turns red.

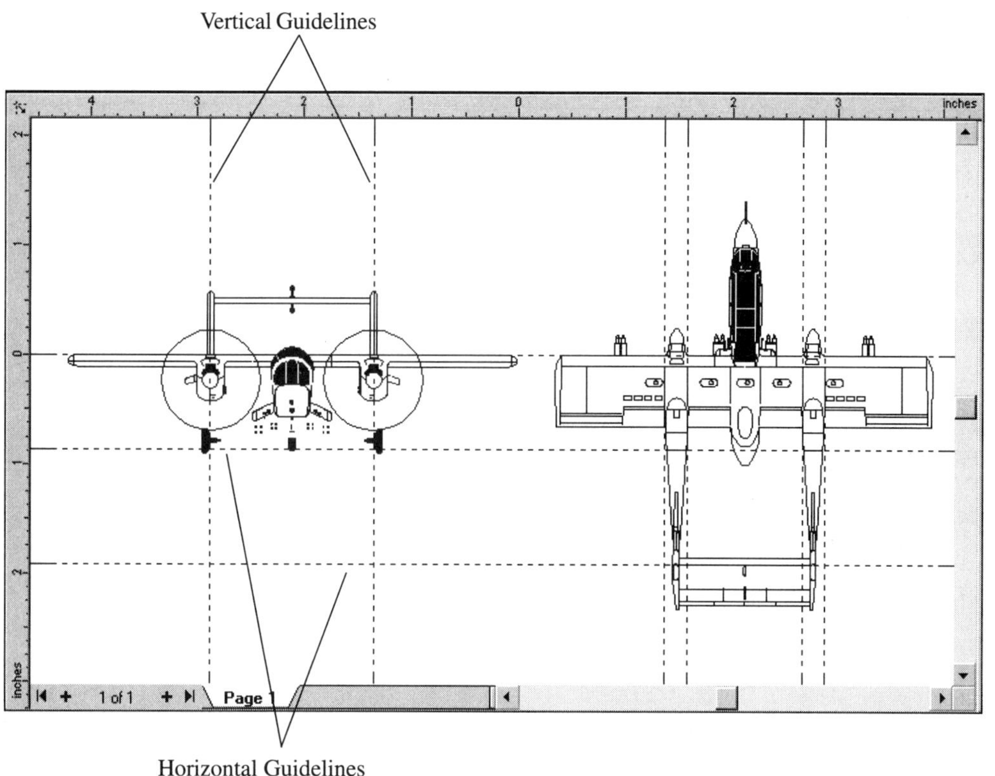

Figure 10. *Horizontal and vertical guidelines are helpful when aligning objects or creating objects of specific sizes.*

To add guidelines to a page:

1. Position the mouse over one of the rulers. Use the horizontal ruler to create horizontal guidelines and vice versa.
2. Press the left mouse button and drag it. A guideline will appear under the mouse pointer (**Figure 11**). Release the mouse button when you are happy with the position of the guideline.

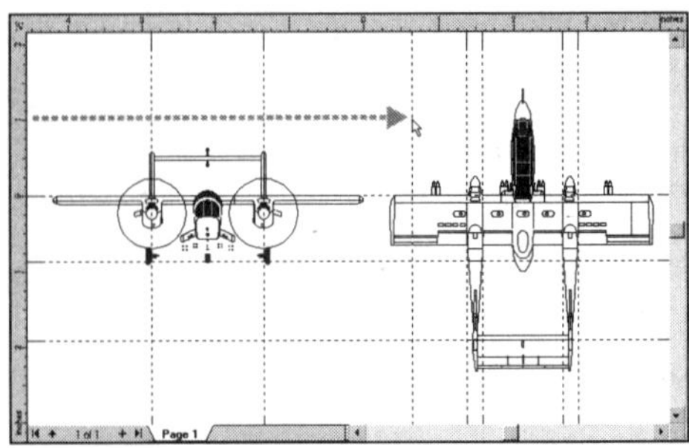

Figure 11. *Position the mouse over a ruler, press the left mouse button, and drag a guideline to the desired position.*

To angle a guideline:

1. With the Pick Tool, click the guideline you want to angle. A center of rotation marker—a circle with a dot in the center—and rotation handles appear around the guideline.
2. Press the left mouse button and drag a rotation handle until the guideline is at the desired angle (**Figure 12**), and then release the mouse button.

or

1. With the Shape Tool, click the guideline you want to angle. Two nodes will appear on the guideline, one at each end.
2. Position the Shape Tool over one of the nodes, press the left mouse button, and drag until the guideline is at the desired angle.

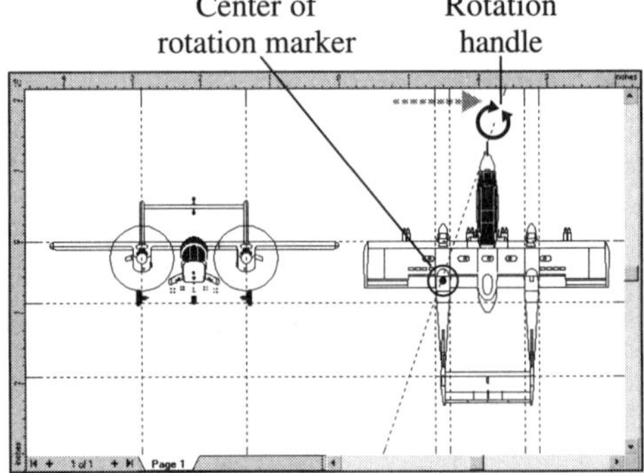

Figure 12. *Drag the guideline handle to angle the guideline.*

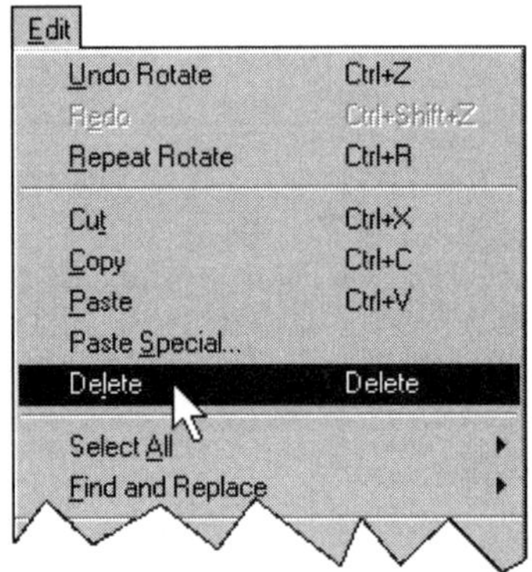

Figure 13. *Choose Delete from the Edit menu or press the Delete key on the keyboard.*

Add Guidelines; Angle a Guideline

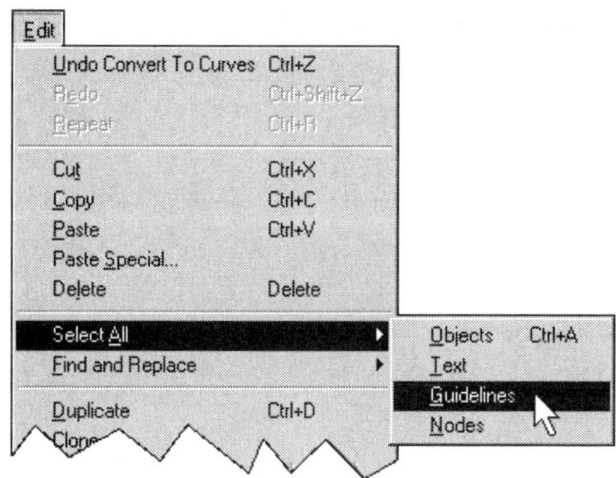

Figure 14. *Choose Guidelines from the Select All fly-out on the Edit menu.*

Figure 15. *After opening the Options dialog box, click on Presets to view that panel.*

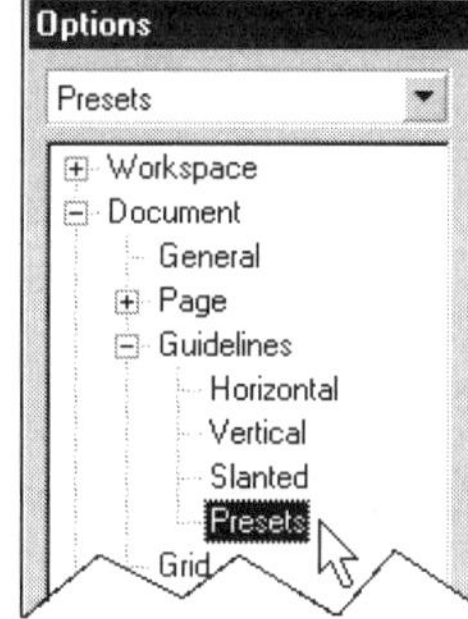

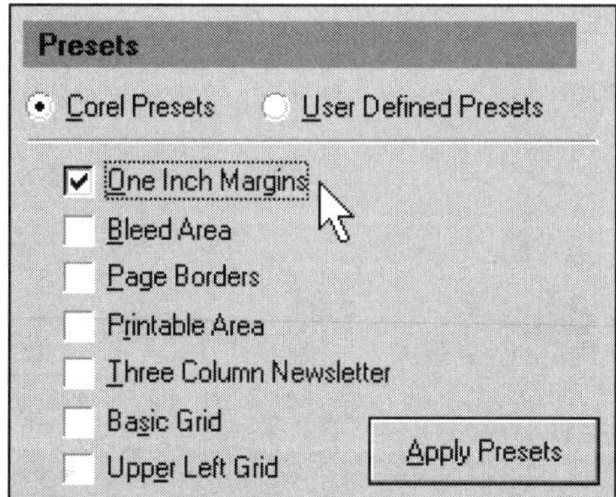

Figure 16. *On the Presets panel of the Options dialog box, you can choose from several guideline preset options.*

To move a guideline:

1. Select the Pick Tool and position the mouse pointer over the guideline.
2. Press the left mouse button and drag the guideline to a new position.

To remove a guideline:

1. Use the Pick Tool to select the guideline you want to remove.
2. Choose Delete from the Edit menu (**Figure 13**) or press the Delete key on the keyboard.

To remove all guidelines:

1. Choose Guidelines from the Select All fly-out on the Edit menu (**Figure 14**).
2. Choose Delete from the Edit menu (**Figure 13**) or press the Delete key on the keyboard.

Tips:

- You can use the Options dialog box can be used to add and move guidelines to specific locations. To open the Options dialog box, double click on a guideline.
- CorelDraw 9 comes with several guideline "presets" that quickly set up guidelines in specific locations. To access the Presets panel in the Options dialog box, double click on a guideline, then select Presets in the tree view window (**Figure 15**). Selcct any of the presets by putting checks in the boxes, then clicking Apply Presets (**Figure 16**).

One of the most important guideline features is *Snap To Guidelines* which makes precise alignment easy by forcing an object to line up with a guideline.

Figure 17. *Click the Snap To Guidelines button on the Property Bar.*

To turn on Snap To Guidelines:

1. Add some guidelines to a document.
2. Click the Snap To Guidelines button near the right end of the Property Bar (**Figure 17**).

   or

   Choose Snap To Guidelines from the View menu (**Figure 18**).
3. Test the Snap To Guidelines feature by selecting the Rectangle Tool and drawing a rectangle near the guidelines. As you draw, the rectangle's edges will "snap to" the guideline.

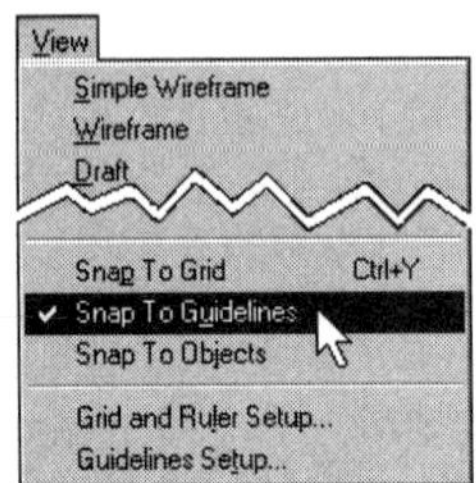

Figure 18. *Choose Snap To Guidelines from the View menu.*

Tip:

- A check mark will appear in front of the Snap To Guidelines item on the View menu when this feature is turned on.

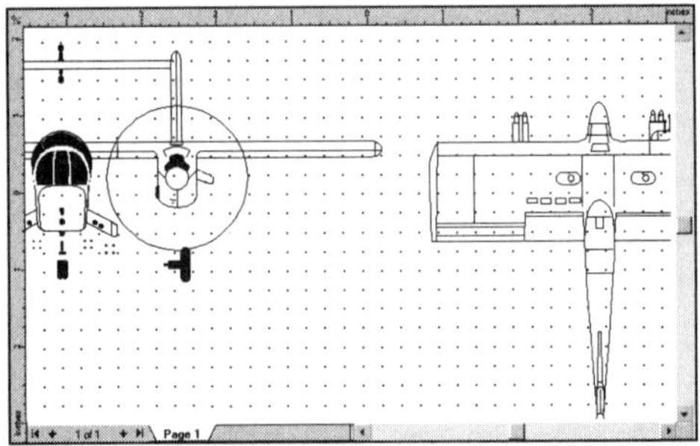

Figure 19. *Grid dots do not print and are helpful when aligning objects.*

Grids are extremely useful for creating precision drawings such as flowcharts, office layout plans, blueprints for buildings, and anything that requires straight lines, uniform shapes, and perfect alignment. The grid dots or lines that appear on the screen when you setup a grid do not print (**Figure 19**).

Figure 20. *Choose Grid and Ruler Setup from the View menu.*

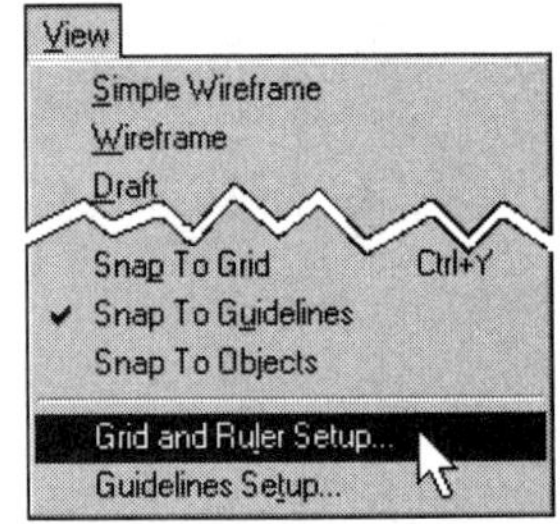

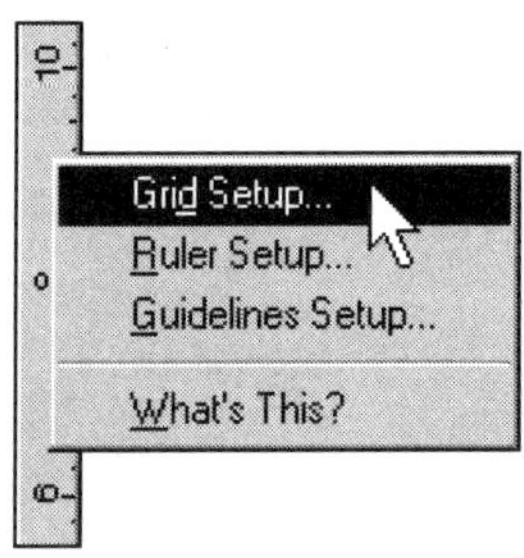

Figure 21. *Choose Grid Setup from the pop-up menu.*

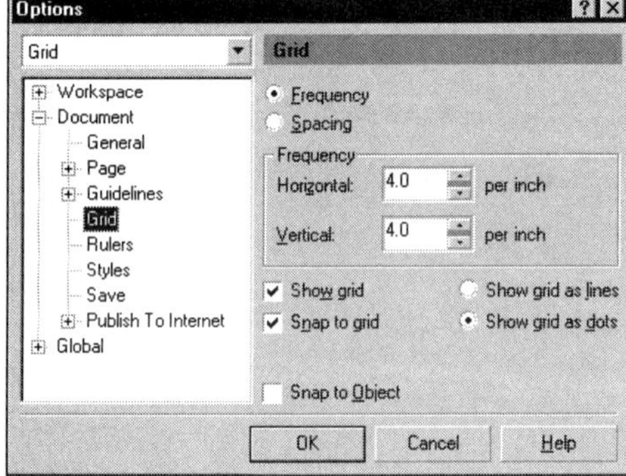

Figure 22. *The Options dialog box opens with Grid selected in the tree view window.*

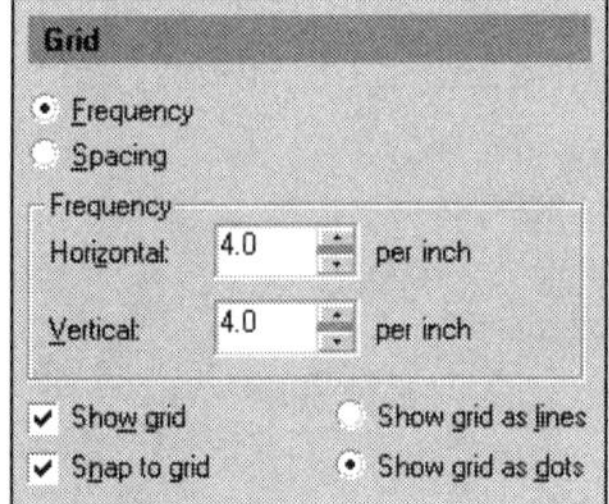

Figure 23. *You can create a grid by setting how many grid dots will appear per measurement unit.*

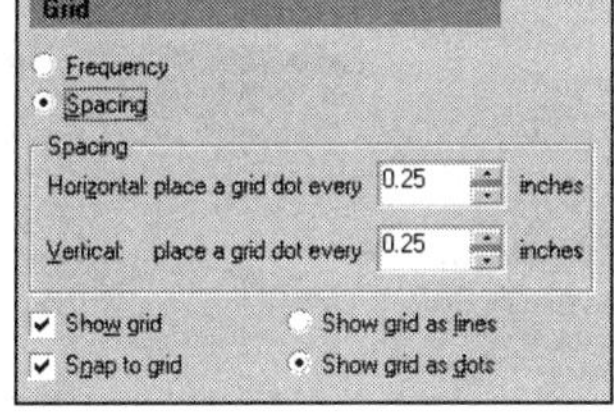

Figure 24. *Or you can create a grid by setting how far apart each grid dot will be.*

To setup a grid:

1. Choose Grid and Ruler setup from the View menu (**Figure 20**).

   or

   a. Right click on a ruler. A pop-up menu will appear (**Figure 21**).

   b. Choose Grid Setup from the pop-up menu.

   The Options dialog box will open with the Grid item selected in the tree view window (**Figure 22**).

2. Using the Grid panel, you can set how many grid dots appear on the screen in two ways:

   - By Frequency: click the option button next to Frequency, then use the Frequency area (**Figure 23**) to type in how many dots will appear per the default unit of measure. In Figure 25, the grid will contain 4 dots per inch (1 dot every 1/4 inch).
   - By Spacing: click the option button next to Spacing, then use the Spacing area (**Figure 24**) to set the placement of each grid dot. In Figure 26, the grid will place 1 dot every .25 inch (1/4 inch).

3. Check the box next to Show grid.
4. Check the box next to Snap to grid.
5. Click OK. The grid will appear on the screen (**Figure 19**).
6. Test out the grid by selecting a drawing tool and creating an object.

Setup a Grid

The Status Bar (**Figure 25**) gives you information about everything you do in CorelDraw—the position of the mouse, what Snap To constraints are on, what kind of object is selected and its details, including size, position, and color. You can tailor the Status Bar to provide the information you need.

By default the Status Bar is one line width high. This saves valuable screen real estate, but does hide information. If you need to see more information about an object, you can make the Status Bar two lines high. This is easy to do using the pop-up menu that appears when you right click on the Status Bar.

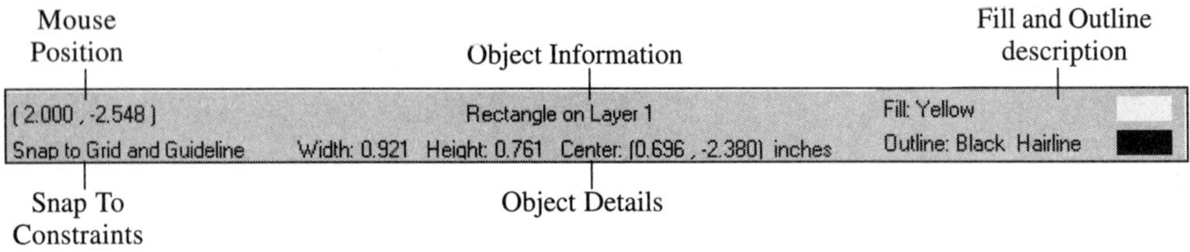

Figure 25. *The Status Bar gives you detailed information about your graphics.*

To make the Status Bar bigger:

1. Right mouse click on the Status Bar. A pop-up menu will appear (**Figure 26**).
2. Choose Two Lines from the Size fly-out on the pop-up menu.

or

Position the mouse pointer over the upper edge of the Status Bar, press the left mouse button, and drag it upward.

Figure 26. *Click Two Lines from the Size fly-out on the pop-up menu.*

Figure 27. *Right mouse click on the Status Bar to display the pop-up menu. Choose Customize to make the Options dialog box open.*

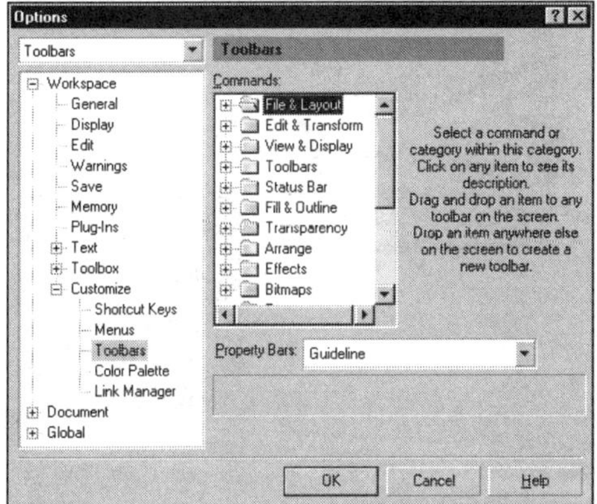

Figure 28. *The Options dialog box opens with File & Layout selected in the Commands list box.*

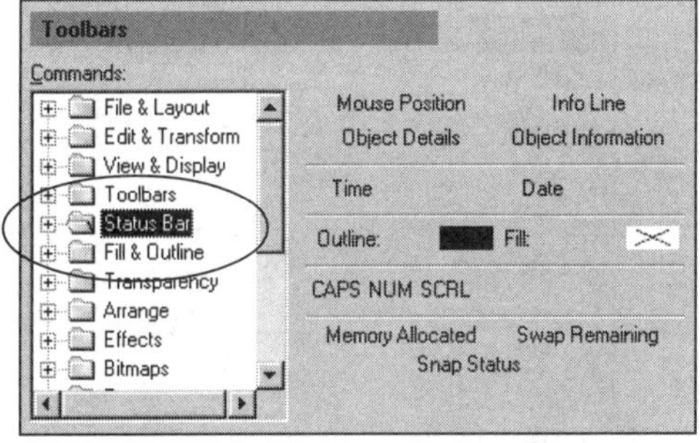

Figure 29. *Click Status Bar in the Commands list box to view the items that can be added to the Status Bar.*

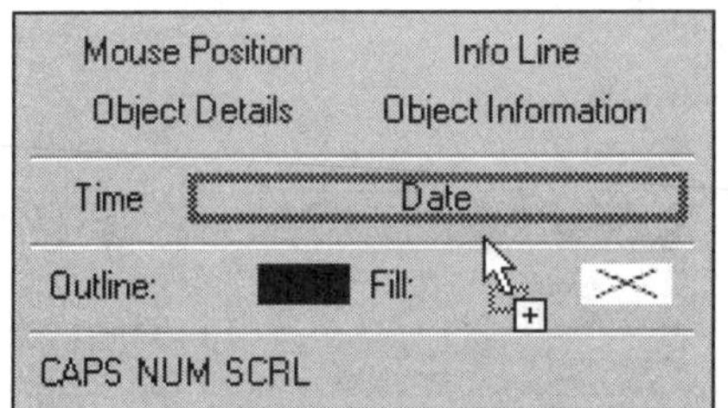

Figure 30. *Position the mouse pointer over the item you want to add to the Status Bar, press the left mouse button, and drag the item to the Status Bar.*

To change the Status Bar information:

1. Right mouse click on the Status Bar. A pop-up menu will appear.
2. Choose Customize from the pop-up menu (**Figure 27**). The Options dialog box will open with File & Layout selected in the Commands list box (**Figure 28**).
3. Click Status Bar in the Commands list box (**Figure 29**). The items you can add to the Status Bar will appear on the right side of the dialog box. You can view many things, including:
   - Mouse Position
   - Object Details and Information
   - Time and Date
   - Keyboard States—whether Caps Lock, Num Lock, or Scroll Lock are on
   - Snap Status—which Snap To features are on
4. To add one of the items to the Status Bar, position the mouse pointer over an item and press the left mouse button. A plus sign will appear attached to the mouse pointer (**Figure 30**).
5. Drag the item onto the Status Bar.
6. Release the mouse button. The item will appear on the Status Bar.
7. When you are finished adding items to the Status Bar, click OK to close the dialog box.

Every object has handles that surround the object when it is selected with the Pick Tool. These handles also serve another purpose—they make up an invisible rectangular boundary around objects. In other words, they are there, working, even if you can't see them. This boundary is used when *aligning* objects. When objects are aligned, they are lined up using a common boundary edge. For instance if two objects are aligned to the left, this means the objects are lined up using the invisible left boundary of each object.

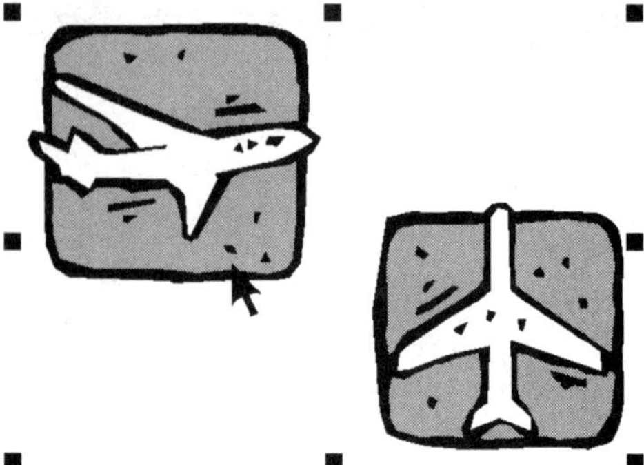

Figure 31. *Use the Pick Tool to select two or more objects to be aligned.*

To align objects:

1. Select two or more objects using the Pick Tool (**Figure 31**).
2. Choose Align and Distribute from the Arrange menu (**Figure 32**) or click the Align and Distribute button at the right end of the Property Bar (**Figure 33**). This will open the Align and Distribute dialog box with the Align tab page in front (**Figure 34**).
3. Select the type of alignment that you want—vertical and/or horizontal. You can align objects in two dimensions (horizontally and vertically) at the same time, or just in one dimension.

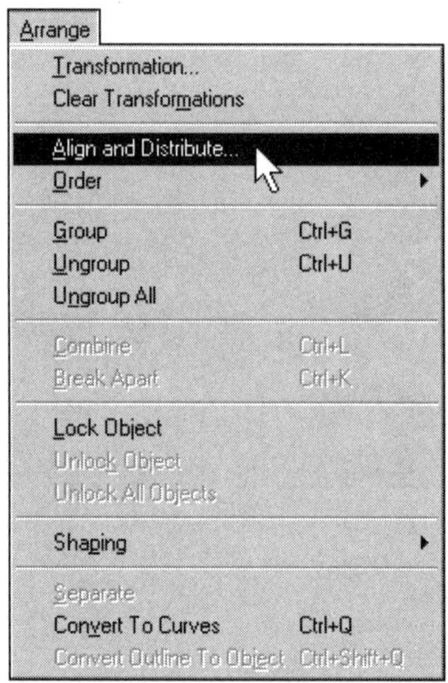

Figure 32. *Choose Align and Distribute from the Arrange menu.*

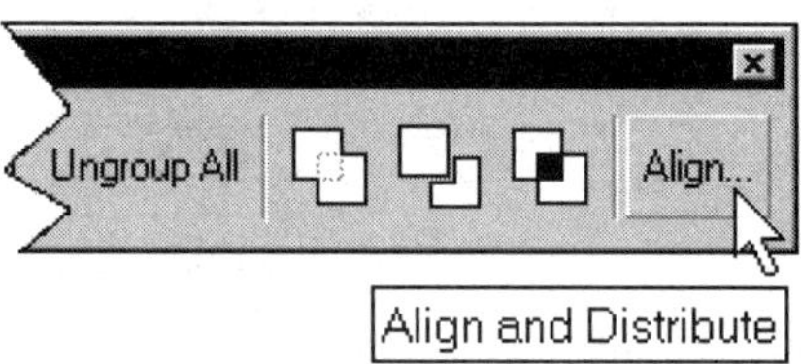

Figure 33. *Click the Align and Distribute button on the Property Bar.*

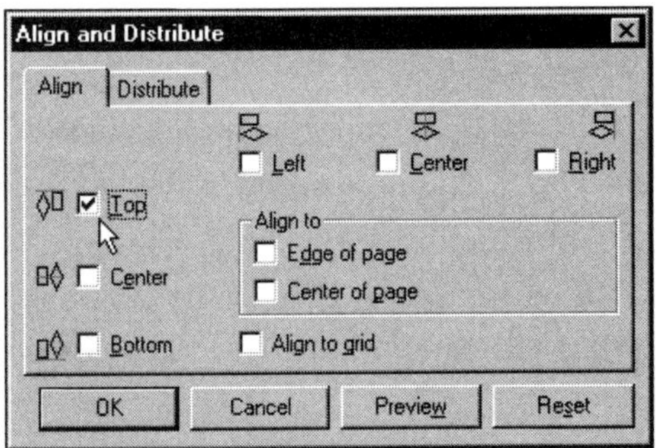

Figure 34. *Put checks in the check boxes next to the type of alignment you want.*

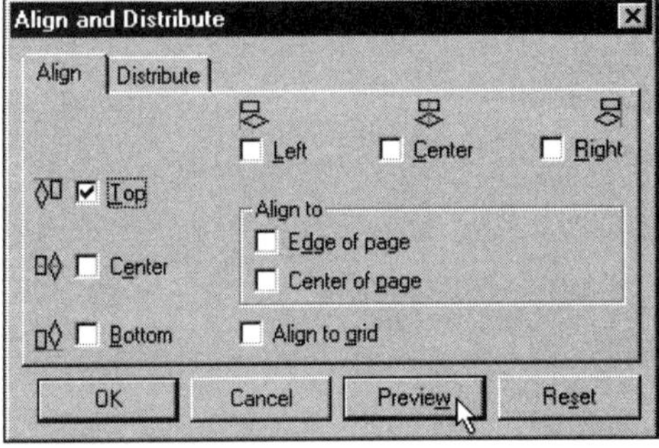

Figure 35. *Click the Preview button to see the objects you selected align in the drawing window. If you like the alignment, click OK, otherwise click Reset and try a different type of alignment. The two jets in this figure have been aligned to the Top (compare them with Figure 31).*

4. Click the Preview button to see the results of what you have chosen without committing yourself (**Figure 35**). If you like what you see, click OK. If you want to select another type of alignment, click Reset. The objects will move back to their original positions and you can try again.

Tips:

- If you select objects by holding down the Shift key and clicking on them—*multiple selecting*—the last object you select will be the target object that CorelDraw will use. For instance, if you use multiple selection and align the objects' right edges, the objects will align to the right edge of the last object you selected.
- If you marquee select the objects, the lowest object on the page is the one that CorelDraw 9 will use as the target to align the other objects.

TYPES OF ALIGNMENT

The Align tab page of the Align and Distribute dialog box shows small pictures by the horizontal and vertical alignment check boxes to give you a hint as to what the alignment will do. These little pictures can be confusing, so below are illustrations that show how the vertical and horizontal alignment works together. In the caption below each illustration, the first word is the vertical alignment and the second word is the horizontal alignment.

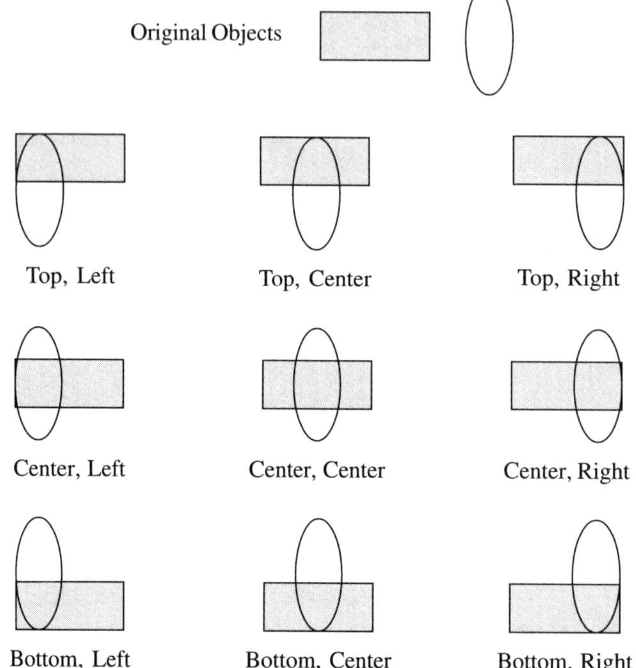

SUMMARY

In this chapter you learned how to:

- Set the zero point
- Change the unit of measure
- Move the rulers
- Add, move, and delete guidelines
- Create angled guidelines
- Use the snap to features
- Setup a grid
- Set Status Bar information
- Align objects

Color and Fills

In this chapter, you will learn how to *fill* closed objects with *uniform*, *fountain*, *pattern*, and *texture* fills, change the outline color of objects, and *sample* a color from one object and apply it to another. The tools you will use are the Color Palette, the Fill Tool and its fly-out, the Interactive Fill Tool, and the new Interactive Mesh Fill, Eyedropper, and Paintbucket Tools (**Figure 1**).

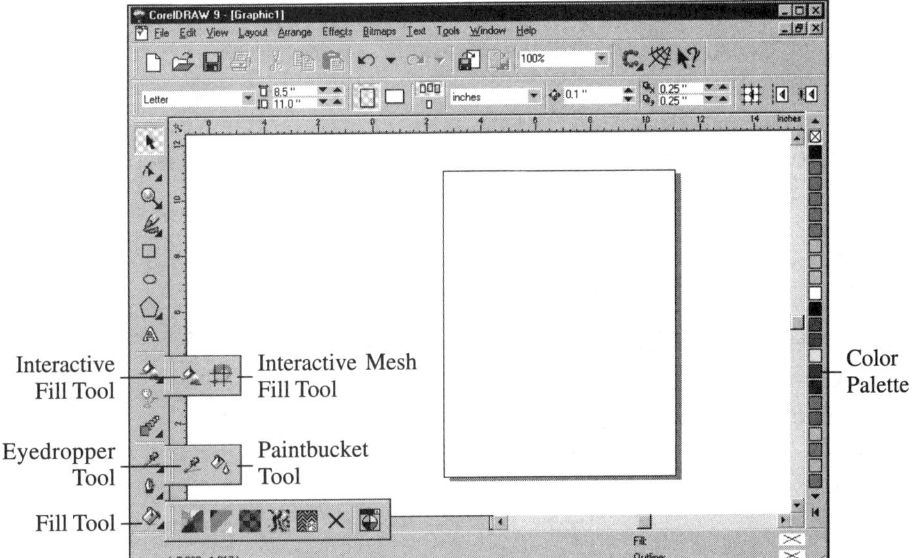

Figure 1. *The Fill Tool, Interactive Fill Tool, Color Palette, and new Interactive Mesh Fill, Eyedropper, and Paintbucket Tools will make your drawings very colorful.*

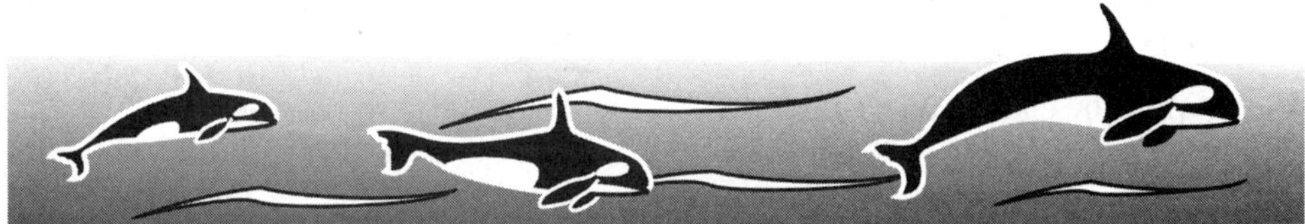

Color can bring a drawing to life and adding a solid color fill—called a *uniform fill*—to an object is very easy. But, before an object can be filled with color, the object has to have a closed path.

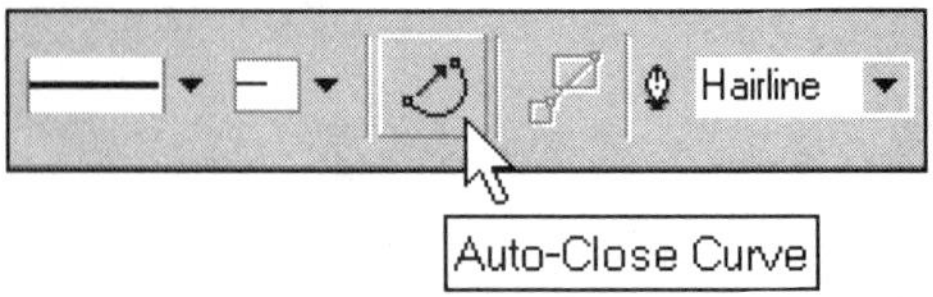

Figure 2. *Click the Auto-Close Curve button on the Property Bar to close the object's path.*

To make sure an object has a closed path:

1. Select the object with the Pick Tool and look up at the right side of the Property Bar. If the Auto-Close Curve button is available (**Figure 2**), then the curve is open; if not, then the curve is closed.
2. To close the curve, press the Auto-Close Curve button.

Figure 3. *Select the closed objects with the Pick Tool.*

To fill objects with a uniform color:

1. Select one or more closed objects with the Pick Tool (**Figure 3**).
2. Click on one of the *color wells* on the Color Palette located at the right side of the screen (**Figure 4**). The objects will fill with that color (**Figure 5**).

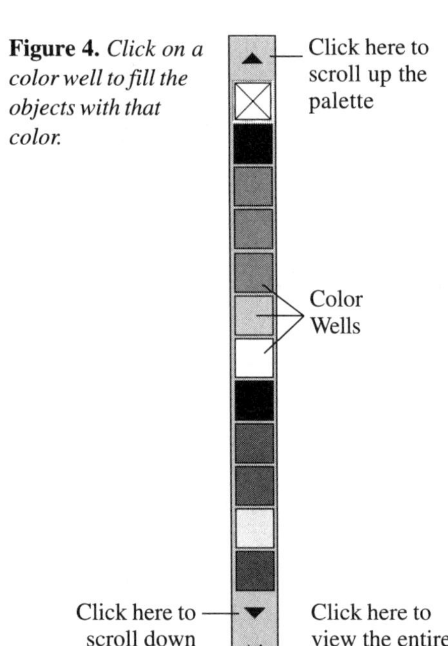

Figure 4. *Click on a color well to fill the objects with that color.*

Tips:

- To see more available colors on the Color Palette, use the up and down arrows at the top and bottom of the palette.
- To view the entire Color Palette, click the left-facing arrow at the bottom of the palette.

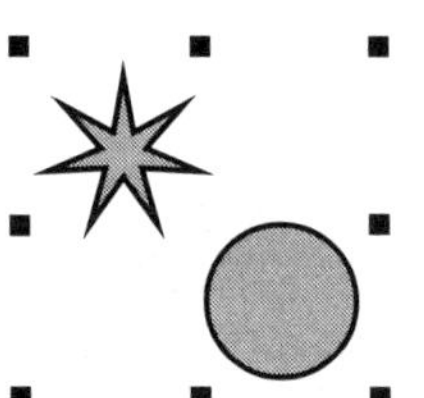

Figure 5. *When you click on a color well, the selected objects fill with that color.*

Figure 6. *Left or right mouse click the color well with an X in it to remove any color fills or outlines from objects.*

To change the outline color of objects:

1. Use the Pick Tool to select the objects you want to change.
2. Right mouse click on one of the color wells on the Color Palette. The objects' outlines will change to that color.

To remove color from objects:

1. Select the objects using the Pick Tool.
2. To remove the fill, *left* mouse click on the color well at the top of the Color Palette that has an X in it (**Figure 6**). To remove the objects' outline color, *right* mouse click on that same color well.

I LOST MY OBJECT!

Be careful when removing both the fill and outline color of an object. If the object is not selected, you won't be able to see it and may lose track of it!

WHERE'S THE COLOR PALETTE?

If you don't see the Color Palette, you can open it by selecting a palette from the Color Palettes fly-out found on the Window menu.

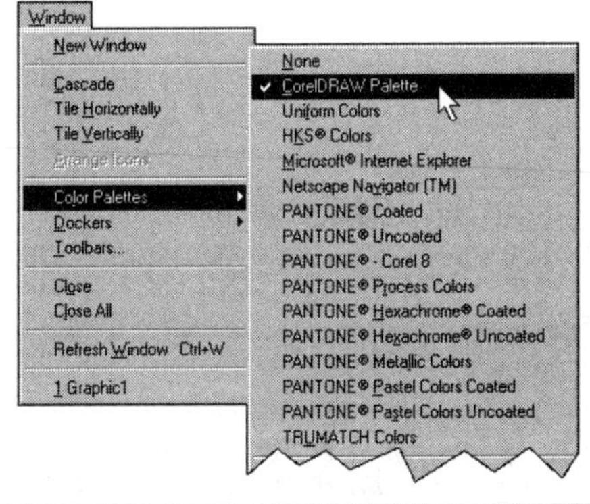

THE POP-UP COLOR PALETTE

A CorelDraw 9 feature, the Pop-up Color Palette lets you quickly find the color you want to use. To open the Pop-up Color Palette, move the mouse pointer over a color well on the Color Palette that is close to the color you want, then press and hold the left mouse button down. The Pop-up Color Palette will appear. Click on a color in the palette to select it.

Two new CorelDraw 9 tools, the Eyedropper and Paintbucket tools, work together to make adding color fills and outlines quick and easy. The Eyedropper Tool is used to *sample* or pick-up the desired color from an object that is already filled. Then, the Paintbucket Tool is used to take that color and apply it to another object's outline or fill.

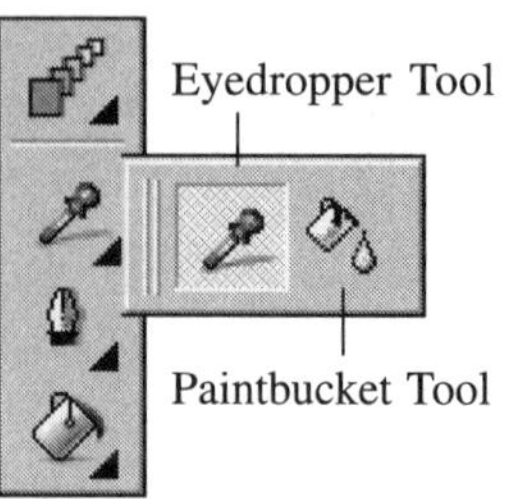

Figure 7. *The new Eyedropper and Paintbucket Tools let you quickly add color to object fills and outlines.*

To sample a fill or outline using the Eyedropper Tool:

1. Select the Eyedropper Tool, using the fly-out menu on the Toolbar (**Figure 7**). The mouse pointer will change to a small eyedropper. The Property Bar will dynamically change to display Eyedropper Tool buttons (**Figure 8**).
2. There are several ways to sample colors using the buttons on the Property Bar:
   - Fill/Outline—samples the entire fill or outline. For instance, if the fill is made up of a pattern, the entire pattern is picked-up.
   - 1x1, 3x3, 5x5—these buttons set the Eyedropper Tool to sample areas of specific dimensions (in pixels) and mix the colors together.
   - Selection—lets you marquee select an area using the Eyedropper Tool, mixing the colors from that area together.

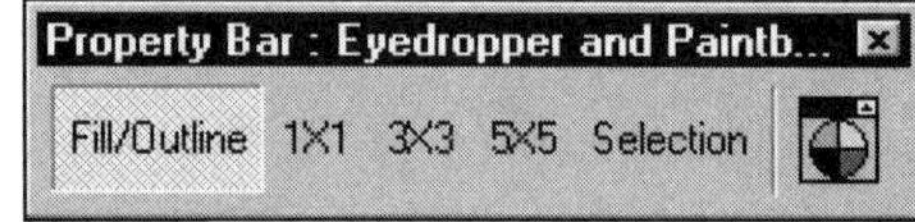

Figure 8. *The Property Bar dynamically changes to display Eyedropper Tool buttons.*

Figure 9. *Use the Eyedropper Tool to sample individual colors or an entire pattern.*

Figure 10. *After you have sampled a color or pattern with the Eyedropper Tool, the color you have picked up is displayed in the Fill or Outline boxes on the Status Bar. In this example, the pattern shown in Figure 9 has been sampled.*

Figure 11. *The closed object waiting to be filled.*

Figure 12. *Use the Eyedropper Tool to select a color or pattern. In this example, the pattern is being sampled.*

Figure 13. *Click on the object you want to fill with the Paintbucket Tool. When the paintbucket passes over a closed object, the sampled fill is displayed in a small square next to the paintbucket.*

> **THE SHIFT KEY LETS YOU TOGGLE**
>
> To toggle between the Eyedropper and Paintbucket Tools when one of them is selected, press the Shift key on the keyboard. This is handy if you need to sample and fill many objects.

3. Position the Eyedropper Tool over the fill or outline you want to select (**Figure 9**).
4. Click the mouse. The color or pattern will be displayed in the Fill or Outline boxes at the right side of the Status Bar (**Figure 10**).

To fill an object using the Paintbucket Tool:

1. Make sure the object you want to fill has a closed path (**Figure 11**).
2. Select a color or pattern using the Eyedropper Tool (**Figure 12**).
3. Select the Paintbucket Tool from the Toolbar (**Figure 7**). The mouse pointer will change to a small paintbucket.
4. Position the paintbucket over the object you want to fill.
5. Click the left mouse button. The object will be filled with the color or pattern (**Figure 13**).

To add outline color using the Paintbucket Tool:

1. Select a color or pattern using the Eyedropper Tool.
2. Select the Paintbucket Tool from the Toolbar (**Figure 7**).
3. Position the paintbucket over the outline you want to change.
4. Click the left mouse button. The object's outline will change to the selected color.

By default, the Color Palette shows a custom set of colors. However, there are many color sets and *color matching systems* to choose from. CorelDraw 9 includes more than one hundred color sets and matching systems available for display in the Color Palette. (To find out about color matching systems, see the sidebar on the next page.)

To display a different color set in the Color Palette:

1. Choose Color Palettes from the Window menu (**Figure 14**). This will open the Color Palettes fly-out.
2. Choose the color set you want to display from the fly-out.

or

1. Choose Color Palette Browser from the Dockers fly-out found on the Window menu (**Figure 15**). The Color Palette Browser docker will open, displaying a tree view window containing hundreds of different color palettes (**Figure 16**).
2. Click on the plus signs next to the palette folders until you find the palette you want to display.
3. Put a check mark in the box next to the name of the palette you want to display. It will simultaneously appear next to the Color Palette you already have open.

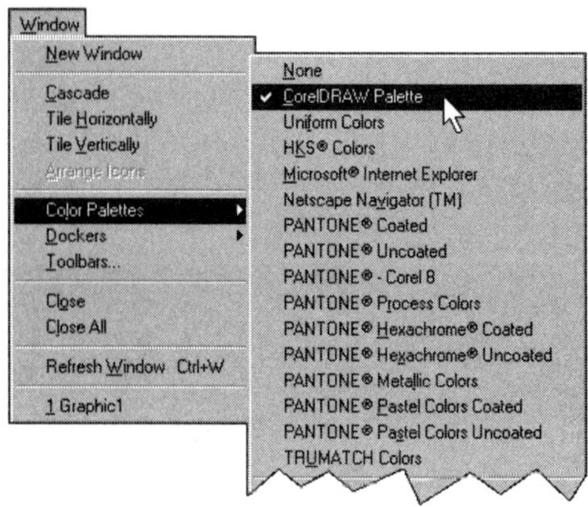

Figure 14. *Choose Color Palettes from the Window menu to display the color sets available on the fly-out.*

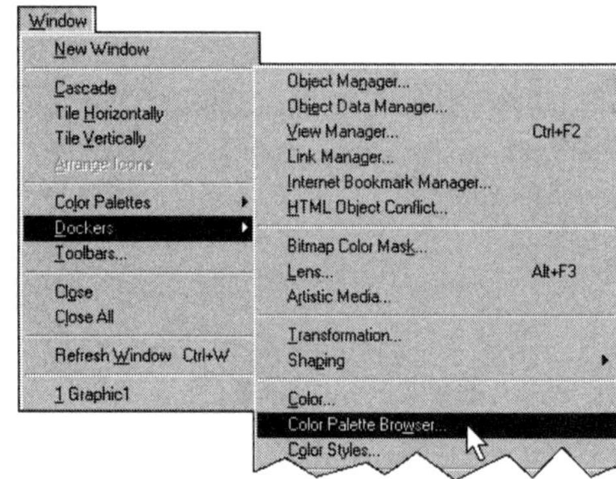

Figure 15. *Choose Color Palette Browser from the Dockers fly-out on the Window menu.*

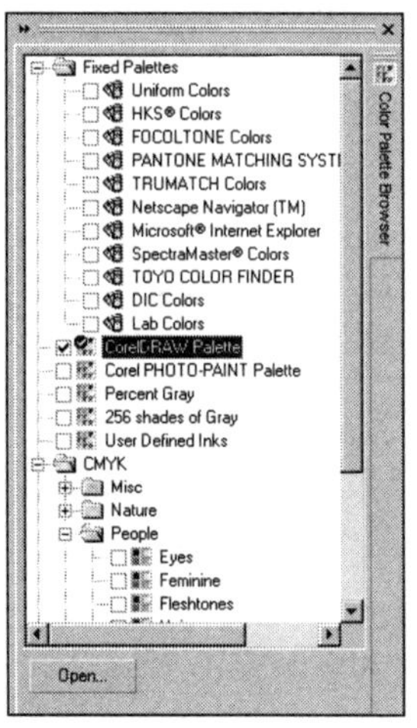

Figure 16. *Use the Color Palette Browser docker to select color palettes for display in your CorelDraw 9 workspace.*

WHAT IS A COLOR MATCHING SYSTEM?

Color matching systems are used by designers to tell commercial printers exactly what color to use for a print job. A matching system assigns numbers to different colors and displays them in *swatch books* that can be bought at art supply stores. Suppose that you want to use "fire engine red" for the title of a brochure. You would look through a color swatch book to find the exact red you have in mind, then tell the printer what that color number is. A few color matching systems are Pantone, Spectramaster, Toyo, and Trumatch.

WHAT IS A COLOR MODEL?

A color model breaks colors down into base or primary colors. If you are familiar with a color wheel, you know that red, yellow, and blue are the primary colors that can be used to make up all the colors our eyes can see. Printers use a different group of primary colors: cyan, magenta, yellow, and black. These four colors make up the *CMYK* color model (black is represented by the letter K because printers refer to this as the *key color*). Other color models include HSB (hue, saturation, and brightness) and RGB (red, green, blue).

SPOT COLOR AND PROCESS COLOR

If you work with a commercial printer, you will probably hear the terms *spot color* and *process color*. Spot color refers to a color matching system such as Pantone, and process color refers to a color model such as CMYK. The conceptual difference is that a color matching system is based on a recipe of specific mixed inks, whereas process color is based on the proportionate break down of real-world colors into each of the primary colors that they contain.

WORLD WIDE WEB COLOR PALETTES

CorelDraw 9 includes two Internet palettes, one for Microsoft Internet Explorer, and another for Netscape Navigator. These palettes include the 256 colors that these Internet browsers correctly display. For more information about graphics and the World Wide Web, check out Chapter 17, *CorelDraw 9 and the Web.*

The Uniform Fill dialog box (**Figure 17**) can be used to choose specific colors from any number of palettes or create custom colors.

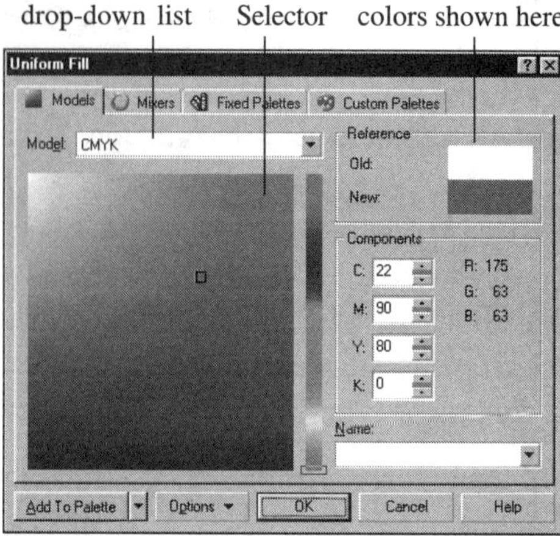

Figure 17. *The Uniform Fill dialog box is used to select colors and create custom colors.*

To use the Uniform Fill dialog box to fill an object with a color:

1. Select the object you want to fill with color.
2. Click the Fill Tool to display the fly-out, then click the Fill Color Dialog button (**Figure 18**) or press Shift+F11 on the keyboard. The Uniform Fill dialog box opens with the Models tab page in front.
3. Use the Model drop-down list to select a color model.
4. Click on the color you want in the Color Selector. The color you select will appear next to New in the Reference area at the upper right of the tab page.
5. Click OK. The dialog box will close and the object will be filled with the color you selected.

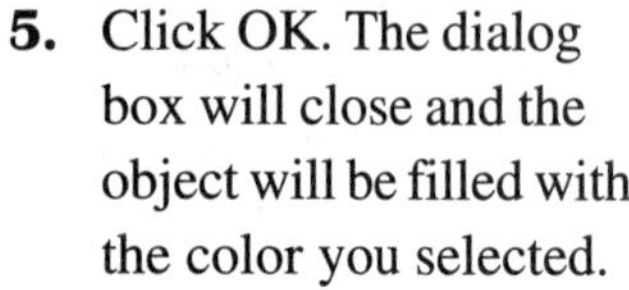

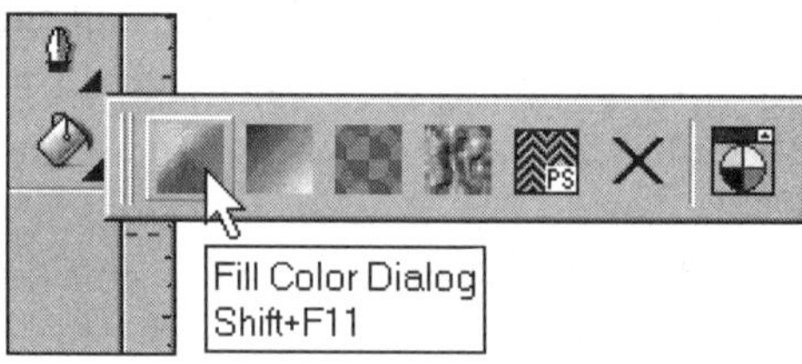

Figure 18. *Click the Fill Tool to display the fly-out, then click the Fill Color Dialog button.*

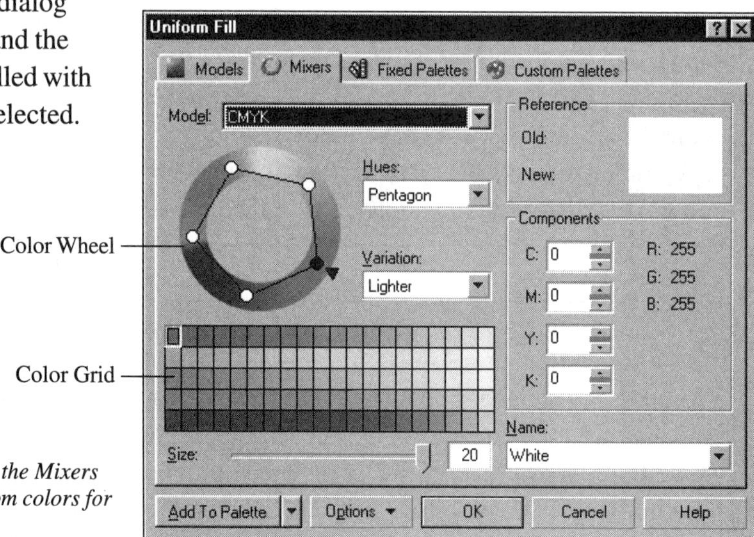

Figure 19. *You can use the Mixers tab page to create custom colors for your drawings.*

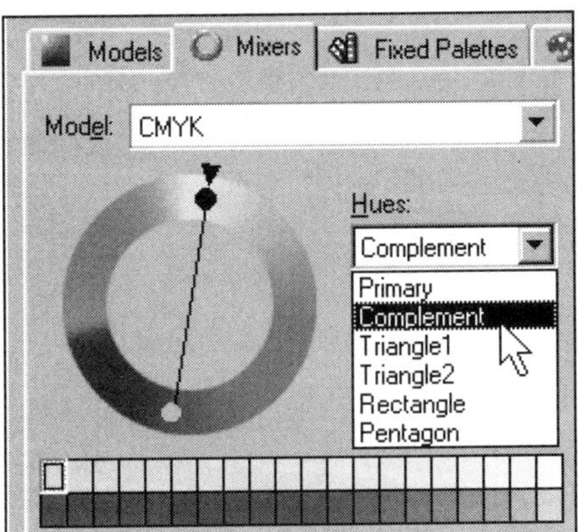

Figure 20. *The Hues drop-down list on the Mixers tab page lets you choose the relationships of the colors selected from the Color Wheel.*

Figure 21. *The custom color is shown in the New box.*

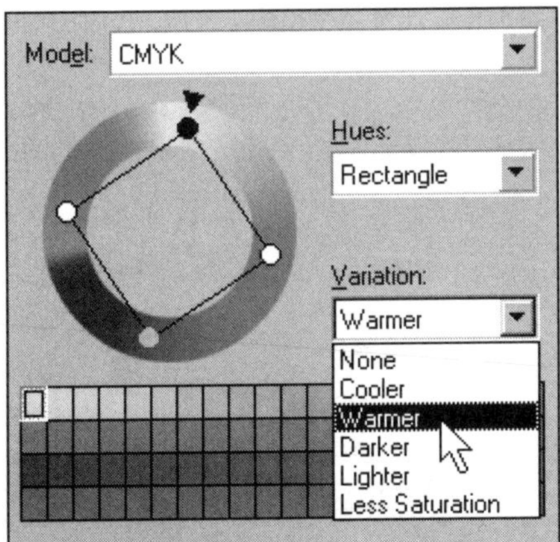

Figure 22. *The Variation drop-down list lets you set the spectrum of colors shown in the Color Grid.*

To create custom colors:

1. Select the object you want to fill with the custom color.
2. Click the Fill Tool to display the fly-out, then click the Fill Color Dialog button. The Uniform Fill dialog box will open with the Models tab page in front (**Figure 17**).
3. Click the Mixers tab to move to that tab page (**Figure 19**).
4. Use the Model drop-down list to select a color model.
5. Use the Hues drop-down list to set the relationships of the colors shown on the grid below the Color Wheel (**Figure 20**). For instance, Complement displays two dots directly across from one another on the color wheel. When you select a color by moving the black dot around the Color Wheel, the complementary color of the one you choose is displayed in the Color Grid.
6. To create a custom color, position the mouse pointer over the black dot on the Color Wheel, press the left mouse button, and drag until the color you want is shown next to New in the Reference area (**Figure 21**).

   or

   Click on a rectangle in the Color Grid to select a custom color.
7. Click OK. The object you selected fills with the custom color.

Tip:

- You can use the Variation drop-down list (**Figure 22**) to display different color spectrums in the Color Grid.

Create Custom Colors

A fountain fill is a gradual blend between two or more colors across a closed path object. There are four types of fountain fills (**Figure 23**):

- Linear—the blend of colors moves in a straight line
- Radial—the blend of colors moves in concentric circles from the center
- Conical—the blend of colors moves in a circular path, radiating from the center
- Square—the blend of colors moves in a series of concentric squares that radiate from the center

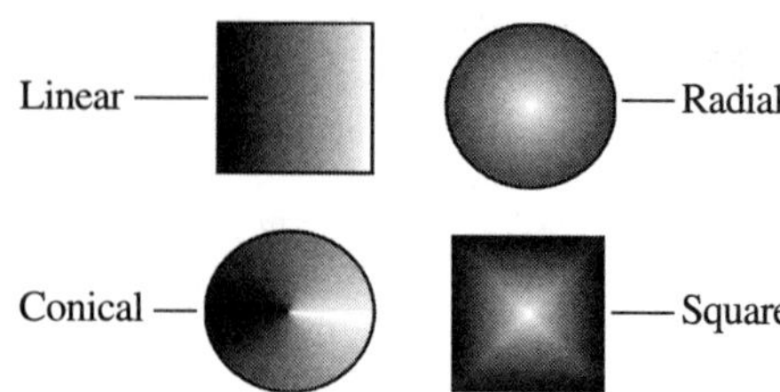

Figure 23. *There are four types of fountain fills.*

Adding special fills is easy with the Interactive Fill Tool (**Figure 24**). All you have to do is click and drag to add the fill.

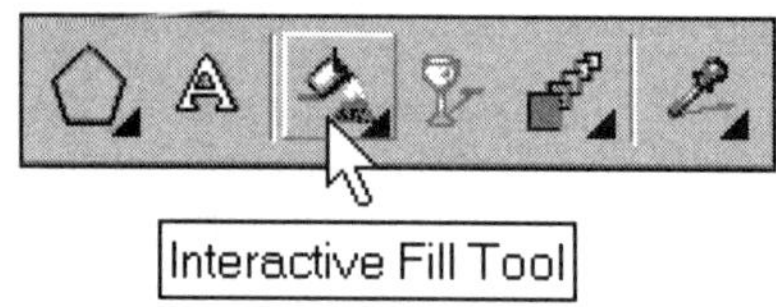

Figure 24. *The Interactive Fill Tool.*

To add a linear fountain fill to an object:

1. Make sure the object is made up of a closed path.
2. Select the Interactive Fill Tool. A little paint bucket appears under the mouse pointer.
3. Click the object to select it.
4. Position the mouse on the side of the object where you want the fill to begin, then press the left mouse button and drag it to the other side of the object where you want the fill to end (**Figure 25**).
5. Release the mouse. The object redraws with a fountain fill (**Figure 26**).

Figure 25. *Click and drag the Interactive Fill Tool to fill an object with a linear fountain fill.*

Figure 26. *When you release the mouse, the object redraws with the new fill.*

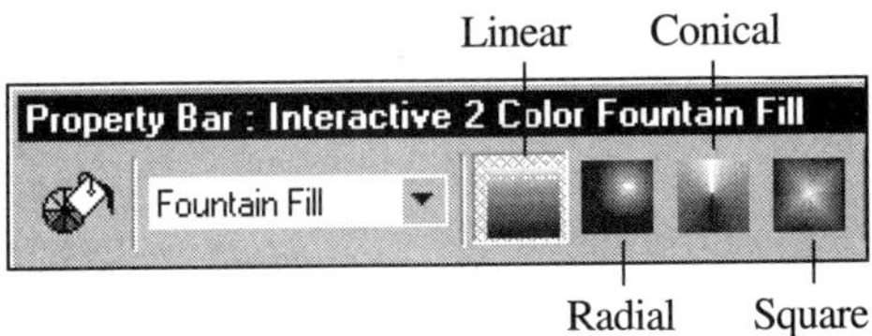

Figure 27. *To change the type of fountain fill, click the appropriate button on the Property Bar.*

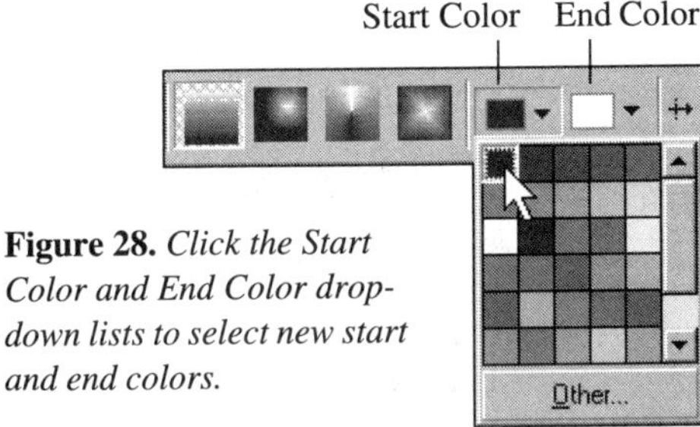

Figure 28. *Click the Start Color and End Color drop-down lists to select new start and end colors.*

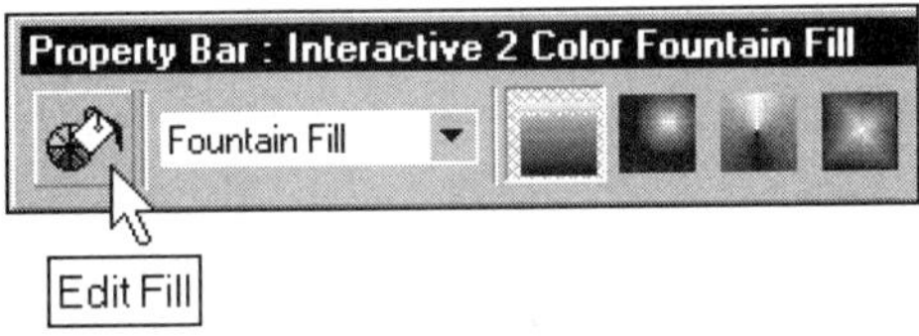

Figure 29. *Click the Edit Fill button found at the left end of the Property Bar.*

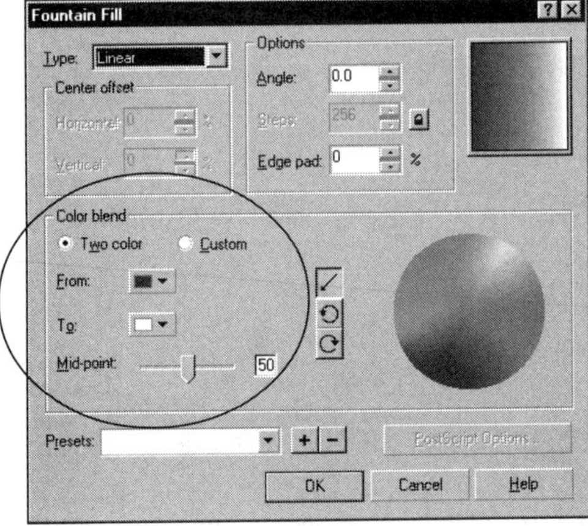

Figure 30. *Use the Fountain Fill dialog box to select new start and end colors.*

To change the type of fountain fill:

1. Fill the closed path object with a linear fountain fill.
2. Select the type of fountain fill that you want—linear, radial, conical, or square—by clicking the appropriate button on the Property Bar (**Figure 27**). The object will redraw with that fill.

To change the fountain fill colors of an object:

1. Select the Interactive Fill Tool, then click the fountain-filled object to select it.
2. Use the Start and End Color drop-down lists on the Property Bar to select new start and end colors (**Figure 28**).

or

1. Select the object using the Interactive Fill Tool.
2. Click the Edit Fill button on the Property Bar (**Figure 29**). The Fountain Fill dialog box appears (**Figure 30**).
3. In the Color blend area, use the From and To drop-down color lists to select new start and end colors.
4. Click OK.

Tip:

- The changes you make will apply only to the selected object.

To move the start color and end color positions:

1. Add a fountain fill to an object using the Interactive Fill Tool (**Figure 31**).
2. Position the Interactive Fill Tool over the start color square. The mouse will change to a cross-hair.
3. Press the left mouse button and drag the color square to the desired position (**Figure 32**), then release the mouse button.
4. Position the mouse over the end color square. Press the left mouse button and drag this square to its new position (**Figure 33**).

Tips:

- You can place the start and end color squares anywhere inside or outside the object. For instance, you could move the start color to the edge of an object and move the end color to the middle.
- You can change where the two colors meet by moving the fountain fill midpoint slider bar up or down along the dashed line between the start and end colors (**Figure 34**).

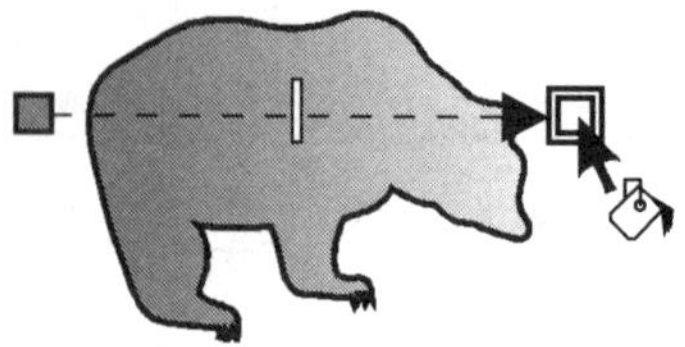

Figure 31. *Add a fountain fill to a closed path object using the Interactive Fill Tool.*

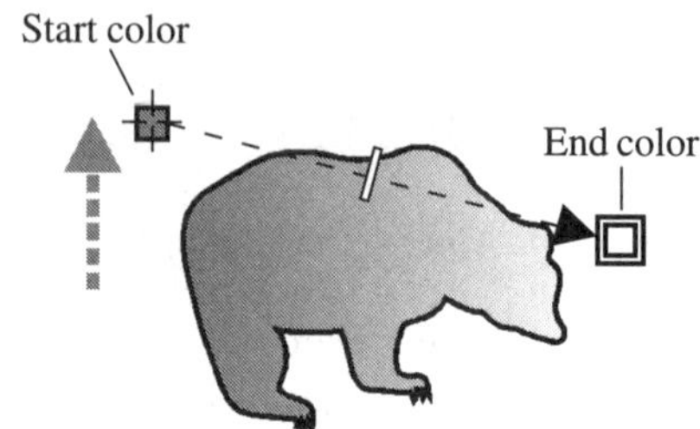

Figure 32. *Press and drag the mouse to move the start color square to its new position.*

Figure 33. *Move the end color square to its new position.*

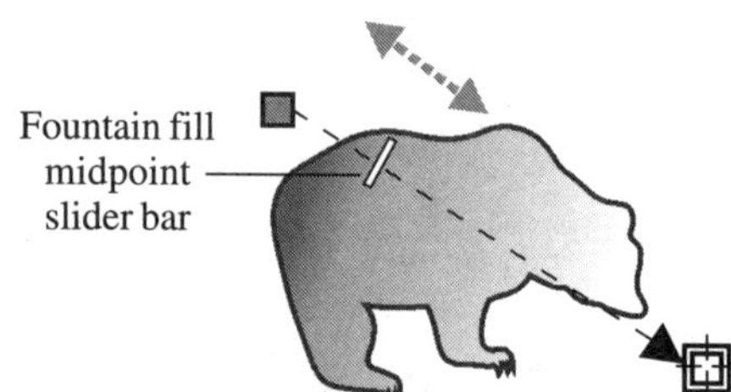

Figure 34. *Move the slider bar up or down along the dashed line to change where the start and end colors meet.*

Figure 35. *Add a fountain fill to an object.*

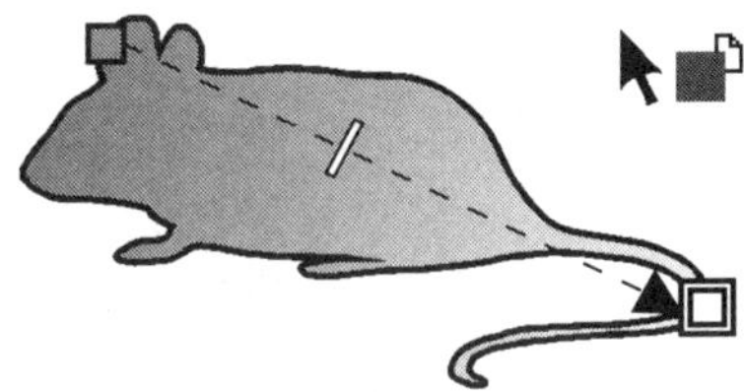

Figure 36. *Drag the intermediate color from the Color Palette using the Interactive Fill Tool.*

Figure 37. *After you release the mouse button, the color is added to the fountain fill.*

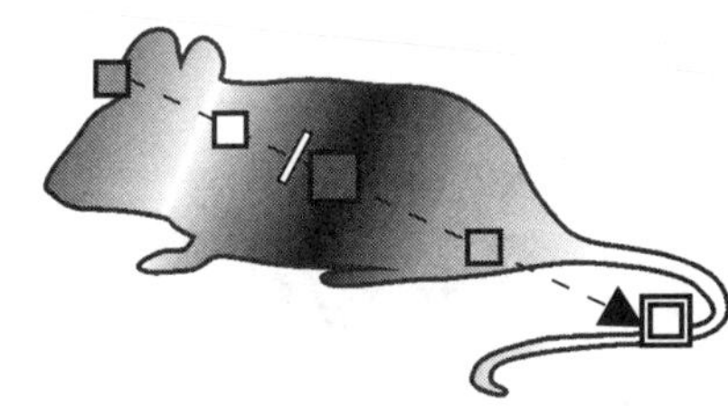

Figure 38. *You can add as many intermediate colors as you want, creating a rainbow effect.*

To add intermediate colors to a fountain fill:

1. Add a fountain fill to an object using the Interactive Fill Tool (**Figure 35**).
2. Find the color on the Color Palette that you want to add between the start and end colors of the fountain fill.
3. Position the mouse over that color, press the left mouse button, and drag that color square onto the dashed line between the start and end color squares. As you drag the color from the palette, a copy of the color square follows the mouse (**Figure 36**).
4. Release the mouse. The color will be added to the fountain fill (**Figure 37**).

Tips:

- You can add as many intermediate colors as you want (**Figure 38**).
- To remove an intermediate color fill, right click on the intermediate color square with the Interactive Fill Tool.
- To quickly change the start or end colors drag a color square from the Color Palette over either the start or end color square.

Patterns are fun and can add interesting effects to your graphics. There are three types of pattern fills you can select: Two Color, Full Color, and Bitmap.

To add a two-color pattern fill to an object:

1. Make sure the object has a closed path, then select it with the Interactive Fill Tool.
2. Select Pattern Fill from the Fill Type drop-down list on the Property Bar (**Figure 39**). Your object will be filled with the default, a two-color pattern, large black dots on a white background (**Figure 40**).
3. To change the pattern, click the Pattern drop-down list on the Property Bar (**Figure 41**) and select another pattern. The graphic will be filled with that new pattern (**Figure 42**).

Tips:

- To change the color of the pattern, use the Front Color and Back Color drop-down lists next to the Pattern drop-down list on the Property Bar.
- You can create your own patterns, by clicking the Other button at the bottom of the Pattern drop-down list (**Figure 41**) and then using the Two-Color Pattern Editor that opens.

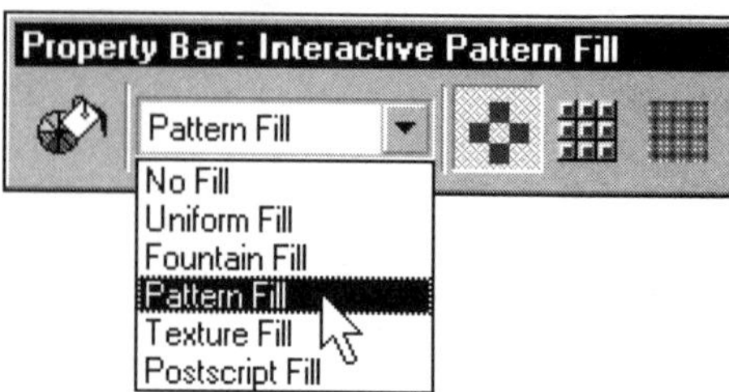

Figure 39. *Select Pattern Fill from the Fill Type drop-down list.*

Figure 40. *When you select Pattern Fill, the selected object will be filled with the default pattern.*

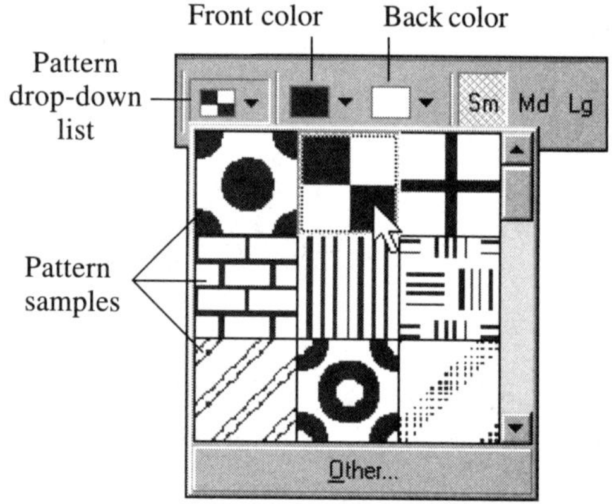

Figure 41. *Click on a pattern sample in the Pattern drop-down list to select that pattern.*

Figure 42. *The selected object will fill with the new pattern.*

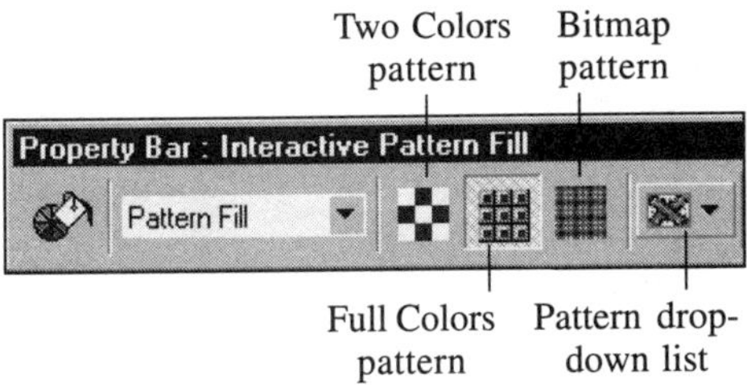

Figure 43. *Click either the Full Colors Pattern Fill button or the Bitmap Pattern Fill button.*

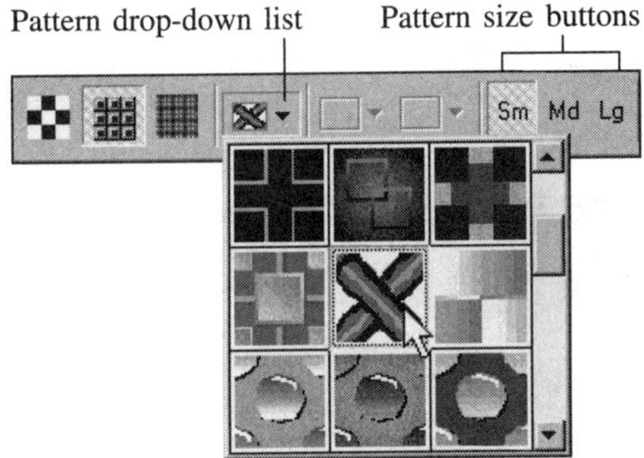

Figure 44. *Click on a pattern from the drop-down list.*

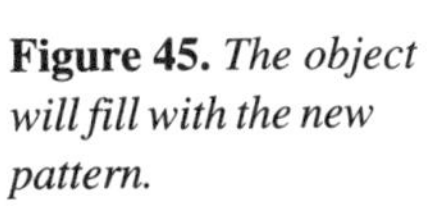

Figure 45. *The object will fill with the new pattern.*

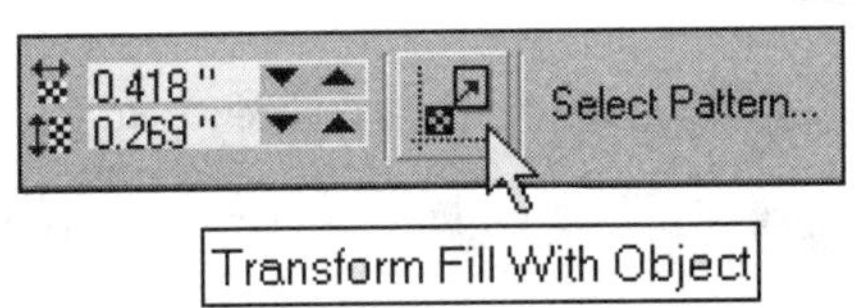

Figure 46. *If you click the Transform Fill With Object button, the pattern will rotate or skew with the object.*

To add a full color or bitmap pattern fill to an object:

1. Make sure the object has a closed path, then select it with the Interactive Fill Tool.
2. Use the drop-down list to choose Pattern Fill on the Property Bar, and click the Full Colors Pattern Fill button or the Bitmap Pattern Fill button on the Property Bar (**Figure 43**).
3. Use the Pattern drop-down list to select a pattern (**Figure 44**). Your graphic will redraw, filled with that pattern (**Figure 45**).

Tips:

- To make the pattern smaller or larger, click the Small (Sm), Medium (Md), or Large (Lg) buttons on the Property Bar.
- If you want to rotate or skew the object and have the pattern rotate or skew with it, click the Transform Fill With Object button on the Property Bar (**Figure 46**). Otherwise, the pattern will remain stationary while the object rotates around it (**Figures 47a–c**).

Figure 47a. *Original object.*

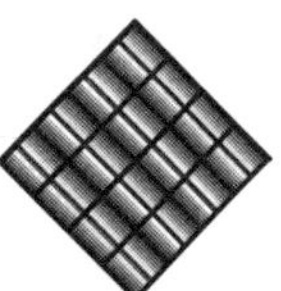

Figure 47b. *Object rotated 45° with the button pressed.*

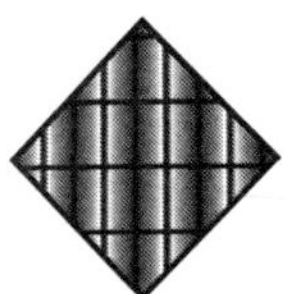

Figure 47c. *Object rotated 45° without the button pressed.*

To create a custom pattern fill:

1. Create the object(s) you want to use as a pattern (**Figure 48**).
2. Choose Pattern from the Create fly-out found on the Tools menu (**Figure 49**). The Create Pattern dialog box opens (**Figure 50**).
3. If the pattern object(s) are made up of two colors or less:
   - Select the Two color radio button in the Type area, then select either a Low, Medium, or High resolution for the pattern.

   If the pattern object(s) are made up of many colors:
   - Select the Full color radio button in the Type area.
4. Click OK to close the Create Pattern dialog box. Vertical and horizontal guidelines will appear attached to the tip of the mouse pointer.
5. Position the mouse pointer at the upper left of the pattern objects.
6. Press the left mouse button and drag a marquee rectangle around the pattern object(s) (**Figure 51**).
7. When you release the mouse button, CorelDraw asks you if you want to create a pattern with the selected area (**Figure 52**). Click OK.
8. Select an object and fill it with your custom pattern, using the Interactive Fill Tool as described on the previous two pages (**Figure 53**).

Figure 48. *Create the object(s) you want to use as a pattern.*

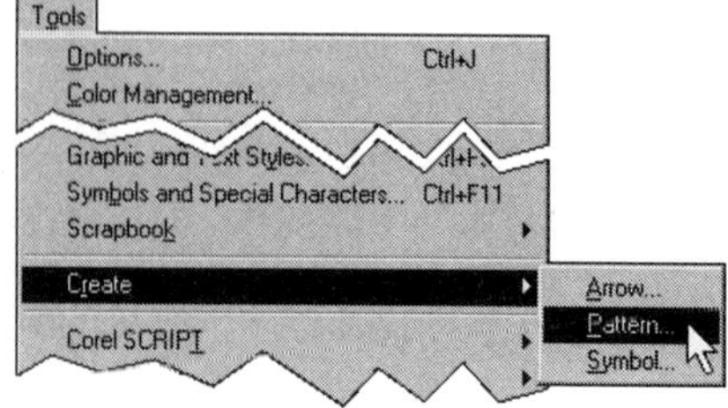

Figure 49. *Choose Pattern from the Create fly-out on the Tools menu.*

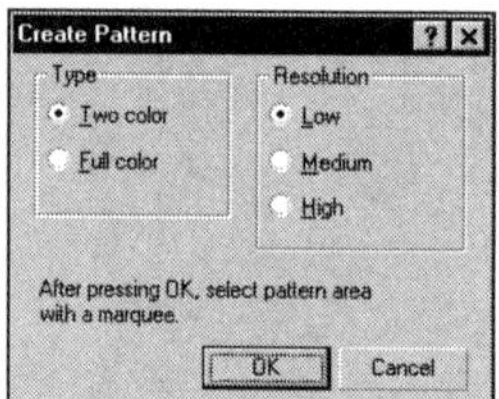

Figure 50. *Use the Create Pattern dialog box to select the type of pattern, Two color or Full color.*

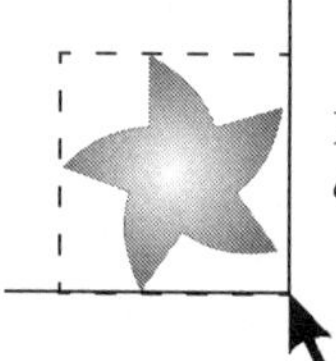

Figure 51. *Drag a marquee around the pattern object(s).*

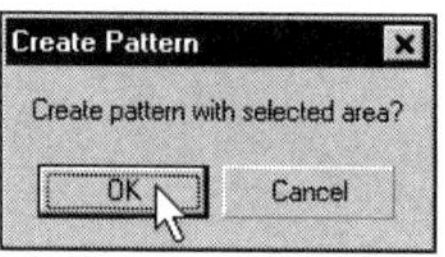

Figure 52. *Click OK in the Create Pattern confirmation box.*

Figure 53. *Fill an object with your custom pattern using the Interactive Fill Tool.*

Figure 54. *Select a closed path object with the Interactive Fill Tool.*

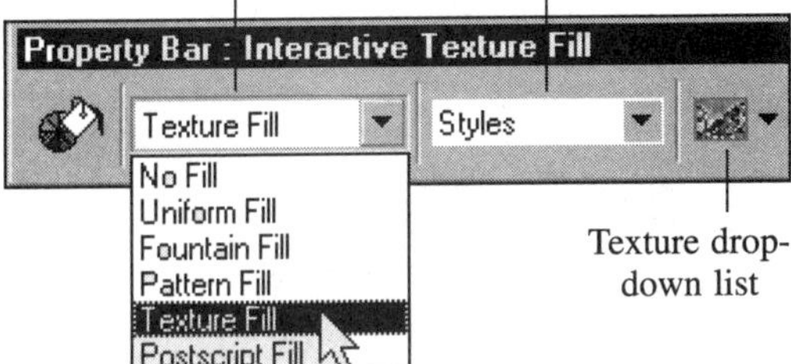

Figure 55. *Select Texture Fill from the Fill Type drop-down list.*

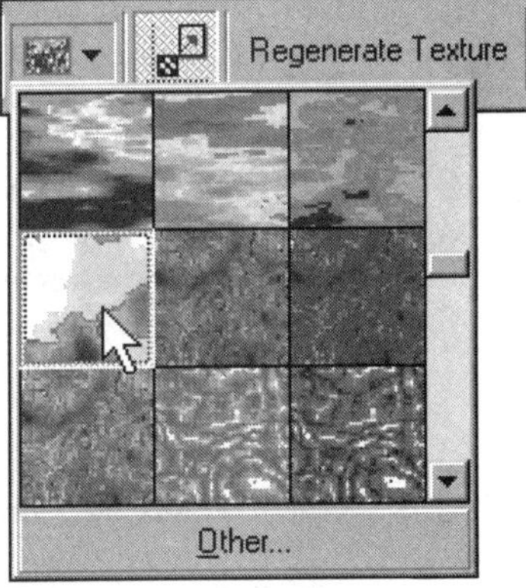

Figure 56. *Click on a texture from the Texture drop-down list.*

Figure 57. *The selected object redraws, filled with the new texture.*

Textures create interesting effects, and you can easily add them to your drawings. CorelDraw 9 comes with hundreds of preset textures that you can modify to suit your needs.

To add a texture fill to an object:

1. Make sure the object has a closed path and select it with the Interactive Fill Tool (**Figure 54**).
2. Select Texture Fill from the Fill Type drop-down list on the Property Bar (**Figure 55**).
3. Use the Texture drop-down list to find a fill (**Figure 56**). Click on the fill of your choice. Your object redraws with that texture (**Figure 57**).

Tip:

- CorelDraw 9 comes with hundreds of textures stored in different libaries. To view the different libraries, use the Texture Libraries drop-down list on the Property Bar (**Figure 55**) to select a library, and then click the Texture drop-down list button to view the textures.

New to CorelDraw 9, the Interactive Mesh Fill Tool (**Figure 58**) quickly lets you add a rainbow of colors to simple objects, lines, or bitmaps.

The Interactive Mesh Fill Tool works by superimposing a dashed grid on a selected object (**Figure 59**). The intersection points of this grid are joined with nodes that can be manipulated with the Shape Tool. (For details about nodes and the Shape Tool, turn to Chapter 6, *Nodes and Paths*.) Add colors to the grid by dragging and dropping a color well from the Color Palette onto one of the mesh nodes or onto a *patch*, one of the areas circumscribed by the mesh outline.

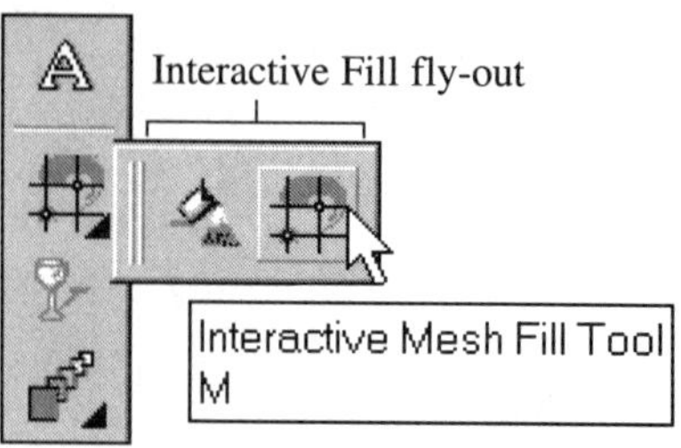

Figure 58. *The new Interactive Mesh Fill Tool is accessed by opening the Interactive Fill fly-out or by pressing M on the keyboard.*

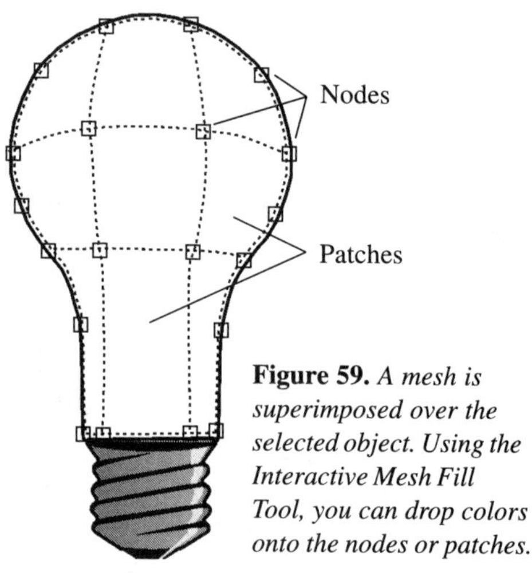

Figure 59. *A mesh is superimposed over the selected object. Using the Interactive Mesh Fill Tool, you can drop colors onto the nodes or patches.*

To fill an object with color using the Interactive Mesh Fill Tool:

1. Select the Interactive Mesh Fill Tool from the Interactive Fill fly-out (**Figure 58**) or press M on the keyboard.
2. Select the object you want to fill. A mesh will be superimposed over the object (**Figure 59**).
3. There are several ways you can use the tool to fill the object with colors:
   a. Position the mouse over a color well on the Color Palette, then press the left mouse button and drag the color onto a patch (**Figure 60**). When you release the mouse button, the patch area will be filled and the color will diffuse out past the mesh surrounding the patch.

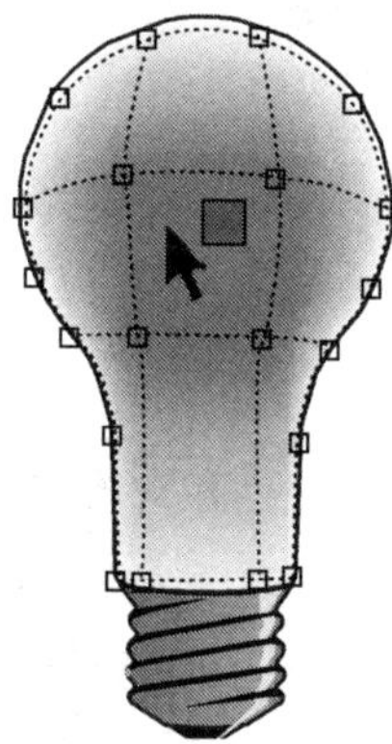

Figure 60. *When a color is dropped onto a patch, the patch area is filled with that color. The color also diffuses out past the mesh surrounding the patch.*

Use the Interactive Mesh Fill Tool

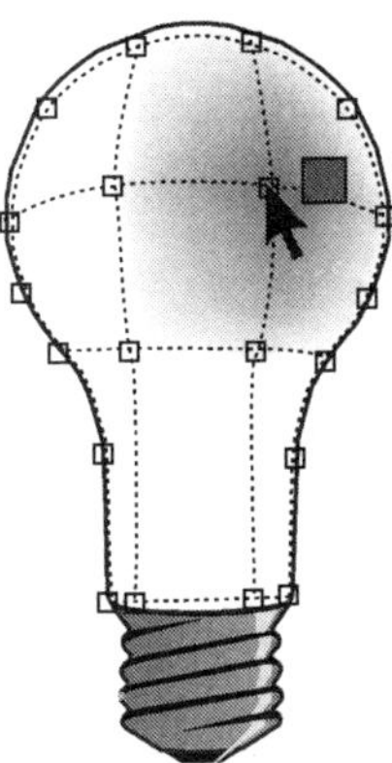

Figure 61. *When the color is dropped onto a node, the area under that node is filled with the color. The color also diffuses out into the surrounding patches.*

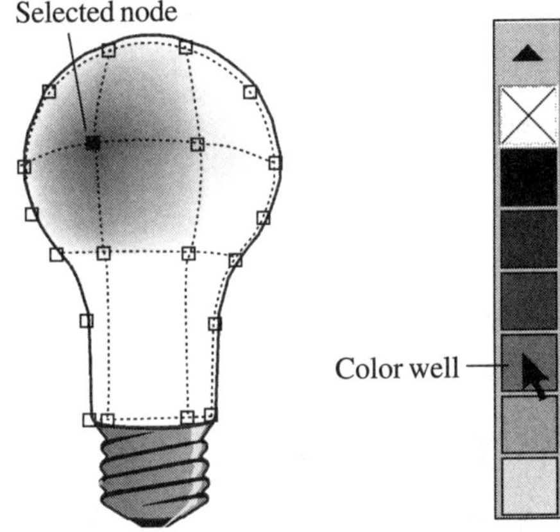

Figure 62. *Select a node, hold down the Ctrl key on the keyboard, then click a color well several times. Each time you click, the color becomes more saturated.*

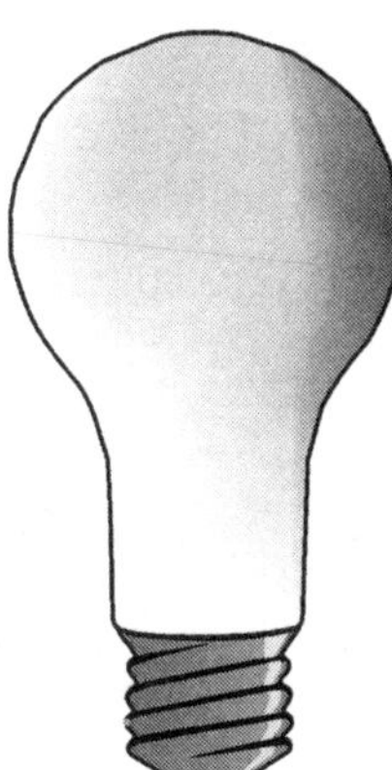

Figure 63. *You can keep adding color and shadings until the object is just right.*

b. Position the mouse over a color well on the Color Palette, then press the left mouse button and drag the color onto a node (**Figure 61**). When you release the mouse button, the area under the node will be filled and the color will blend out into the surrounding patches.

c. Use the Interactive Mesh Fill Tool to select a node, then position the mouse over a color well. Hold down the Ctrl key, and click (you may need to click several times to see results). Each time you click, the color becomes a shade darker. Keep clicking until you see the desired shade (**Figure 62**).

You can continue adding color to an object until it's just right (**Figure 63**).

Tips:

- If you add a color and don't like the effect it creates, undo the action by pressing Ctrl+Z on the keyboard or clicking the Undo button on the Property Bar.
- You can select several nodes at once using marquee selections.

You can also affect how the colors are blended with the Interactive Mesh Fill tool by reshaping the mesh and moving its nodes.

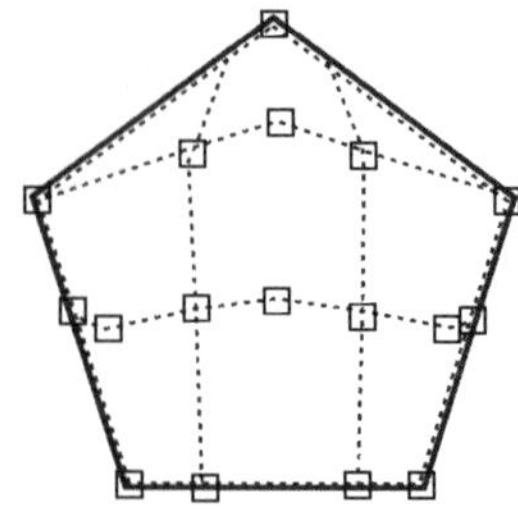

Figure 64. *Select the object with the Interactive Mesh Fill Tool.*

To move the mesh or its nodes:

1. Select the object you want to fill using the Interactive Mesh Fill Tool. A mesh will appear superimposed over the object (**Figure 64**).
2. Position the mouse over the dashed mesh or node you want to move.
3. Press the left mouse button and drag the mesh or node to its new location (**Figure 65**). When you fill the object, the colors will follow the contours of the manipulated mesh (**Figure 66**).

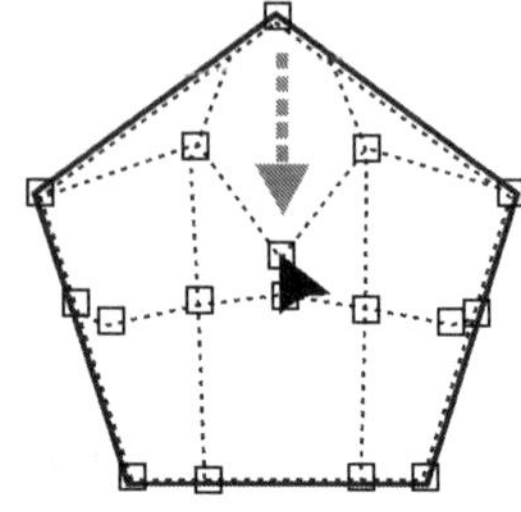

Figure 65. *Position the mouse over the node or dashed mesh you want to move, press the left mouse button, and drag.*

Figure 66. *You can move the mesh and nodes to create familiar shapes. When colors are added to the manipulated mesh, the shapes appear.*

Tip:

- You can add nodes, change their type, delete nodes, and manipulate them just as described in Chapter 6, *Nodes and Paths*.

Summary:

In this chapter you learned how to:

- Add uniform fills to objects
- Change objects' outline color
- Use the new Eyedropper and Paintbucket Tools
- Add fountain fills to objects
- Change the fountain fill colors
- Add intermediate colors to a fountain fill
- Add pattern fills to objects
- Add texture fills to objects
- Use the new Interactive Mesh Fill Tool

Working with Text

Pictures can be worth a thousand words, but sometimes you also need words to convey your message to the world. For instance, it's hard to imagine brochures, pamphlets, or postcards without some text.

Text comes in two flavors in CorelDraw 9. *Artistic text* is used for single text lines such as titles or for text to which you want to add a special effect, such as *fitting text to a path*. *Paragraph text* is used for text-intensive projects such as brochures, ads, or newsletters. Any text created in CorelDraw 9, whether it's artistic or paragraph, makes up a *text object*.

In this chapter, you will learn how to add artistic and paragraph text, change fonts, change spacing between characters and lines, and convert artistic text to paragraph text and back again. From there, you will import text into a document, make it flow between text frames, add bullets to a list, and quickly create drop caps.

CorelDraw Ships with Over 1,000 Fonts

Included on CorelDraw CD-ROM disk 1 are more than 1,000 typefaces you can load onto your computer system. To view new fonts and load them on your system, use the Font application found in the Windows Control Panel. The fonts are located alphabetically under the Font folder on the CD-ROM. A word of warning, though. Windows can only handle about 500 fonts on a system at one time. If you load this many fonts on your computer, the time it takes Windows to boot up will become quite long.

To add artistic text:

1. Select the Text Tool (**Figure 1**) or press F8 on the keyboard. The mouse pointer will change to a cross-hair with a tiny "A" attached to it.
2. Click on the place where you wish the artistic text to start. A vertical line will appear where you clicked. This is called the *insertion marker*.
3. Type your text. As you type, the corresponding characters will appear on the screen (**Figure 2**).
4. When you are finished typing, select the Pick Tool. Eight black handles will appear around the text object, showing that it is selected (**Figure 3**).

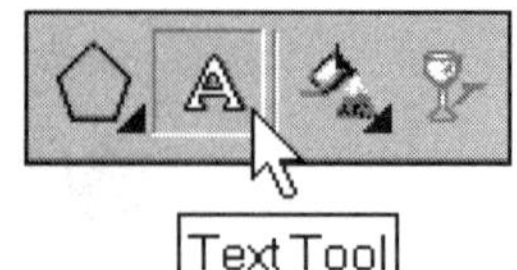

Figure 1. *The Text Tool.*

Figure 2. *As you type, the corresponding characters appear on the screen.*

Figure 3. *When you finish typing and select the Pick Tool, eight handles appear around the text object.*

WHAT ARE THOSE SQUIGGLY RED LINES UNDER MY WORDS?

As you type, CorelDraw 9 checks your spelling. If there are any squiggly red lines underneath a word after you have finished typing, this means that the word could be spelled incorrectly (or is not in the program's dictionary). To check spellings that CorelDraw 9's dictionary suggests, select the Text Tool, then right mouse click on the word. A pop-up menu with spelling suggestions will appear (**Figure 4**). Click the correctly spelled word to replace the misspelled one in the text object.

Figure 4. *Use the Text Tool to right mouse click on the word, then select a suggested word from the pop-up menu.*

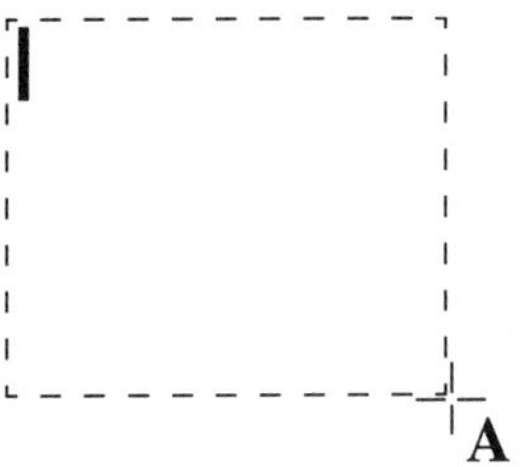

Figure 5. *Press the left mouse button and drag the Text Tool to create a marquee.*

Figure 6. *As you type, the corresponding characters appear in the dashed frame. (A. A. Milne wrote this sentence.)*

Figure 7. *When paragraph text is selected there are six black handles and two text handles around the text frame.*

To add paragraph text:

1. Select the Text Tool.
2. Position the mouse cross-hair on the place where you would like the text to start.
3. Press the left mouse button and drag it diagonally. As you drag a dashed rectangle will appear (**Figure 5**). When you release the mouse button, an insertion marker will appear at the upper left of the marquee. Six black handles will appear to the right and left of the marquee and two *text handles* will also appear—one at the top and one at the bottom.
4. Type your text. As you type, the corresponding characters will appear in the dashed frame (**Figure 6**).
5. When you are finished, select the Pick Tool. The dashed rectangle will change to a paragraph text frame (**Figure 7**).

Fonts Used in This Book

The drop caps used in each chapter of this book are all available on CorelDraw CD-ROM disk 1. If you see a font you like, look in Appendix A for the font name.

To convert artistic text to paragraph text:

1. Select the artistic text object with the Pick Tool (**Figure 8**).
2. Choose Convert To Paragraph Text from the Text menu (**Figure 9**). A paragraph text frame will appear around the text (**Figure 10**).

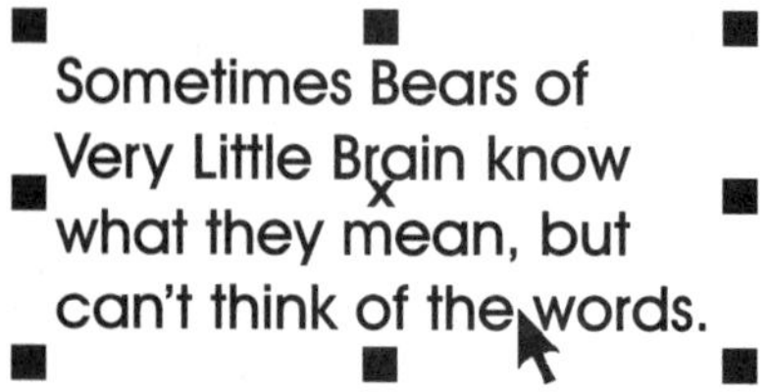

To convert paragraph text to artistic text:

1. Select the paragraph text object with the Pick Tool.
2. Choose Convert To Artistic Text from the Text menu (**Figure 11**). The paragraph frame will disappear from around the text and the eight black handles will remain.

> **YOU CAN ALSO USE THE POP-UP MENU**
>
> There's another way to change artistic text to paragraph text and vice versa. Instead of using the Text menu as described in the two methods above, select "Convert to Paragraph Text" or "Convert to Artistic Text" from the pop-up menu that appears when you right click on a text object.

Sometimes Bears of
Very Little Brain know
what they mean, but
can't think of the words.

Figure 8. *Select the artistic text object with the Pick Tool.*

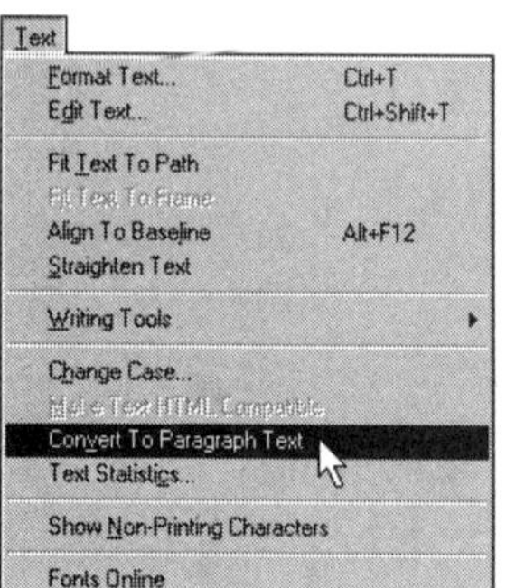

Figure 9. *Choose Convert To Paragraph Text from the Text menu.*

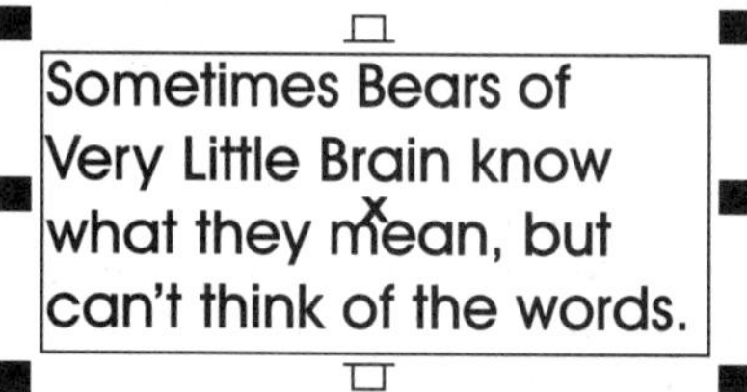

Figure 10. *A paragraph text frame appears around the text.*

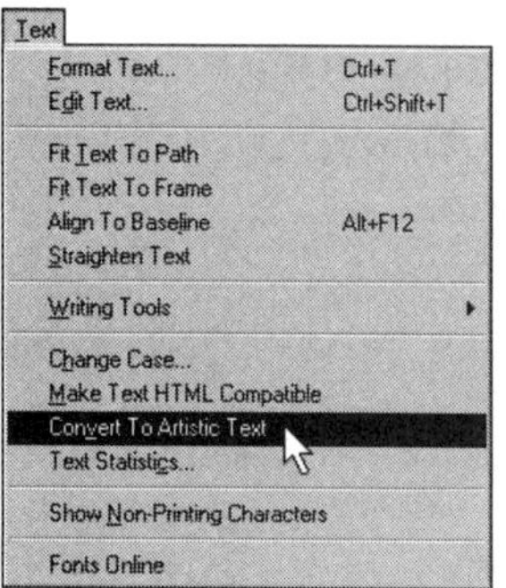

Figure 11. *Choose Convert To Artistic Text from the Text menu.*

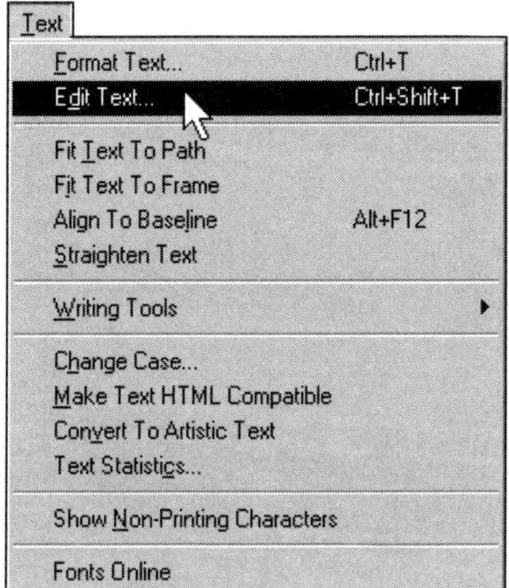

Figure 12. *Choose Edit Text from the Text menu or press Ctrl+Shift+T on the keyboard.*

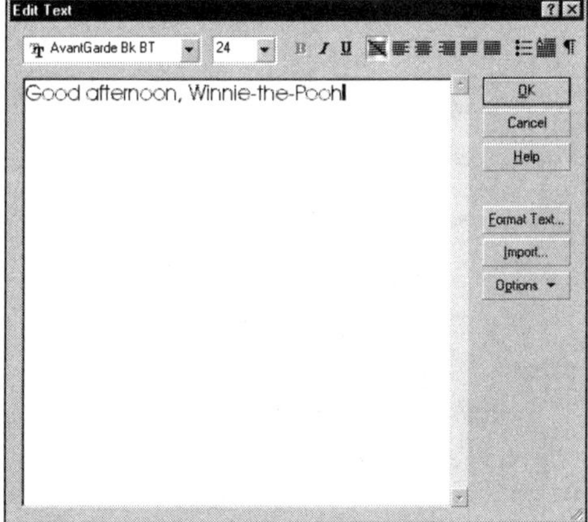

Figure 13. *Use the Edit Text dialog box to edit your text.*

> **WATCH THE STATUS BAR**
>
> When a text object is selected the Status Bar will always tell you whether it's artistic or paragraph text and what font and font size are being used.

To edit artistic or paragraph text:

1. Select the text object with the Pick Tool.
2. Choose Edit Text from the Text menu (**Figure 12**) or press Ctrl+Shift+T on the keyboard. The Edit Text dialog appears (**Figure 13**).
3. Edit the text in the window, then click OK.

or

1. Select the Text Tool, then position the mouse over the text to be edited.
2. Click the left mouse button. The insertion marker will appear there.
3. Edit the text.

Tips:

- The second text editing method should only be used for editing small amounts of text. If you need to edit a large section of text, use the Edit Text dialog box.
- You must use the Edit Text dialog box to edit artistic text that has had any of the following special effects applied to it: Perspective, Envelope, or Extrude. (To check out these special effects, take a look at Chapter 15, *Special Effects*.)

Edit Text

When you add text, CorelDraw 9 uses a default font (AvantGarde), font size (24 points), justification (none), and character and line spacing (100% of character size). To change these attributes, you will need to *format* the text using the Format Text dialog box.

To change the font of a text object:

1. Select the text object with the Pick Tool (**Figure 14**).
2. Choose Format Text from the Text menu (**Figure 15**) or press Ctrl+T on the keyboard. The Format Text dialog box will open with the Font tab page in front (**Figure 16**).
3. Use the Font drop-down list box to select a font (**Figure 17**). A preview of that font will appear in the preview pane.
4. Click OK. The text will redraw in the new font (**Figure 18**).

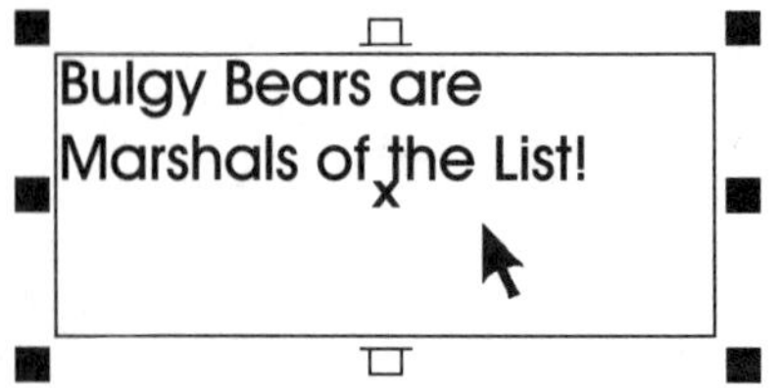

Figure 14. *Select the text object with the Pick Tool.*

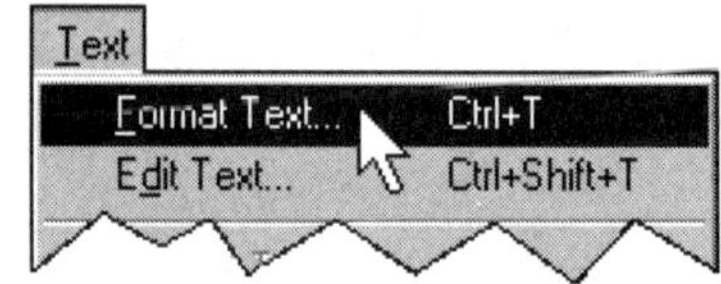

Figure 15. *Choose Format Text from the Text menu or press Ctrl+T on the keyboard.*

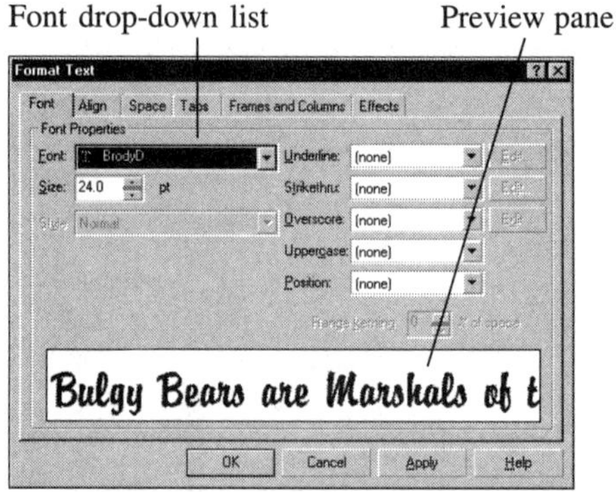

Figure 16. *Click a font name in the Font list to see a sample of it in the preview pane.*

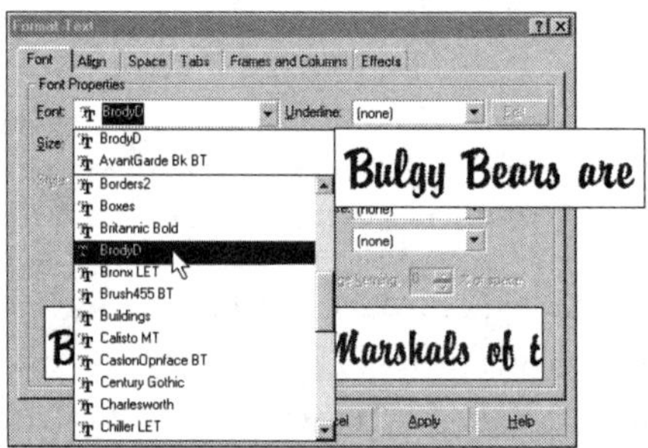

Figure 17. *Select a font from the drop-down list.*

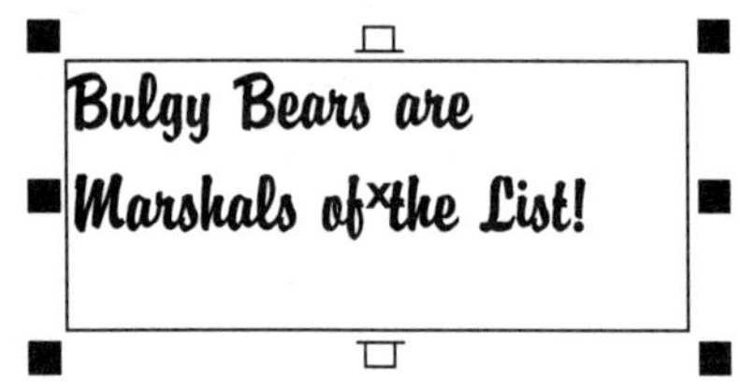

Figure 18. *After you click OK, the text redraws using the newly selected font.*

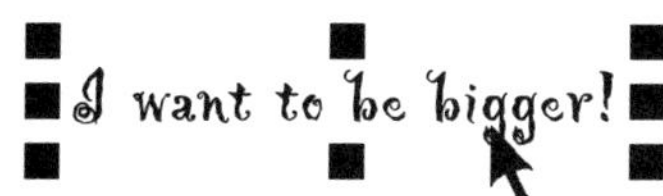

Figure 19. *Select the text object you want to change with the Pick Tool.*

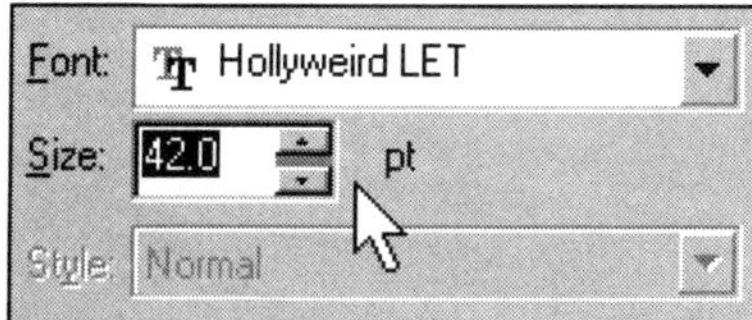

Figure 20. *Use the Size text box found in the Format Text dialog box to enter a new font size.*

Figure 21. *After you click OK, the text redraws in the new size.*

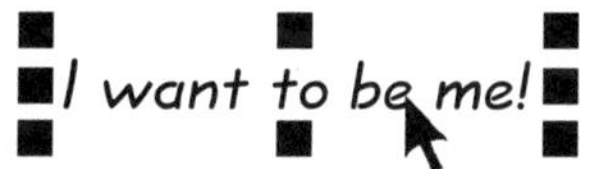

Figure 22. *Select the text object with the Pick Tool.*

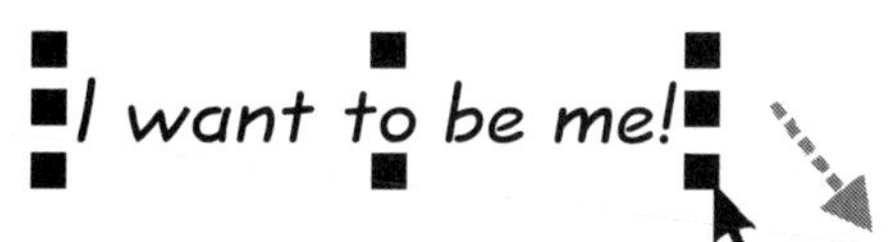

Figure 23a. *Stretching text proportionally.*

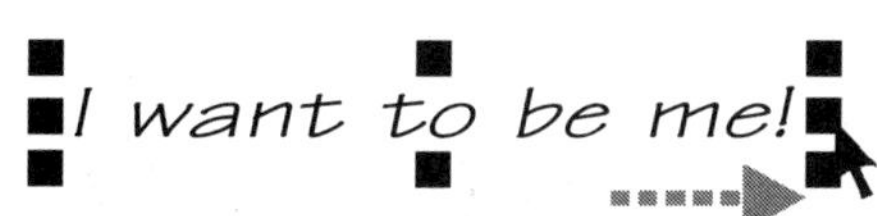

Figure 23b. *Stretching text horizontally.*

To change the size of paragraph or artistic text characters:

1. Select the text object with the Pick Tool (**Figure 19**).
2. Open the Format Text dialog box by pressing Ctrl+T on the keyboard or choosing Format Text from the Text menu (**Figure 15**).
3. Type a number in the Size text box (**Figure 20**). The default unit for type is points (24 point type is ¼" (6 millimeters) high).
4. Click OK. Your text will redraw with that point size (**Figure 21**).

Another way to change artistic or paragraph text character size:

1. Select the artistic text object with the Pick Tool (**Figure 22**). This will display the eight black handles that surround the text object.
2. If you are resizing artistic text, drag the appropriate handle to stretch the text proportionally, horizontally, or vertically (**Figures 23a–c**). If you are resizing paragraph text, hold down the Alt key and drag a corner handle.

Figure 23c. *Stretching text vertically.*

To change the formatting of individual characters:

1. Zoom in on the text object using the Zoom Tool.
2. Select the Text Tool, then position the mouse to the left of the character you want to change (**Figure 24**).
3. Press the left mouse button and drag it to the right to select the character (**Figure 25**).
4. Open the Format Text dialog box by choosing Format Text from the Text menu or pressing Ctrl+T on the keyboard. Change the character's attributes—font and/or font size—then click OK. The letter will redraw with the changes you have made (**Figure 26**).

Tip:

- You can change the formatting of several letters at once by dragging the mouse to select several letters.

Change Ime!

Figure 24. *Position the insertion marker before the character you want to change.*

Change me!

Figure 25. *Press the left mouse button and drag the insertion marker until the letter is selected.*

Figure 26. *After you click OK, the letter redraws with the new formatting.*

WHAT KIND OF JUSTIFICATION DO YOU WANT?

There are five ways you can justify a text block in CorelDraw 9. Below is a sample of each type.

I am left justified.	I am center justified.	I am right justified.	I am full justified.	I am force justified.

Figure 27. *Select the text object with the Pick Tool.*

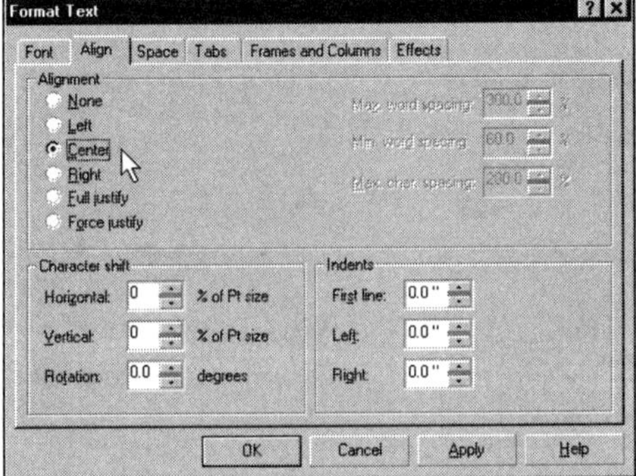

Figure 28. *Use the Align tab page of the Format Text dialog box to change the text's justification.*

Figure 29. *When you click OK, the text redraws with the new centered justification.*

To change the text object's justification:

1. Select the text object with the Pick Tool (**Figure 27**).
2. Choose Format Text from the Text menu or press Ctrl+T on the keyboard. The Format Text dialog box will open with the Font tab page in front.
3. Click on the Align tab to bring that page to the front (**Figure 28**).
4. On the upper-right side of the Align tab page, use the Alignment area to select the type of justification.
5. Click OK. Your text will change to assume that type of justification (**Figure 29**).

THE FORMAT TEXT DIALOG BOX IS CONTEXT SENSITIVE

If you compare Figure 28 with Figure 33, you will notice that the tabs available in the dialog box are different. The reason for this is that the Format Text dialog box is context sensitive. It displays different options depending upon the selected text object. In Figure 28, a paragraph text object is selected, whereas in Figure 33, an artistic text object is selected.

The space between characters is called *kerning* and the distance from the bottom of one line of text to the bottom of the next is called *leading*. These are terms that desktop publishers use all the time. There are several ways to change kerning and leading in CorelDraw 9.

Figure 30. *Select the text object with the Shape Tool.*

To let CorelDraw kern the space equally between all characters:

1. Create the text objcct.
2. Select the Shape Tool, then use it to click on the text object (**Figure 30**). This will select the text object and two arrows will appear connected to the object—one on the lower left pointing downward, and one on the lower right pointing to the right.
3. Position the Shape Tool over the arrow on the lower-right corner.
4. Press the left mouse button and drag the mouse to the right to add space between the letters (**Figure 31**) or drag the mouse to the left to decrease the amount of space between the letters (**Figure 32**).

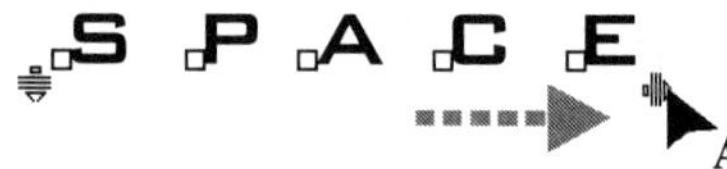

Figure 31. *Drag the lower right arrow to the right to add more space between characters.*

or

1. Create the text object.
2. Select it using the Pick Tool, then open the Format Text dialog box by pressing Ctrl+T on the keyboard or choosing Format Text from the Text menu.
3. Click on the Space tab to move to that tab page (**Figure 33**).

Figure 32. *Drag the lower-right arrow to the left to decrease the space between characters.*

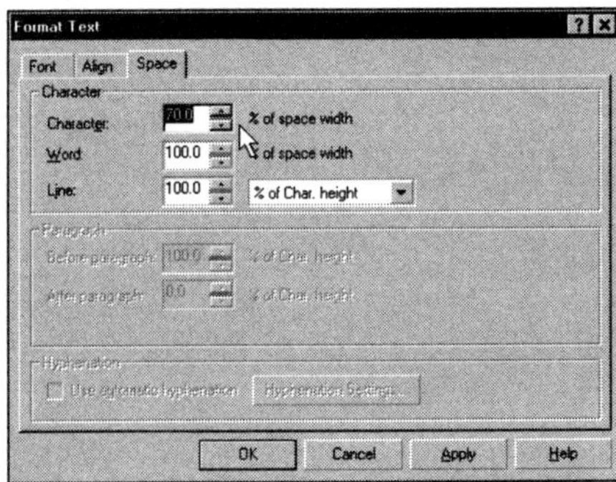

Figure 33. *Use the Space tab page of the Format Text dialog box to set the amount of space between characters.*

4. Use the text box next to Character in the upper-left corner to set the percentage of space width (this is based on the size of the font).
5. Click OK.

Tip:

- You can also set the amount of space between words using the Format Text dialog box. To change the inter-word spacing, type a number into the Word text box (it is located directly under the Character text box) on the Space tab.

To kern individual characters:

Figure 34. *Select the text object with the Shape Tool. A node will appear at the lower left of each character.*

1. Use the Zoom Tool to zoom in on the text object.
2. Select the text object with the Shape Tool. A node will appear at the lower left of each character (**Figure 34**).
3. Position the mouse pointer over the node that corresponds to the character you want to move.
4. Press the left mouse button and drag that character to its new position (**Figure 35**). As you drag, a blue dashed version of the character will appear.

Figure 35. *Position the Shape Tool over the node that corresponds to the character you want to move, then press the left mouse button and drag the character to its new position.*

Tip:

- If you want to move several letters at once, you can select several nodes by holding down the Shift key while clicking on each node or pressing the left mouse button and dragging a marquee around the desired nodes.

To let CorelDraw evenly set the leading:

1. Select the text object with the Shape Tool (**Figure 36**).
2. Position the mouse over the arrow at the lower-left corner of the text object.
3. Press the left mouse button and drag the mouse down to add more space between lines (**Figure 37**) or up to decrease the space between lines (**Figure 38**).

or

1. Select the text object with the Pick Tool.
2. Open the Format Text dialog box by choosing Format Text from the Text menu or by pressing Ctrl+T on the keyboard.
3. Click the Space tab to bring that tab page to the front (**Figure 39**).
4. Enter a number in the Line text box. You can use the drop-down list next to the text box to base the line spacing on the percentage of the character height, a specific set number of points, or a percentage of the point size.
5. Click OK. The lines of text will redraw with the new interline spacing.

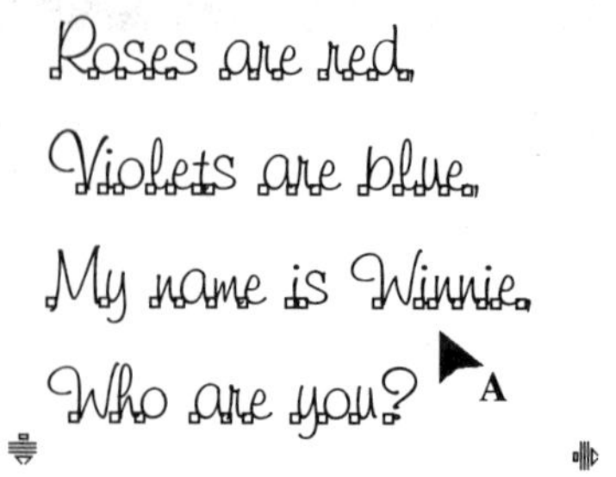

Roses are red.
Violets are blue.
My name is Winnie.
Who are you?
A

Figure 36. *Select the text object with the Shape Tool.*

Roses are red.
Violets are blue.
My name is Winnie.
Who are you?
A

Figure 37. *Drag the arrow at the lower left of the text object down to add more space between lines.*

Roses are red.
Violets are blue.
My name is Winnie.
Who are you?
A

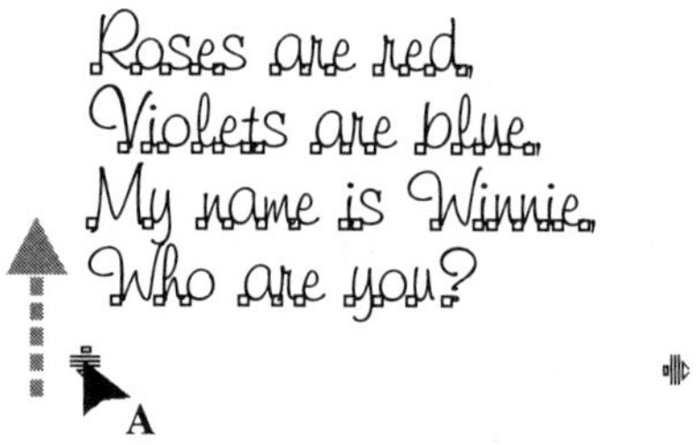

Figure 38. *Drag the arrow at the lower left of the text object up to decrease the space between lines.*

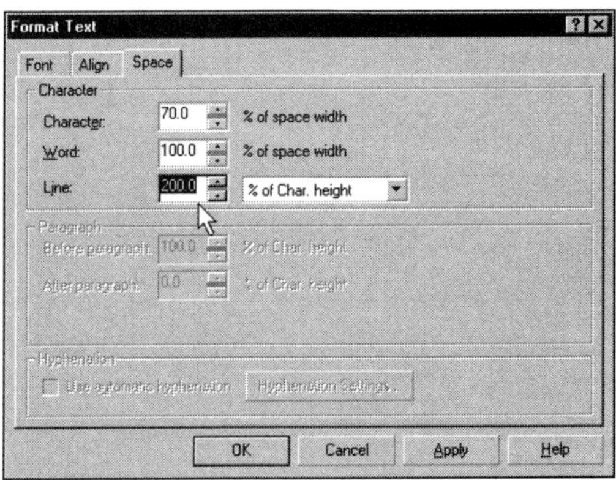

Figure 39. *Use the Space tab of the Format Text dialog box to set the amount of space between lines.*

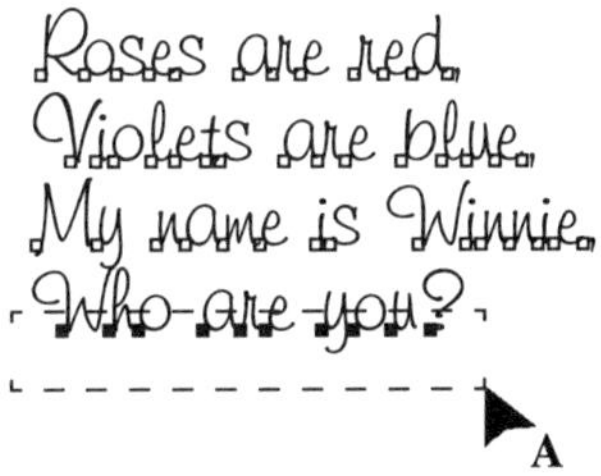

Figure 40. *Select several text nodes at once by dragging the Shape Tool to create a marquee.*

To change the leading between individual lines:

1. Select the text block with the Shape Tool.
2. Drag a marquee around the nodes that make up one line (**Figure 40**). This will select them all.
3. Position the mouse pointer over one of the selected nodes, then press the left mouse button and drag the line to its new position (**Figure 41**). As you drag, a dashed blue outline of the line being moved will appear.
4. Release the mouse button. The line of text will redraw in its new position (**Figure 42**).

Figure 41. *Press the left mouse button down and drag the selected text nodes to their new position.*

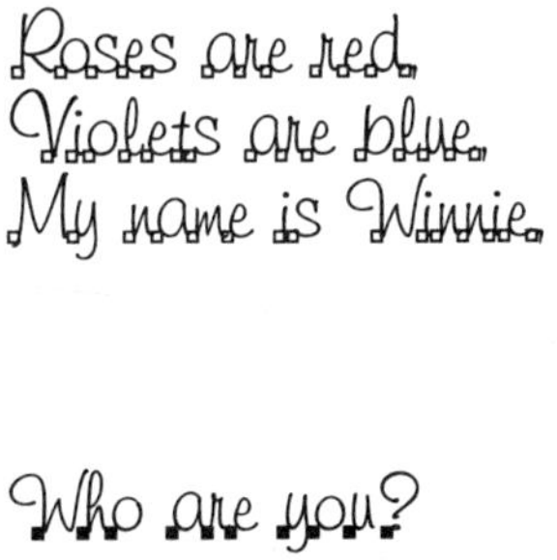

Figure 42. *When you release the mouse, the line of text redraws in the new position.*

If you already have the text for a brochure or newsletter saved in a word processing program, there's no need to retype it into a CorelDraw 9 project. You can import it into the project as paragraph text and manipulate it just as if you were using a page layout program—you can flow text between blocks and around objects, and add bullets and drop caps.

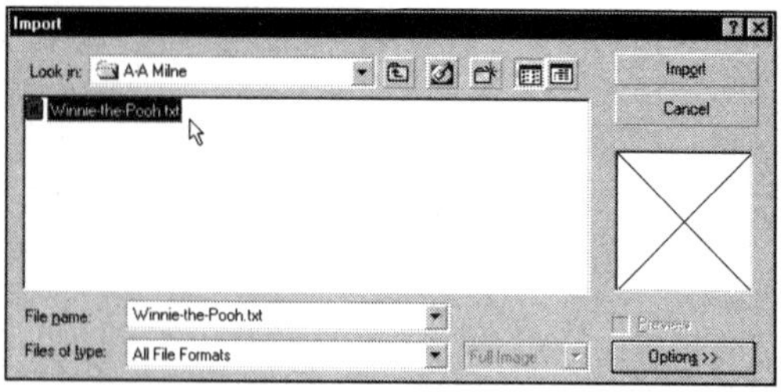

Figure 43. *Use the Import dialog box to select the text you want to bring into a project.*

To import text into a project:

1. Press Ctrl+I on the keyboard or choose Import from the File menu. The Import dialog box will appear (**Figure 43**).
2. Use the Look in drop-down list to move to the folder where the text document is located, and then click on the file name to select it.
3. Click Import.
4. The text will appear in your document in one large text frame (**Figure 44**). You can now work with it like any paragraph text object.

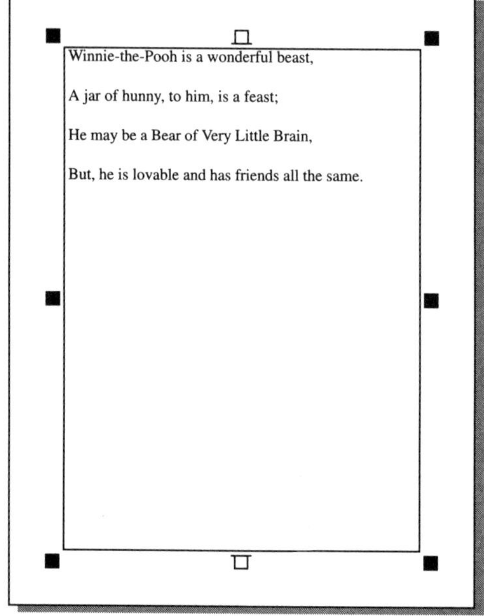

Figure 44. *When the text is imported, it appears in a large text frame.*

TEXT FILE FORMATS

CorelDraw 9 comes with filters that translate text from many word processing programs into CorelDraw paragraph text. To check to see if the word processing program you use can be translated, use the Files of type drop-down list found in the Import dialog box (**Figure 43**).

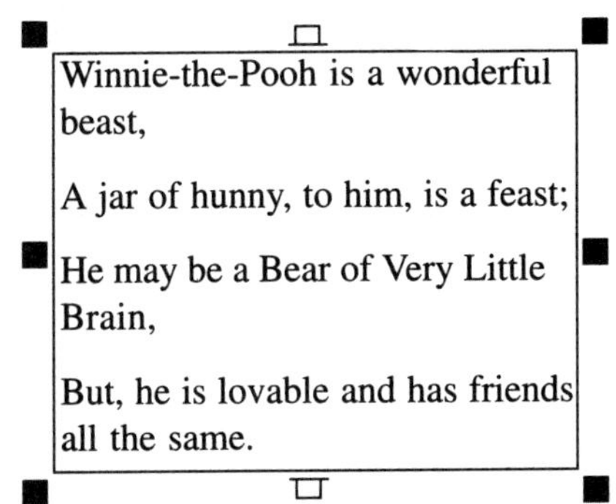

Figure 45. *Select the paragraph text object with the Pick Tool.*

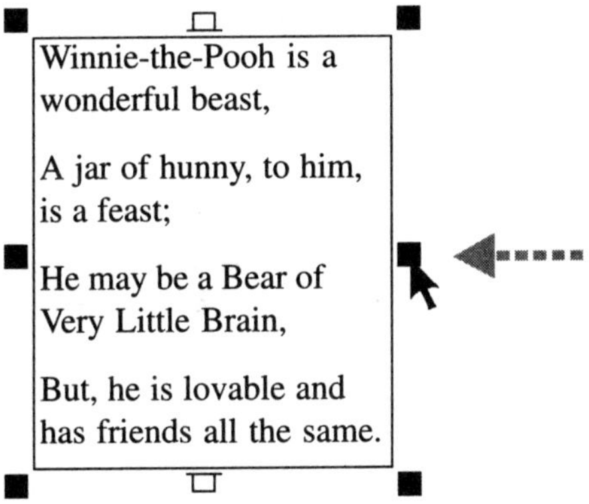

Figure 46. *Drag the handles until the paragraph text object is the right size.*

To reshape a paragraph text object:

1. Select the paragraph text object with the Pick Tool (**Figure 45**). Six black handles and two text handles will appear around the object.
2. Drag the handles until the paragraph text object is the desired shape (**Figure 46**).

The Pick Tool and Text Object Handles

You may have noticed that the Pick Tool affects artistic text objects and paragraph text objects differently. When you drag a handle of an artistic text object, the text changes size and shape. Whereas, when you drag a handle of a paragraph text object, the text stays the same size and rearranges itself depending upon the size of the text frame. To proportionally change the size of paragraph text, hold down the Alt key while dragging a corner handle.

To flow text between paragraph text frames:

1. Create the paragraph text or import a text file.
2. Select the paragraph text object with the Pick Tool (**Figure 47**). Notice the two text handles, one at the top and one at the bottom of the frame.
3. If you reshape the text object so all the text is not showing, the bottom text handle will change to display a *text flow tab* (**Figure 48**).
4. Position the mouse over the bottom text handle and click. The pointer will change to a page with an arrow attached to it.
5. Position the mouse where you want the paragraph text to continue.
6. Press the left mouse button and drag a new text frame (**Figure 49**). When you release the mouse button, the extra text from the first text frame will flow into the new text frame (**Figure 50**).

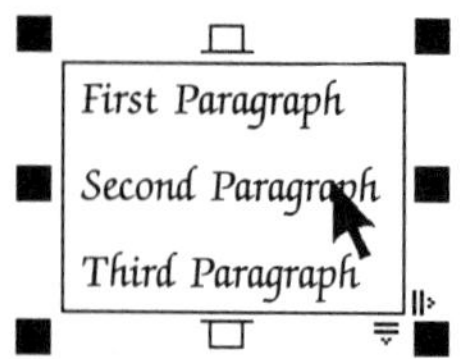

Figure 47. *Select the paragraph text block with the Pick Tool.*

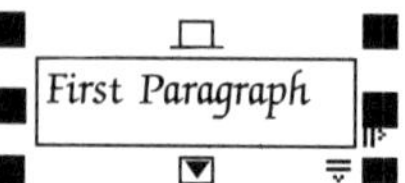

Figure 48. *If there is more text than the text frame can show, a text flow tab appears in place of the lower text handle.*

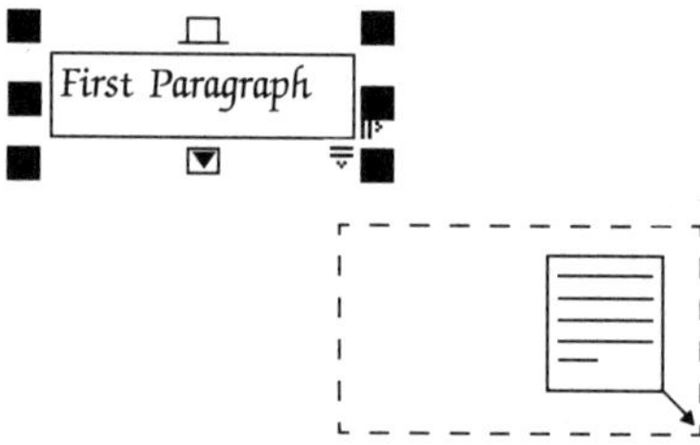

Figure 49. *Position the mouse where you would like the flow of text to appear and drag a new text frame.*

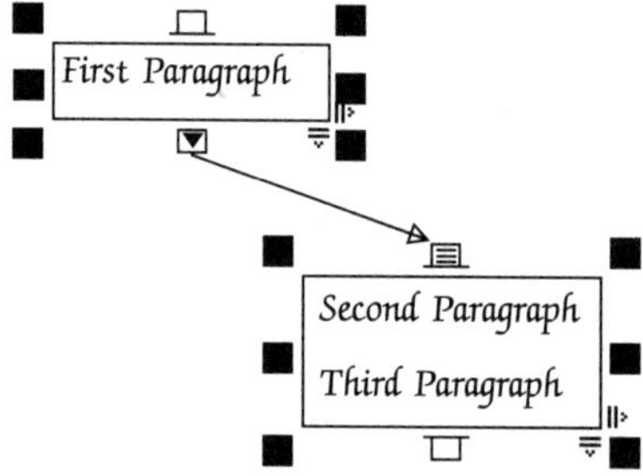

Figure 50. *When you release the mouse button, the text flows into the new text frame and a blue arrow appears indicating the link between the two text frames.*

Tip:

- You can flow text between paragraph text frames on different pages of text-intensive projects, such as brochures and multiple page newsletters. If you add or delete text from a linked paragraph text frame, the text will automatically adjust, flowing between the linked frames.

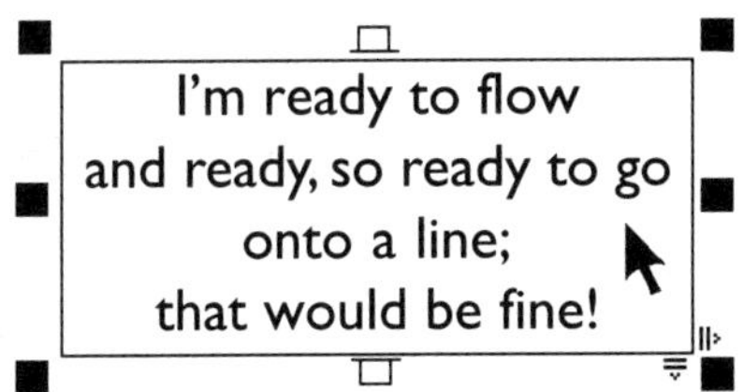

Figure 51. *Select the paragraph text with the Pick Tool, then resize the paragraph text frame so a flow tab appears at the bottom of the text as shown in Figure 52.*

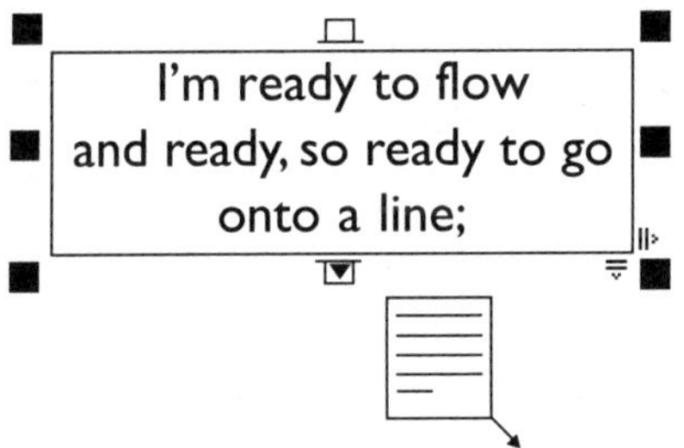

Figure 52. *With the paragraph text frame resized, the fourth line of text is hidden and a text flow tab appears. When you click the text flow tab, the mouse pointer changes to a page with an arrow attached to it.*

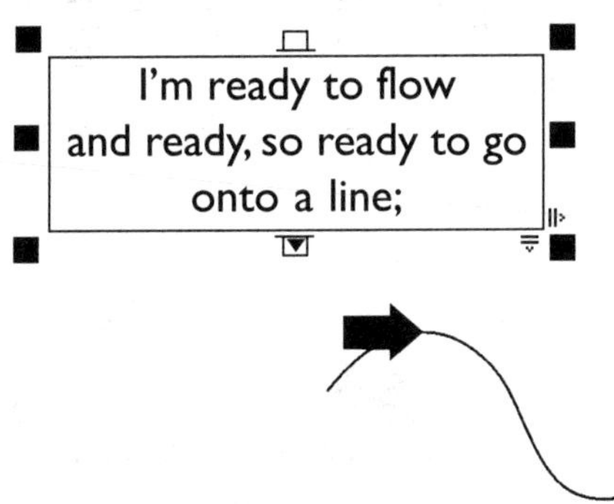

Figure 53. *The mouse is in the right place when it changes to a large black arrow.*

With CorelDraw 9, there's more to flowing paragraph text than just from frame-to-frame. There are two new features that are really neat and easy to use: flowing paragraph text onto an open path, such as a curvy line, and inside a closed object, such as a circle or star.

To flow paragraph text onto a path:

1. Create the paragraph text or import a text file.
2. Select the paragraph text object with the Pick Tool (**Figure 51**).
3. Resize the paragraph text frame so a text flow tab appears.
4. Position the mouse pointer over the text flow tab and click (**Figure 52**). The pointer will change to a page with an arrow attached to it.
5. Position the mouse over the line onto which you want to flow text (**Figure 53**). When you are in the right position, the mouse pointer will change to a large black arrow.
6. Click the left mouse button. The text will flow onto the line (**Figure 54**).

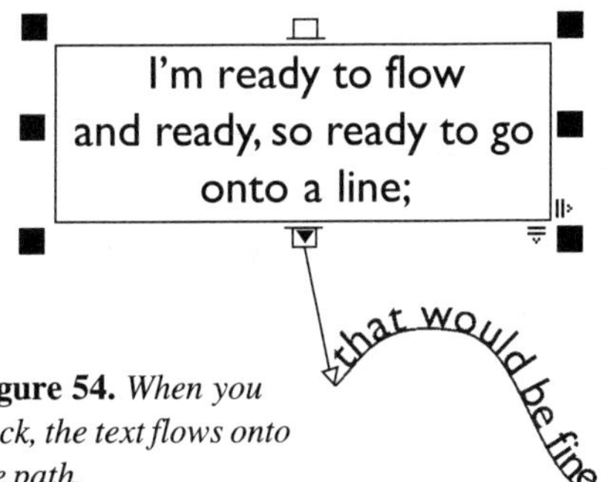

Figure 54. *When you click, the text flows onto the path.*

Flow Paragraph Text onto a Path

To flow paragraph text into an object:

1. Create the paragraph text or import a text file.
2. Select the paragraph text object with the Pick Tool (**Figure 55**).
3. Resize the paragraph text frame so a text flow tab appears.
4. Position the mouse pointer over the text flow tab and click (**Figure 56**). The pointer will change to a page with an arrow attached to it.
5. Position the mouse over the object into which you want to flow text (**Figure 57**). When you are in the right position, the mouse pointer will change to a large black arrow.
6. Click the left mouse button. The text will flow into the object (**Figure 58**).

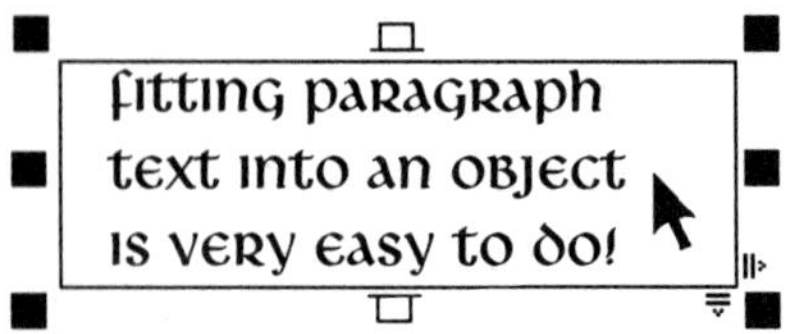

Figure 55. *Select the paragraph text object with the Pick Tool, then resize the paragraph text frame so a flow tab appears at the bottom of the text as shown in Figure 56.*

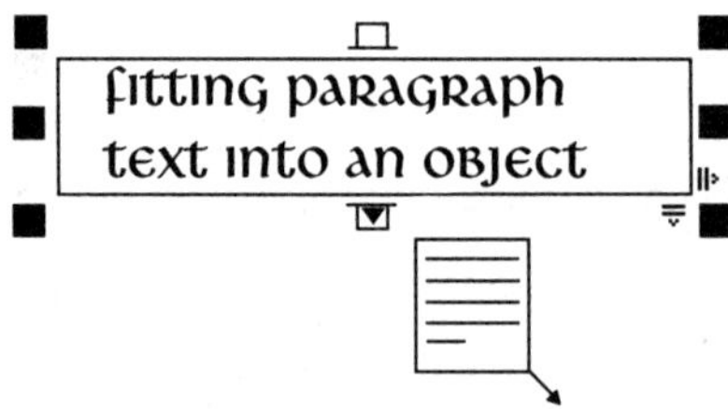

Figure 56. *With the paragraph text frame resized, the third line of text is hidden and a text flow tab appears. When you click the text flow tab, the mouse pointer changes to a page with an arrow attached to it.*

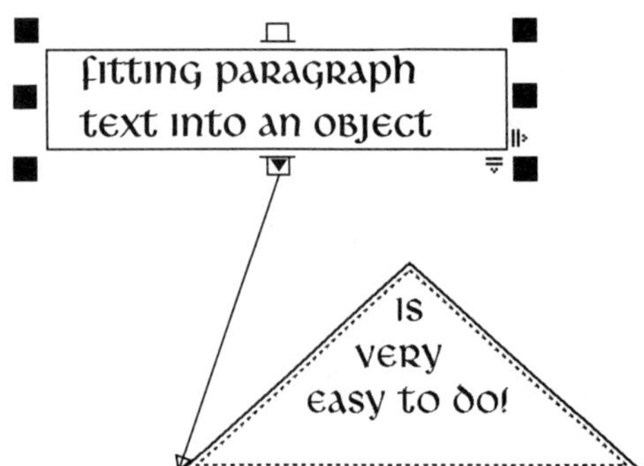

Figure 58. *When you click the left mouse button, the paragraph text appears inside the object in a paragraph text frame shaped like the object.*

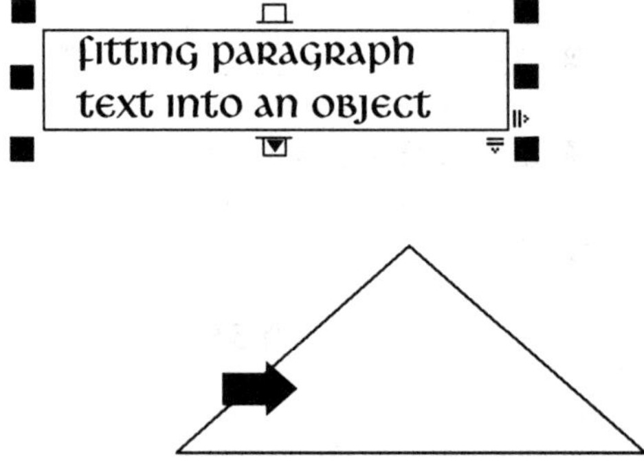

Figure 57. *The mouse is in the right place when it changes to a large black arrow.*

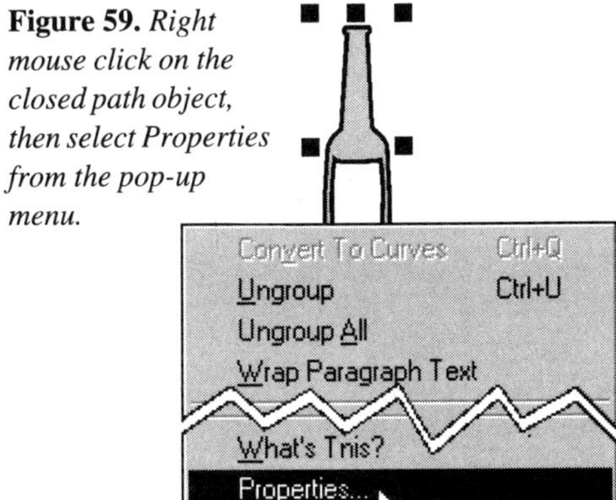

Figure 59. *Right mouse click on the closed path object, then select Properties from the pop-up menu.*

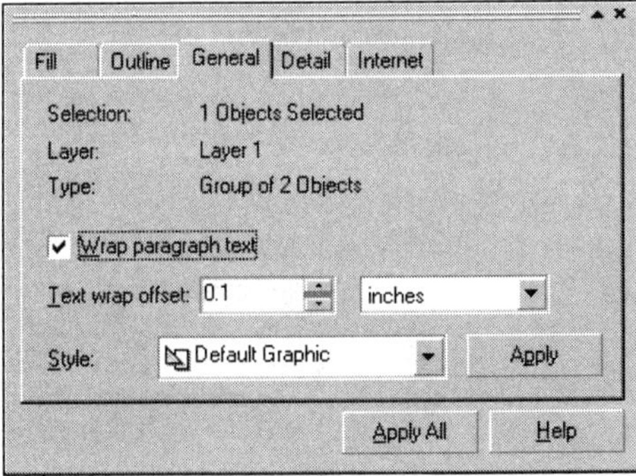

Figure 60. *Use the General tab page of the Object Properties dialog box to set paragraph text wrapping.*

Figure 61. *When you draw a text frame using the Text Tool, a dashed outline also appears around the object.*

To make new text flow around an object:

1. Make sure the object has a closed path.
2. Select the Pick Tool and right mouse click on the object. A pop-up menu will appear (**Figure 59**).
3. Choose Properties from the menu. The Object Properties dialog box will open.
4. Click the General tab to move that page to the front (**Figure 60**).
5. Put a check in the box before Wrap paragraph text and enter an amount in the Text wrap offset text box. The text wrap offset is the distance the wrapped text will be from the object.
6. Click OK.
7. Select the Text Tool and drag a text frame around the object (**Figure 61**). A dashed rectangle will appear, showing the text frame and a dashed outline will also appear around the object.
8. Type your text. As you type the text will flow around the object (**Figure 62**).

Figure 62. *As you type, the text flows around the object.*

To make existing text flow around an object:

1. Convert the text object to paragraph text if it is artistic text and select it (**Figure 63**).
2. Make sure the object you want to flow the text around has a closed path, then right mouse click on it with the Pick Tool. Select Properties from the pop-up menu (**Figure 64**).
3. Click on the General tab to move that tab page to the front (**Figure 60**).
4. Put a check in the box before Wrap paragraph text and enter an amount in the Text wrap offset text box.
5. Drag the paragraph text on top of the object. The text will automatically wrap around the object (**Figure 65**).

Tips:

- If you aren't sure whether a text object is paragraph or artistic text, just select it and check the Status Bar.
- You can wrap one paragraph of text around as many objects as you like at a time.
- If you like the text wrap offset 0.1" default, just choose Wrap Paragraph Text from the pop-up menu instead of going into the Object Properties dialog box.

Figure 63. *If the text is artistic, convert it to paragraph.*

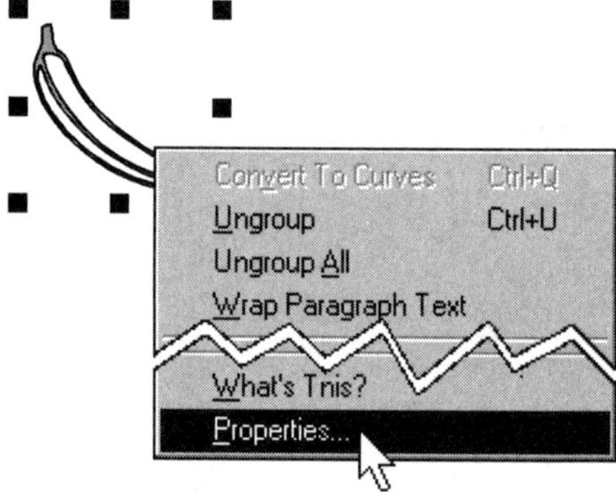

Figure 64. *Right mouse click on the object and select Properties from the pop-up menu.*

Figure 65. *As you drag the paragraph text object over the object, the text rearranges itself around the object.*

Make Existing Text Flow Around an Object

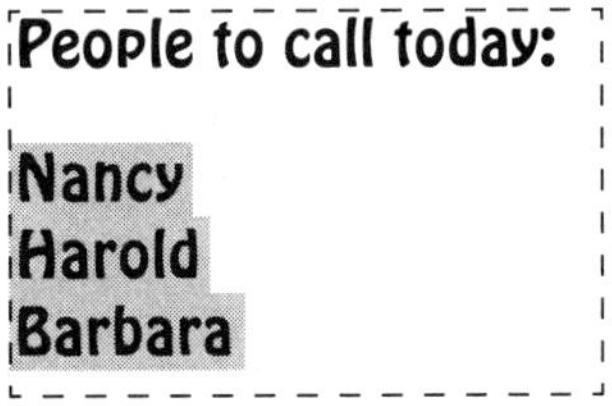

People to call today:

Nancy
Harold
Barbara

Figure 66. *Use the Text Tool to select the lines of text to which you want to add bullets.*

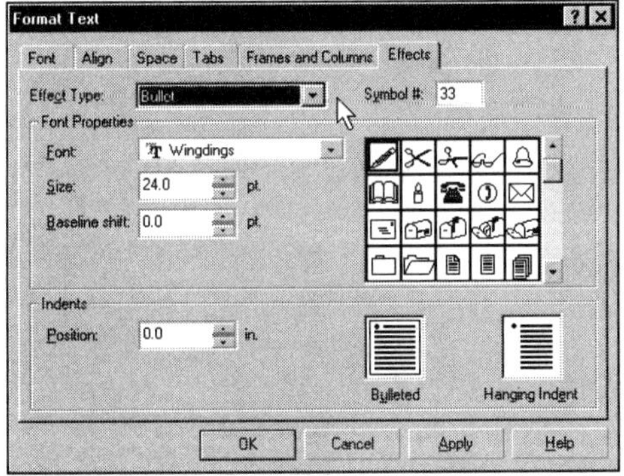

Figure 67. *Select the Bullet option button on the Effects tab page of the Format Text dialog box.*

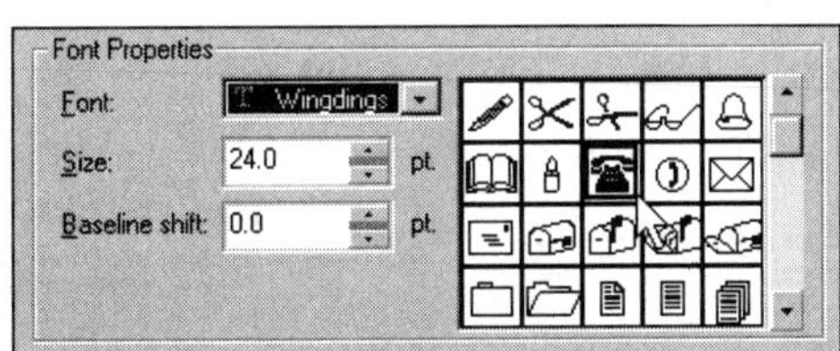

Figure 68. *Select a bullet style from the list and set its size.*

To add bullets to paragraph text:

1. Select the Text Tool, then use it to highlight the text to which you want to add bullets (**Figure 66**).
2. Open the Format Text dialog box by choosing Format Text from the Text menu or pressing Ctrl+T on the keyboard.
3. Click the Effects tab to bring that page to the front (**Figure 67**).
4. Use the Effect Type drop-down list to select Bullet.
5. Use the Font drop-down list in the Font Properties area to choose a font.
6. Choose a bullet style from the list on the right side of the tab page (**Figure 68**).
7. Set the Bullet size using the Size text box under the Font drop-down list.
8. In the Indents area, use the Position text box to enter the amount the text will be indented from the bullet.
9. Click OK. The selected lines of text will redraw with bullets in front of them (**Figure 69**).

Figure 69. *After you click OK, the selected text redraws with bullets.*

To add a drop cap to paragraph text:

1. Select the Text Tool and position it at the beginning of the paragraph where you want the drop cap (**Figure 70**).
2. Open the Format Text dialog box by pressing Ctrl+T on the keyboard or choosing Format Text from the Text menu.
3. Move to the Effccts tab page by clicking on the Effects tab.
4. Use the Effect Type drop-down list to select Drop cap, then set how many lines the cap will drop (**Figure 71**).
5. Click OK. The paragraph text will redraw with the dropped cap (**Figure 72**).

Tip:

- You can change the drop cap's font by selecting the character with the Text Tool, then using the Font tab page of the Format Text dialog box.

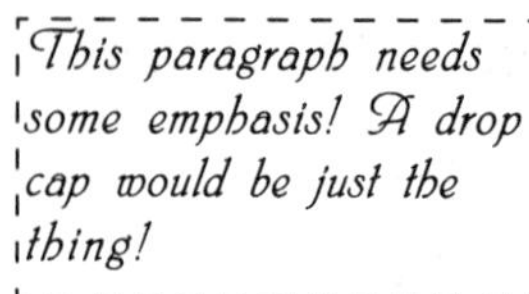

Figure 70. *Place the insertion marker at the beginning of the paragraph where you want the drop cap.*

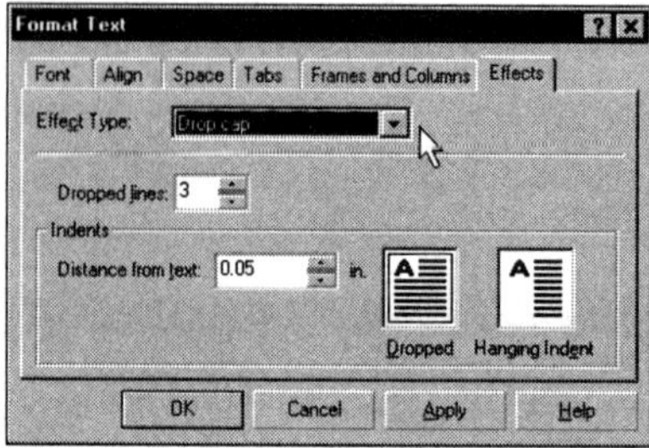

Figure 71. *Select the Drop cap option button on the Effects tab page.*

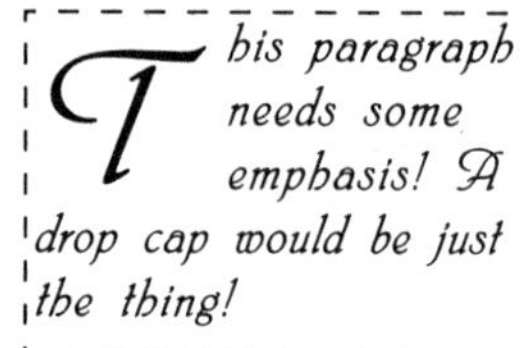

Figure 72. *When you click OK, the text redraws with the drop cap.*

Summary

In this chapter you learned how to:

- Add and edit artistic and paragraph text
- Convert artistic text to paragraph text and vice versa
- Change font, font size, and formatting
- Change character and line spacing
- Import text
- Flow text around objects
- Add bullets
- Add drop caps

Fun with Text

In the last chapter, you learned how to add text to your projects. This chapter takes text one step further, making it into a design element that enhances your graphics.

This chapter will show you how to *skew* and *rotate* text objects and create shadows two different ways—by duplicating the text object and using the Interactive Drop Shadow Tool. Then you will fit artistic text to a path. From there, you will add *bevels* and *extrusions* to text using the CorelDraw 9 Interactive Extrusion Tool, then rotate the text for amazing three-dimensional effects. Next, you will modify characters' shapes using the Shape Tool. Finally, you will take what you have learned in previous chapters to highlight text with eye-popping neon effects. (You'll have to use your imagination here because the black and white illustrations in this book don't do them justice!)

When a text object is skewed, it is slanted either vertically or horizontally, using *skewing handles* (**Figure 1**). A text object that is rotated is spun around a central point called the *center of rotation marker*, using *rotation handles* (**Figure 4**). Skewing and rotation handles become visible when you double-click an object with the Pick Tool. They are double-headed arrows that surround the object in a rectangular formation. The skewing handles are the top, bottom, left, and right center arrows. The rotation handles are the curved arrows at the corners. Rotation and skewing are measured in degrees.

Figure 1. *When you double-click on an object with the Pick Tool, skewing handles appear around its perimeter.*

To skew text:

1. Double-click on the text object with the Pick Tool. Double-headed arrows—skewing handles—will appear around the object (**Figure 1**).
2. To skew the text horizontally, position the mouse pointer over the top or bottom skewing handles, then press the left mouse button and drag sideways (**Figure 2**). As you drag, a dashed rectangle appears around the text object and the mouse pointer changes to a double-headed arrow. To skew the text vertically, position the mouse over the left or right skewing handles, then press the left mouse button and drag up or down (**Figure 3**).

Figure 2. *If you drag the top or bottom skewing handle sideways, the text object slants horizontally.*

Figure 3. *If you drag the left or right skewing handle up or down, the text slants vertically.*

Skew Text

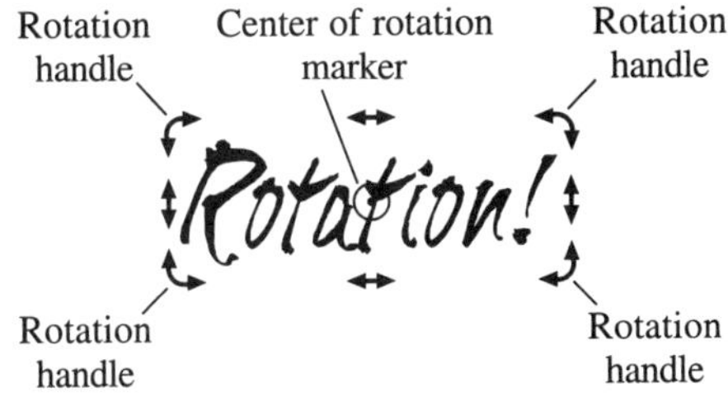

Figure 4. *Double-click on the text object to make the rotation and skewing handles appear.*

Figure 5. *Drag one of the rotation handles to rotate the text object.*

Figure 6. *Move the center of rotation marker to the position where you want the text object to rotate around.*

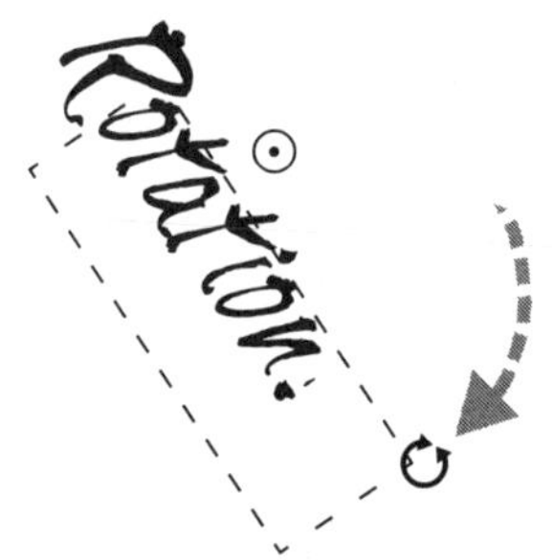

Figure 7. *As you drag the text object, notice how it rotates around the center of rotation marker.*

To rotate text:

1. Double-click on the text object with the Pick Tool. The rotation and skewing handles will appear (**Figure 4**). In addition, at the center of the text object, a circle with a dot in the center will appear. This is the center of rotation marker.
2. Position the mouse pointer over one of the rotation handles, press the left mouse button and drag in a clockwise or counterclockwise direction (**Figure 5**). When you drag, a dashed rectangle appears around the text object and the mouse pointer changes to a round double-headed arrow.
3. Release the mouse button. The text redraws in its new, rotated position.

Tip:

- Experiment with moving the center of rotation marker. To move the marker, place the mouse over it, then press the left mouse button and drag it to a new position (**Figure 6**). Next, rotate the text object and notice how it moves around the marker (**Figure 7**).

> **ROTATING AND SKEWING OTHER OBJECTS**
>
> You can rotate and skew any kind of object—rectangles, polygons, etc.—using the rotation and skewing handles. Just double-click on the object to access the special handles.

Rotate Text

Another way to rotate and skew text is to use the Free Transform Tool found on the Shape Tool fly-out (**Figure 8**). The Free Transform Tool works with the Property Bar to give you quick access to a Free Rotation Tool, Free Angle Reflection Tool, Free Scale Tool, and Free Skew Tool (**Figure 9**).

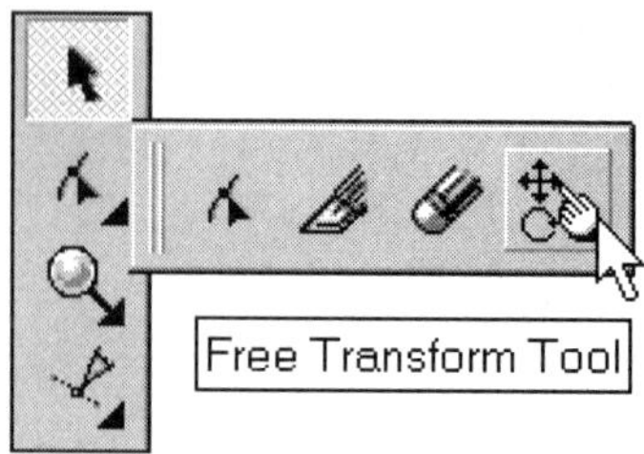

Figure 8. *Select the Free Transform Tool from the Shape fly-out.*

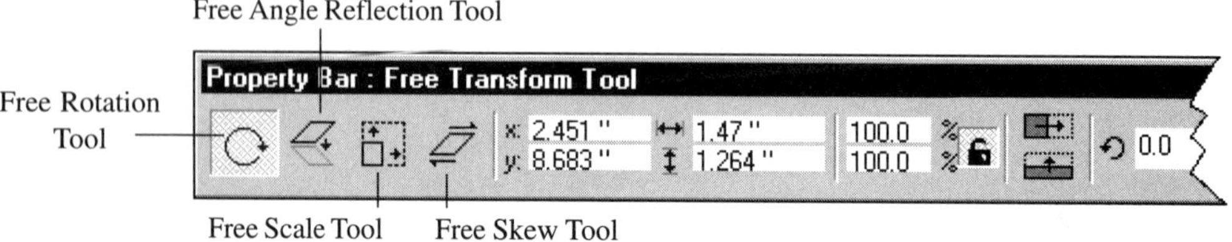

Figure 9. *When the Free Transform Tool is selected, the Property Bar dynamically changes to gives fast access to several handy tools.*

To rotate text using the Free Rotation Tool:

1. Use the Shape Tool fly-out to select the Free Transform Tool. The mouse pointer will change to a cross-hair.
2. Click the Free Rotation Tool button on the Property Bar (**Figure 9**).
3. Click on the object with the mouse to select it (**Figure 10**). (You'll know it's selected when the object's nodes appear.)
4. Position the mouse cross-hair over the object where you would like the center of rotation to be.

Figure 10. *Select the object using the mouse cross-hair.*

Figure 11. *Position the cross-hair where you want the center of rotation, then press the left mouse button and drag to rotate the text object.*

Figure 12. *When you release the mouse button, the text redraws in its new rotated position.*

Figure 13. *Select the text object using the cross-hair.*

Figure 14. *Drag the mouse cross-hair to skew the text.*

Figure 15. *When you release the mouse button, the text redraws skewed.*

5. Press the left mouse button and drag the mouse in the direction you would like to rotate the text object (**Figure 11**). A dashed-blue line will appear, showing the center of rotation and a blue outlined version of the text will appear, rotating as you drag the mouse.
6. Release the mouse button when you are finished rotating the text (**Figure 12**).

To skew text using the Free Skew Tool:

1. Use the Shape Tool fly-out to select the Free Transform Tool.
2. Click the Free Skew Tool button on the Property Bar (**Figure 9**).
3. Click on the object with the mouse to select it (**Figure 13**).
4. Position the mouse cursor over the object where you would like the skew to originate from.
5. Press the left mouse button and drag the mouse in the direction you want to skew the object (**Figure 14**). A blue outline of the text object will appear showing how far the object has been skewed.
6. Release the left mouse button when the object is skewed the way you want it (**Figure 15**).

Shadows give the impression of three dimensionality. Adding shadows to text highlights it, making it stand out. There are many ways to create shadows with CorelDraw 9. The first method described here uses duplication to make shadows. The second method uses the Interactive Drop Shadow Tool.

To create text shadows using duplication:

1. Use the Text Tool to create some artistic text.
2. Change the typeface to a favorite font by selecting the text with the Text Tool, and then using the Font drop-down list on the Property Bar (**Figure 16**). In addition, make the text large enough so it is easy to see. (The font used in Figure 16 is Brush 455 BT.)
3. Open the Options dialog box by pressing Ctrl+J on the keyboard or choosing Options from the Tools menu (**Figure 17**). The dialog box will open with Workspace selected in the tree view window.
4. Click Edit in the tree view window to access the duplicate placement text boxes (**Figure 18**).

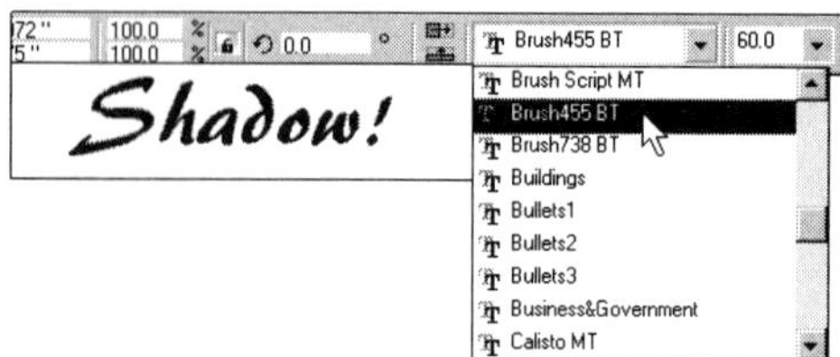

Figure 16. *You can use the Property Bar to change the font and font size.*

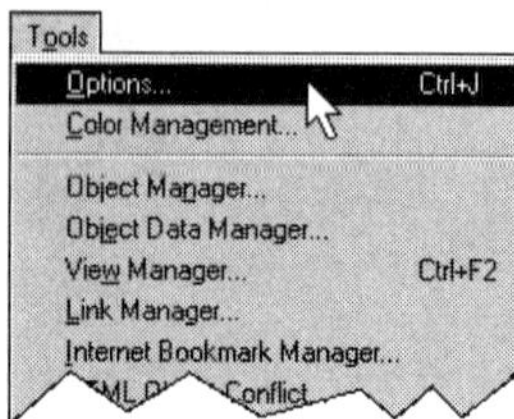

Figure 17. *Choose Options from the Tools menu.*

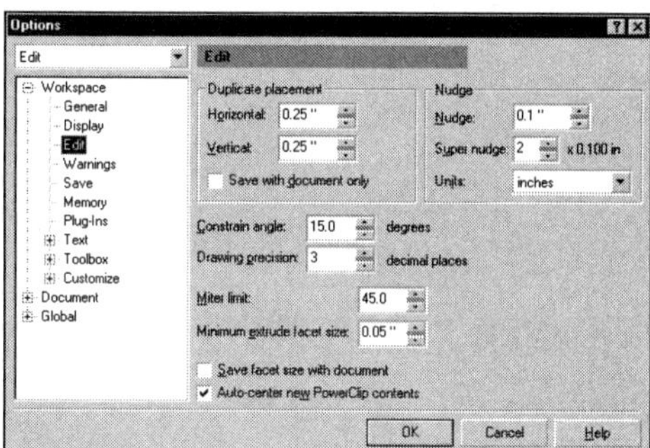

Figure 18. *Click Edit in the tree view window to access the duplicate placement text boxes.*

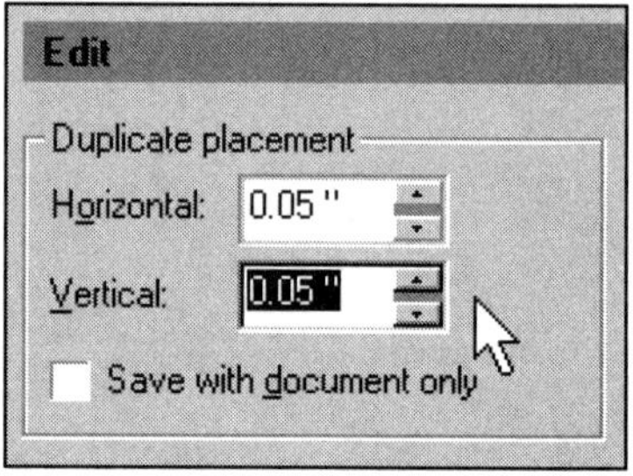

Figure 19. *In the Duplicate placement area, change both the Horizontal and Vertical settings.*

Create Text Shadows using Duplication

Figure 20. *Select the text object with the Pick Tool.*

Figure 21. *Left click on a color well to change the fill color of the text.*

Figure 22. *The duplicate will appear selected to the right and a little above the original.*

Figure 23. *After clicking the color well to fill the duplicate with a different color, the shadowed text becomes apparent.*

5. In the Duplicate placement area (**Figure 19**), change the Horizontal and Vertical settings to 0.05 inch (0.13 centimeter), then click OK.
6. Select the text object with the Pick Tool. Eight black handles will appear around the object (**Figure 20**).
7. Change the fill color of the text by left mouse clicking on one of the color wells in the color palette (**Figure 21**). Light gray is a good choice since this text will become the shadow.
8. Duplicate the text object by pressing Ctrl+D on the keyboard or choosing Duplicate from the Edit menu. A duplicate of the text object will appear, selected, slightly up and to the right of the original (**Figure 22**). It may be slightly difficult to see.
9. Change the fill color of the duplicate by clicking the left mouse button on a color well. Pick a color that is darker than the shadow color, bright blue, for instance. You've just created shadowed text (**Figure 23**)!

Creating drop shadows using the Interactive Drop Shadow Tool is fast and fun!

To create shadows using the Interactive Drop Shadow Tool:

1. Select the Interactive Drop Shadow Tool from the Interactive Tool fly-out (**Figure 24**). A small rectangle with a drop shadow will become attached to the mouse pointer.
2. Select the text object to which you want to add a drop shadow by clicking on it (**Figure 25**). (You'll know the object is selected when you see its nodes.)
3. Position the mouse near the center of the text object.
4. Press the left mouse button and drag the pointer in the direction where you want the drop shadow to appear (**Figure 26**). A blue-outlined representation of the drop shadow will appear with a dashed blue rectangle around it, letting you see where it will be placed.
5. If you want to change how visible the drop shadow is, move the slider bar on the drop shadow arrow (**Figure 26**).
6. Release the mouse button. The text will redraw with a fabulous drop shadow (**Figure 27**).

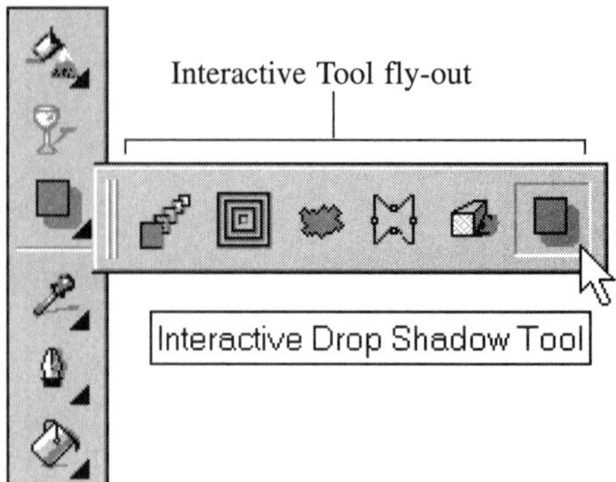

Figure 24. *Select the Interactive Drop Shadow Tool from the Interactive Tool fly-out.*

Figure 25. *Select the text object with the mouse pointer.*

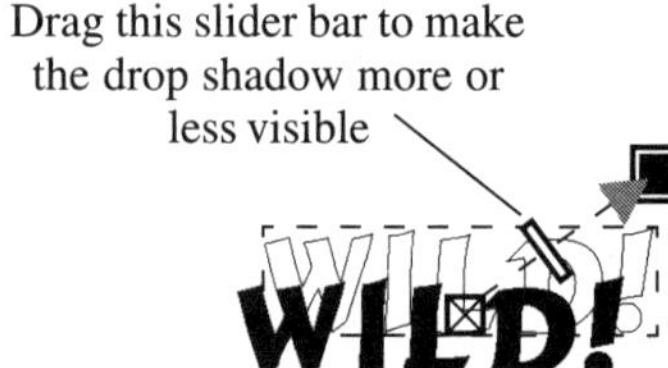

Figure 26. *Drag the mouse in the direction where you would like the drop shadow. A blue-outlined representation of the drop shadow appears to help with placement.*

Figure 27. *When you release the mouse button, the text object redraws with a great drop shadow.*

The Interactive Drop Shadow Tool

The Property Bar offers several drop shadow styles. To access these shadows, use the Drop Shadow Feathering Direction, Feathering Edges, and Perspective Type drop-down lists (**Figure 28**). In addition, the small rectangular slider bar that is available when you use the Interactive Drop Shadow Tool (**Figure 26**) and the corresponding text box on the Property Bar let you set how visible the drop shadow is. Experiment with the different drop shadow styles (**Figures 29a-e**). Don't forget that you can use the Interactive Drop Shadow Tool on any object you create in CorelDraw 9.

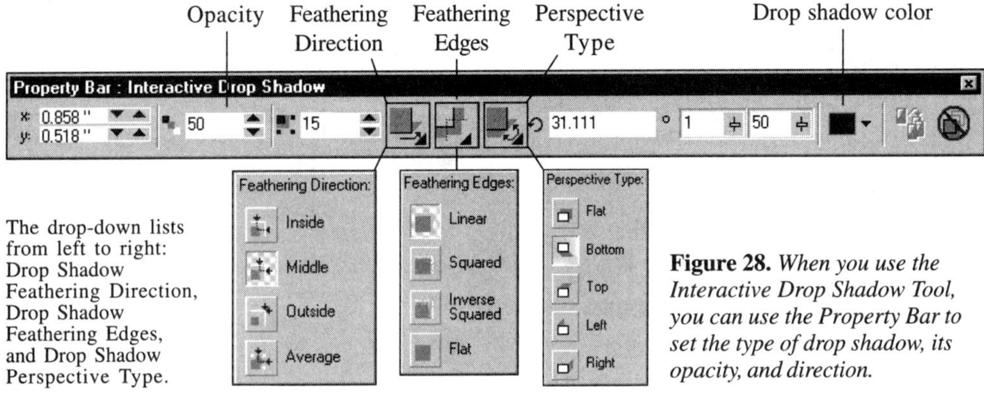

Figure 28. *When you use the Interactive Drop Shadow Tool, you can use the Property Bar to set the type of drop shadow, its opacity, and direction.*

Figure 29a. *This is an average drop shadow applied to text with a texture fill.*

Figure 29b. *This example uses an inside drop shadow direction and linear drop shadow edges.*

Figure 29c. *To create this example, use a middle drop shadow direction and flat drop shadow edges.*

To change the drop shadow color:

1. Create the drop shadow using the Interactive Drop Shadow Tool as described on the previous page.
2. Use the Drop Shadow Color drop-down palette to select a new color (**Figure 28**). The drop shadow will redraw using the new color.

Figures 29d–e. *These examples use an outside drop shadow direction and inverse squared drop shadow edges.*

The term *fitting text to a path* means that a line of text is bound to the path of an object. As the text moves along the object's path it assumes the shape of the path. You can fit text to a path interactively or use the Text menu.

To fit artistic text to a path interactively:

1. With the Pick Tool, select the object to which you want to fit the text (**Figure 30**). (The object can have a closed path, or it can be a line.)
2. Select the Text Tool.
3. Position the Text Tool on the object's path. You'll know you're in the right place when the mouse changes from the Text Tool's cross-hair to an I-beam.
4. Click the left mouse button. The insertion marker will appear at the top of the object (**Figure 31**).
5. Type your text. As you type, the text will follow the outline of the object (**Figure 32**).

To fit existing text to a path:

1. Create an object to which you want to fit the text (**Figure 33**).
2. Create some artistic text and change it to your favorite font and color (**Figure 34**). (This example is set in the font Pipeline.)

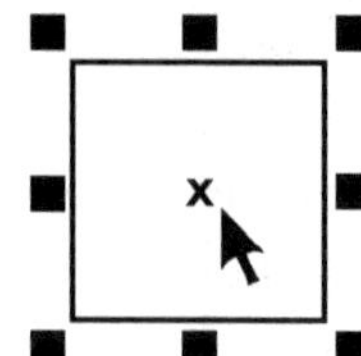

Figure 30. *Use the Pick Tool to select the object to which you want to fit the text.*

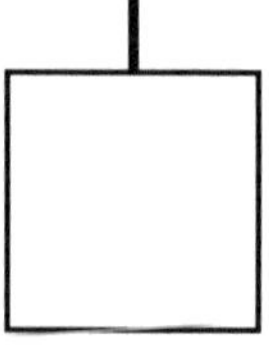

Figure 31. *When you click on the selected object's path with the Text Tool, the insertion marker appears at the top of the object.*

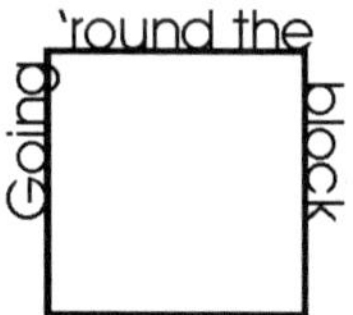

Figure 32. *As you type, the text wraps itself around the object.*

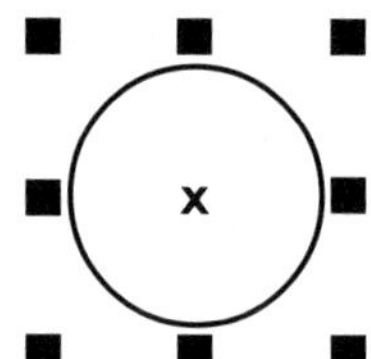

Figure 33. *Create the object to which you want to fit the text.*

Figure 34. *Create the text you want to fit to the object's path.*

Figure 35. *You can use the Pick Tool to drag a marquee around the two objects to select them.*

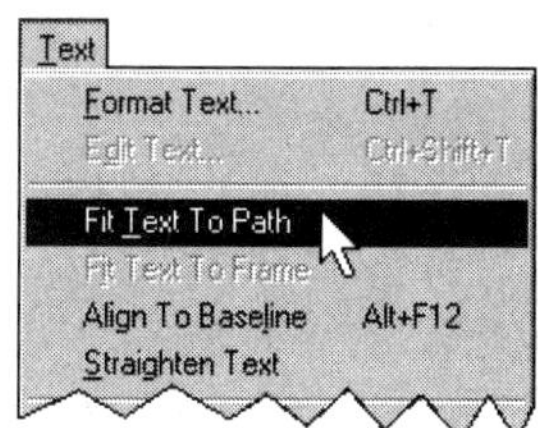

Figure 36. *Choose Fit Text To Path from the Text menu.*

Figure 37. *When you choose Fit Text to Path, the text fits itself to the object's path.*

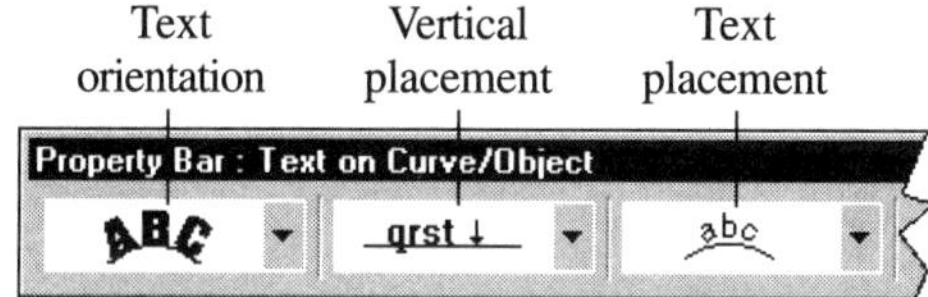

Figure 38. *You can use the Property Bar to change the placement of the text on the path.*

Figure 39. *The orientation of this text is "standing" upright. Compare it to the text in Figure 37 which is sideways.*

Figure 40. *The vertical placement of this text is under the path. Compare it to the text in Figure 37 which is placed on top of the path.*

Figure 41. *The text placement of this text is centered on the left side of the path.*

3. Select both objects either by holding down the Shift key while you click or by pressing the left mouse button and dragging to marquee select with the Pick Tool (**Figure 35**).
4. Choose Fit Text To Path from the Text menu (**Figure 36**). The text will redraw, following the path of the object (**Figure 37**).

Tip:

- Once the text is fit to the path, you can select it using the Pick Tool, and then change its position on the path using the Property Bar (**Figure 38**). (Click on the text to select it, otherwise you may select the path that it is fit to. When the text is selected the Status Bar will read something such as "Text on a Path on Layer 1.") A few of the changes you can make using the Property Bar include:
  - **Text orientation**—lets you specify how the text "stands," giving it an upright or sideways appearance (**Figure 39**).
  - **Vertical placement**—lets you set where on the path the text sits, on top, underneath, etc. (**Figure 40**).
  - **Text placement**—lets you set where the text is centered on the path, top, bottom, left, or right (**Figure 41**).

Extrusions give a two-dimensional drawing the appearance of three dimensions. CorelDraw 9's Interactive Extrude Tool (**Figure 42**) makes it easy to create *vector extrusions* or *bitmap extrusions*.

A vector extrusion is created by projecting points from the edges of a two-dimensional object (**Figure 43a**), and joining them together to converge toward a vanishing point (**Figure 43b**). The illusion of three dimensions is created by the addition of objects on top of the original or *control* object (the two-dimensional object that has been extruded). After creating a vector extrusion, bevels, fills and *ambient lighting* can be added to enhance the extrusion effect (**Figure 43c**).

A bitmap extrusion actually lets you work with a three-dimensional object, not just a two-dimensional object with other objects placed on top of it (**Figure 44a**). When a bitmap extrusion is *rendered*, bevels, ambient and *spot lighting*, and texture fills can be added to the object (**Figure 44b**). The object can also be rotated in three dimensions, letting you view it from any side or angle (**Figure 44c**).

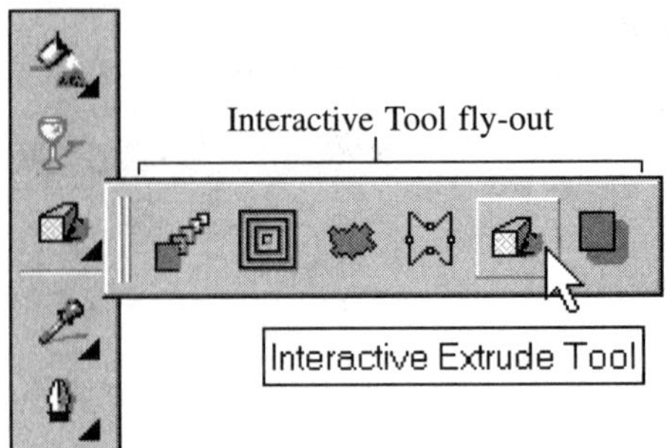

Figure 42. *The Interactive Extrude Tool can be found on the Interactive Tool fly-out.*

Figure 43a. *The original text object.*

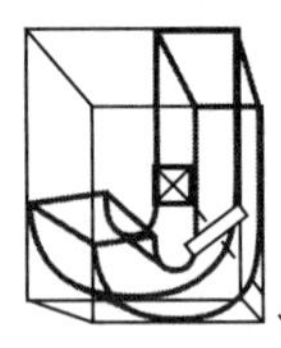

Figure 43b. *The original object being extruded.*

Figure 43c. *The extruded object with a bevel, fill, and light added to enhance the effect.*

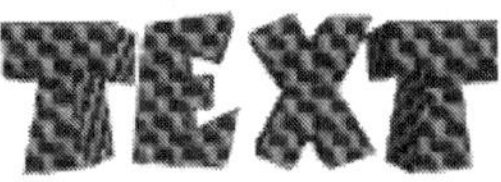

Figure 44b. *A bevel, texture, and spot lighting added to the bitmap extrusion.*

Figure 44a. *The three-dimensional bitmap extrusion.*

Vector and Bitmap Extrusions

Figure 44c. *The rotated extrusion.*

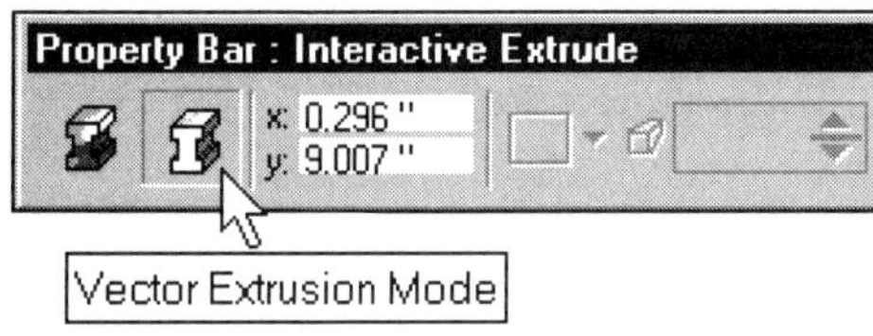

Figure 45. *Click the Vector Extrusion Mode button at the left end of the Property Bar.*

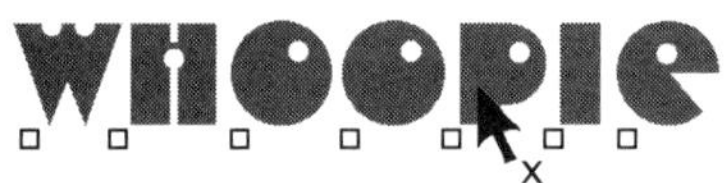

Figure 46. *Select the text object with the mouse pointer.*

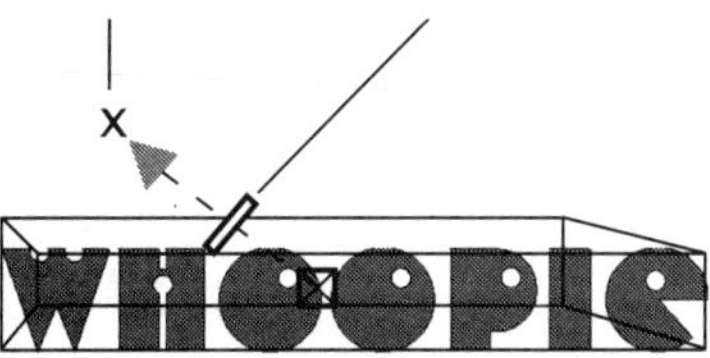

Figure 47. *Drag the mouse to create the extrusion. Use the 3D rectangle to help with placement.*

To create a vector extrusion:

1. Select the Interactive Extrude Tool by opening the Interactive Tool fly-out and clicking the Interactive Extrude Tool button (**Figure 42**). An X will appear attached to the mouse pointer.
2. Click the Vector Extrusion Mode button at the left end of the Property Bar (**Figure 45**).
3. Select the text object to which you want to add the extrusion (**Figure 46**). You'll know the object is selected when you can see its nodes. (An outline added to the text will make the extrusion look better.)
4. Position the mouse pointer near the center of the text object.
5. Press the left mouse button and drag the extrusion in the direction you want it to go (**Figure 47**). A red and blue 3D rectangle will appear and help you place the extrusion.
6. Release the mouse button. The text object will redraw showing the extrusion (**Figure 48**).

Figure 48. *When you release the mouse button, the text redraws with the extrusion.*

Now that you've created a vector extrusion, you can add colors, bevels, and lighting effects to your extruded object.

To add color to a vector extrusion with the Interactive Extrude Tool:

1. Select the extruded object with the Pick Tool.
2. Click the Color button on the Property Bar to access the drop-down box (**Figure 49**).
3. Click one of the color fill buttons on the drop-down box to add color to your image. The choices are:
   - **Use Object Fill**—this option uses the fill color of the original object to color the extrusion.
   - **Use Solid Color**—this option lets you select a solid fill color for the extrusion. Click the Using drop-down palette to select a color (**Figure 50**).
   - **Use Color Shading**—this option fills the extrusion with a fountain fill made up of two colors you select from the From and To drop-down palettes (**Figure 51**).
4. When you are finished making color selections, press Enter on the keyboard. The extrusion will fill with the color you selected (**Figures 52a–c**).

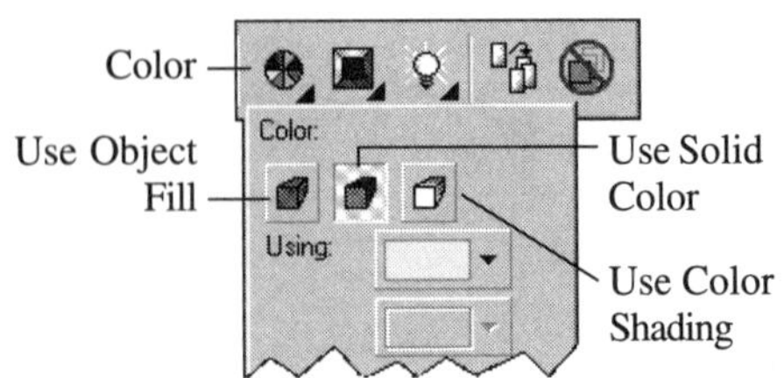

Figure 49. *The Color drop-down box lets you choose what color the extrusion is filled with.*

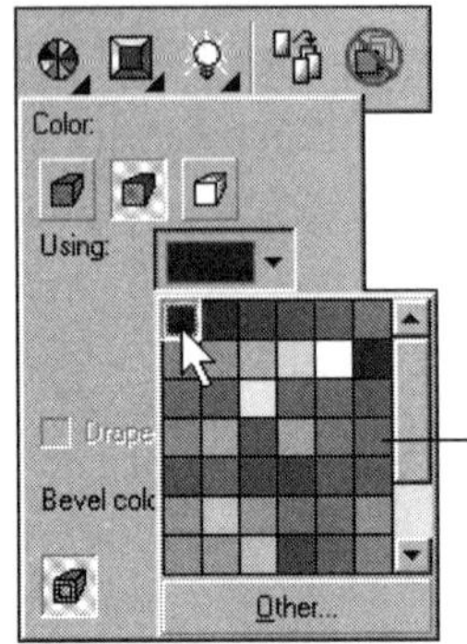

Figure 50. *The Using drop-down palette lets you select a solid color for the extrusion.*

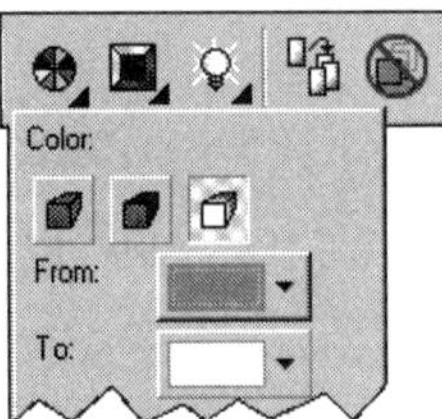

Figure 51. *When you click the Use Color Shading button, the drop-down box dynamically changes to display From and To drop-down palettes.*

Figure 52a. *Object Fill selected.*

Figure 52b. *Solid Color selected.*

Figure 52c. *Color Shading selected.*

Figure 53. *Select the extruded object with the Pick Tool.*

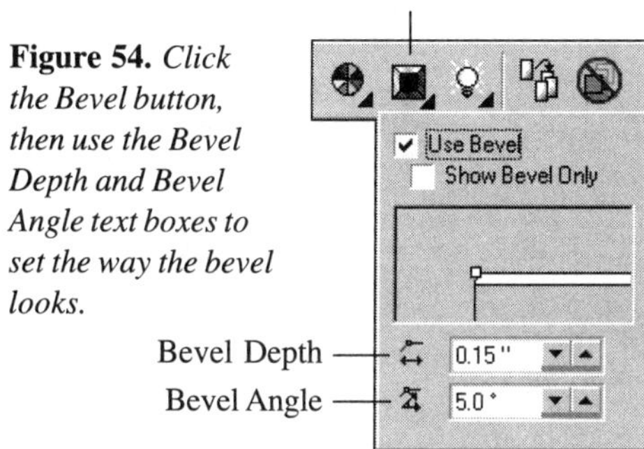

Figure 54. *Click the Bevel button, then use the Bevel Depth and Bevel Angle text boxes to set the way the bevel looks.*

Figure 55. *After you press Enter, the extruded object redraws with the bevel.*

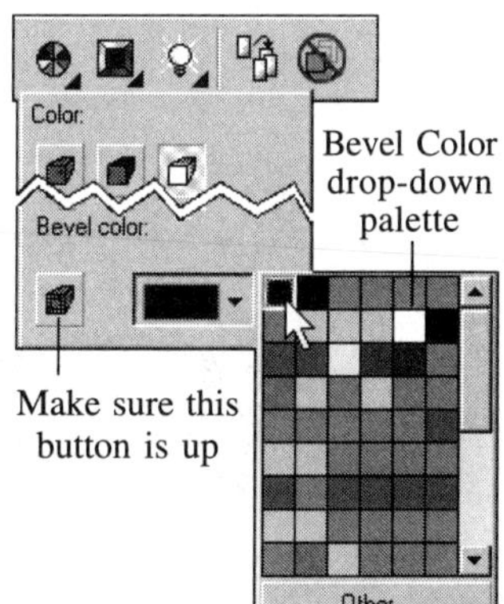

Figure 56. *Use the Bevel Color drop-down palette to set the bevel's color.*

To add pattern, fountain or bitmap fills, or textures to a vector extrusion:

1. Select the extruded object with the Interactive Fill Tool.
2. Use the Fill Type drop-down list on the Property bar to select the type of fill you want to use—Uniform, Fountain, Pattern, or Texture.
3. Depending on the type of fill you select, follow the directions for applying that fill as described on pages 142–151 in Chapter 10.

To add a bevel to a vector extrusion:

1. Select the extruded object with the Pick Tool (**Figure 53**).
2. Click the Bevel button on the Property Bar (**Figure 54**). The Bevel drop-down box will appear.
3. Put a check mark in the Use Bevel check box.
4. Type in the thickness of the bevel in the Bevel Depth text box.
5. Set the bevel angle using that text box.
6. Press Enter on the keyboard. The extruded object will assume the bevel you have set (**Figure 55**).
7. To set the bevel's color, click the Color button, make sure the Use Extrude Fill for Bevel button is *up* (not selected), and then use the Bevel Color drop-down palette to select a color (**Figure 56**).

To add lighting effects to a vector extrusion:

1. Select the extruded object with the Pick Tool (**Figure 57**).
2. Click the Lighting button near the right end of the Property Bar (**Figure 58**). The Lighting drop-down box will appear.
3. Click the little Lightbulb #1 button to turn that light on. A black dot with a "1" in the center will appear in the Preview Pane on the grid (**Figure 59**).
4. Position the mouse over the small black dot, press the left mouse button, and drag the dot to the position on the grid where you would like the light. As you make changes to the lighting, the extrusion will also change (**Figure 60**).
5. Use the Intensity slider bar to set how bright the light is.
6. If you want to add more lighting, click the other Lightbulb buttons and repeat steps 4–5.
7. When you are finished, press Enter on the keyboard to close the Lighting drop-down box.

Tip:

- If you want to export a vector extrusion after you are finished creating it, you will need to group it first. To find out how to group objects, turn to page 214.

Figure 57. *Select the extruded object with the Pick Tool.*

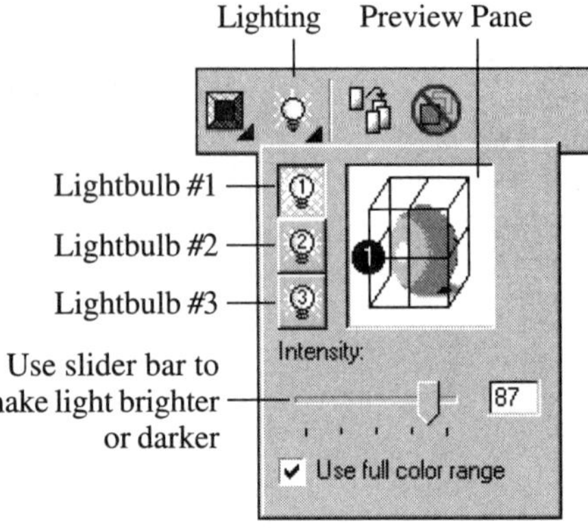

Figure 58. *The Lighting drop-down box lets you add lighting effects to a vector extrusion.*

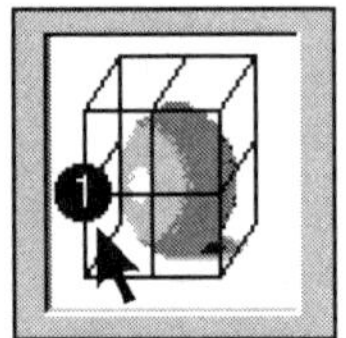

Figure 59. *Move the Lightbulb #1 dot to the position you need on the grid in the Preview Pane.*

Figure 60. *Lighting effects can really change how a vector extrusion looks.*

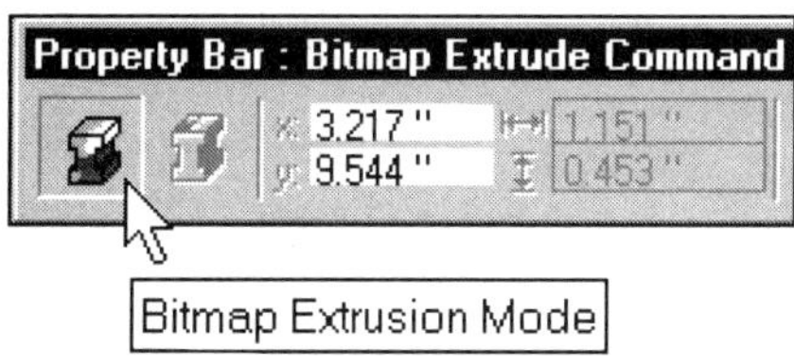

Figure 61. *Click the Bitmap Extrusion Mode button on the Property Bar.*

Figure 62. *The extrusion effect will become visible once a spot light is added.*

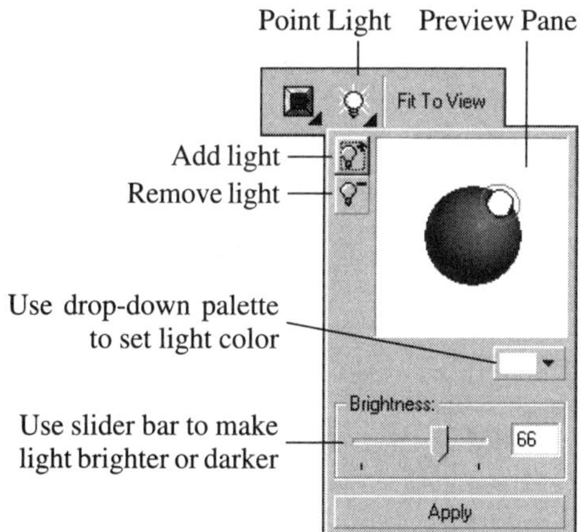

Figure 63. *Use the Point Light drop-down box to set up spot lighting effects.*

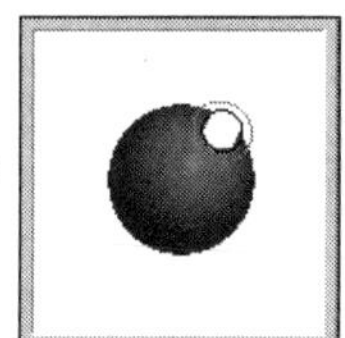

Figure 64. *Move the white dot with the mouse to set where the spot light is positioned.*

Figure 65. *The same bitmap extrusion shown in Figure 62 with a spot light added.*

To create a bitmap extrusion:

1. Select the Interactive Extrude Tool by opening the Interactive Tool fly-out and clicking the Interactive Extrude Tool button (**Figure 42**). An X will appear attached to the mouse pointer.
2. Click the Bitmap Extrusion Mode button at the left end of the Property Bar (**Figure 61**).
3. Double click on the object you want to extrude. The object will become extruded and look rather blob-like (**Figure 62**). To see the extrusion, you will need to add a spot light.

To add a spot light to a bitmap extrusion:

1. Select the bitmap extrusion with either the Pick or Interactive Extrude Tools.
2. Click the Point Light button to open the drop-down box (**Figure 63**).
3. Click the Add Light button. A white dot will appear over the dark circle in the Preview Pane (**Figure 64**).
4. Move the white dot to the position where you would like the light.
5. Click Apply. The spot light will be added to the extrusion (**Figure 65**).

Tip:

- You can add as many spot lights as you want.

To add a texture to a bitmap extrusion:

1. Select the bitmap extrusion with the Pick Tool (**Figure 66**).
2. Use the Texture drop-down list on the Property Bar to select a texture (**Figure 67**). The extrusion will redraw, displaying the texture (**Figure 68**).

Figure 66. *Select the extrusion with the Pick Tool.*

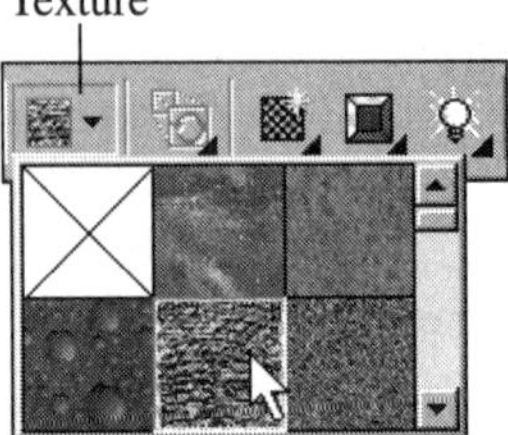

Figure 67. *Click the Texture button to select a texture from the drop-down list.*

Figure 68. *The bitmap extrusion redraws with the texture.*

To bevel a bitmap extrusion:

1. Select the bitmap extrusion with the Pick Tool (**Figure 69**).
2. Use the Front Bevel or Back Bevel drop-down boxes to select a bevel style (**Figure 70**).
3. To set the bevel width and angle, click the Bevels button on the Property Bar and use those text boxes (**Figure 71**). The bevel will appear on the object (**Figure 72**).

Figure 69. *Select the extrusion with the Pick Tool.*

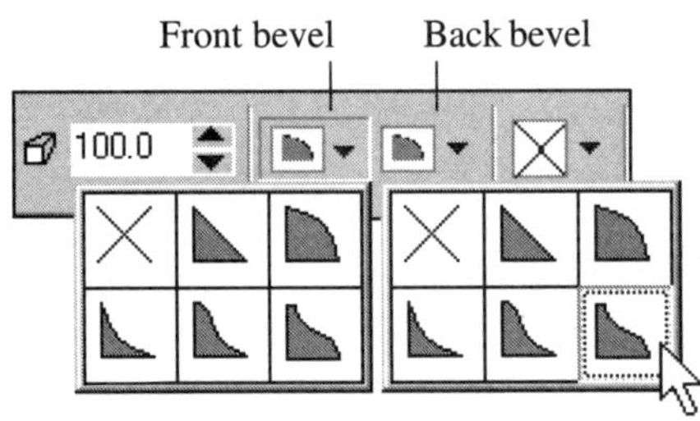

Figure 70. *Use the drop-down lists to select front and/or back bevels.*

Tips:

- Try several bevel styles; you'll be surprised at the different shapes.
- You won't be able to see the back bevel until the object is rotated.

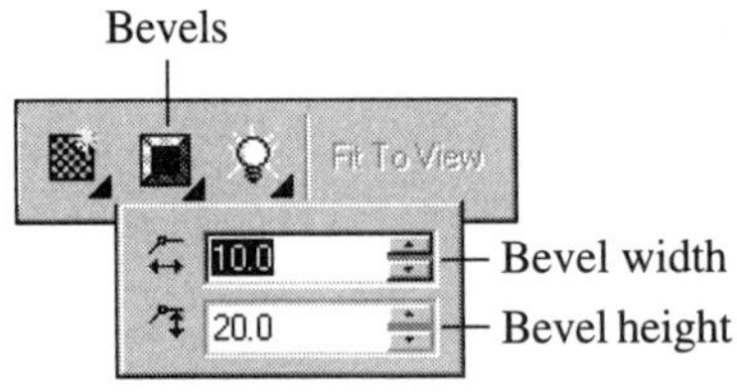

Figure 71. *Set the bevel's width and height using the text boxes on the Bevels drop-down box.*

Figure 72. *A bevel added to the bitmap extrusion.*

Figure 73. *Drag the mouse to rotate the vector extrusion.*

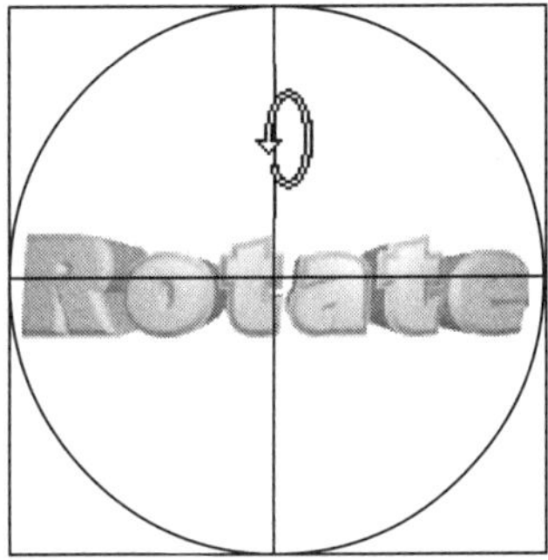

Figure 74. *Drag the mouse to rotate the bitmap extrusion.*

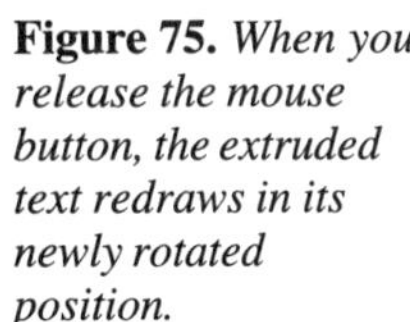
Figure 75. *When you release the mouse button, the extruded text redraws in its newly rotated position.*

Figure 76. *As you drag the mouse, the text rotates. When you deselect the object, you see the full effect of the rotation.*

To rotate a vector or bitmap extrusion:

1. Select the vector or bitmap extrusion with the Interactive Extrude Tool.
2. Double-click on the extrusion. If you are rotating a vector extrusion, a green dashed circle with triangular handles will appear on the object and the mouse pointer will change to two swirling arrows (**Figure 73**). If you are rotating a bitmap extrusion, a circle with north/south lines surrounded by a rectangle will appear on the object and the mouse pointer will change to a swirling arrow (**Figure 74**)
3. To rotate a vector extrusion:
   - **a.** Position the mouse pointer over the dashed circle, press the left mouse button, and drag to rotate the text.
   - **b.** Release the mouse button when you finish the rotation (**Figure 75**).

   To rotate a bitmap extrusion:
   - **a.** Position the mouse pointer over either the circle, or north or south lines, press the left mouse button, and drag to rotate.
   - **b.** Release the mouse button when you finish the rotation (**Figure 76**).

To modify character shape:

1. Create some artistic text and select a favorite font. (Figure 77 uses the font OzHandicraft BT.)
2. Select the text object with the Pick Tool (**Figure 77**).
3. Convert the text to curves by pressing Ctrl+Q on the keyboard or choosing Convert To Curves from the Arrange menu (**Figure 78**).
4. Select the Shape Tool. Many, many nodes will appear around the text (**Figure 79**).

> **CONVERTING TEXT TO CURVES**
>
> Once text has been converted to curves, you can no longer edit it using the Text Tool. The reason for this is that CorelDraw 9 “sees” text converted to curves only as closed path shapes—it does not recognize the shapes as text anymore.

> **WORKING WITH CURVES**
>
> When text is converted to curves, it is like any other object that is made up of curves. It has nodes and can be modified with the Shape Tool. For detailed information about nodes and working with curves, take a look at Chapter 6, *Nodes and Paths.*

Figure 77. *Select the text object with the Pick Tool.*

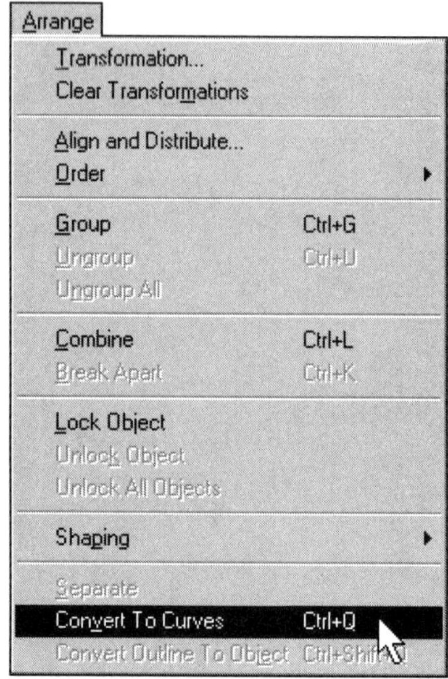

Figure 78. *Choose Convert To Curves from the Arrange menu.*

Figure 79. *When the text is selected with the Shape Tool after it has been converted to curves, many nodes appear around the perimeter of each letter.*

Figure 80. *Use the Shape Tool to marquee select all the nodes.*

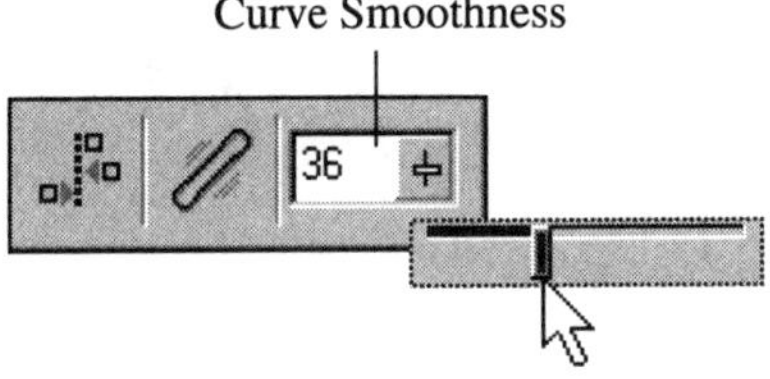

Figure 81. *Use the Curve Smoothness slider bar to reduce the number of nodes. The higher the number, the smoother (fewer nodes) the curve.*

Figure 82. *After you use the Curve Smoothness slider bar, the text shapes redraw with fewer nodes.*

Figure 83. *Use the Shape Tool to drag the nodes, just as you would with any object.*

5. Move the mouse to the left and above the text, press the left mouse button, and drag a marquee to select all the nodes (**Figure 80**).
6. Move the Curve Smoothness slider bar to the right. This slider bar is found at the right end of the Property Bar (**Figure 81**). This will remove a few of the nodes, making the curves easier to work with (**Figure 82**).
7. Click the mouse anywhere outside the text to deselect the nodes.
8. Position the Shape Tool over a node where you would like to alter the shape of the text.
9. Press the left mouse button and drag the node, just as you would reshape any curve (**Figure 83**).
10. Continue moving nodes until the shape of the characters is what you want (**Figure 84**).

Tip:

- If you create an effect you don't like, you can always go undo it by pressing Ctrl+Z on the keyboard. CorelDraw will undo up to the last 99 actions you have performed.

Figure 84. *Continue dragging nodes until you achieve the effect you want.*

Special Project:

The Neon Effect

neon

Figure 85. *Create some artistic text in a favorite font.*

Highlighting text with a bright neon effect is a great way to get attention. All the effect consists of are different color outlines blended together.

To create the neon effect:

1. Create some artistic text and change it to a favorite font in a large point size (**Figure 85**). (Figure 85 uses Brush 738 BT.)
2. Change the text's fill color to red by left mouse clicking on that color well in the Color Palette.
3. Select the text with the Pick Tool and convert it to curves by pressing Ctrl+Q on the keyboard or choosing Convert To Curves from the Arrange menu (**Figure 78**).
4. Click on the Outline Pen Dialog button on the Outline Tool fly-out menu (**Figure 86**). The Outline Pen dialog box will open (**Figure 87**).
5. Use the drop-down list next to Color to change the outline color to red, and change the Width to 0.05 inches (1.25 millimeters).
6. Move down the dialog box to the Corners area and select the rounded corner option, and in the Line caps area select rounded caps (**Figure 88**).
7. Put a check mark in the Scale with image box, then click OK.

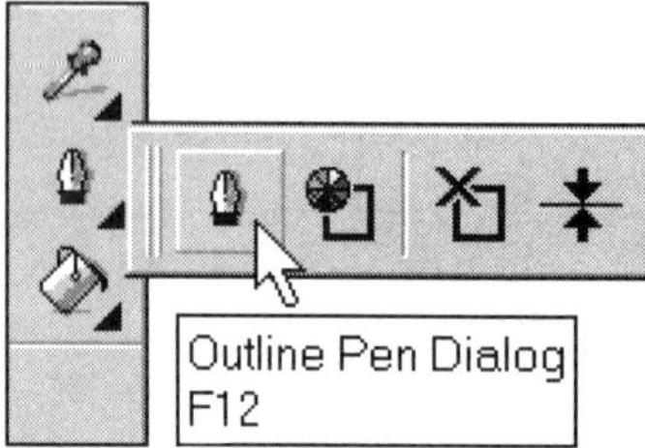

Figure 86. *Click the Outline Pen Dialog button on the Outline Tool fly-out menu.*

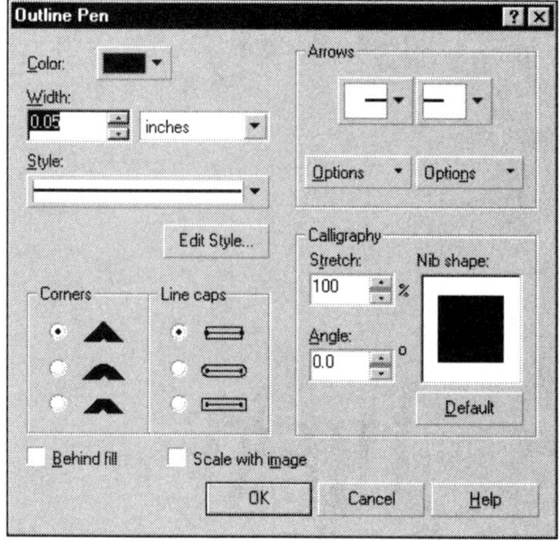

Figure 87. *Use the Outline Pen dialog box to set the outline color, width, corners, and end caps.*

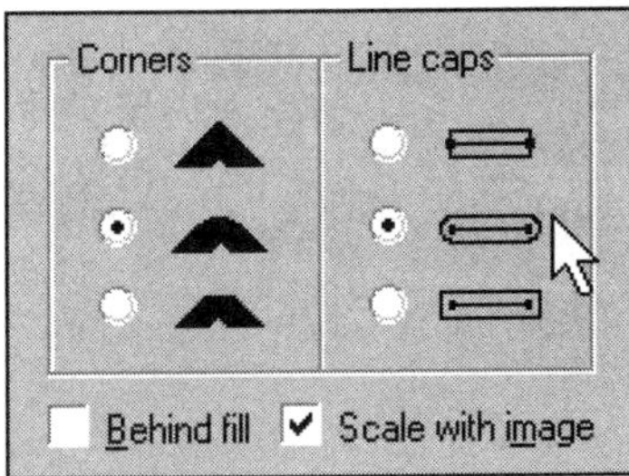

Figure 88. *Click the rounded corners and rounded caps option buttons, then put a check mark in the box next to Scale with image.*

Figure 89. *Click the color well with the X in it to remove the fill from the duplicate.*

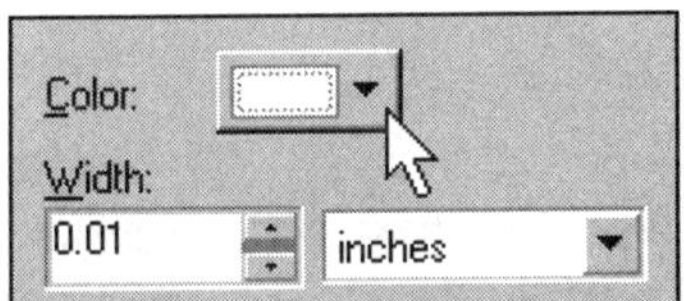

Figure 90. *In the Outline Pen dialog box, use the drop-down list to change the Color to white, then change the Width setting to 0.01 inches.*

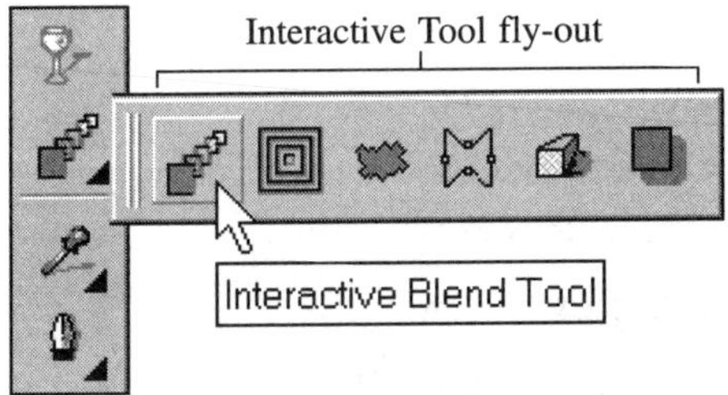

Figure 91. *Select the Interactive Blend Tool from the Interactive Tool fly-out.*

8. Choose Options from the Tools menu or press Ctrl+J on the keyboard to open the Options dialog box (**Figure 17**).
9. Click Edit in the Tree View window.
10. On the Edit panel in the Duplicate placement area, change both the Horizontal and Vertical settings to 0, then click OK (**Figure 18**).
11. With the text object selected, press Ctrl+D on the keyboard or choose Duplicate from the Edit menu. A duplicate of the text object will appear selected directly on top of the original.
12. On the Color Palette, left mouse click the color well with the X in it to remove the fill color from the duplicate (**Figure 89**).
13. Open the Outline Pen dialog box again by clicking the Outline Tool to open the fly-out menu and clicking the Outline Pen Dialog button.
14. Use the drop-down list next to Color to change the outline color to white (**Figure 90**).
15. Change the Width setting to 0.01 inches (0.25 millimeters), then click OK.
16. Select the Interactive Blend Tool from the Interactive Tool fly-out (**Figure 91**).

(continued)

17. Double click on the text objects to select both of them. The Status Bar will read: 2 Objects Selected on Layer 1.
18. Position the mouse pointer at the center of the text objects.
19. Press the left mouse button and drag to the right about 1" (2.5 centimeters) (**Figure 92**).
20. Release the mouse button. The outlines of the text objects will blend together, creating the neon effect (**Figure 93**).

Figure 92. *Drag the mouse to the right just a little way.*

Figure 93. *When you release the mouse button, the two text objects blend together, creating the neon effect.*

Tip:

- You can apply the same techniques to lines and other objects such as the rectangle surrounding the summary box below.

SUMMARY

In this chapter you learned how to:

- Skew and rotate text
- Use the Free Transform Tool
- Fit text to a path
- Use the Interactive Drop Shadow and Extrude Tools
- Create vector extrusions
- Add color, bevels, and lighting effects to vector extrusions
- Create bitmap extrusions
- Add textures, bevels, and spot lighting to bitmap extrusions
- Rotate extrusions
- Give text a neon effect

Layers

When two objects are drawn, CorelDraw 9 automatically *stacks* the second object on the first. When a third object is drawn, it is stacked on the second, and so on. This positioning is called the *stacking order*. If the objects do not overlap, the stacking order isn't apparent (**Figure 1**). But, if they do overlap, it's easy to see (**Figure 2**).

You've probably noticed the Status Bar displaying messages such as "Rectangle on Layer 1." By default, CorelDraw 9 places all objects on one *layer*. Layers are invisible planes that stack vertically, one on top of the other (**Figure 3**). Layers help keep a drawing's distinct elements separate. You can add as many layers as you need to a project.

Figure 1. *When objects don't overlap, the stacking order is not apparent.*

Figure 2. *As soon as the objects overlap, the stacking order is easy to see.*

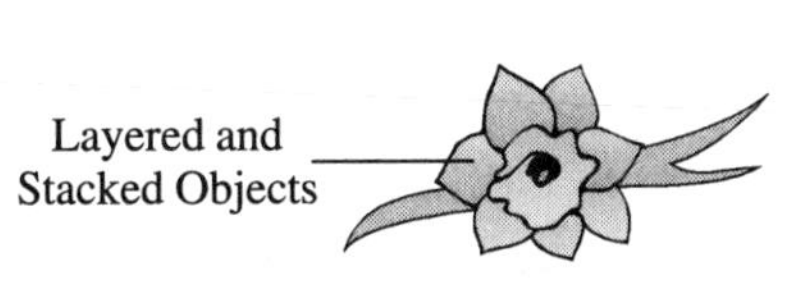

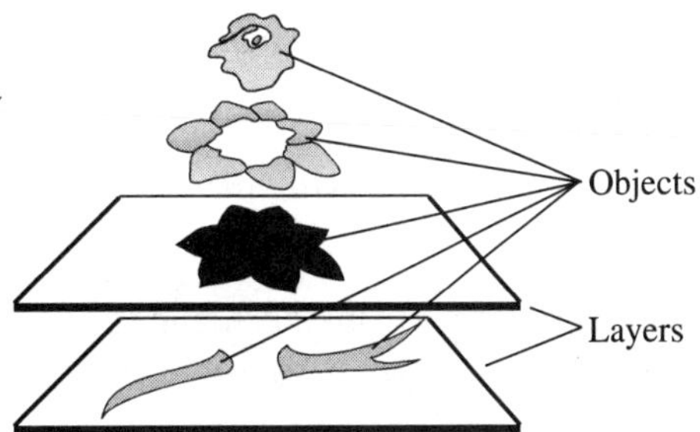

Figure 3. *Objects are drawn on layers and are positioned vertically in a stacking order. Layers are stacked, also, in their own stacking order.*

It's easy to manipulate the stacking order of objects using the Order commands on the Arrange menu (**Figure 4**).

To bring an object to the front:

1. Select the object using the Pick Tool (**Figure 5**).
2. Press Shift PageUp on the keyboard or choose Order on the Arrange menu to open the fly-out, then select To Front. The object will move to the front (**Figure 6**).

To position an object in front of a specific object:

1. Select the object you want to position using the Pick Tool (**Figure 7**).
2. On the Arrange menu, choose Order to open the fly-out, then click In Front Of. The mouse pointer will change to a large black, right-facing arrow.
3. Position the black arrow over the object you want to place the selected one in front of and click. The selected object will move in front of the clicked object (**Figure 8**).

To bring an object forward one object:

1. Select the object using the Pick Tool.
2. Choose Order from the Arrange menu, then select Forward One on the fly-out menu.

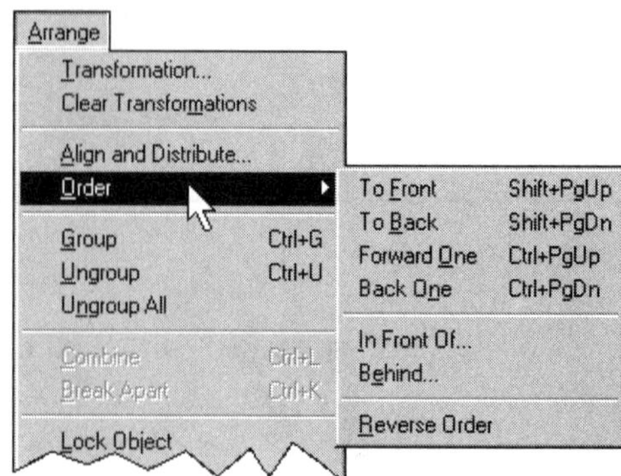

Figure 4. *Use the Order fly-out on the Arrange menu to change the stacking order of objects.*

Figure 5. *Select the object.*

Figure 6. *When you select To Front, the object moves to the front of the stack.*

Figure 7. *Select the object you want to position.*

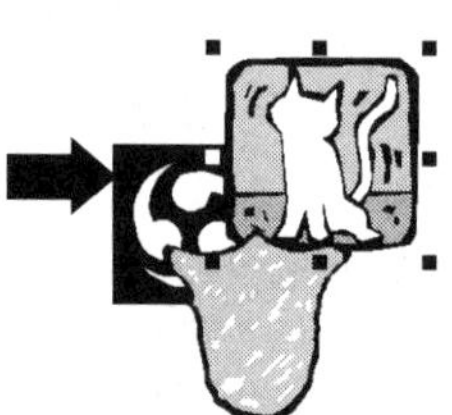

Figure 8. *The selected object moves in front of the object you click with the black arrow.*

Figure 9. *Select the object you want to send to the back.*

To move an object behind all objects:

1. Select the object using the Pick Tool (**Figure 9**).
2. Press Shift PageDown on the keyboard or choose Order from the Arrange menu, then choose To Back on the fly-out. The object will move to the back (**Figure 10**).

Figure 10. *When you select To Back, the object moves to the back of the stack.*

To position an object behind a specific object:

1. Select the object you want to position with the Pick Tool (**Figure 11**).
2. Choose Order from the Arrange menu, then select Behind from the fly-out. The mouse pointer will change to a large black, right-facing arrow.
3. Place the black arrow over the object you want to place the selected one behind and click. The selected object will move behind the clicked one (**Figure 12**).

Figure 11. *Select the object you want to position.*

To move an object back one object:

1. Select the object using the Pick Tool.
2. Choose Order from the Arrange menu, then select Back One on the fly-out.

Figure 12. *The selected object moves behind the object you click with the black arrow.*

Using the Object Manager docker, you can create individual layers to work on (**Figure 13**). The settings for a layer determine whether it can be seen, printed, or drawn on, and whether it is a *master layer*. A master layer is used for multiple page documents, where you want the same graphics to appear in the same place on each page. For instance, if you were designing a company newsletter, you could place the company logo on every page automatically by placing the logo on a master layer.

You can create as many layers as you want, and you can change the stacking order of the layers using the Object Manager docker.

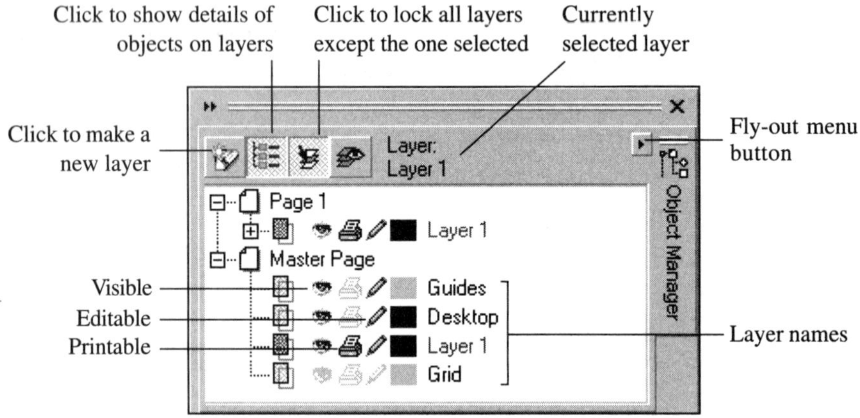

Figure 13. *The Object Manager docker.*

To open the Object Manager docker:

Choose Object Manager from the Dockers fly-out on the Window menu (**Figure 14**).

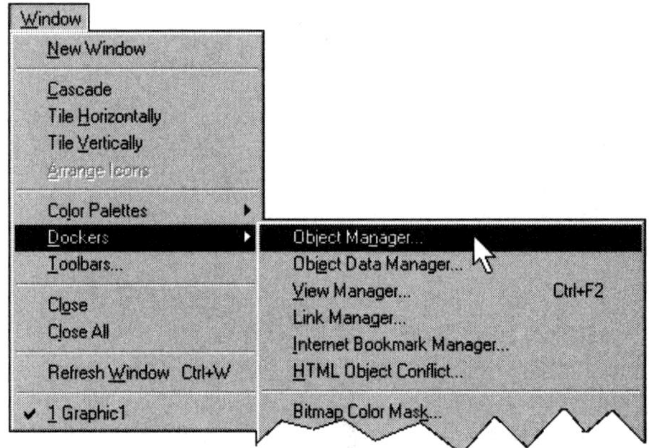

Figure 14. *Choose Object Manager from the Dockers fly-out on the Window menu.*

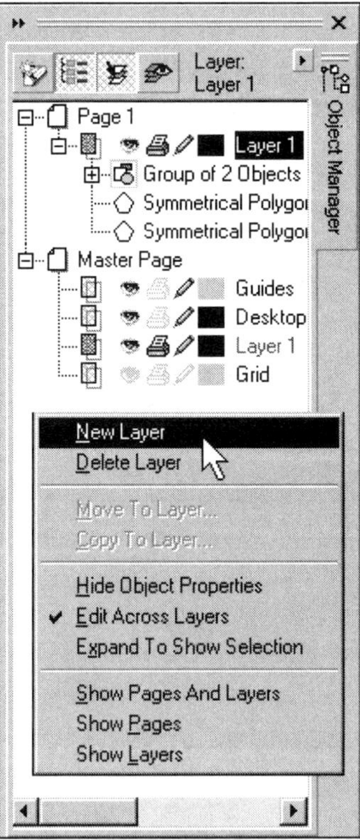

Figure 15. *Right click on a blank area of the docker and select New Layer from the pop-up menu.*

To create a new layer:

1. Right click on a blank area of the Object Manager docker then select New Layer from the pop-up menu (**Figure 15**) or click the New Layer button at the top left of the docker (**Figure 13**). The new layer will appear above the topmost layer in the Object Manager docker (**Figure 16**).
2. Type a name for the layer.
3. Press Enter on the keyboard.

To change the current layer:

Click the name of the layer you want to make current. The layer name will become highlighted (**Figure 17**). The name of the selected layer will appear at the top of the Object Manager docker after "Layer." Any objects you create will be added to that layer.

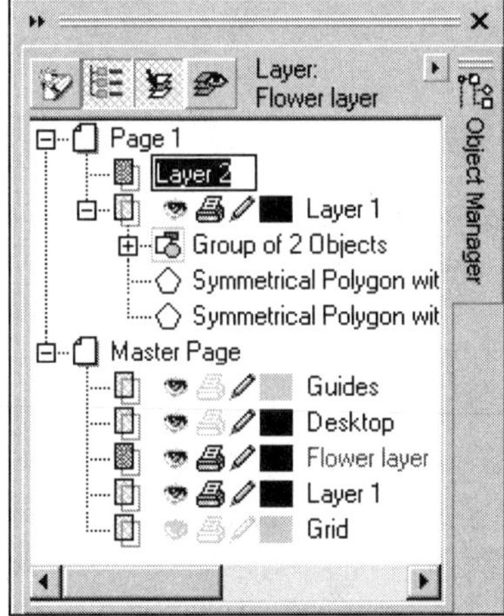

Figure 16. *The new layer appears above the topmost layer.*

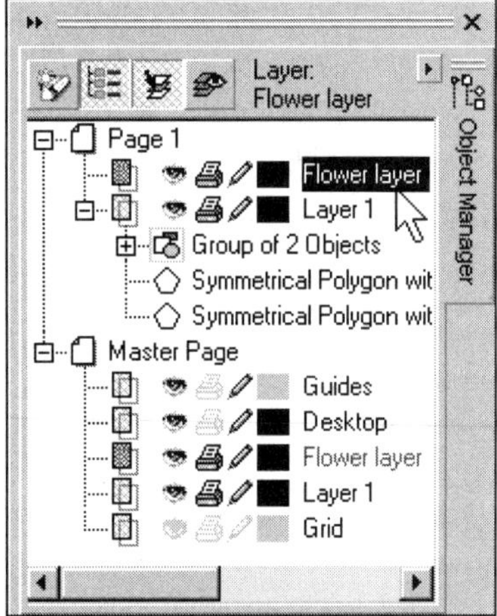

Figure 17. *When you click a layer's name, it becomes the current layer.*

To change a layer's settings:

1. Select the layer you want to change by clicking on it (**Figure 18**).
2. Right click on the layer's name. A pop-up menu will appear (**Figure 19**).
3. Select the setting you want to change from the pop-up menu. A check mark in front of a setting means that it is selected.
4. Click OK.

or

Click the appropriate icon to the left of the layer whose settings you want to change (**Figure 20**). If the icon is grayed out, then that setting is turned off.

Tips:

- Notice that there are Grid and Guides layers. The default color for these layers is blue. If you want grids or guidelines to appear in another color, such as red or black, double click on the colored rectangle. A color drop-down list will appear letting you select a new color.
- If you finish with a layer and do not want to inadvertently move any objects on that layer, click on the pencil icon to make the layer uneditable.

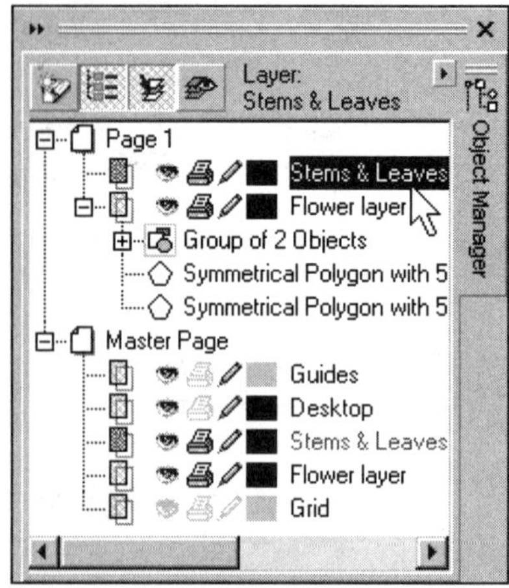

Figure 18. *Select the layer whose settings you want to change.*

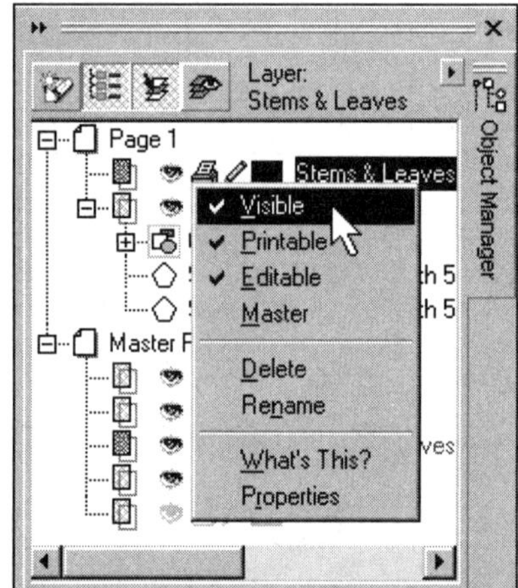

Figure 19. *Select the setting you want to change from the pop-up menu.*

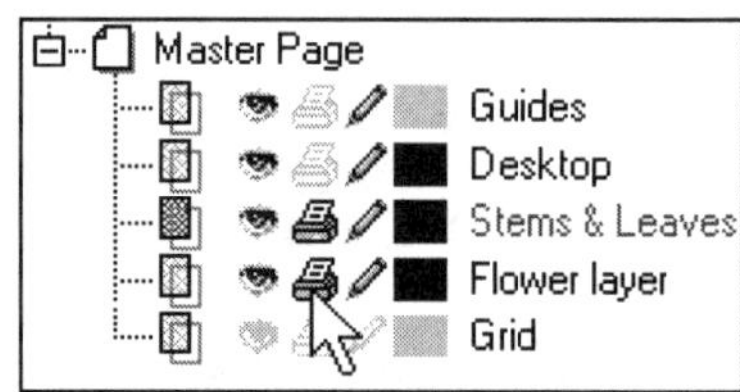

Figure 20. *Click the appropriate icon to change the setting.*

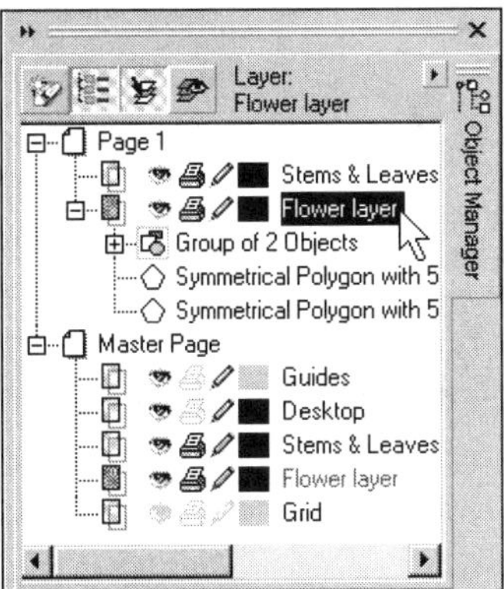

Figure 21. *Position the mouse over the layer you want to move.*

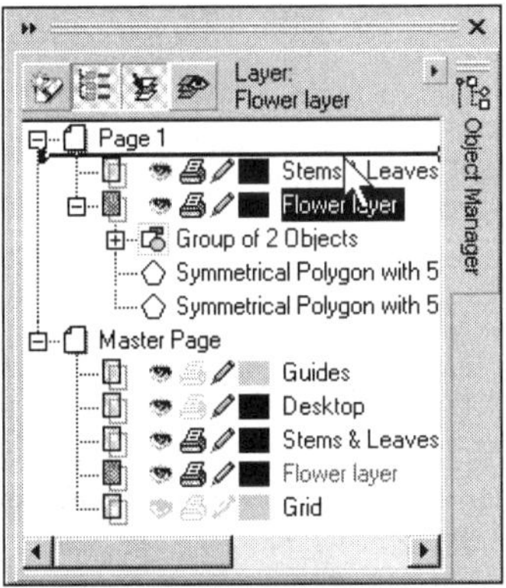

Figure 22. *A black bar appears as you drag, indicating the layer's possible new position.*

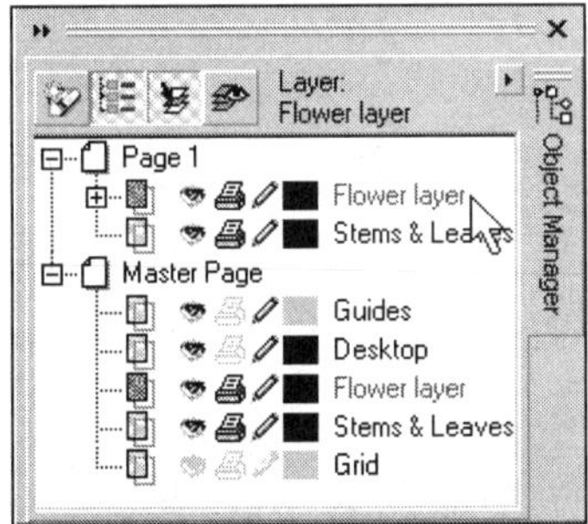

Figure 23. *When you release the mouse button, the layer moves to its new position.*

To reorder layers:

1. Position the mouse pointer over the layer you want to move (**Figure 21**).
2. Press the left mouse button and drag it up or down the list. A black bar will appear as you drag, indicating the layer's possible position (**Figure 22**).
3. Release the mouse when the bar is where you want to place the layer. The layer will move to that position and become the current layer (**Figure 23**).

Using Layers to Create Plans

Layers can be very helpful when creating technical plans for items such as buildings, gardens, and cars. For instance, when creating a plan for a house, you could create plumbing, electrical, and framing layers. Drawings of pipes would be placed on the plumbing layer, wiring diagrams would be placed on the electrical layer, and window layouts would be placed on the framing layer.

When it came time to print the plans, you could print one sheet that contained all the layers and print separate pages, one for each layer. That way, you could hand each contractor a page for her particular specialty.

To move or copy an object to a different layer:

1. Select the object (or objects) with the Pick Tool (**Figure 24**). The object you select will appear highlighted in the Object Manager docker.
2. Position the mouse over the selected object(s) in the Object Manager docker, and then press the left mouse button and drag the objects onto the name of the layer where you want to move them (**Figure 25**).
3. Release the mouse button. The objects will move to the new layer (**Figure 26**).

Tip:

- Watch the Status Bar—it will always tell you what layer a selected object is on.

To delete a layer:

Select the layer with the Pick Tool then right mouse click. A pop-up menu will appear (**Figure 27**). Choose Delete.

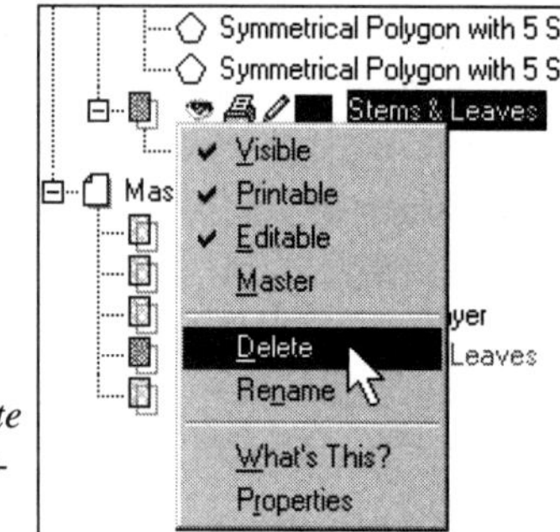

Figure 27. *Choose Delete from the pop-up menu.*

Figure 24. *Select the object you want to move to another layer. In this example, the leaf is selected.*

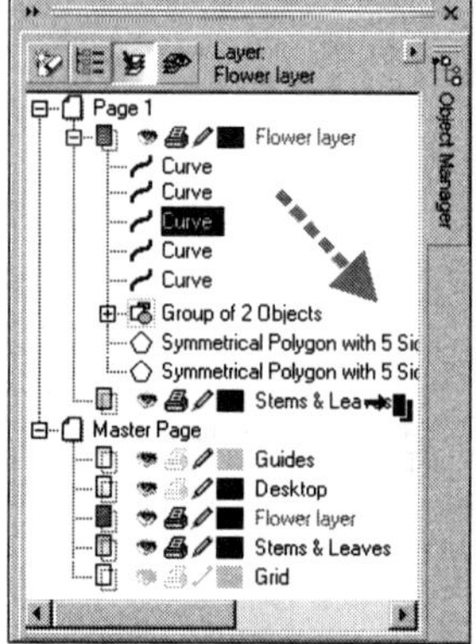

Figure 25. *When you drag the object onto a layer's name, the mouse pointer changes to a horizontal arrow with attached pages.*

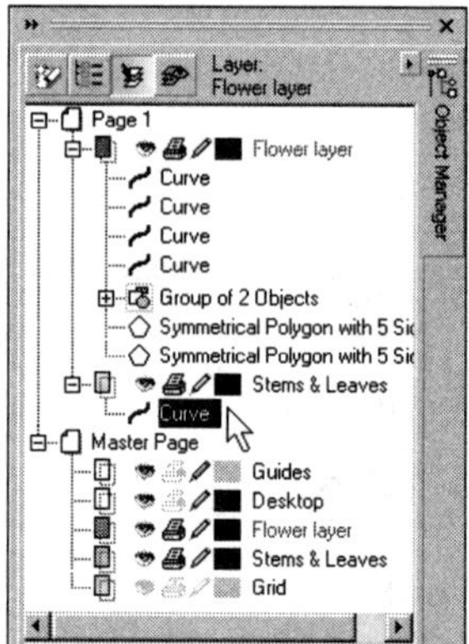

Figure 26. *The object moves to the new layer when the mouse button is released.*

Figure 28. *Add horizontal and vertical guidelines to mark the page margins.*

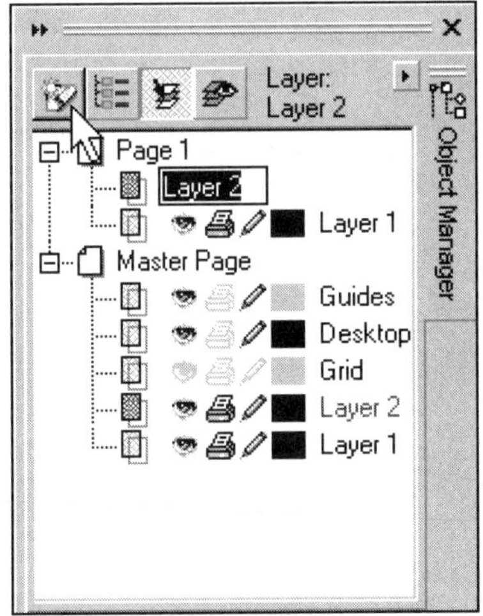

Figure 29. *Click the New Layer button to create a new layer.*

Special Project:

Set Up a Newsletter with Logo

Creating a master layer makes all the difference when you set out to create a document that will use the same graphics on every page.

To set up a newsletter:

1. Start a new document by pressing Ctrl+N on the keyboard or choosing New from the File menu (see page 25).
2. Add three horizontal guidelines to the page to mark the page margins, placing the first 0.5 inch down from the top, the next 2 inches from the top, and the third 1 inch from the bottom. Then add two vertical guidelines for the right and left margins, positioning each one 0.5 inch from the edge of the page (**Figure 28**).
3. Open the Object Manager docker by choosing Object Manager from the Layout menu.
4. Add a new layer to the project by clicking the New Layer button at the upper left of the Object Manager docker window (**Figure 29**).
5. Enter a name for the new layer, if you wish, then press Enter on the keyboard. The default name you will see is Layer 2.

6. Right click on the new layer's name. A pop-up menu will appear.
7. Select Master from the pop-up menu (**Figure 30**). Notice that the Current Layer is the new layer. (In Figure 30 it is named Layer 2.) This means that any objects you add will go onto the master layer.
8. Add a logo to the upper-left corner of the page above the guideline that is 2 inches from the top of the page (**Figure 31**). This example uses a piece of clipart, a finch, from CorelDraw 9 CD-ROM #2. If you want to use it, the finch is located under Clipart\Birds\Songbrds\Finch2.Cdr.
9. Draw a straight line, using the Freehand Tool, along the horizontal guideline below the logo (see page 88).
10. Draw another horizontal line at the bottom of the page where the vertical guidelines intersect with the horizontal guideline.
11. Use the Text Tool to type the date. Center that text below the lower horizontal line. At this point, your page should look something like the one in **Figure 32**.

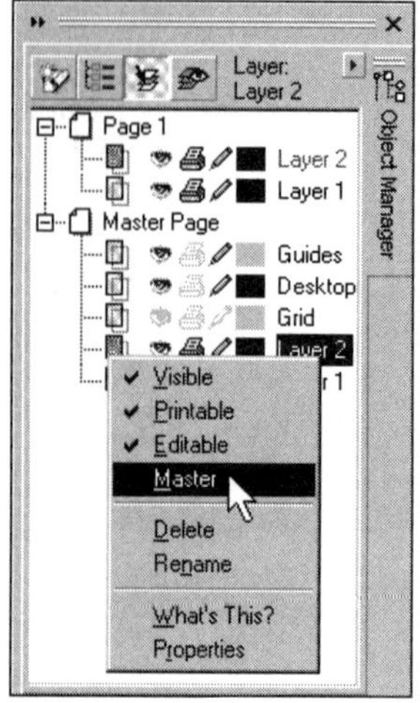

Figure 30. *Select Master from the pop-up menu to make the new layer a master layer.*

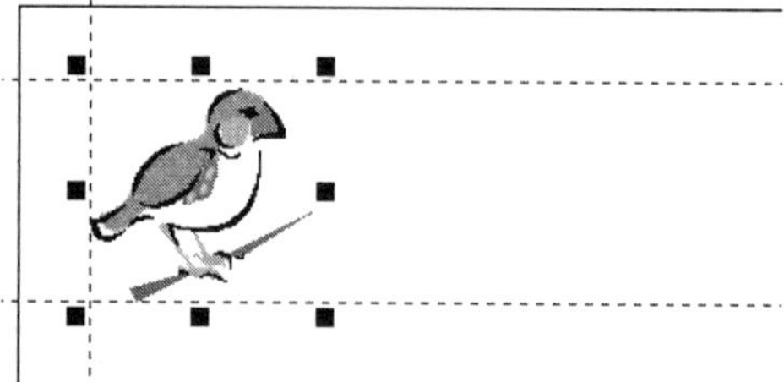

Figure 31. *Add a logo to the upper-left corner of the page between the two horizontal guidelines.*

Figure 32. *The full page with all the items needed on the master layer.*

Special Project: Set Up a Newsletter

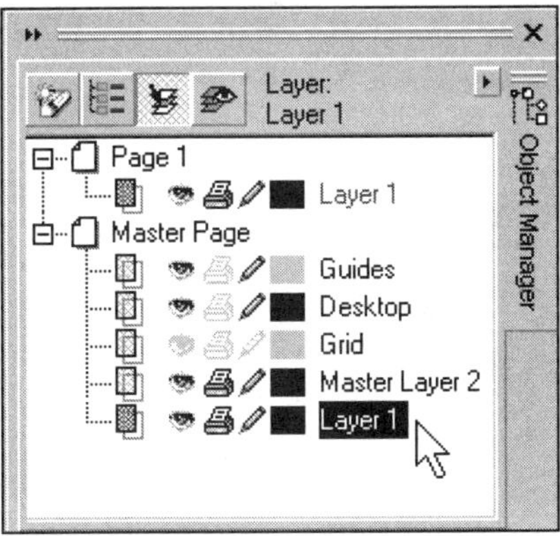

Figure 33. *Click Layer 1 to make that layer the Current Layer. Any objects added after this change will be placed on Layer 1.*

Figure 34. *Use the Text Tool to add a title next to the logo.*

Figure 35. *Use the Text Tool to drag a paragraph text frame from one vertical guideline to the other.*

12. In the Object Manager docker, click Layer 1 to make it the Current Layer (**Figure 33**). Any object you add from now on will be added to Layer 1.
13. Move back to the top of the page and create a title for the newsletter with the Text Tool. Use a favorite font and size the text to fit the space next to the logo (**Figure 34**).
14. Add a page to the document (see page 115). Notice that the document moves to that page and that the finch, the two horizontal lines, and the date are visible on the page, but the newsletter title is not present.
15. Move back to page 1 (see page 117).
16. Select the Text Tool and drag a paragraph frame that is the width of the page from vertical guideline to vertical guideline (**Figure 35**).
17. Open the Format Text dialog box by choosing Format Text from the Text menu or pressing Ctrl+T on the keyboard.

18. Click the Frames and Columns tab to move to that tab page (**Figure 36**).

19. Change the Number of columns to 3 and set the Gutter width to 0.5 inch. Click the option button next to Maintain current frame width, then click OK. Three columns with 0.5 inch gutters will appear within the paragraph text frame (**Figure 37**).

20. Type your newsletter text and add a drop cap to the first paragraph, if you desire (see page 176). Use the paragraph frame's text flow tab to flow text onto page 2 (see page 170 for directions on how to make paragraph text flow from one frame to the next).

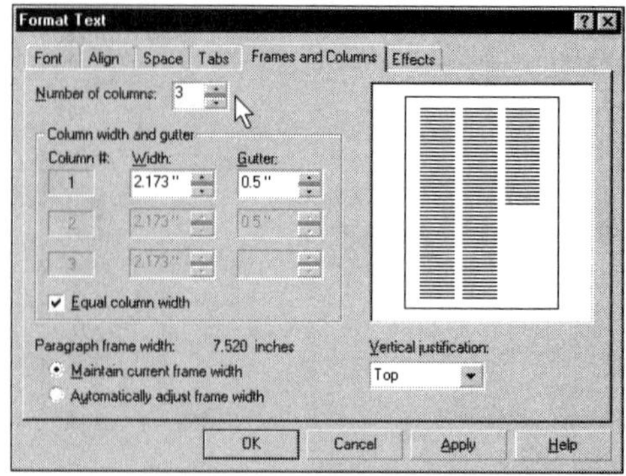

Figure 36. *Use the Frames and Columns tab page to set up three columns for your newsletter text.*

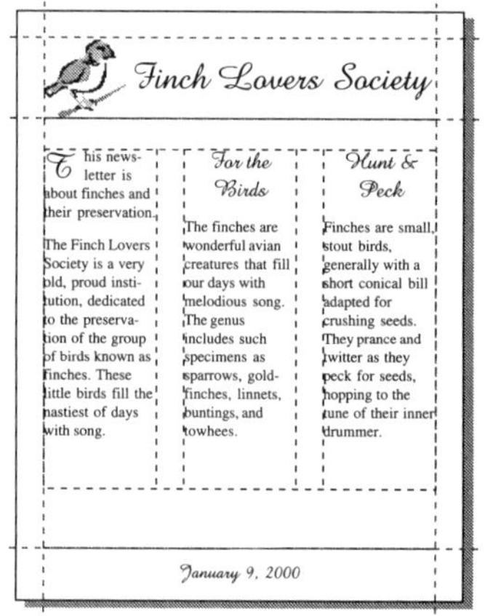

Figure 37. *As you type the newsletter text, it will flow from column to column.*

Tip:

- You can add many elements to a newsletter such as dividing lines between columns, page numbers, and pictures to accompany articles.

SUMMARY

In this chapter you learned how to:

- Bring objects to the front
- Bring an object forward one
- Send objects to the back
- Send an object back one
- Create layers
- Change layer settings
- Create a master layer
- Set up a newsletter

Transformations

It's amazing what you can do with a few clicks of the mouse. The transformation commands—group, combine, rotate, mirror, scale, weld, and blend—are among the most powerful and easy to use tools in CorelDraw 9.

In this chapter you will learn how to group and lock objects, weld objects together, and use the Combine command to create cut-outs. Next, you will discover the Transform docker and use it to change an object's size and flip an object vertically and horizontally. From there, the chapter will move on to rotating and cloning objects, and then finish with a special project that shows you how to create the "woodcut" effect.

Changing More than One Object at a Time

Any of the transformations discussed in this chapter, such as grouping, rotating, sizing, mirroring, etc., can be performed on more than one object or group of objects at a time. Just select the objects you want to change and follow the steps outlined in this chapter.

Also, remember that text is an object, too. So, you can transform objects that contain shapes such as circles and triangles, as well as text objects.

Grouping objects binds them together so they can be manipulated as a unit. For instance, if you want to move several objects yet keep them in the same positions relative to each other, you would group the objects, then move them as a unit. Another use for grouping is formatting. Any type of formatting applied to grouped objects will effect all the objects in the group. For example, you could add a blue fill to all the objects in a group just by selecting the group, then clicking the blue color well on the Color Palette.

Figure 1. *Marquee select the objects you want to group.*

To group objects:

1. Select the objects with the Pick Tool by either holding down the Shift key while clicking on the objects or pressing the left mouse button down to drag a marquee (**Figure 1**).
2. Choose Group from the Arrange menu (**Figure 2**) or press Ctrl+G on the keyboard. The next time you select the grouped objects, you'll notice that the eight black handles appear around the group.

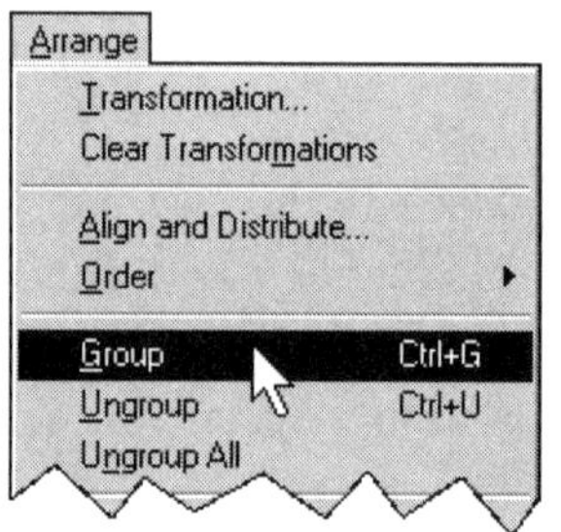

Figure 2. *Select Group from the Arrange menu.*

To ungroup objects:

1. Select the grouped objects with the Pick Tool.
2. Choose Ungroup from the Arrange menu (**Figure 3**) or press Ctrl+U on the keyboard.

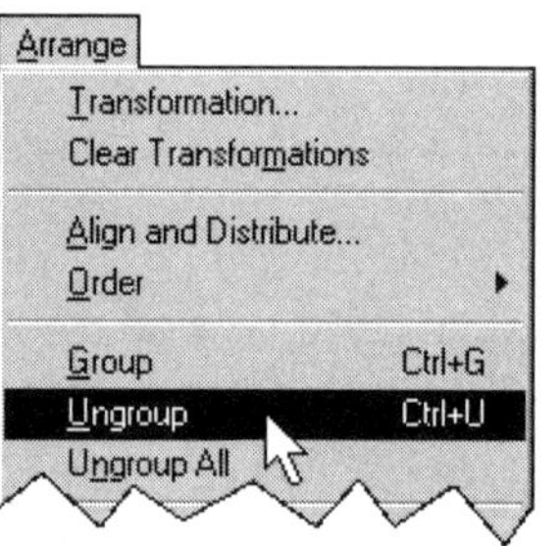

Figure 3. *Select Ungroup from the Arrange menu.*

To ungroup all objects on a page:

Choose Ungroup All from the Arrange menu (**Figure 4**).

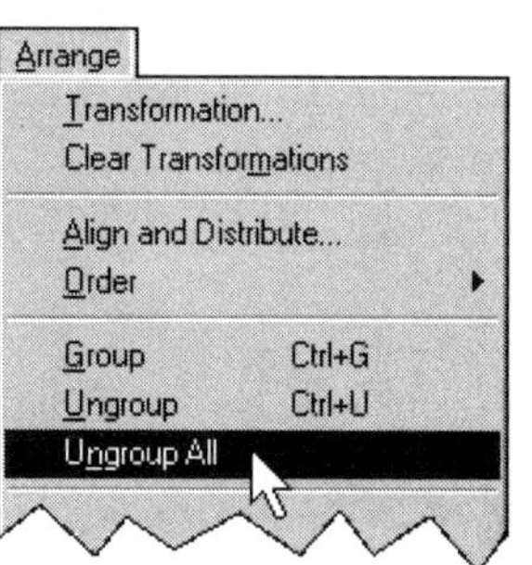

Figure 4. *Choose Ungroup All from the Arrange menu.*

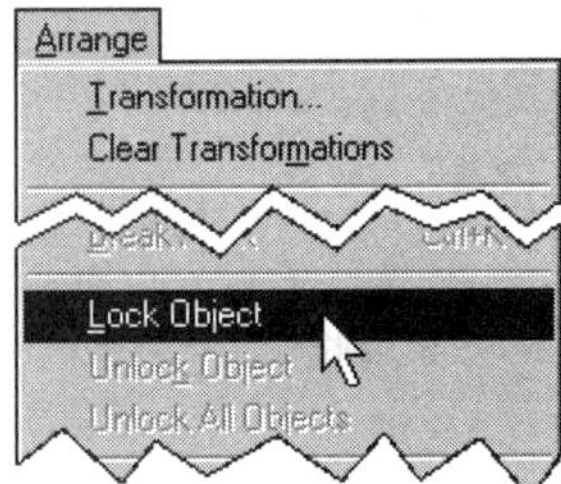

Figure 5. *Choose Lock Object from the Arrange menu.*

Locking objects sets them on the page so they cannot be selected, moved, or altered in any way. This feature is very handy when working with several layered objects. The objects that you have finished with or don't want to select by mistake can be locked down, leaving the other objects available for selection and manipulation.

Figure 6. *When the object is locked, its handles change to tiny padlocks.*

To lock objects:

1. Select the object(s) that you want to lock down with the Pick Tool.
2. Choose Lock Object from the Arrange menu (**Figure 5**). The handles of the object(s) will change to little padlocks (**Figure 6**).

Tips:

- You can lock every type of object in CorelDraw, including a single object, several selected objects, a group or set of groups.
- If you want to modify a locked object, you will need to unlock it first.

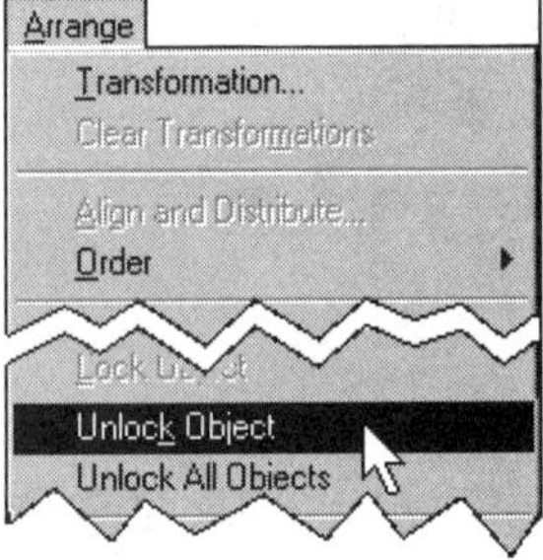

Figure 7. *Choose Unlock Object from the Arrange menu.*

To unlock an object:

1. Select the locked object with the Pick Tool.
2. Choose Unlock Object from the Arrange menu (**Figure 7**).

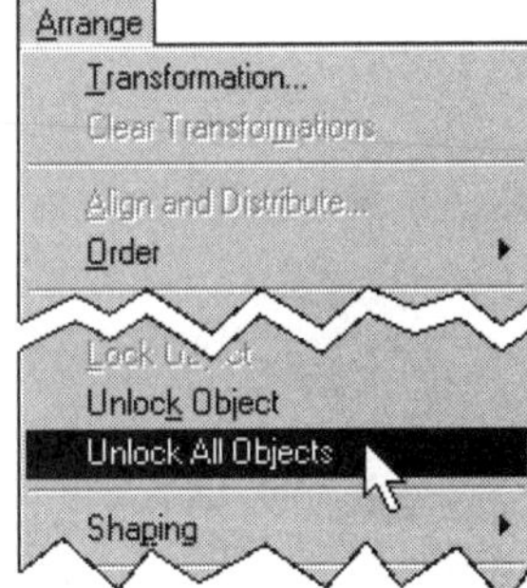

Figure 8. *Choose Unlock All Objects from the Arrange menu.*

To unlock all objects on a page:

Choose Unlock All Objects from the Arrange menu (**Figure 8**).

Chapter 12 showed you how to use the rotation handles and the Free Transform Tool to rotate a text object (see page 180). You can use the same techniques on any object or group of objects. CorelDraw 9 also provides a Transformation docker (**Figure 9**) for precision.

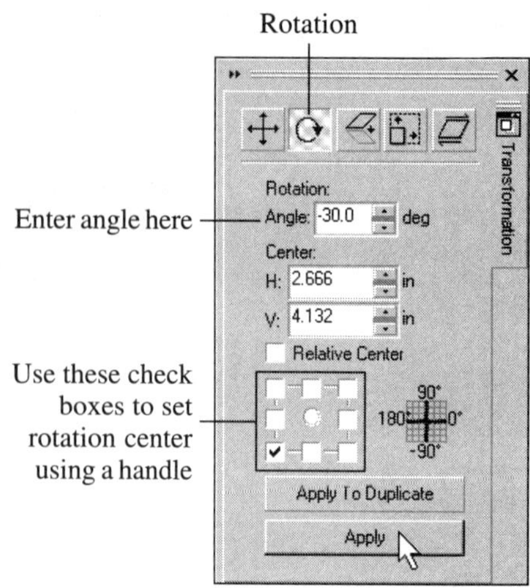

Figure 9. *The Transformation docker.*

To rotate an object:

1. Select the object using the Pick Tool (**Figure 10**).
2. Choose Transformation from the the Arrange menu (**Figure 11**). The Transformation docker will open.
3. Click the Rotation button near the top of the docker window (**Figure 9**).
4. Enter the number of degrees you want to rotate the object in the Angle text box.
5. If you want to rotate the object using one of its handles as the center of rotation, use the check boxes that correspond to the object's eight black handles.
6. Place a check mark in one of these boxes to move the center of rotation.
7. Click either Apply To Duplicate to rotate a duplicate of the original object or Apply to rotate the original object. The object or its duplicate will rotate (**Figure 12**).

Figure 10. *Select the object using the Pick Tool.*

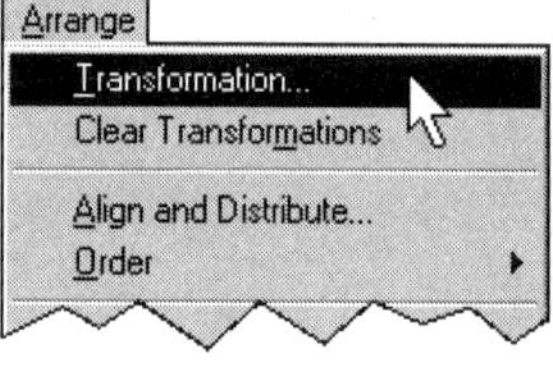

Figure 11. *To open the Transformation docker, choose Transformation from the Arrange menu.*

Figure 12. *The object redraws rotated.*

Rotate an Object

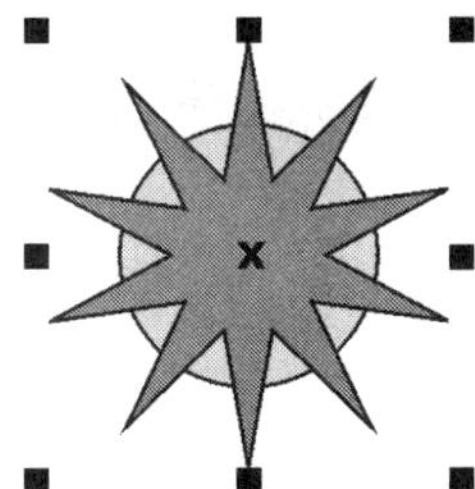

Figure 13. *A ten-pointed, dark gray star centered on top of a light gray circle is selected. The circle will be used as the target object.*

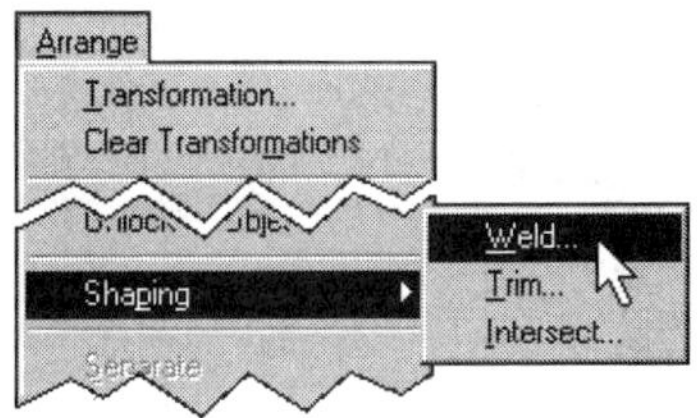

Figure 14. *Choose Weld from the Shaping fly-out on the Arrange menu.*

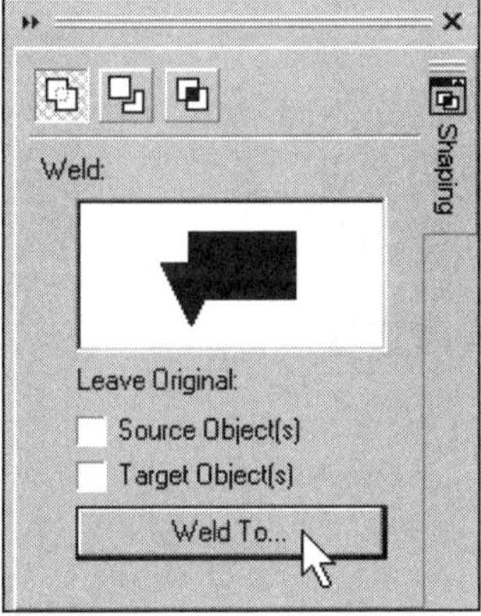

Figure 15. *Use the Shaping docker to bind several objects into one object.*

Figure 16. *When the circle—the target object—is clicked the two objects weld together, creating one object with a single outline. Notice that what remains of the dark gray star has taken on the light gray fill color of the circle.*

Welding lets you connect several objects together to create one object. If you weld objects together that overlap, they will bind together, creating an object with one outline. If you weld objects together that do not overlap, they will create a weld group that looks like separate objects but acts like a single object. The way welding works is like this: one object—called the *target object*—is used as the anchor to which the other objects are welded.

To weld objects together:

1. Select the objects you want to weld to the target object (**Figure 13**).
2. Choose Weld from the Shaping fly-out on the Arrange menu (**Figure 14**). The Shaping docker will appear (**Figure 15**).
3. If you want to keep a copy of the target object put a check in the Target Object(s) check box.
4. If you want to keep copies of the objects that are being welded to the target object, put a check in the Source Object(s) check box.
5. Click Weld To. A tiny representation of a welded object will appear attached to the mouse pointer.
6. Click on the target object. The selected objects will weld themselves to the target object (**Figure 16**).

When you *combine* objects, the lines and shapes fuse to create new shapes and any overlapping areas are removed, creating *clipping holes* that let you see what's underneath.

A perfect use for the combine transformation is the popular black/white graphic effect. With this effect, half of the drawing is white on black and the other half is black on white. (Check out the border on page 213.)

To create a black/white graphic:

1. Create a closed path object and fill it with black by clicking on the black color well in the Color Palette (**Figure 17**). You can use the same graphic shown in this example by opening the Symbols docker and selecting image #61 from the Animals1 collection.
2. Use the Rectangle Tool to draw a rectangle that covers the right half of the graphic (**Figure 18**).
3. Fill the rectangle with black. The rectangle will obscure the graphic beneath it (**Figure 19**). (As you learned in the last chapter, the second object drawn is automatically stacked on top of the first object.)
4. Select the Pick Tool, press the left mouse button, and drag a marquee to select both objects (**Figure 20**).

Figure 17. *Create a closed path object.*

Figure 18. *Use the Rectangle Tool to draw a rectangle that covers half the object.*

Figure 19. *Fill the rectangle with black.*

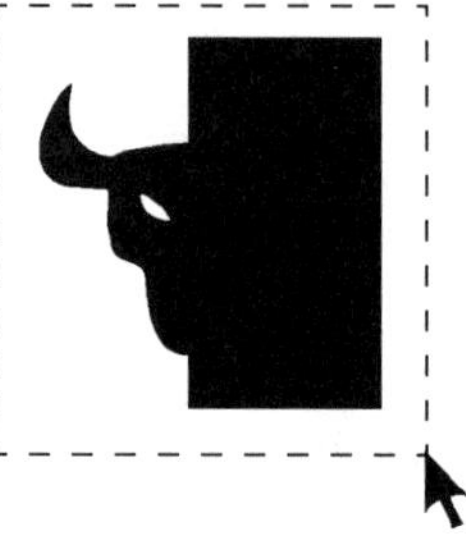

Figure 20. *Use the Pick Tool to drag a marquee to select both objects.*

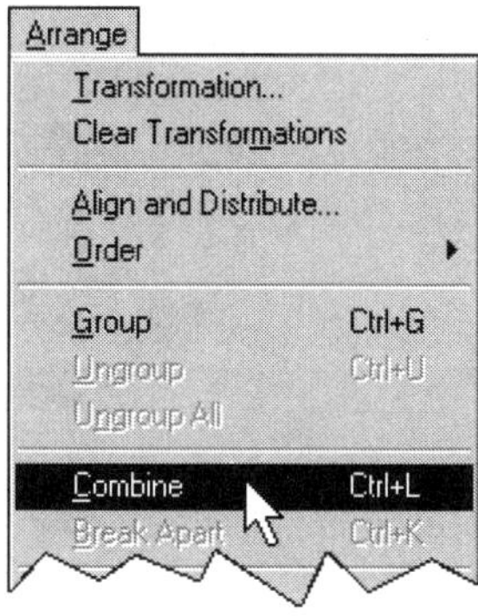

Figure 21. *Choose Combine from the Arrange menu.*

Figure 22. *The half covered by the rectangle becomes a cut-out.*

Figure 23. *A second rectangle added to the left, filled with white, and sent to the back of the stack finishes the drawing.*

Figure 24. *A filled square placed behind the drawing adds interest.*

Figure 25. *You can use the same techniques on artistic text.*

5. Choose Combine from the Arrange menu (**Figure 21**) or press Ctrl+L on the keyboard. The half of the graphic covered by the rectangle will become a cut-out (**Figure 22**).
6. Finish the drawing by creating a matching rectangle for the left side of the image. Send it to the back (press Shift PageDown on the keyboard) and fill it with white (**Figure 23**).
7. Marquee select all the objects and group them by pressing Ctrl+G on the keyboard or choosing Group from the Arrange menu (**Figure 2**).

Tips:

- To add another interesting effect to the drawing, create a large square that completely covers the grouped objects. Send the square to the back of the stack (press Shift+PageDown), then fill it with a color such as blue or red, or a texture fill (see page 151). The cut-out, created by the combined objects, lets the large square's fill shine through (**Figure 24**).
- Experiment using these same techniques on text. Create some artistic text, add a color fill, then position a colored rectangle over half the text. Select the two objects and combine them (**Figure 25**).

To separate objects that have been fused with the Combine command, use the *Break Apart* command. Break Apart is the exact opposite of Combine.

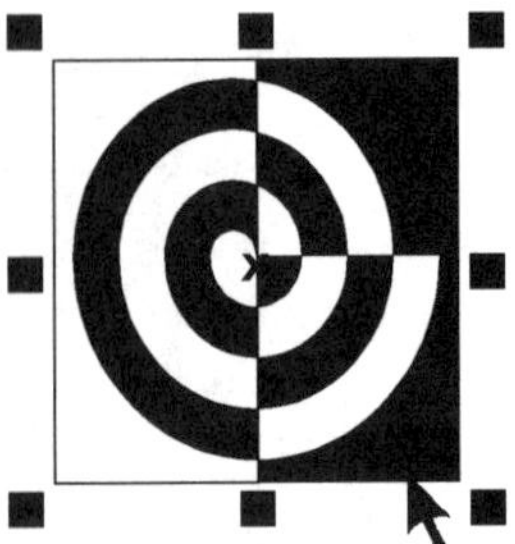

Figure 26. *Select the combined objects.*

To break objects apart:

1. Select the combined objects with the Pick Tool (**Figure 26**).
2. Choose Break Apart from the Arrange menu (**Figure 27**) or press Ctrl+K on the keyboard. The objects will resume their original shape (**Figure 28**). You can now work with them as individual objects.

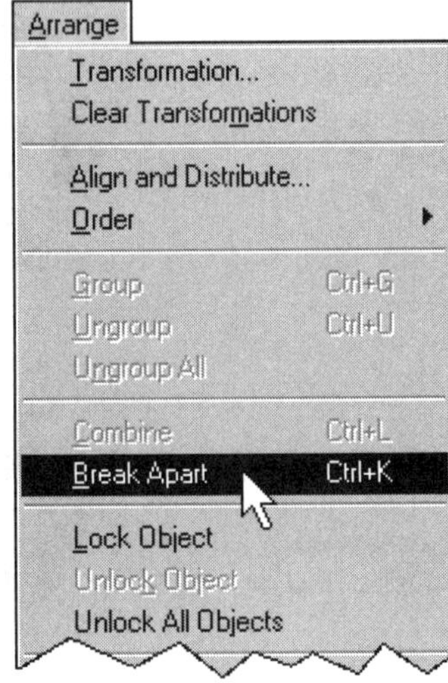

Figure 27. *Choose Break Apart from the Arrange menu.*

Figure 28. *The objects redraw in their original form.*

> **WORKING WITH CLIPART IMAGES**
>
> Many clipart images are created by grouping and/or combining several objects. By ungrouping or breaking these graphics apart, you can modify clipart to suit your needs and taste. Once you've made changes, you can regroup or recombine the graphics.
>
> You can check to see if a graphic has been combined or grouped by selecting the drawing with the Pick Tool, then opening the Arrange menu. If Ungroup and/or Break Apart are available, then the graphic has been grouped and/or combined.

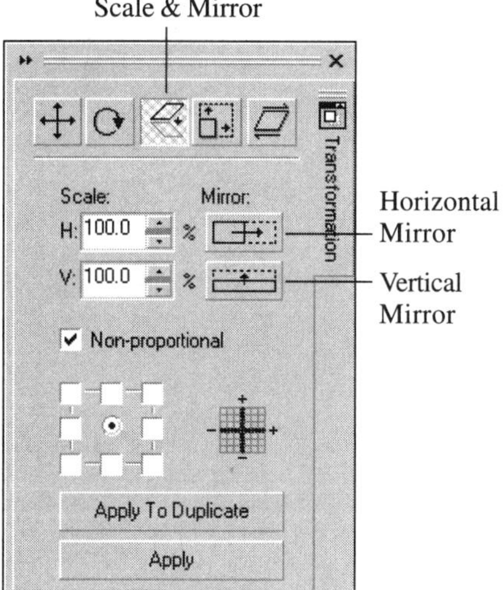

Figure 29. *The Transformation docker.*

Figure 30. *Select the object you want to mirror, then drag either the center left or center right handle.*

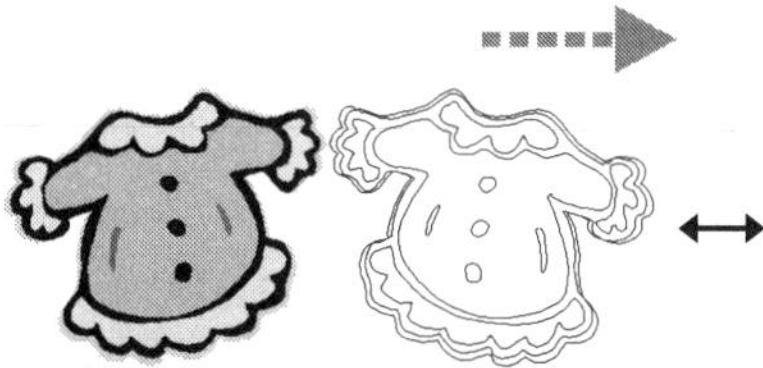

Figure 31. *When you press the Ctrl key and drag the handle, the object flips horizontally.*

Mirroring an object flips it vertically or horizontally (or both). You can mirror objects using their handles or using the Transformation docker (**Figure 29**).

To mirror an object horizontally:

1. Select the object with the Pick Tool. Eight black handles will appear around the object (**Figure 30**).
2. Press the Ctrl key while dragging either the left center or right center handle sideways (**Figure 31**). The object will flip horizontally.

or

1. Select the object with the Pick Tool.
2. Choose Transformation from the Arrange menu (**Figure 32**) or press Alt+F9 on the keyboard. The Transformation docker will open (**Figure 29**).
3. Click the Scale & Mirror button near the top center of the docker.
4. Click the Horizontal Mirror button, then click Apply To Duplicate to leave the original object and mirror a duplicate, or click Apply to flip the original object.

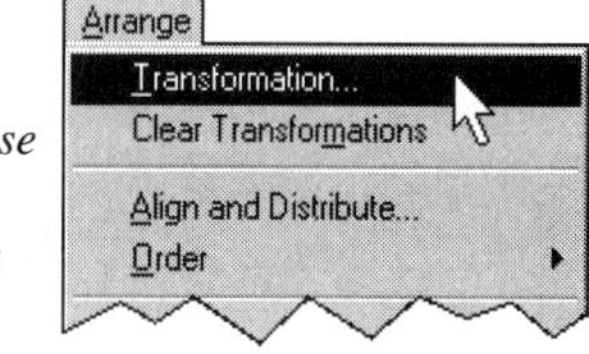

Figure 32. *Choose Transformation from the Arrange menu.*

Mirror an Object Horizontally

To mirror an object vertically:

1. Select the object with the Pick Tool (**Figure 33**).
2. Press the Ctrl key while dragging either the top center or bottom center handle up or down (**Figure 34**). The object will flip vertically.

or

1. Select the object with the Pick Tool.
2. Open the Transformation docker by pressing Alt+F9 on the keyboard or choosing Transformation from the Arrange menu (**Figure 32**).
3. Click the Vertical Mirror button, then click either the Apply To Duplicate button or the Apply button (**Figure 29**). In **Figure 35**, Apply To Duplicate has been clicked.

Tip:

- You can easily create a border like the one at the bottom of this page by rotating and mirroring duplicates of original objects. In this case, duplicates of two fish have been mirrored and rotated several times.

Figure 33. *Select the object with the Pick Tool, then drag either the top center or bottom center handle.*

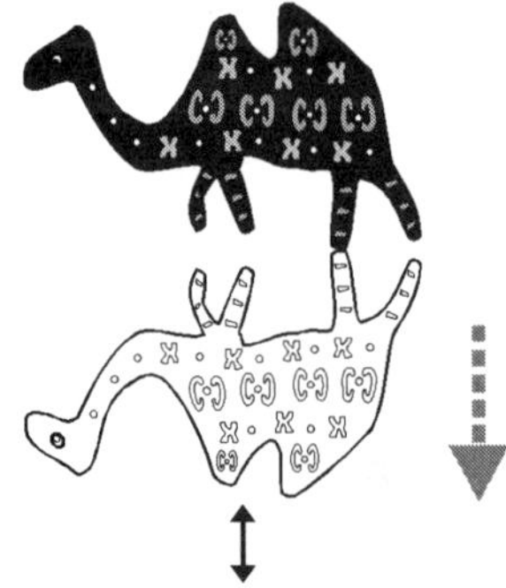

Figure 34. *When you drag the top handle down past the bottom of the object, it flips vertically.*

Figure 35. *After the Apply To Duplicate button is clicked, a copy of the original appears flipped vertically.*

Figure 36. *Select the object you want to scale.*

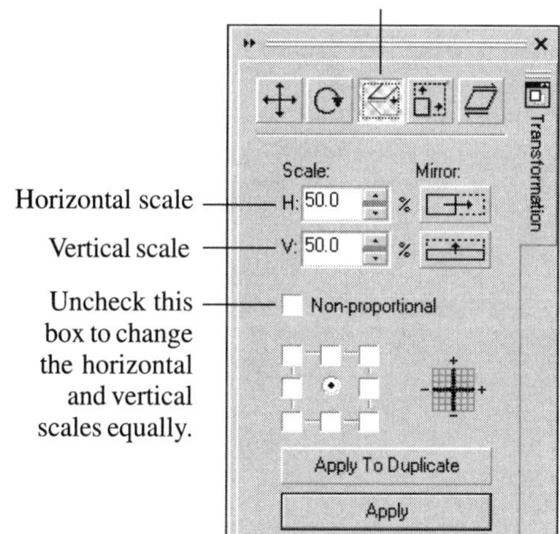

Figure 37. *Enter the percentage you want to scale the object to in the H and V text boxes.*

Figure 38. *The original object scaled down by 50%.*

Scaling an object makes its vertical or horizontal dimension (or both) larger or smaller. In Chapter 4, you learned how to use an object's handles to scale it (see page 54). But, you can also use the Transformation docker to resize objects with more accuracy.

To scale an object:

1. Select the object with the Pick Tool (**Figure 36**).
2. Open the Transformation docker by pressing Alt+F9 on the keyboard or choosing Transformation from the Arrange menu (**Figure 32**).
3. Click the Scale & Mirror button.
4. Enter the horizontal or vertical percentage to which you want to scale the object in the text boxes next to H and V. 100% represents the current size of the object, whereas 50% would be half the size and 200% would be twice the size. You can scale an object both horizontally and vertically at the same time.
5. To change the object's horizontal and vertical scales equally, remove the check mark from the check box next to Non-proportional (**Figure 37**).
6. Click either the Apply To Duplicate button to scale a duplicate of the original or the Apply button to scale the original object. The object or its duplicate will redraw in its new size (**Figure 38**).

Special Project:

Create the Woodcut Effect

The woodcut look is a very popular highlighting/shadowing technique that is easy to create with CorelDraw 9 (**Figure 39**). All it really consists of are simple triangles that are blended and then grouped together.

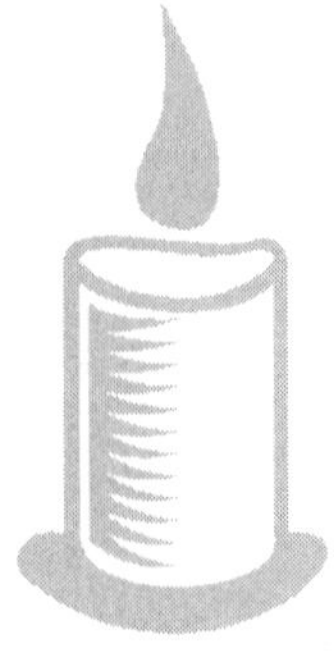

Figure 39. *Triangles are used to create the woodcut-look shadow on the left side of this candle.*

To create the woodcut effect:

1. Right mouse click on the Polygon tool and select Properties from the pop-up menu. The Options dialog box will open with Polygon Tool selected in the tree view window.
2. Make sure the Polygon option button is selected and Number of points/sides is set to 3 (**Figure 40**), then click OK to close the dialog box.
3. Select the Polygon Tool.
4. Press the left mouse button and drag the mouse diagonally to draw a long thin triangle (**Figure 41**).

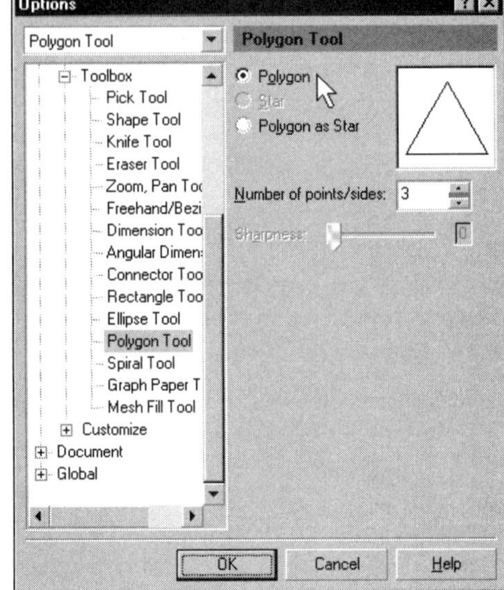

Figure 40. *Use the Polygon Tool panel of the Options dialog box to set the default to a polygon with 3 points.*

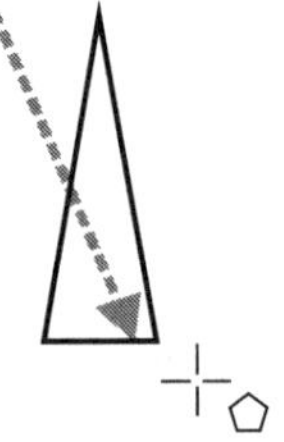

Figure 41. *Drag the mouse diagonally to draw a long thin triangle using the Polygon Tool.*

5. Use the Pick Tool to select the triangle and either choose Duplicate from the Edit menu or press Ctrl+D on your keyboard. A duplicate triangle will appear selected to the right and above the original triangle (**Figure 42**).
6. Drag the duplicate triangle further to the right of the original (**Figure 43**).
7. Shift click to select both triangles.
8. Choose Align and Distribute from the Arrange menu (**Figure 44**). The Align and Distribute dialog box will open (**Figure 45**).
9. Put a check mark in the Bottom check box to align the triangles to their bottoms, then click OK. The triangles will redraw, aligned (**Figure 46**).

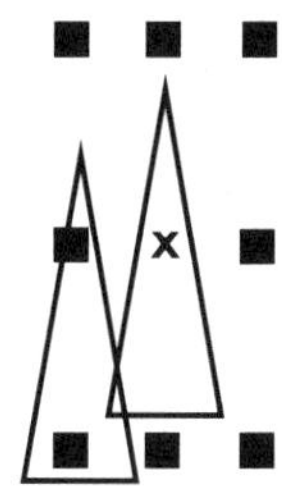

Figure 42. *Use Duplicate on the Edit menu or press Ctrl+D on the keyboard to create a copy of the original triangle.*

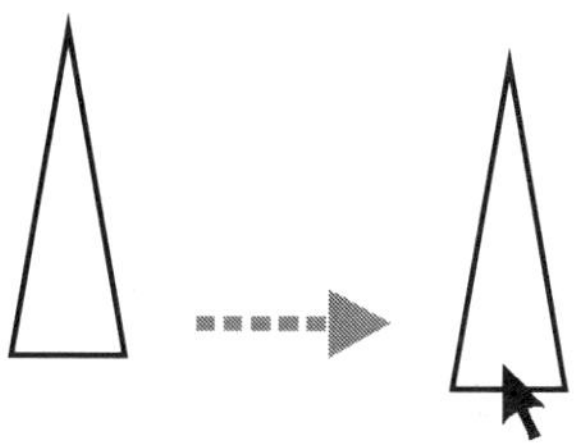

Figure 43. *Use the Pick Tool to drag the duplicate further to the right of the original.*

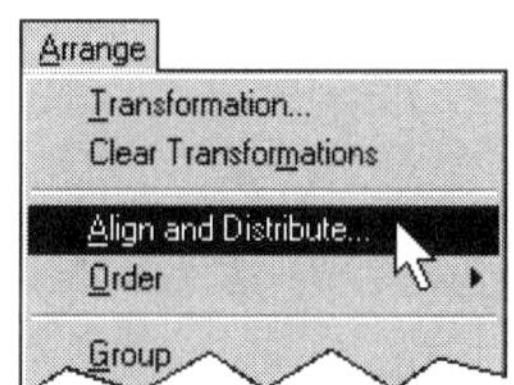

Figure 44. *Choose Align and Distribute from the Arrange menu.*

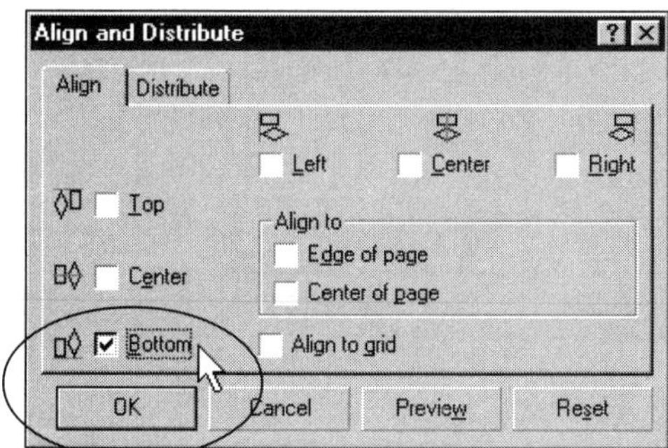

Figure 45. *Click Bottom in the Align and Distribute dialog box, then click OK.*

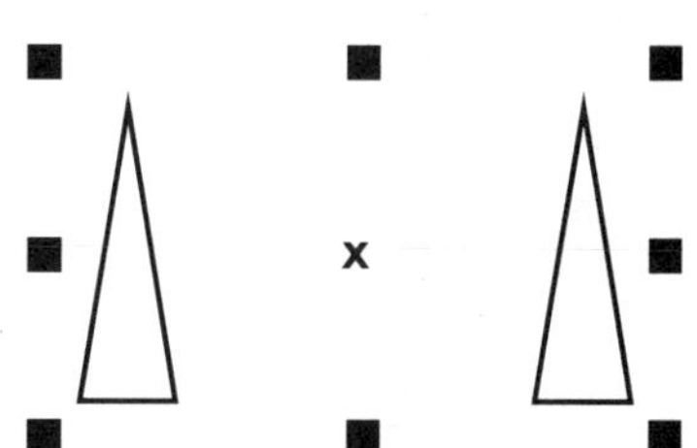

Figure 46. *The bottoms of the triangles are now exactly aligned.*

Next, you need to *blend* the two triangles. Blending creates a specific number of intermediate objects or *steps* between two selected objects. In this case, you are going to use a blend to create several triangles between the two selected triangles.

To blend the two triangles:

1. Choose the Interactive Blend Tool from the Interactive Tool fly-out (**Figure 47**). The Property Bar will dynamically change to display blend settings (**Figure 48**).
2. Use the Property Bar to enter a small number of steps in the Steps text box. **Figure 48** shows 5 as the number of steps.
3. Position the mouse over the left triangle, press the left mouse button, and drag the pointer over to the right triangle (**Figure 49**).
4. Release the mouse button. Several intermediate triangles will appear between the original triangles. For the woodcut effect, the triangles should overlap near the bottom. If your triangles do not overlap at all, add more steps using the Steps text box. If you have too many triangles and they overlap up near the top points, use the Steps text box to reduce the number of steps.

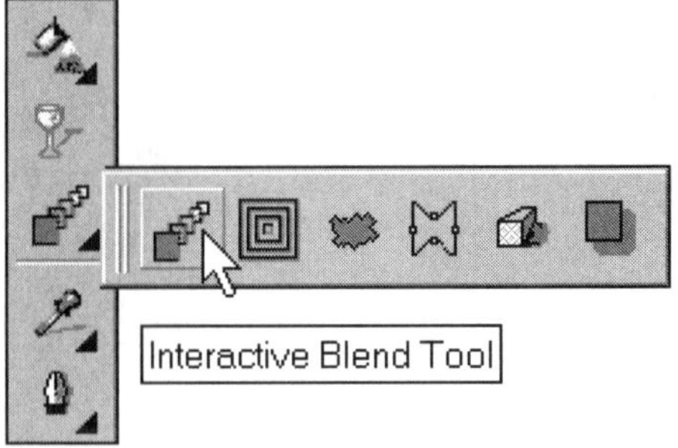

Figure 47. *Choose the Interactive Blend Tool from the Interactive Tool fly-out.*

Steps text box

Property Bar : Interactive Blend Tool			
x: 6.518 "	↔ 0.603 "		5
y: 7.324 "	↕ 1.008 "		↔ 1.0 "

Figure 48. *The Steps text box on the Property Bar is used to create any number of intermediate objects, or steps, between two selected objects.*

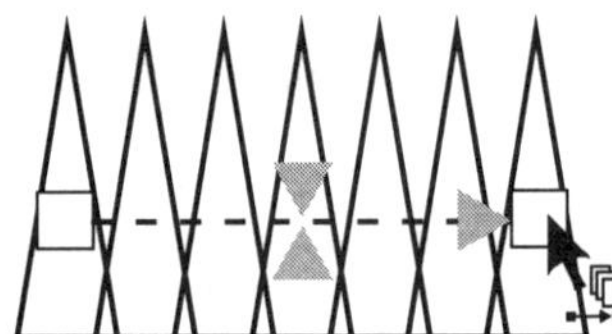

Figure 49. *Drag the Interactive Blend Tool from the left triangle to the right triangle. When you release the mouse button, several intermediate triangles appear between the original two.*

> **KEEP AN EYE ON THE STATUS BAR**
>
> Remember that the Status Bar tells all. After blending the triangles it will state, "Blend Group on Layer 1."

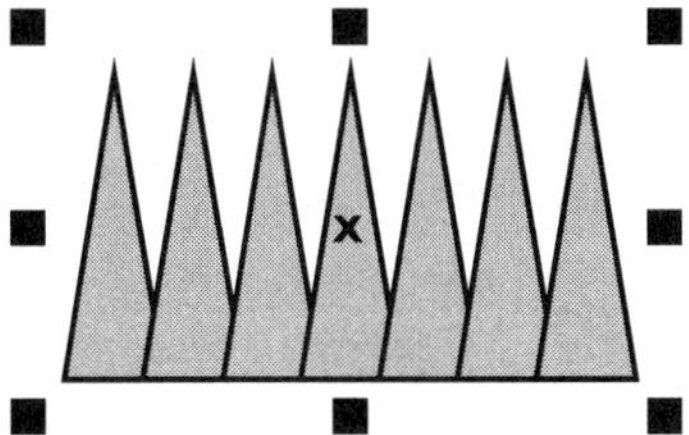

Figure 50. *Fill the triangles with a color that complements the object you are shadowing or highlighting.*

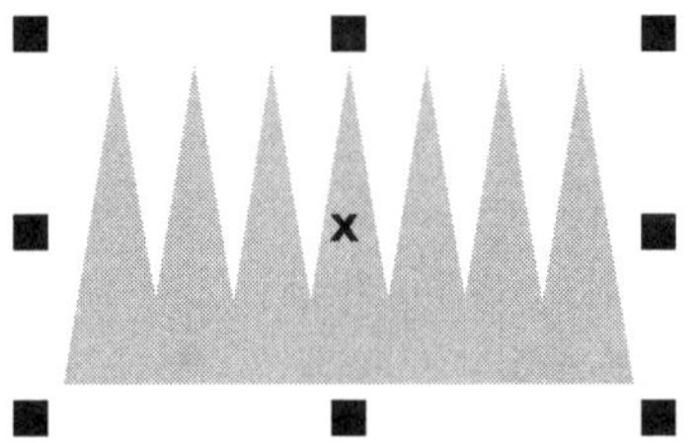

Figure 51. *Right mouse click the color well with an X in it to remove the triangles' outlines.*

Figure 52. *Look at the graphic you want to highlight or shadow and figure out how the grouped triangles need to be rotated and scaled.*

Finishing the woodcut effect is easy. The final steps involve grouping and filling the triangles with a uniform color, then rotating and scaling them.

To finish the woodcut effect:

1. With all the triangles selected, choose Group from the Arrange menu (**Figure 2**) or press Ctrl+G on the keyboard.
2. Click a color well in the Color Palette to fill the grouped triangles with color (**Figure 50**). To create a woodcut highlight, add a fill to the grouped object that is a few shades lighter than the object being highlighted. To create a shadow, add a fill that is a few shades darker.
3. Right mouse click the color well with the X in it. This will remove the outline from the grouped triangles (**Figure 51**).
4. Look at the object to which you are going to add the woodcut effect and judge how the triangles need to be rotated and scaled (**Figure 52**).

(continued)

> **ADDING COLOR TO OBJECTS**
>
> It's easy to add a uniform color to objects. Just select the objects and click the color well of your choice. For more information about filling objects with color, see Chapter 10.

5. Rotate (see page 216) and scale (see page 223) the grouped triangles to the appropriate size, then add them to the graphic (**Figure 53**).

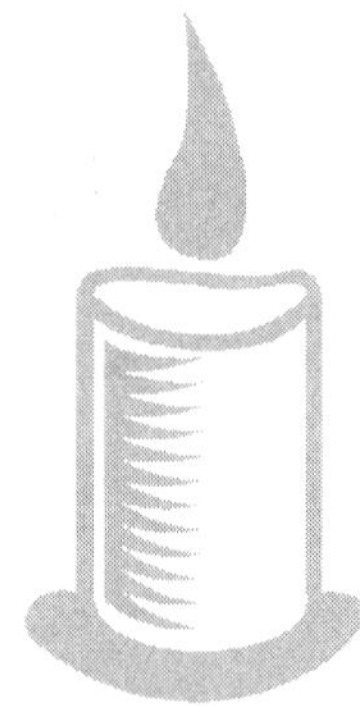

Figure 53. *Add the rotated and scaled triangles to the graphic.*

Tips:

- If the sides of the grouped triangles need to bend to give the impression of a rounded shape, convert the triangles to curves (see page 70) then use the Shape Tool to manipulate their nodes.
- You can add woodcut highlights and shadows to many kinds of graphics. In addition, extra triangles can be used to create the illusion of three dimensional shape or to add emphasis (**Figures 54a–c**).

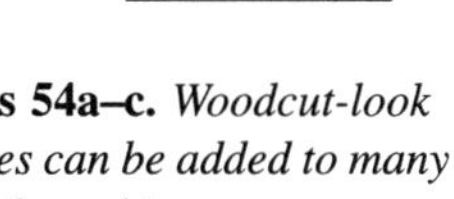

Figures 54a–c. *Woodcut-look triangles can be added to many styles of graphics.*

SUMMARY

In this chapter you learned how to:

- Group and ungroup objects
- Lock and unlock objects
- Rotate objects
- Weld objects together
- Combine and break objects apart
- Scale and Mirror objects
- Create a woodcut effect using the skills you've learned

Special Effects

Previous chapters showed you how to transform objects with such techniques as duplicating, filling graphics with color and patterns, skewing, grouping, and blending. This chapter takes those transformations and helps you put them together to create exciting special effects. These effects are not hard to do, now that you know the basics, and they will add a professional touch to your graphics. As you move through the chapter, don't hesitate to experiment! If you think a technique you learned previously might add an interesting effect, try it out.

This chapter starts out showing you how to use *envelopes*, containers that distort an object's shape, creating nifty effects. To do this you'll use the Interactive Envelope Tool. Then, you will use the Interactive Blend Tool, to morph one object into another. From there, you will learn how to add perspective to objects and create objects by drawing their shadows. Next, you'll use the Interactive Transparency Tool to make objects see-through. Then, you'll use the Interactive Distortion Tool, to quickly stretch and reshape objects. From there, you'll discover how to use the new Interactive Contour Tool to create amazing effects. Finally, you'll find out how to add motion trails to objects, giving them the illusion of motion.

Envelopes are used to distort the shape of objects. An envelope works like a container placed around an object. The object is forced to take on the shape of the container, becoming distorted in the process. The shape of an envelope is manipulated using the Shape Tool or the Interactive Envelope Tool and the nodes that appear at various points around the envelope itself.

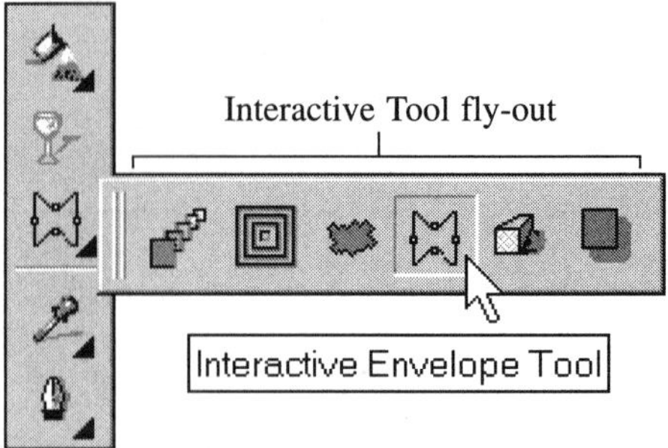

Figure 1. *The Interactive Envelope Tool is found on the Interactive Tool fly-out.*

The Interactive Envelope Tool, found on the Interactive Tool fly-out (**Figure 1**), works with the Property Bar (**Figure 2**) to give you quick access to all the envelope features.

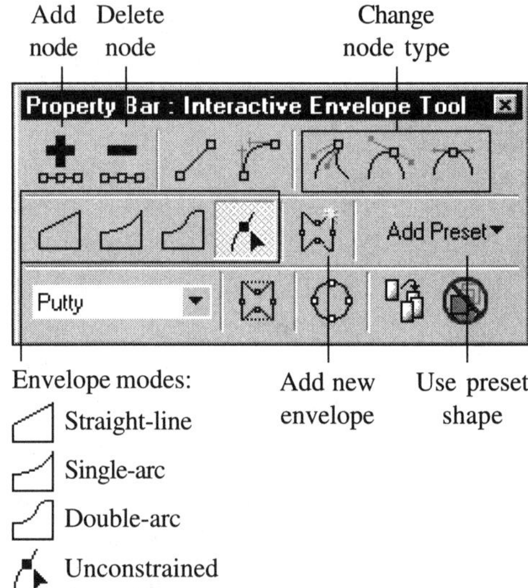

Figure 2. *The Property Bar works with the Interactive Envelope Tool to make enveloping features handy.*

To use the Interactive Envelope Tool shape an object:

1. Select the Interactive Envelope Tool from the Interactive Tool fly-out (**Figure 1**).
2. Select the object you want to shape with the Interactive Envelope Tool (**Figure 3**). You'll know it's selected when you see a red-dashed rectangular envelope with nodes appear around the object.
3. Select the envelope mode you want to use by clicking the appropriate button on the Property Bar:
   - **Straight-line**—a straight line is maintained between each of the corner nodes (**Figure 4a**)
   - **Single-arc**—a curved line is allowed between each pair of corner nodes (**Figure 4b**)

Figure 3. *Use the Interactive Envelope Tool to select the object you want to shape.*

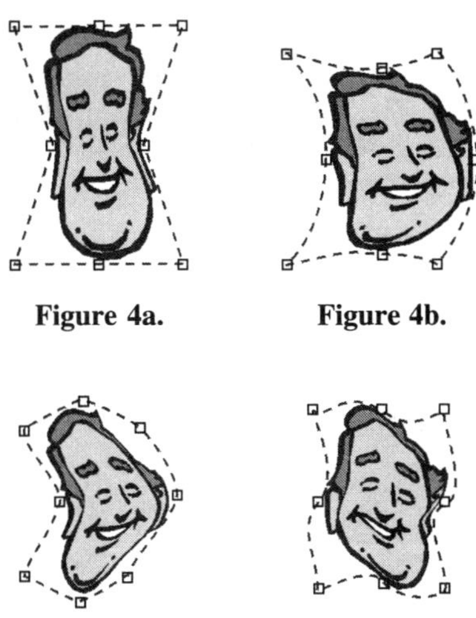

Figure 4a. Figure 4b.

Figure 4c. Figure 4d.

Figure 5. *Use the Interactive Envelope Tool to drag the nodes and shape the envelope. (This is a straight-line mode envelope.)*

Figure 6. *Could this be the man in the moon?*

- **Double-arc**—a wavy line is allowed between each pair of corner nodes (**Figure 4c**)
- **Unconstrained**—you can edit the envelope path, dragging nodes and control points, as if it were an outline drawn with the Freehand or Bézier Tools (**Figure 4d**)

4. Drag the nodes with the Interactive Envelope Tool until the envelope is the desired shape (**Figure 5**).

Tips:

- When working in unconstrained mode, you can add nodes, change node types, and manipulate the envelope's outline just like any ordinary path, using the Shape Tool and Property Bar (for more about nodes see Chapter 6).
- You can also create an envelope that mimics a shape. In **Figure 6**, a moon outline was placed behind the face. The face was then selected and an unconstrained mode envelope was added around the face. The next step was to shape the envelope using the moon outline as a guide. As the envelope was shaped, the face also changed shape.
- If you want to put several objects in an envelope, you must group them first.

Presets let you quickly apply a specific envelope shape to an object. They're easy to use and can quickly get you on the road to creating your own custom envelopes.

Figure 7. *Select the object with the Interactive Envelope Tool.*

To apply a preset envelope to an object:

1. Select the Interactive Envelope Tool from the Interactive Tool fly-out.
2. Select the object to which you want to add a preset envelope shape (**Figure 7**). An envelope, represented by eight nodes connected by a dashed red line, will appear around the object.
3. Use the Add Preset drop-down list on the Property Bar to select an envelope shape (**Figure 8**). The object will redraw using the envelope to reshape it (**Figure 9**). The different presets can really change how an object looks (**Figures 10a–d**).

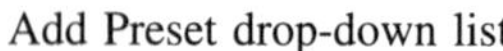

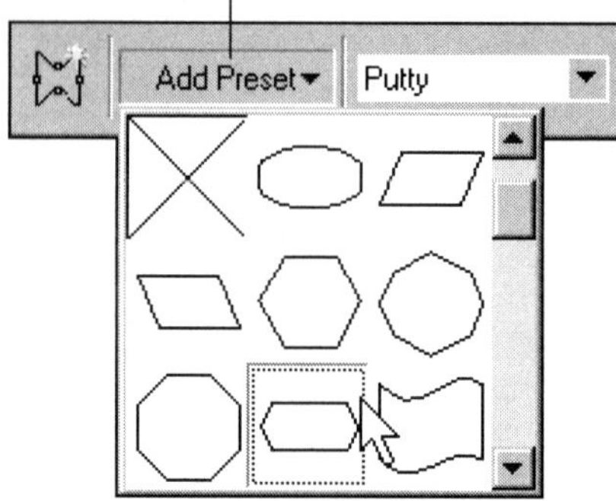

Figure 8. *Select an envelope shape from the Add Preset drop-down list.*

Figure 9. *The object redraws using the envelope to reshape it.*

Figures 10a–d. *Try some of the different preset envelope shapes. You never quite know how they will reshape an object.*

Mapping Mode drop-down list

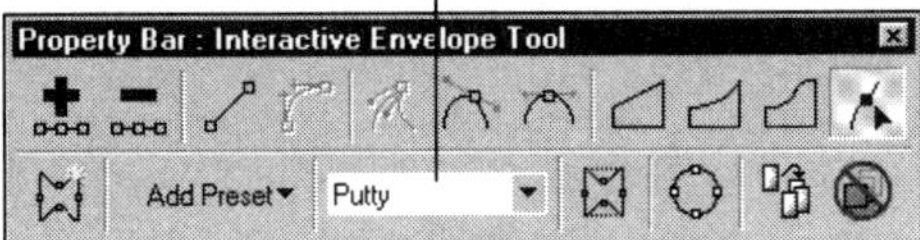

Figure 11. *The mapping modes found on the drop-down list effect the way an object is changed by an envelope.*

Mapping Mode drop-down list

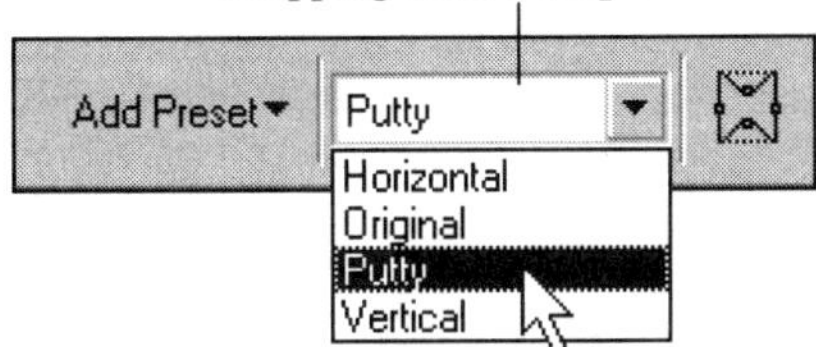

Figure 12. *When the Interactive Envelope Tool is selected, you can use the Property Bar to select a mapping mode.*

Figure 13. *This is the way the original figure looked before the preset envelope shown was applied.*

You may have already noticed one other drop-down list available on the Property Bar: the Mapping Mode drop-down list (**Figure 11**). The mapping mode effects how the object is changed by the envelope. Its effects are especially obvious when applied to an object using a preset envelope shape.

To add a mapping mode to an envelope:

1. Select the object to which you want to add the envelope with the Interactive Envelope Tool.
2. Select a mapping mode using the drop-down list on the Property Bar (**Figure 12**).
3. Select a preset envelope shape from the Preset drop-down list on the Property Bar (**Figure 8**). The object will assume the envelope shape and mapping mode. **Figure 13** shows the original image before a preset envelope is applied. **Figures 14a–d** use the same envelope shape with one of the four different mapping modes.

Figure 14a. *This figure uses the horizontal mapping mode.*

Figure 14b. *This figure uses the original mapping mode.*

Figure 14c. *This figure uses the putty mapping mode.*

Figure 14d. *This figure uses the vertical mapping mode.*

Special Project:

Shape an Envelope like an Object

In Chapter 6, you learned how to make a heart by manipulating a circle's nodes. You can add special emphasis to that heart by adding the word "love" to the heart in a heart-shaped envelope.

Figure 15. *Create a heart.*

To add the word "love" to a heart:

1. Create the heart as described in Chapter 6 (**Figure 15**).
2. Use the Text Tool to type the word "LOVE." Choose a favorite font and size the text to the width of the heart (**Figure 16**). (The font used in this example is Apollo MT.)
3. Select the Interactive Envelope Tool (**Figure 1**), then select the text. A rectangular envelope will appear around the text object.
4. On the Property Bar click the Add Preset button to display a list of pre-designed envelope shapes. Scroll down the list until you find the heart shape (**Figure 17**).

Figure 16. *Create the word "LOVE," then size it to the width of the heart.*

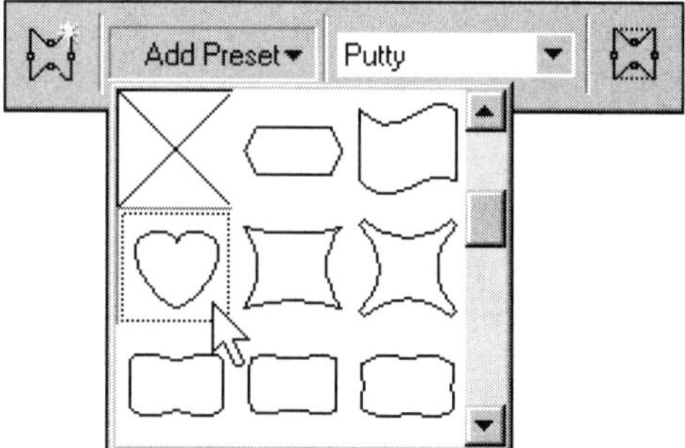

Figure 17. *Select the heart-shaped envelope from the Add Preset drop-down list on the Property Bar.*

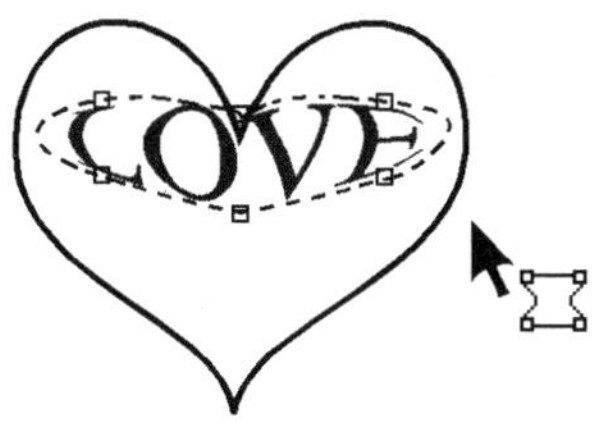

Figure 18. *When you click the preset heart shape, a heart-shaped envelope appears and the text assumes the envelope shape.*

Figure 19. *Drag the envelope's nodes and control points to shape the envelope, using the heart as a guide.*

Figure 20. *When you finish shaping the envelope, the text assumes the shape of the heart.*

Figure 21. *Add your favorite fill colors to the heart and enveloped text.*

5. Click the heart shape. A small heart-shaped envelope will appear around the text (**Figure 18**) and the text will assume this shape.
6. Using the envelope's nodes and control points, reshape the envelope using the heart you created earlier as a guide (**Figure 19**).
7. When you are finished reshaping the envelope (**Figure 20**), fill the heart with a favorite color (red is always a good choice for a heart), then fill the type with another color (**Figure 21**).

Tips:

- To add a new envelope effect on top of one that has already been applied to an object, click the Add New Envelope button on the Property Bar (**Figure 22**).
- To export the heart and shaped text, you will need to group the two objects together. (For details about grouping objects, turn to page 214.)

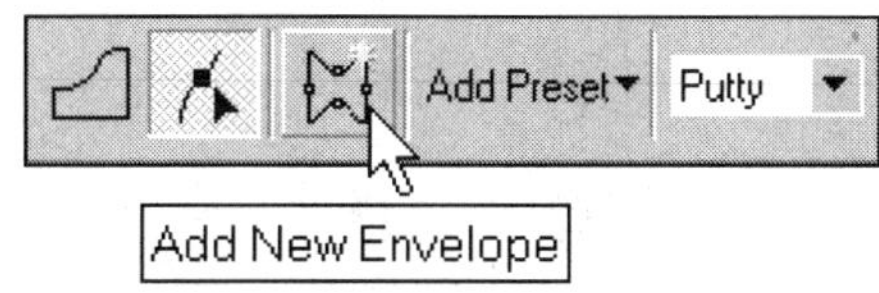

Figure 22. *Click the Add New Envelope button on the Property Bar to add a new envelope to an object that has already been manipulated by one.*

Blends create a specific number of intermediate objects, or steps, between two selected objects. You can use a blend to quickly create several copies of the same object—which you did in the last chapter when creating the woodcut effect—or to blend two different objects together to create a morph. Blends can also be blended together to create multiple blends. With multiple blends you can create highlights and make objects sparkle.

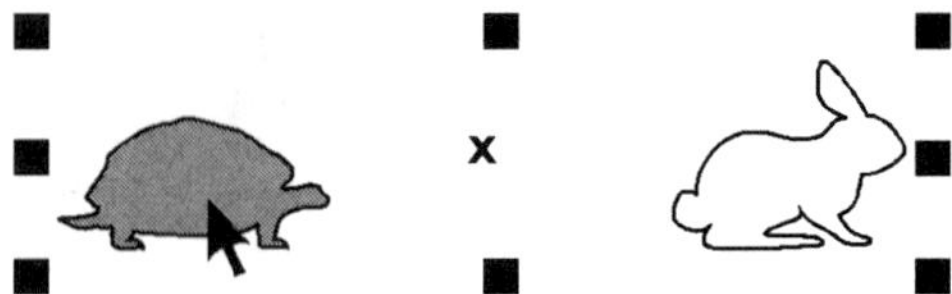
Figure 23. *Select the two objects you want to blend.*

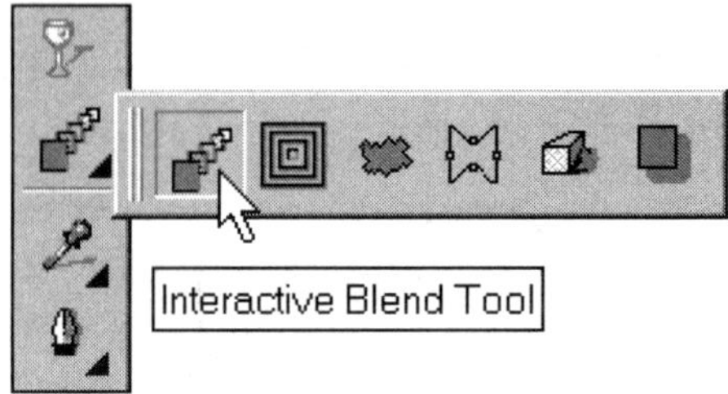

Figure 24. *Select the Interactive Blend Tool from the Interactive Tool fly-out.*

To blend two objects together using the Interactive Blend Tool:

1. Select the two objects you want to blend with the Pick Tool (**Figure 23**).
2. Select the Interactive Blend Tool (**Figure 24**). Three tiny pages and an arrow will attach to the mouse pointer.
3. Position the mouse over the first object, press the left mouse button, and drag over to the second object. A dashed arrow will appear as you drag (**Figure 25**).
4. Release the mouse button. The blended steps will appear between the two objects (**Figure 26**).

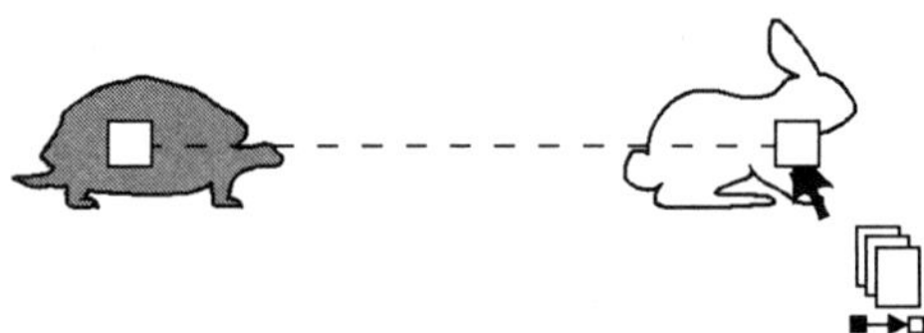
Figure 25. *Drag the Interactive Blend Tool from the first object to the second.*

Figure 26. *When you release the mouse button, blended objects appear between the original objects.*

Tip:

- You can use the Property Bar to increase or decrease the number of steps created by the Interactive Blend Tool and set whether the blend will rotate (**Figure 27**).

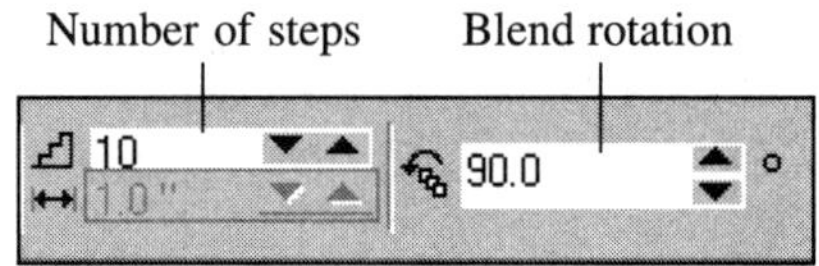

Figure 27. *You can use the Property Bar to change the number of steps and set which way the blend will rotate.*

Figure 28. *The sized objects waiting to be filled with color and blended together.*

Figure 29. *The objects have been filled with color and moved into position for the blends to come.*

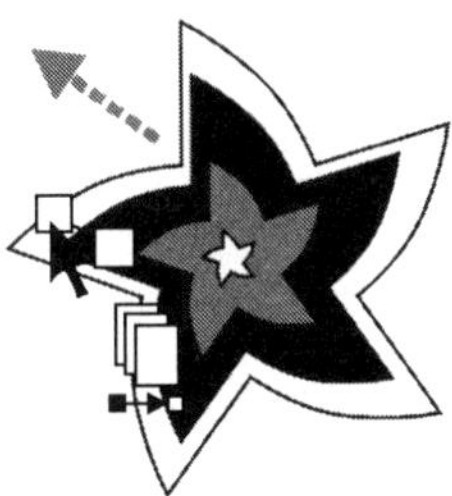

Figure 30. *Press the mouse button and drag the Interactive Blend Tool from the first object to the second to create the first blend.*

Figure 31. *The completed blend of the black star outwards to the big white star.*

When creating a multiple blend, you will need to draw, in advance, all the objects you want to blend together. Then, the objects can be filled with the colors of your choice and blended together one-by-one. This example uses a simple star and makes it sparkle.

To create a multiple blend:

1. Create the objects you want to use in the multiple blend (**Figure 28**). In this example a big star has been duplicated 3 times for a total of 4 stars. The duplicates have been scaled down so they will fit inside each other.
2. Fill the objects with the various colors you want to use and position them where you want the blends to start and end (**Figure 29**). In this example, the stars have been filled with (starting from the outer-most star) white, black, 50% black, and white, and aligned to their centers using the Align and Distribute dialog box. (See pages 132–133 for directions on using this dialog box.)
3. Position the mouse over the first object, press the left mouse button, and drag over to the second object (**Figure 30**). In the example, a blend has been created from the black star outwards to the big white star (**Figure 31**).

(continued)

4. Position the mouse over the next object you want to blend, press the left mouse button and drag to the blend target object (**Figure 32**). In the example, a second blend has been created from the grey star outwards to the black star (**Figure 33**).

Figure 32. *Drag the Interactive Blend Tool from the next selected object to the target object to create a second blend.*

5. Repeat step 4 until you have blended all the objects you want to blend together (**Figure 34**). The third and final blend for the star example is blended from the tiny white star in the center outwards to the grey star.

Figure 33. *The completed blend of the grey star outwards to the black star.*

Figure 34. *The final blend for the star is a blend from the tiny white star in the center outwards to the grey star.*

Tips:

- Let your imagination soar! You can use blends to create almost any kind of highlight or shaping (**Figures 35a–c**).
- If you create a blend that you don't like or didn't mean to create, just press Ctrl+Z on the keyboard to undo it.
- After you have created a multiple blend, you can still change the number of steps for each individual blend. Just use the Pick Tool to select one of the original objects, then enter a new number in the Number of steps text box on the Property Bar (**Figure 27**).

Figures 35a–c. *Many of the intricate highlights and shapes in these drawings have been created with blends.*

Setting an object's perspective lets you add the illusion of distance and depth to your drawings.

To add perspective to an object:

1. Select the object with the Pick Tool (**Figure 36**).
2. Choose Add Perspective from the Effects menu (**Figure 37**). A red, dotted, rectangular grid with four handles, one at each corner, will appear on the object (**Figure 38**).
3. Position the mouse over one of the handles, press the left mouse button, and drag the handle to change the shape of the grid. As you drag, the object will change perspective (**Figure 39**).
4. Release the mouse button when you are finished.

Tips:

- As you drag a handle, an X will appear somewhere on the drawing page. This is the vanishing point. You can also drag the X to change the object's perspective.
- You can add perspective to as many objects as you want at one time. Just group the objects together before selecting.
- To return the object to its original shape (without perspective), drag one of the handles onto another handle or choose Clear Perspective from the Effects menu.

Figure 36. *Use the Pick Tool to select the object.*

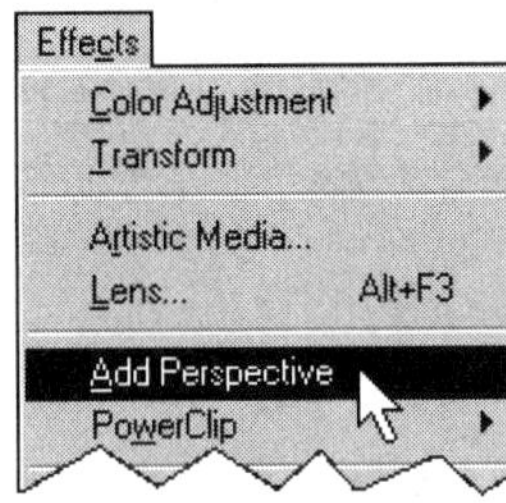

Figure 37. *Choose Add Perspective from the Effects menu.*

Figure 38. *A dotted rectangular grid with a handle on each corner appears on top of the object.*

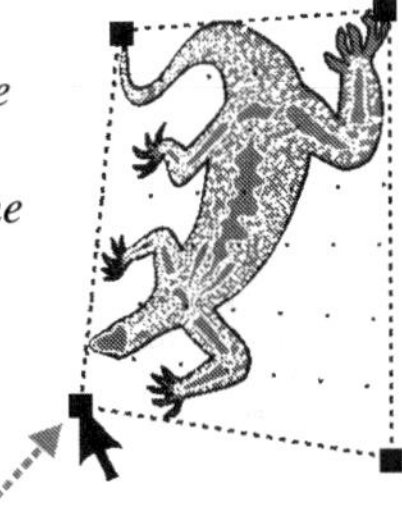

Figure 39. *As you drag the mouse, the perspective of the object changes, making it look like it's going off into the distance.*

Shadows make drawings appear more realistic, as if they were three dimensional. One use for shadows is understated emphasis. You can use shadows to create the outline of an object that is filled with the same color as the background (**Figure 40**).

Figure 40. *A shadow can be used to create text or any other object.*

To create an object defined by its shadow:

1. Choose Options from the Tools menu or Press Ctrl+J on the keyboard to open the Options dialog box.
2. In the tree view window, click Edit to view the Edit panel.
3. In the Nudge area on the right side of the dialog box, change the value in the Nudge text box to 0.01 inch (**Figure 41**) and click OK.
4. Select the object you want to shadow with the Pick Tool (**Figure 42**).
5. Fill it with the same color you will use for the background, and right mouse click on the color well with the X in it to remove the object's outline (**Figure 43**). (This example uses 30% black for the background and object fill.)
6. Choose Copy from the Edit menu or press Ctrl+C on the keyboard. This copies the object to the Windows clipboard.

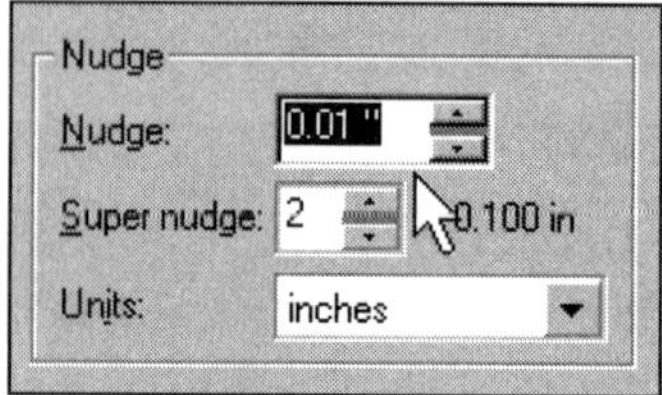

Figure 41. *Change the Nudge setting to 0.01 inch (0.025 centimeter).*

Figure 42. *Select the object you want to define with its shadow.*

Figure 43. *Fill the object with the chosen background color and remove any outline.*

Figure 44. *Use the right mouse button to drag a copy of the object.*

Create a Shadow Object

Figure 45. *Click Copy Here on the pop-up menu.*

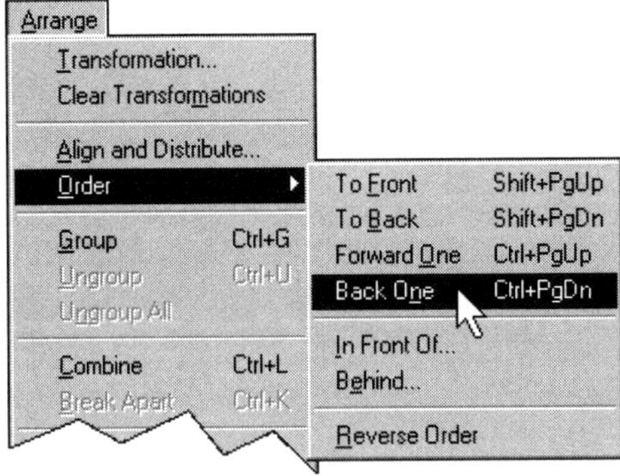

Figure 46. *Choose Back One from the Order fly-out on the Arrange menu.*

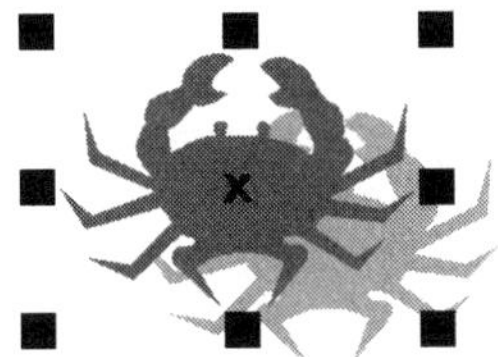

Figure 47. *Change the original object's color to a few shades darker than the background color.*

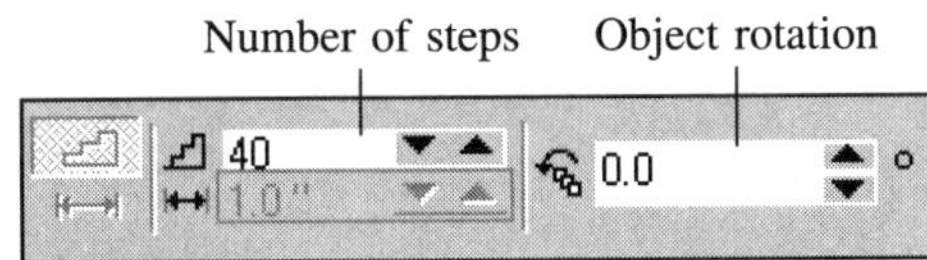

Figure 48. *Set the number of steps to 40 and the object rotation to 0.*

7. Position the mouse pointer over the object and press the right mouse button. Drag the wireframe version of the object down and to the right of the original object (**Figure 44**).
8. Release the mouse button. A pop-up menu will appear asking whether you want to copy or move the object. Choose Copy Here (**Figure 45**).
9. Press Ctrl+PageDown on the keyboard or choose Back One from the Order fly-out on the Arrange menu (**Figure 46**). This moves the copied object behind the original object.
10. Use the Pick Tool to select the original object.
11. Change the original object's fill color to a color that is a few shades darker than the original color (**Figure 47**). (This example uses 60% black.)
12. Select the Interactive Blend Tool from the Interactive Tool fly-out.
13. Use the Property Bar to set the Number of steps to 40 and enter 0 in the Object rotation text box (**Figure 48**).
14. Position the mouse pointer over the original object, press the left mouse button and drag the mouse to the copy.
15. Release the mouse button. The two objects blend together (**Figure 49**).

(continued)

Create a Shadow Object

16. Select the Pick Tool.
17. Press Ctrl+V on the keyboard or choose Paste from the Edit menu. A copy of the original object appears selected.
18. Left mouse click in the white color well to fill the copy with white (**Figure 50**).
19. You need to nudge the white filled copy up and slightly to the left to create a highlight. To do this, you are going to use CorelDraw's built-in nudge feature. Press the up arrow key [↑] once to nudge the object up 0.01 inch. Then press the left arrow key [←] once to nudge the object left 0.01 inch. You may not even notice the object move.
20. Press Ctrl+V on the keyboard or choose Paste from the Edit menu again. Another copy of the original appears (**Figure 51**).
21. Use the Rectangle Tool to draw a rectangle that is larger than the objects you've just created. Fill the rectangle with the background color you originally decided on.
22. Position the rectangle directly over the objects you have made.
23. Press Shift+PageDown on the keyboard to send the rectangle to the back of the stack or choose To Back from the Order fly-out on the Arrange menu. The object's shadow will become apparent (**Figure 52**).

Figure 49. *When you release the mouse button, the two objects blend together.*

Figure 50. *Fill the copy with white.*

Figure 51. *Choosing Paste from the Edit menu creates another copy of the original object.*

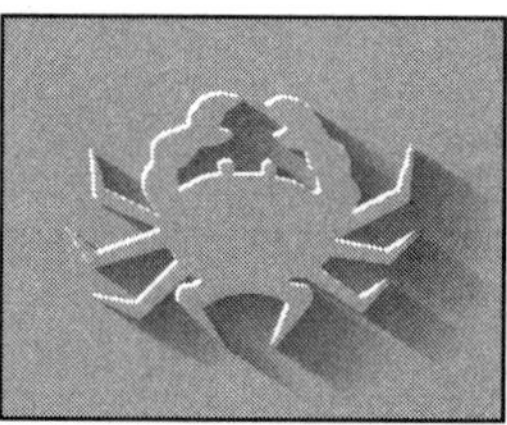

Figure 52. *After adding a rectangle filled with the background color, the object's shadow becomes apparent.*

Create a Shadow Object

You can put one object inside another using the PowerClip command. When you use PowerClip, one object becomes a container, while the other object becomes the contents. Any part of the contents that does not fit in the container gets "clipped" off.

Figure 53. *Select the object you want to use as the "contents."*

To powerclip two objects:

1. Select the object you want to use as the "contents" with the Pick Tool (**Figure 53**).
2. Choose Place Inside Container from the PowerClip fly-out on the Effects menu (**Figure 54**). The mouse pointer changes to a large black arrow.
3. Click on the container object. The contents object will redraw inside the container object (**Figure 55**).

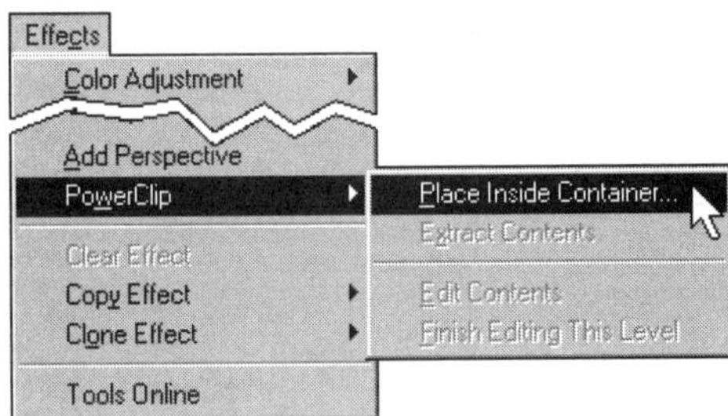

Figure 54. *Choose Place Inside Container from the PowerClip fly-out on the Effects menu.*

Figure 55. *When you click on the container object, the contents object redraws inside it.*

Tips:

- The container object can be any closed path object you create in CorelDraw, such as stars, polygons, and artistic text.
- The contents object can be any object created in CorelDraw or any imported object, such as bitmap images. (For more about bitmaps, see Chapter 16.)
- Let your imagination soar when using the PowerClip command! You never know what will look interesting together (**Figures 56a–c**).

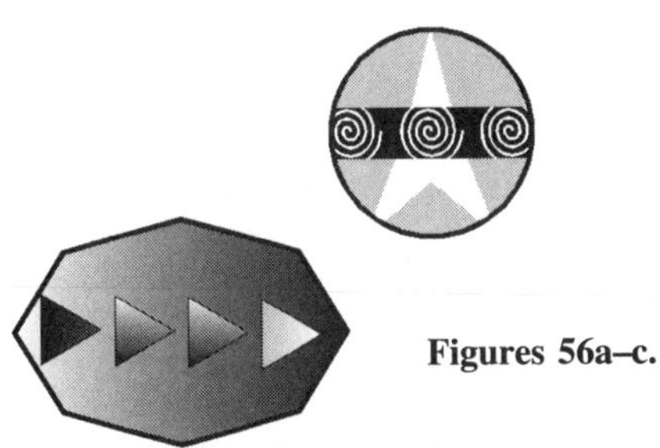

Figures 56a–c.

The Interactive Transparency Tool lets you create objects that are, well, transparent. If a transparent object is placed on top of another object, the object underneath the transparency remains visible, though the object's appearance is changed by the see-through quality of the transparency. The Interactive Transparency Tool works just like the Interactive Fill Tool (see page 144), adding transparent uniform, fountain, pattern, and texture "fills" to objects. In actuality, these "fills" are *greyscale masks*. A mask covers part of an object and is used to make changes only to that particular part.

To create a transparency:

1. Select the Interactive Transparency Tool from the toolbar (**Figure 57**). A tiny glass will appear attached to the mouse pointer.
2. Click the object you want to make transparent with the Interactive Transparency Tool (**Figure 58**). (You'll know the object is selected when you see its nodes.)
3. Position the mouse pointer where you want the transparency to start.
4. Press the left mouse button and drag the mouse to where you want the transparency to end (**Figure 59**).
5. Release the mouse button. The object will redraw, looking gray and hazy (**Figure 60**). If you position the transparent object over another object, you'll see that the transparent object is see-through (**Figure 61**).

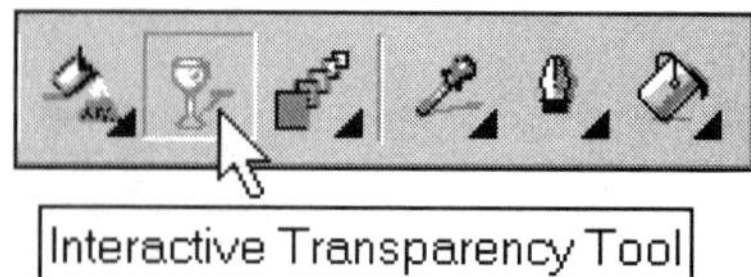

Figure 57. *Select the Interactive Transparency Tool from the toolbar.*

Figure 58. *Select the object you want to make transparent.*

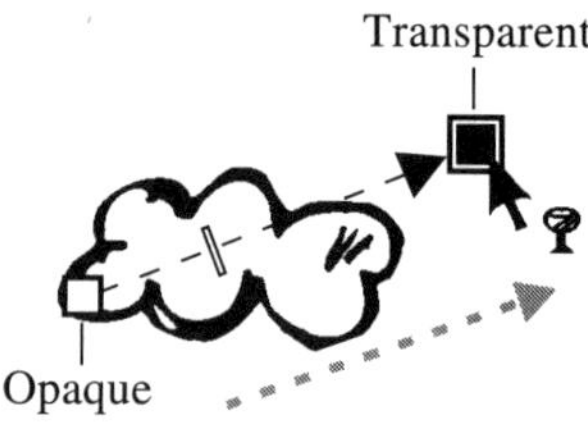

Figure 59. *Drag the Interactive Transparency Tool to make the object transparent.*

Figure 60. *When you release the mouse button, the object redraws as a transparency. A fountain transparency is the default.*

Figure 61. *If you drag the object you've been working with over another object, you can see that it's transparent.*

When you select the Interactive Transparency Tool, the Property Bar changes to give you quick access to a variety of transparency features (**Figure 62**). There are four types of transparencies you can create:

- **Uniform**—an even transparency that covers an object
- **Fountain**—transparency gradually increases across an object
- **Pattern**—a transparent pattern that covers an object
- **Texture**—a transparent texture that covers an object

Using the Property Bar, it is also possible to set how a transparency's colors interact with the colors of the objects below the transparency. And if you create a transparency and don't like it, just click the Remove button to start fresh.

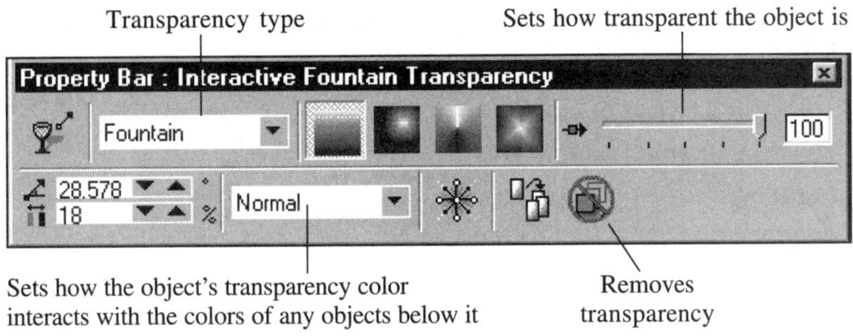

Figure 62. *The Property Bar offers many transparency options.*

Experiment with the different types of transparency to see what kinds of effects you can create. **Figure 63** shows two objects, a bear and the word "bear," before the bear is made transparent and placed over the text. **Figures 64a–e** show a few types of transparency.

Figure 63. *The original bear before it is placed on top of the word "bear" and a transparency mask is applied.*

Figure 64a. *Uniform transparency.*

Figure 64b. *Inverse uniform transparency.*

Figure 64c. *Fountain transparency.*

Figure 64d. *Pattern transparency.*

Figure 64e. *Texture transparency.*

The Interactive Distortion Tool (**Figure 65**) lets you add amazing effects to objects fast. Just like the other interactive tools, the Property Bar offers access to several features that help you create some interesting effects (**Figure 66**). There are three types of distortion: Push and Pull, Zipper, and Twister. Distortions can be applied to any object created in CorelDraw 9 as well as to artistic text.

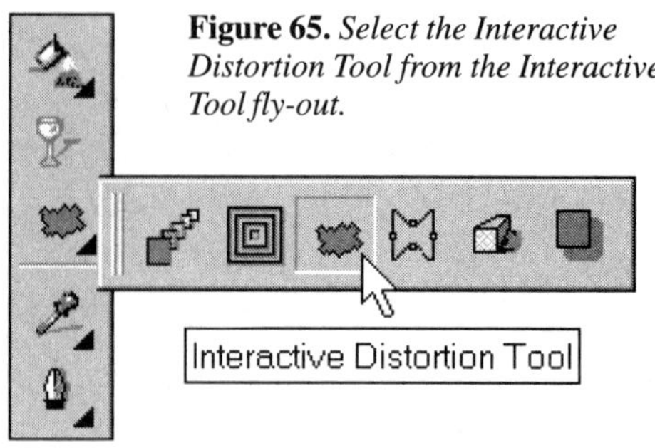

Figure 65. *Select the Interactive Distortion Tool from the Interactive Tool fly-out.*

Push and Pull Distortion

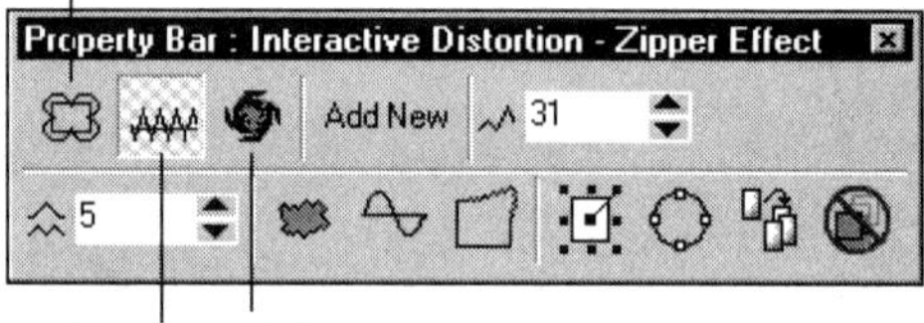

Zipper Distortion

Twister Distortion

Figure 66. *The Property Bar gives quick access to different distortion features depending upon which distortion type is selected.*

To create a push or pull distortion:

1. Select the Interactive Distortion Tool from the Interactive Tool fly-out (**Figure 65**). A tiny rumpled rectangle becomes attached to the mouse pointer.
2. Click the Push and Pull Distortion button on the Property Bar (**Figure 66**).
3. Select the object you want to distort (**Figure 67**). (You'll know it's selected when you see its nodes.)
4. Position the mouse pointer near the center of the object.
5. Press the left mouse button and drag to the right to create a push distortion (**Figure 68**) or drag to the left to create a pull distortion (**Figure 69**).
6. Release the mouse button when you are satisfied with the results.

Figure 67. *Select the object with the Interactive Distortion Tool.*

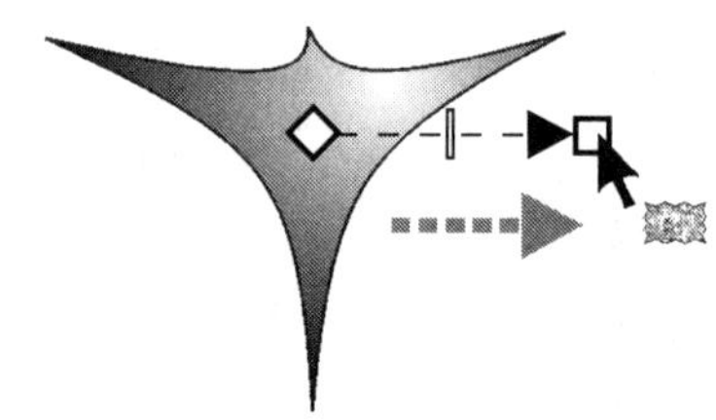

Figure 68. *Drag the Interactive Distortion Tool to the right to create a push distortion.*

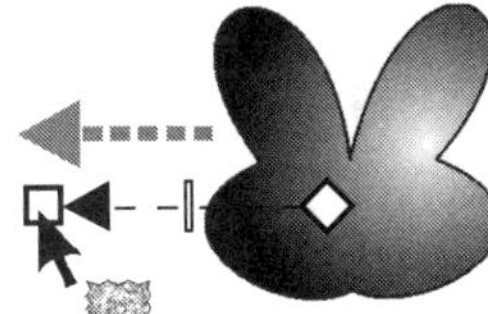

Figure 69. *Drag the Interactive distortion Tool to the left to create a pull distortion.*

Figure 70. *Drag the Interactive Distortion Tool in any direction to create a zipper distortion.*

Figure 71. *Drag the Interactive Distortion Tool clockwise to create a clockwise twister distortion.*

Figure 72. *Drag the Interactive Distortion Tool counterclockwise to create a twister distortion that swirls in the other direction.*

To create a zipper distortion:

1. Select the Interactive Distortion Tool (**Figure 65**).
2. Click the Zipper Distortion button on the Property Bar (**Figure 66**).
3. Select the object you want to distort (**Figure 67**). (You'll know it's selected when you see its nodes.)
4. Position the mouse pointer where you want the distortion to start, then press the left mouse button and drag to create the distortion (**Figure 70**).
5. Release the mouse button when you like what you see.

To create a twister distortion:

1. Select the Interactive Distortion Tool (**Figure 65**).
2. Click the Twister Distortion button on the Property Bar (**Figure 66**).
3. Select the object you want to distort (**Figure 67**). (You'll know it's selected when you see its nodes.)
4. Position the mouse pointer where you want the distortion to start, then press the left mouse button and drag either clockwise (**Figure 71**) or counterclockwise (**Figure 72**) to create the distortion.
5. Release the mouse button when you have finished the distortion.

When you add contours to an object with the new Interactive Contour Tool (**Figure 73**), CorelDraw uses the object's outline to create *contour lines*. You can set how thick these lines are, their color, and in which direction they move: either to the center of the object, inside the object, or outside the object.

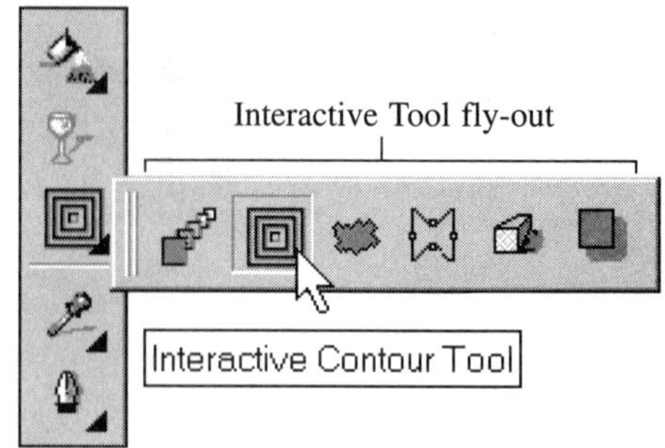

Figure 73. *Select the Interactive Contour Tool from the Interactive Tool fly-out.*

To add contours to an object:

1. Select the Interactive Contour Tool from the Interactive Tool fly-out (**Figure 73**).
2. Click on the object you want to contour to select it (**Figure 74**).
3. Position the mouse pointer near the edge of the object.
4. Drag in towards the center of the object to create inside contours (**Figure 75**) or drag out, away from the object, to create outside contours (**Figure 76**).

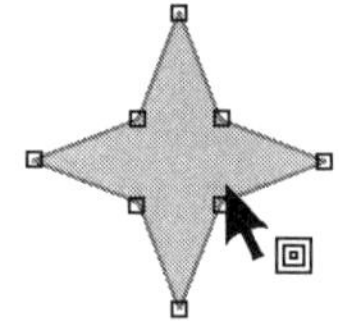

Figure 74. *Select the object you want to contour. You'll know it's selected when tiny nodes appear around the object.*

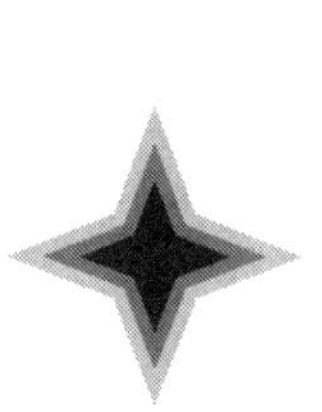

Figure 75. *Drag inwards to create inside contours.*

Figure 76. *Drag outwards to create outside contours.*

When you select the Contour Tool, the Property Bar dynamically changes to display the different contour features you can set and select (**Figure 77**).

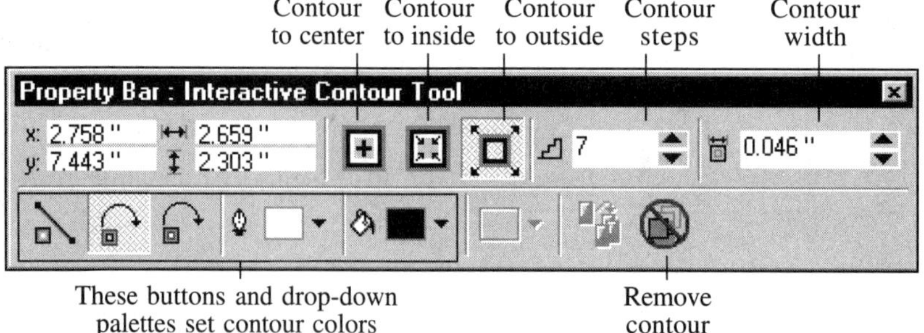

Figure 77. *The Property Bar gives quick access to contour features.*

The Interactive Contour Tool

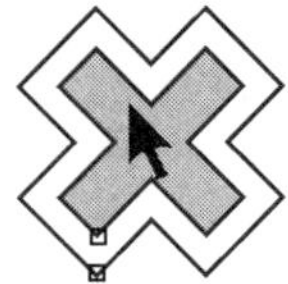

Figure 78. *Select the contoured object. This object has one contour line on the outside.*

Figure 79. *The object redraws with the new number of contour steps. This object now has three outside contour lines.*

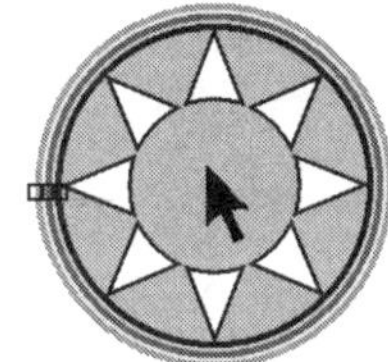

Figure 80. *Select the contoured object. This object has two contour lines on the outside that are .05" thick.*

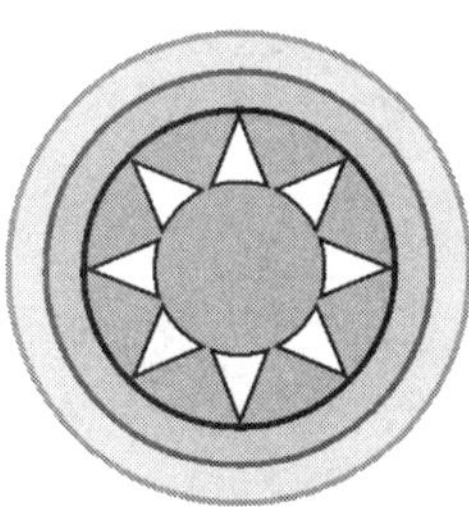

Figure 81. *The object redraws with the new contour line width. This object's two contour lines are now .1" thick.*

To change the number of contour steps:

1. Select the contoured object with the Pick Tool. (**Figure 78**).
2. Enter a new number in the Contour Steps text box on the Property Bar (**Figure 77**).
3. Press Enter on the keyboard. The object will redraw with the new number of contours (**Figure 79**).

To change the width of the contour lines:

1. Select the contoured object with the Interactive Contour Tool (**Figure 80**).
2. Enter a new measurement in the Contour Width text box on the Property Bar (**Figure 77**).
3. Press Enter on the keyboard. The object will redraw with the new contour width (**Figure 81**).

Tip:

- Don't hesitate to experiment with the settings on the Property Bar! You can create some really nifty effects with the Interactive Contour Tool (**Figures 82a–c**).

Figures 82a–c. *There are many ways to contour objects. If you set the contour steps to a large number and the contour width to a very small number, the contour will create a highlighting effect.*

The Lens docker (**Figure 83**) lets you simulate the effects created by camera lenses, including fish eye, brightening, transparency, and color inversion. Any closed path object, such as a square, star, or artistic text object, can be used as the lens that views the drawing behind it.

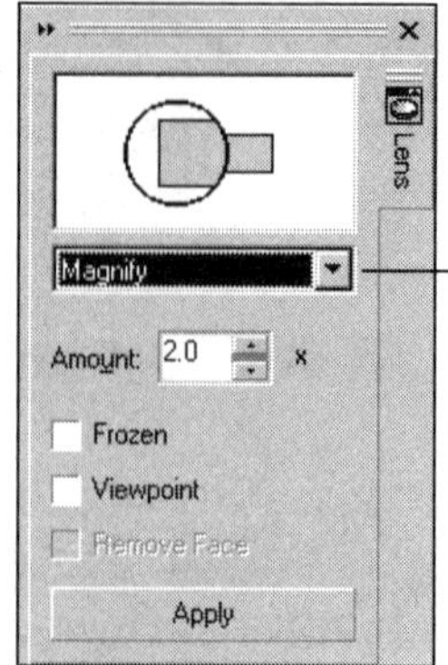

Figure 83. *The Lens docker lets you add interesting viewing effects.*

Lens Type drop-down list

To add a lens effect to a graphic:

1. Choose Lens from the Effects menu (**Figure 84**) or press Alt+F3 on the keyboard.
2. Select the object that is going to become the lens with the Pick Tool and position it on top of the graphic that will be viewed with the lens (**Figure 85**).
3. Use the Lens Type drop-down list on the Lens docker to select a lens effect.
4. Click Apply. The lens graphic redraws, completing the effect on the graphic behind it (**Figure 86**). Try out the different lenses available on the Lens Type drop-down list (**Figure 87a–c**).

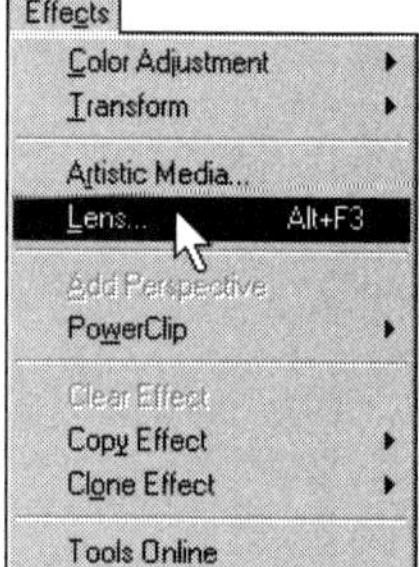

Figure 84. *Choose Lens from the Effects menu.*

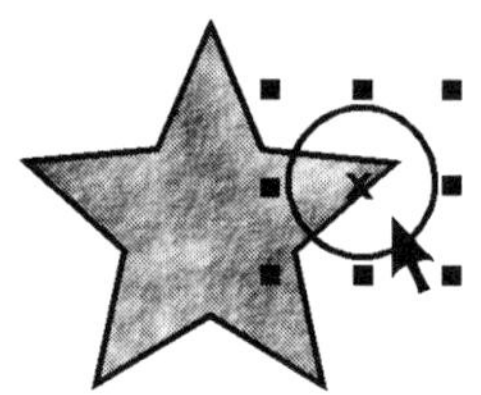

Figure 85. *Position the lens object on top of the graphic to be viewed.*

Figure 86. *The star viewed through a magnifying lens.*

Figure 87a. *A fish eye lens.*

Figure 87b. *A transparency lens.*

Figure 87c. *A brightening lens.*

Add Lens Effects

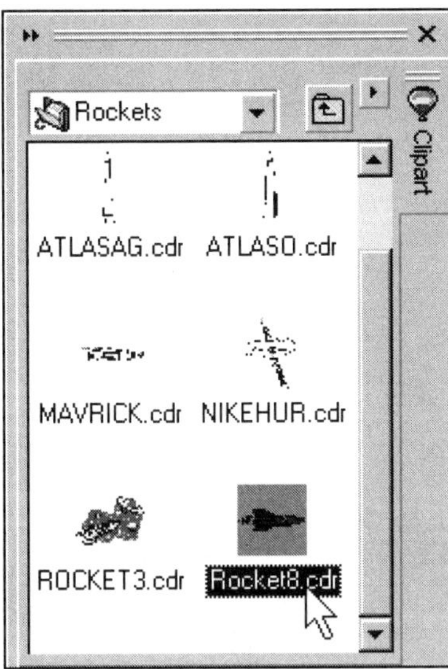

Figure 88. *Select the clipart rocket from the Scrapbook docker.*

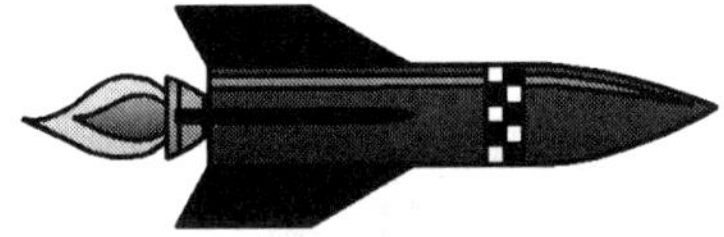

Figure 89. *Resize the rocket and zoom in so you can see it clearly.*

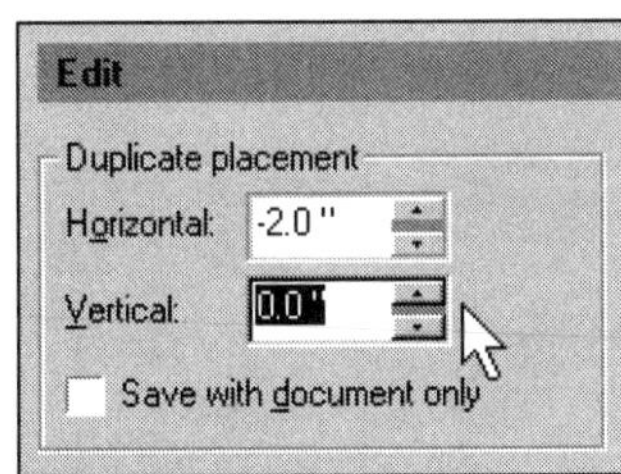

Figure 90. *On the Edit panel of the Options dialog box, use the Duplicate placement area to change the Horizontal setting to -2.0 inches and the Vertical setting to 0.*

Special Project:

Making Drawings Move

Showing motion is hard when all you have is a still page. Motion blurs, which are fading trails behind objects, help give the impression of motion. These trails are simply blends.

This example uses a clipart rocket, available on CorelDraw 9 CD-ROM disk 2 as Clipart\Space\Rockets\Rocket8.Cdr.

To make a rocket fly:

1. Import the clipart rocket using the Scrapbook docker (**Figure 88**). (For more about importing clipart see pages 258–259.)
2. Resize the rocket so it is about 3 inches (7.6 centimeters) long and zoom in to see it clearly (**Figure 89**).
3. Select the rocket and ungroup it by pressing Ctrl+U on the keyboard or by choosing Ungroup from the Arrange menu. The Status Bar will state "17 Objects Selected on Layer 1."
4. Open the Options dialog box by choosing Options from the Tools menu, then click Edit in the tree view window to move to that panel.
5. In the Duplicate placement area of the Edit panel, change the Horizontal setting to -2.0 inches (-5 centimeters) and the Vertical setting to 0 (**Figure 90**), then click OK.

6. Select the upper, black rocket fin, then choose Duplicate from the Edit menu or press Ctrl+D on the keyboard. A duplicate fin will appear 2 inches (5 centimeters) to the left of the rocket (**Figure 91**).
7. Notice that the bottom edge of the duplicate fin is curved. That edge needs to be straight so that it follows the straight red tube of the rocket. Drag a horizontal guideline down and align it exactly with the edge of the red rocket tube (**Figure 92**).
8. Choose Snap to Guidelines from the Arrange menu, then select the Shape Tool.
9. Zoom in so you can see the duplicate tail fin clearly, then click on it with the Shape Tool to select it. Nodes will appear around the fin (**Figure 93**).
10. Drag the nodes on the bottom edge of the fin up to the guideline to straighten it out (**Figure 94**).
11. Zoom out so you can see the rocket again.
12. Select the Pick Tool, then select the tail fin.

Figure 91. *The duplicate tail fin appears 2 inches (5 centimeters) to the left of the rocket.*

Figure 92. *Add a horizontal guideline, aligning it with the top edge of the red rocket tube.*

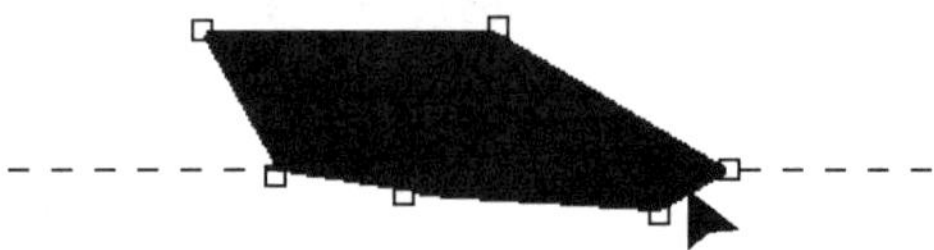

Figure 93. *When you select the tail fin copy, nodes appear around its perimeter.*

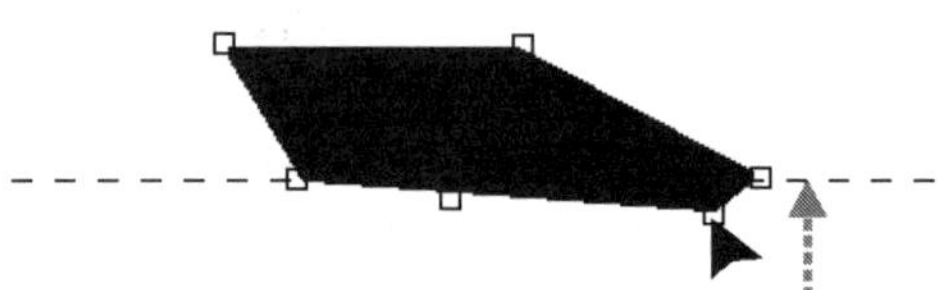

Figure 94. *Drag the nodes on the bottom of the tail fin copy up to the guideline.*

Special Project: Making Drawings Move

Figure 95. *Fill the tail fin copy with 30% black and remove the outline.*

Figure 96. *Drag the gray copy on top of the original black tail fin.*

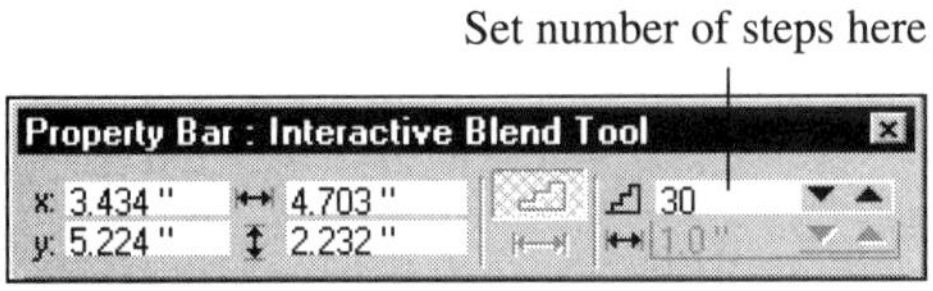

Set number of steps here

Property Bar : Interactive Blend Tool
x: 3.434 " ↔ 4.703 " 30
y: 5.224 " ↕ 2.232 " 1.0 "

Figure 97. *Use the Property Bar to set the number of steps to 30.*

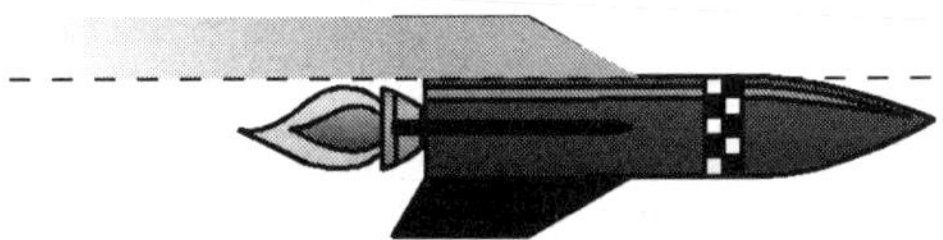

Figure 98. *When the copied tail fins are blended, a fading trail appears.*

13. Fill the fin with 30% black and remove the outline by right mouse clicking on the color well with an X in it (**Figure 95**).
14. Choose Copy from the Edit menu or press Ctrl+C on the keyboard.
15. Press Ctrl+V on the keyboard or choose Paste from the Edit menu. A copy of the gray tail fin will appear selected.
16. Use the Pick Tool to drag the gray copy on top of the original rocket tail fin (**Figure 96**).
17. Select the tail fin to the left of the rocket and fill it with the background color.
18. Select the Interactive Blend Tool from the Interactive Tool fly-out (**Figure 24**).
19. Use the Property Bar to set the number of steps to 30 (**Figure 97**).
20. Position the mouse pointer over the gray fin that is on the rocket.
21. Press the left mouse button and drag the mouse to the tailfin at the left of the rocket.
22. Release the mouse button. The gray and background color tail fins will blend, creating a fading trail (**Figure 98**).

23. Choose To Back from the Order fly-out on the Arrange menu or press Shift+PageDown on the keyboard. The blended trail will move behind the black tail fin (**Figure 99**). Congratulations! You just made your first motion trail!

24. Repeat steps 6–23, making a blended trail for the bottom fin (**Figure 100**).

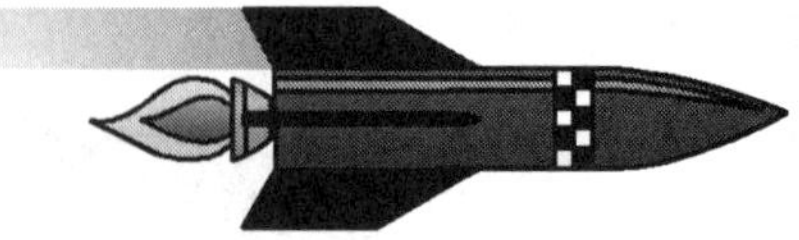

Figure 99. *When the blended tail copies are sent to the back of the stack, they become a motion trail.*

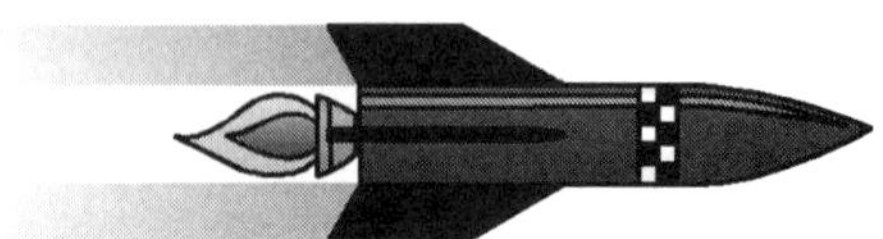

Figure 100. *Adding a second motion trail makes the rocket take off!*

Tip:

- There are other ways to show motion. You can also create motion trails using lines and curves (**Figures 101a–c**).

Figures 101a–c.

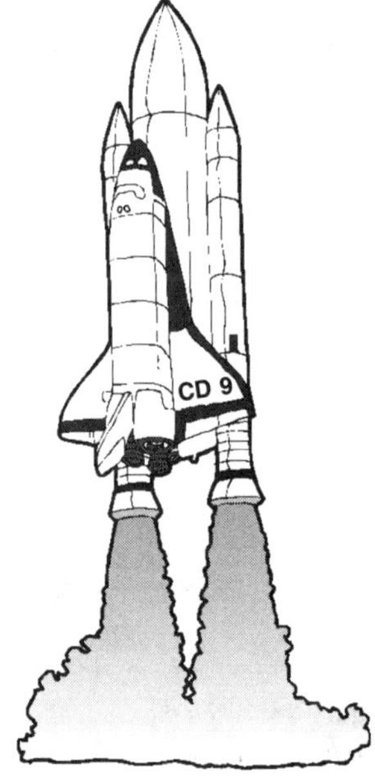

SUMMARY

In this chapter you learned how to:

- Use envelopes
- Shape envelopes using objects as guides
- Use the Interactive Blend, Transparency, and Distortion Tools
- Add perspective to objects
- Emphasize objects with shadows
- Create PowerClips
- Use the new Interactive Contour Tool
- Add lens effects
- Make motion trails

Symbols, Clipart, and Bitmaps

16

CorelDraw 9 ships with over 25,000 pieces of clipart. What an amazing library of beautiful images to have at your fingertips! (For the location of all the clipart used in this book, see Appendix A.)

CorelDraw 9 includes the ability to create photographic or painterly effects with *bitmaps*. Bitmaps are images made up of tiny dots called pixels. If you zoom in on a bitmap, you will see a pattern of tiny colored squares.

CorelDraw 9 is primarily a vector-based drawing program that gives you all the tools you need to create professional-quality graphics. Throughout this book, you've created vector graphics—drawings made with lines and fills created with mathematical formulas. With the addition of bitmap technology, you can take your drawings one step further, giving them photo-quality realism.

In addition to enhancing your drawings, CorelDraw 9 offers a new digital camera interface that lets you easily import your photographs into CorelDraw. Once a photo is imported, you can touch it up and add dazzling filter effects.

In CorelDraw, you can add symbols from such symbols fonts as Wingdings and ZapfDingbats to your documents, and manipulate them as you would any other graphical object. In fact, CorelDraw ships with thousands of symbols, organized into collections.

To add symbols to a document:

1. Choose Symbols and Special Characters from the Tools menu (**Figure 1**) or press Ctrl+F11 on the keyboard. The Symbols and Special Characters docker will open (**Figure 2**).
2. Use the drop-down list to select a collection of symbols. The collection will appear in the sample window.
3. Scroll down the sample window until you find the symbol you want.
4. Position the mouse over the symbol, press the left mouse button, and drag the symbol on to the drawing window (**Figure 3**). You can now work with the symbol like any other CorelDraw graphic.

Tips:

- You can set the size of a symbol using the Symbol Size text box.
- If you know the number of the symbol you want to use in a particular collection, just type the number in the # text box. The symbol will appear selected in the sample window.

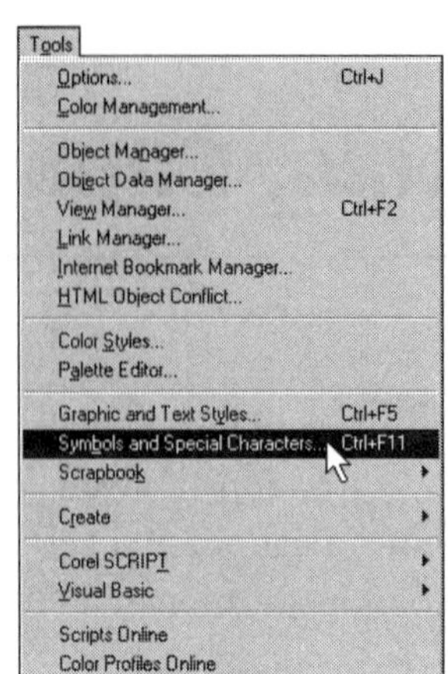

Figure 1. *Choose Symbols and Special Characters from the Tools menu.*

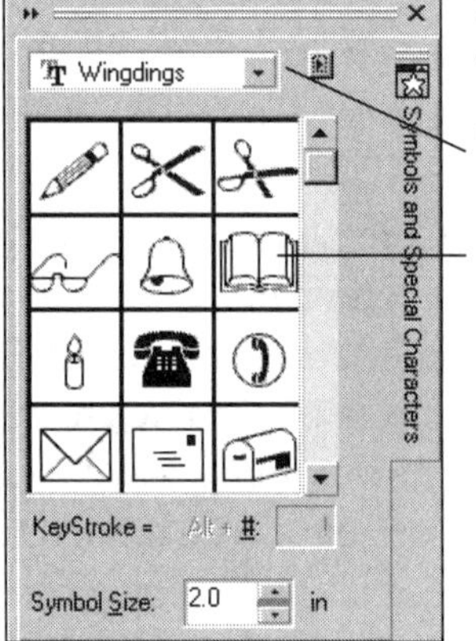

Figure 2. *The Symbols docker.*

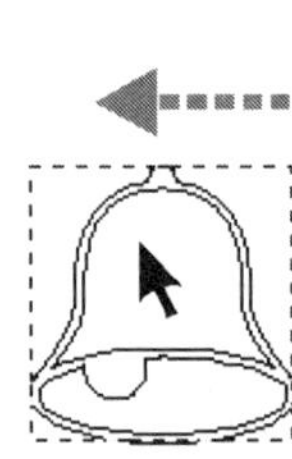

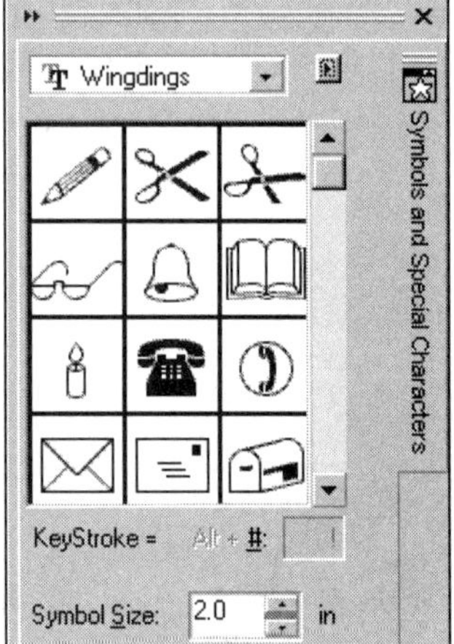

Figure 3. *Drag a symbol on to the drawing window.*

Symbols as Graphical Elements

Figure 4. *Select the object that is to become a symbol.*

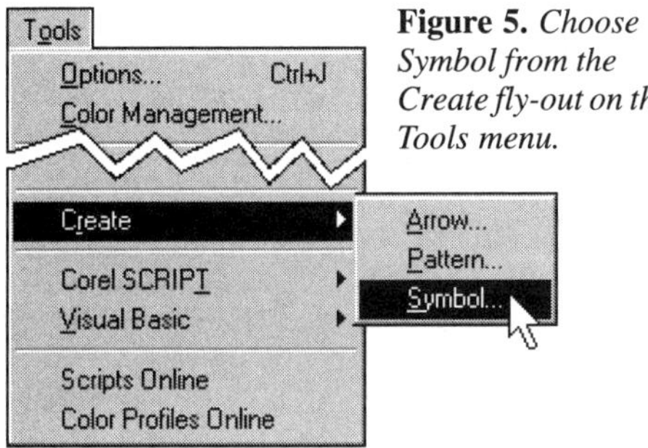

Figure 5. *Choose Symbol from the Create fly-out on the Tools menu.*

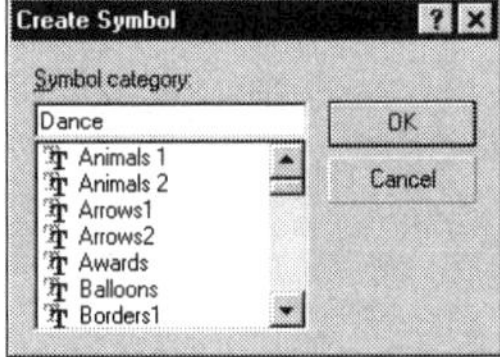

Figure 6. *Select the category where you want to place the new symbol or type a new category name in the text box.*

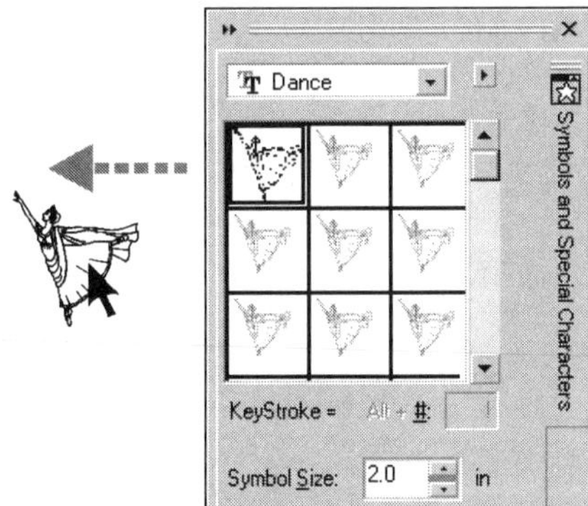

Figure 7. *You can now select the new symbol using the Symbols docker.*

With CorelDraw 9, you can create custom symbols and add them to any symbol collection or start a new collection of your own.

To create a custom symbol:

1. Use the Pick Tool to select the object that you want to become a symbol (**Figure 4**).
2. Choose Symbol from the Create fly-out on the Tools menu (**Figure 5**). The Create Symbol dialog box will open (**Figure 6**).
3. Use the scroll bars to select the symbol category where you want to place the new symbol or type a new category name in the text box.
4. Click OK. When you open the Symbols and Special Characters docker and use the drop-down list to move to the category where you placed the new symbol, you will see that the symbol is there (**Figure 7**). You can now drag the symbol onto the drawing window and work with it like any other CorelDraw graphic.

Tip:

- The graphic you select to make into a symbol must be made up of only one object. To make a multiple object graphic into one object, ungroup it (if it is grouped), then choose Combine on the Arrange menu.

The Clipart docker makes it easy to import the clipart and bitmaps that ship on the CorelDraw 9 CD-ROM disks.

To import clipart:

1. Choose Clipart from the Scrapbook fly-out on the Tools menu (**Figure 8**). The Clipart docker will open with the Clipart folder displayed in the file window (**Figure 9**).
2. If you do not have the correct CD-ROM loaded in your CD-ROM drive, the Find CD dialog box appears (**Figure 10**). Insert the correct CD-ROM disk, then click OK.
3. Use the file window the same way you would use Windows Explorer. Double-click on the Clipart folder. The contents of the folder—many more folders, organized by category—will appear (**Figure 11**).
4. Scroll down the list of folders until you find one that may contain an item you want to import, then double-click that folder.
5. Use the scroll bar to move down the list of importable files.
6. When you find a file to import, position the mouse pointer over the item, press the left mouse button, and drag the object onto the page (**Figure 12**).
7. Release the mouse button. The graphic will appear (**Figure 13**).

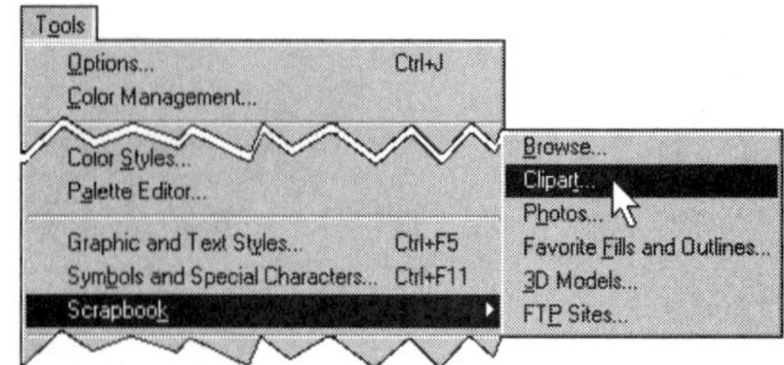

Figure 8. *Choose Clipart from the Scrapbook fly-out on the Tools menu.*

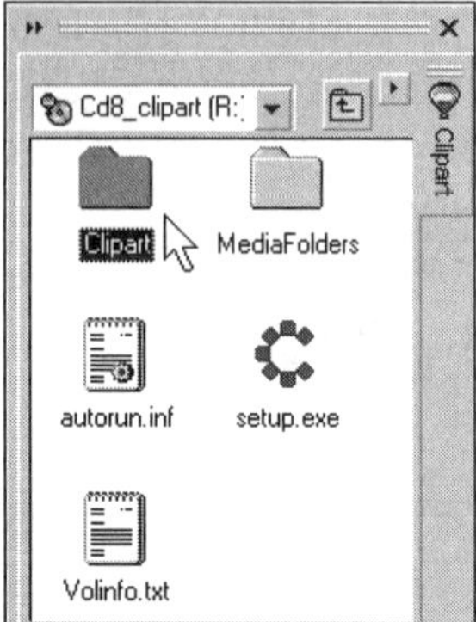

Figure 9. *When the Clipart docker opens, the Clipart folder is present in the window.*

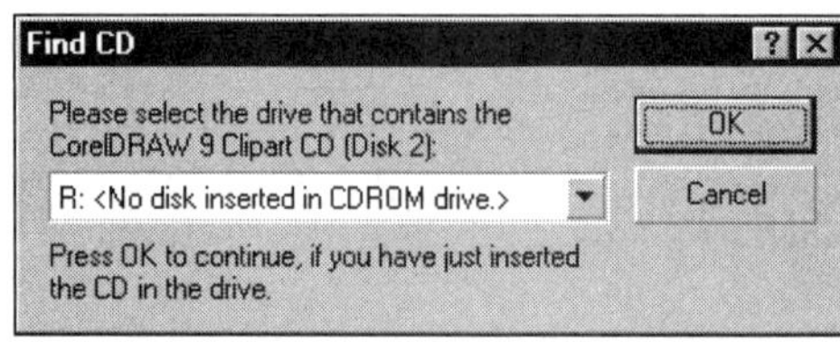

Figure 10. *Put the correct disk in your CD-ROM drive and click OK.*

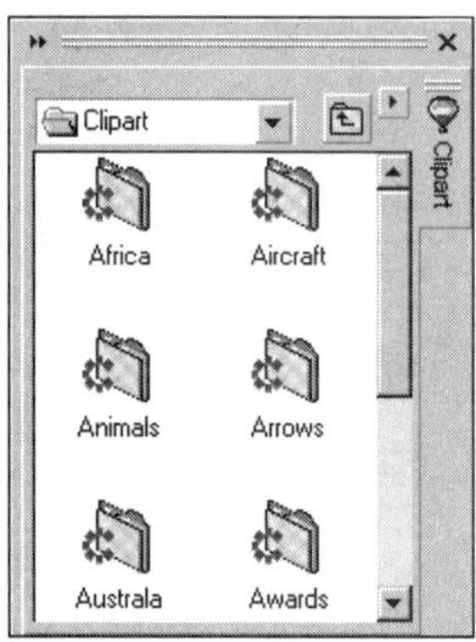

Figure 11. *The clipart is organized into categories by folder. Double-click to access the contents of a folder.*

Import Clipart

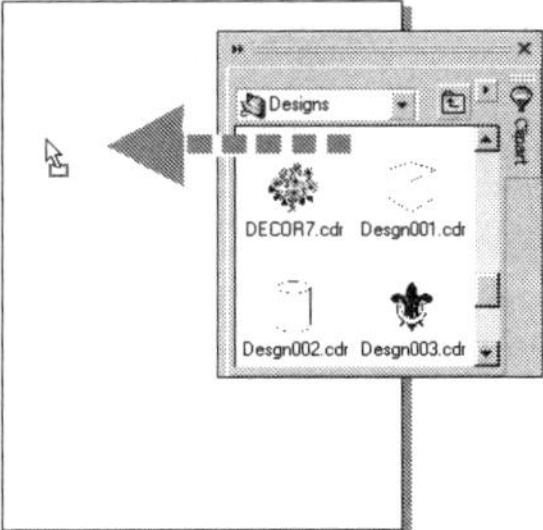

Figure 12. *Drag the clipart from the Clipart docker onto the page.*

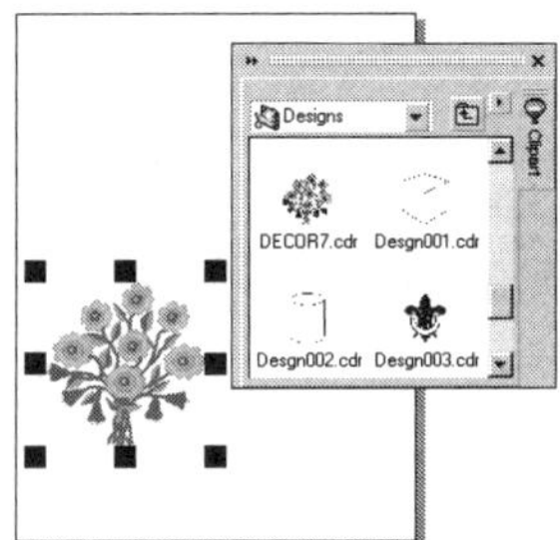

Figure 13. *When you release the mouse, the clipart is added to your project.*

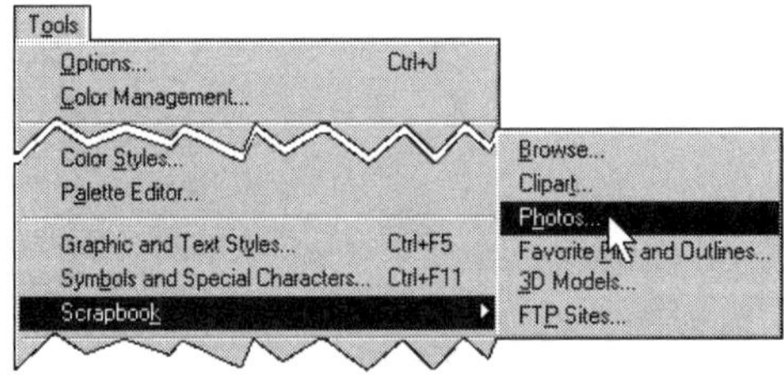

Figure 14. *Choose Photos from the Scrapbook fly-out on the Tools menu.*

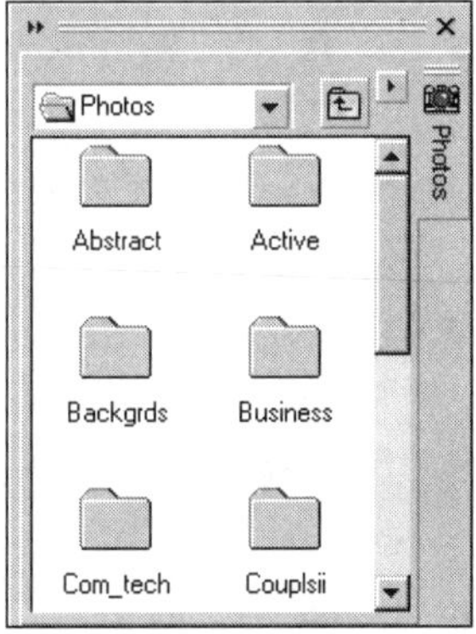

Figure 15. *Double-click on a folder to access the bitmap images.*

Tips:

- If you double-click on a clipart image in the Clipart docker (instead of dragging the image from the docker window), CorelDraw will automatically create a new document and place the clipart image on that page.
- Graphics files can be rather large. Importing graphics may use a lot of your computer's resources, causing it to slow down.
- When you import an item using the Clipart tab page, the graphic will be grouped. To work with the graphic, ungroup it, then alter it as you please.

To import bitmaps:

1. Choose Photos from the Scrapbook fly-out on the Tools menu (**Figure 14**). The Photos docker will open with the Photos folder open (**Figure 15**).
2. Double-click on a folder to access its contents.
3. Scroll down the list of importable bitmaps until you find the right one.
4. Position the mouse over the bitmap you want to import, press the left mouse button, and drag it out onto the page (**Figure 12**).

The Bitmaps menu offers many interesting tools and *filters* that you can use to manipulate bitmaps. Filters let you add special effects such as blurring, sharpening, and geometric distortions to bitmaps.

To convert a vector drawing to a bitmap:

1. Select the vector drawing you want to convert with the Pick Tool (**Figure 16**).
2. Choose Convert to Bitmap from the Bitmaps menu (**Figure 17**). The Convert to Bitmap dialog box will open (**Figure 18**).
3. Use the Color drop-down list to select the number of colors and put a check in the Dithered box. *Dithering* will keep the transitions between colors smooth in drawings that contain blends or fountain fills.
4. Select a Resolution using the drop-down list and put a check in the Anti-aliasing box. *Anti-aliasing* blends the pixels at the boundaries between colors for a smoother look.
5. Click OK. The drawing will be converted. You may notice some difference in the quality of the converted drawing. Lines may appear dotty since they are being created with pixels (**Figure 19**). (Compare Figure 16 with Figure 19.)

Figure 16. *Select the vector drawing with the Pick Tool.*

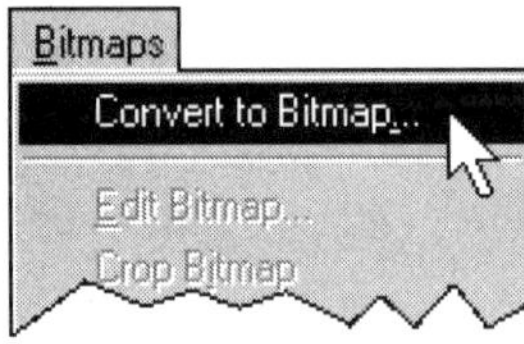

Figure 17. *Choose Convert to Bitmap from the Bitmaps menu.*

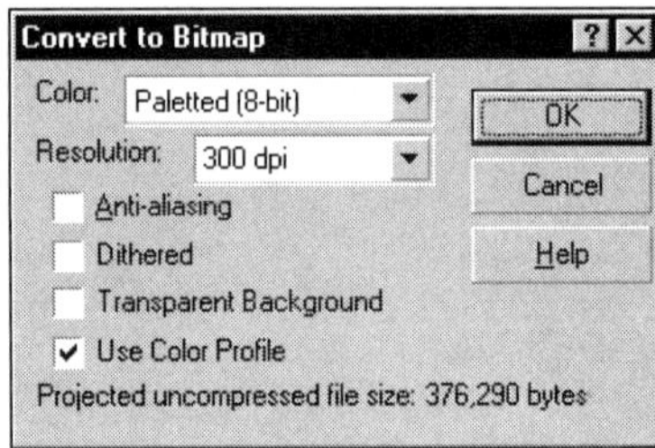

Figure 18. *Use the Convert to Bitmap dialog box to set the bitmap's number of colors and resolution.*

Figure 19. *The bitmapped image may appear more dotty since the lines are now created with pixels.*

Figure 20. *Select the bitmap image with the Pick Tool.*

Figure 21. *When you click on an area of the bitmap with the mouse, a tracing of the bitmap is created.*

Figure 22. *Use the Pick Tool to move the traced vector drawing off of the bitmap.*

With the auto-trace feature, you can quickly create vector drawings from bitmapped images.

To auto-trace a bitmap:

1. Select the bitmap image with the Pick Tool (**Figure 20**). The Status Bar will display something along the lines of "Color Bitmap on Layer 1."
2. Select the Freehand Tool or Bézier Tool from the Toolbox.
3. Position the mouse over the area you want to auto-trace. The mouse will change to a cross-hair with three dots attached to it.
4. Click the left mouse button. CorelDraw will trace an outline of the area (**Figure 21**).
5. Select the Pick Tool. The traced outline will automatically be selected.
6. Move the outline off the bitmap (**Figure 22**). You can now manipulate the traced outline as you would any other vector graphic.

Tip:

- The auto-trace feature only works on high contrast areas. If an area is made up of similar soft shades, auto-trace will not work.

Many filters on the Bitmaps menu will not be available unless the selected bitmap is converted to a color model. (Color models are discussed on page 141.) Some available color models include grayscale, RGB, and CMYK. Typically, grayscale is used to display an image in up to 256 shades of gray, RGB is used to display images on a computer monitor, and CMYK is used for color printing.

To convert a bitmap from one color model to another:

1. Select the bitmap with the Pick Tool.
2. Choose Mode from the Bitmaps menu. A fly-out will appear (**Figure 23**).
3. Select the color model you want to use from the fly-out.

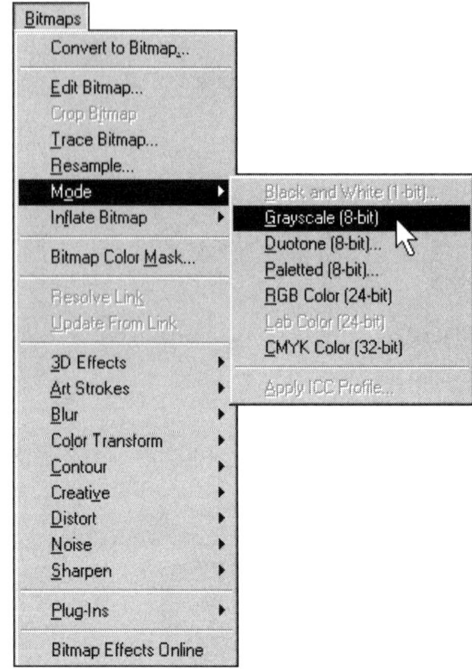

Figure 23. *Choose a color model from the Mode fly-out on the Bitmaps menu.*

File Size and Bitmaps

When choosing the number of colors and resolution for your bitmap, keep in mind that the higher you put the settings, the larger the file will be when saved. The simplest bitmapped image can be quite large (over 1MB) and for larger files, the sky's the limit.

Converting Vector Drawings to Bitmapped Images

Once a vector drawing has been converted to a bitmap and saved, there's no easy way to convert it back to vector format. You could use the auto-trace feature to recreate the drawing, but that can take time. Instead, save a copy of the drawing before converting it to a bitmap.

Figure 24. *Select the bitmap using the Pick Tool.*

Using bitmap filters is easy. All you need to do is select the filter from the Bitmaps menu, then move the controls in the dialog box that appears for that specific filter. Two examples—adding an impressionist touch and adding *noise*—are given here to get you started. To see other filter options, check out the filter effects shown on page 266.

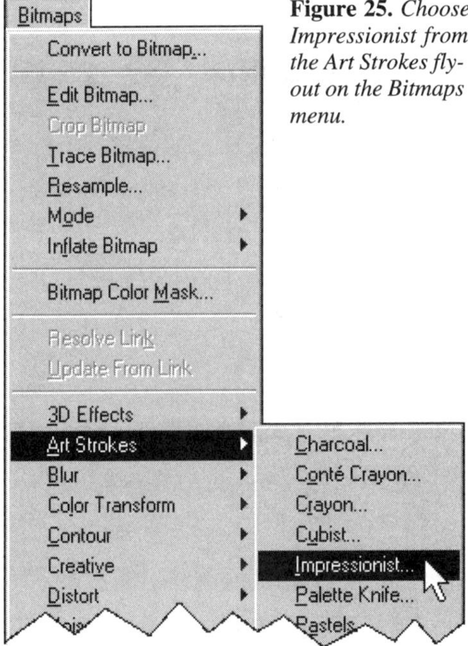

Figure 25. *Choose Impressionist from the Art Strokes fly-out on the Bitmaps menu.*

To make a bitmap look like an impressionist painting:

1. Select a bitmap with the Pick Tool (**Figure 24**).
2. Choose Impressionist from the Art Strokes fly-out on the Bitmaps menu (**Figure 25**). The Impressionist dialog box appears (**Figure 26**).
3. In the Technique area, use the sliders to set the effect. Higher settings translate to longer strokes, more color, and increased brightness.
4. Click the preview button to see what you have created (**Figure 27**).
5. If you like what you see, click OK, otherwise click Reset. The bitmap will revert to its original form.

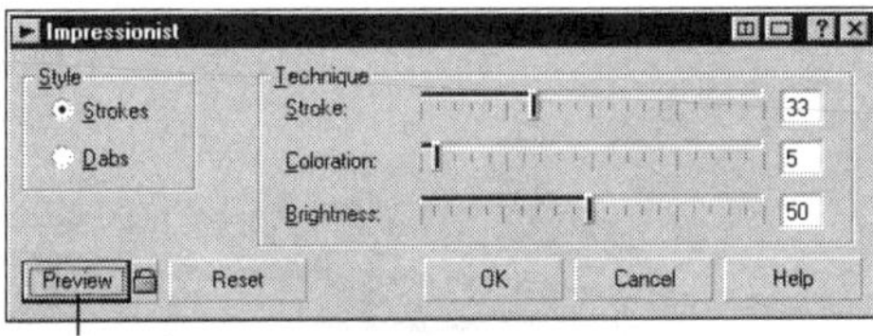

Preview button

Figure 26. *Use the Impressionist dialog box to set the effect.*

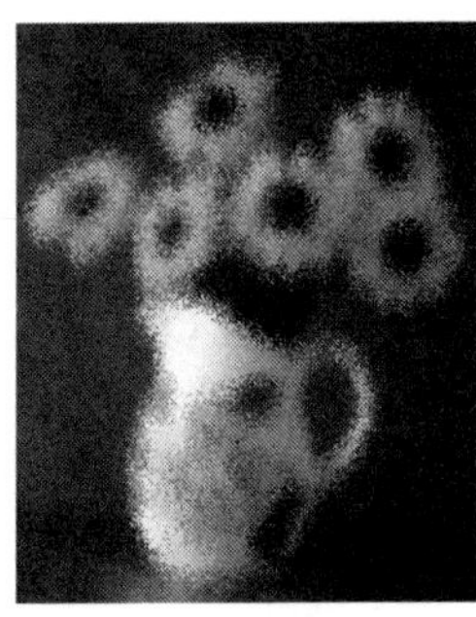

Figure 27. *Click the preview button to see the effect created by the settings.*

The Add Noise filter adds random pixels to a bitmap to give it a speckled appearance. It can be used to simulate a photograph taken on high-speed film.

Figure 28. *Select the bitmap with the Pick Tool.*

To add noise to a bitmap:

1. Select a bitmap with the Pick Tool (**Figure 28**).
2. Choose Add Noise from the Noise fly-out on the Bitmaps menu (**Figure 29**). The Add Noise dialog box will open (**Figure 30**).
3. Set the amount of noise using the Level and Density sliders. In addition, move to the Noise type area and select from the three options: Gaussian, Spike, and Uniform.
4. Click the the preview button to see the effect you have created (**Figure 31**).
5. If the effect is what you want, click OK. Otherwise, click Reset. The drawing will return to its original form.

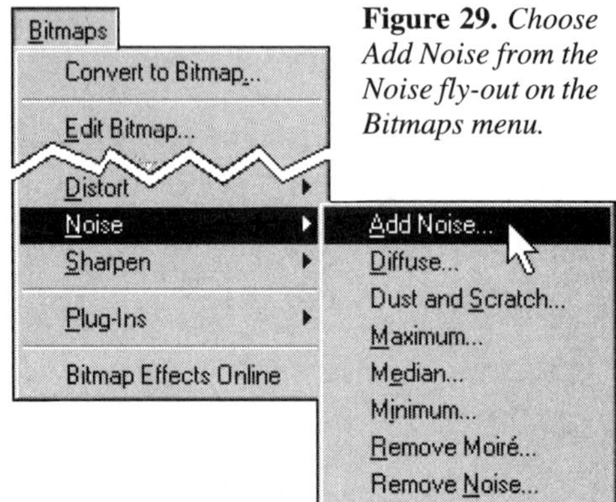

Figure 29. *Choose Add Noise from the Noise fly-out on the Bitmaps menu.*

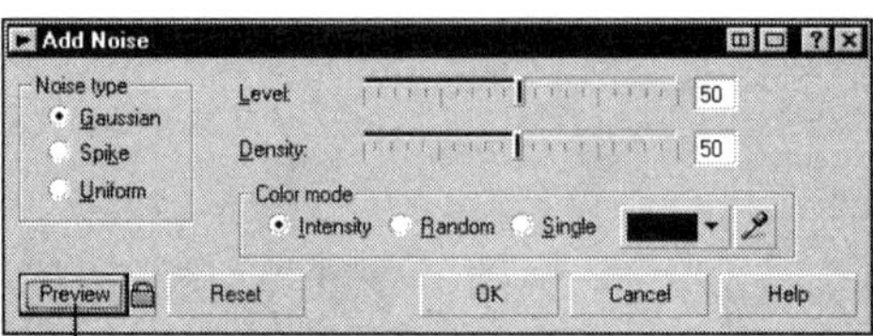

Preview button

Figure 30. *Use the Add Noise dialog box to set the amount and density of random pixels.*

Tip:

- The three types of noise that you can choose from, Gaussian, Spike, and Uniform, are based on mathmatical formulas. Each formula creates a different pattern of dots that make up the "noise" added to a bitmap.

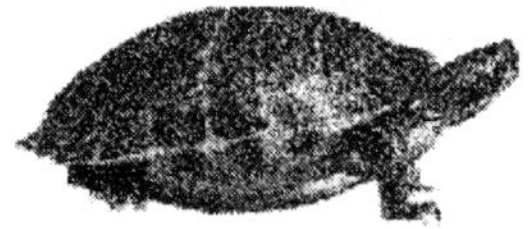

Figure 31. *Click the preview button to see the effect created by the settings.*

Figure 32. *Select the bitmap with the Pick Tool.*

Vignettes, pictures with gradually shaded edges that emphasize a face or object, are easy to create with the CorelDraw 9 Vignette bitmap filter.

To create a vignette:

1. Select a bitmap with the Pick Tool (**Figure 32**).
2. Choose Vignette from the Creative fly-out on the Bitmaps menu (**Figure 33**). The Vignette dialog box will open (**Figure 34**).
3. Set the shape of the vignette—ellipse, circle, rectangle, or square—by selecting the appropriate radio button in the Shape area.
4. Use the Offset and Fade sliders in the Adjust area to set how much of the image is visible and the amount that the edges of the image fade.
5. Click the preview button to see the effect you have created (**Figure 35**).
6. If you like what you see, click OK, otherwise, click Reset. The drawing will return to its original form.

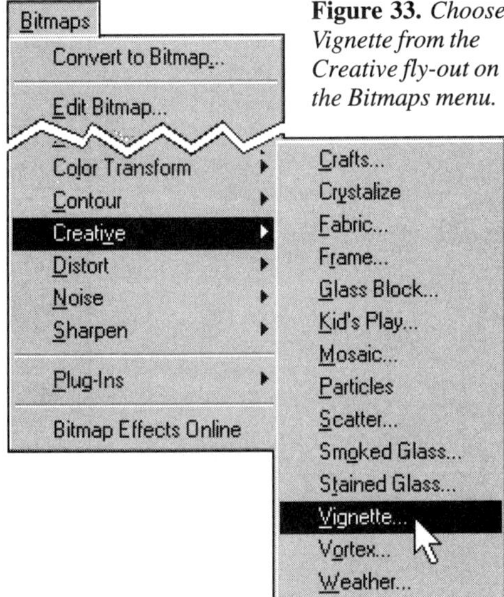

Figure 33. *Choose Vignette from the Creative fly-out on the Bitmaps menu.*

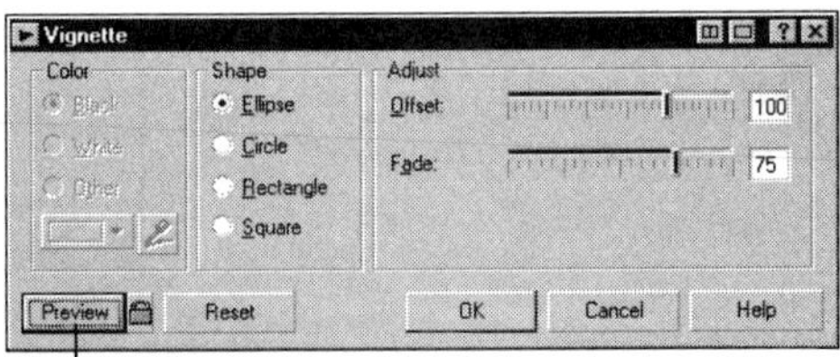

Figure 34. *Use the Vignette dialog box to set the effect.*

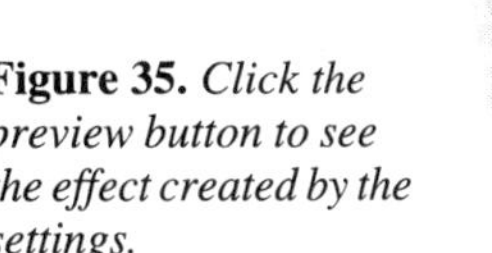

Figure 35. *Click the preview button to see the effect created by the settings.*

BITMAP FILTER EFFECTS

There are many filters that come with CorelDraw 9. You can use them to create interesting painterly effects. **Figures 36a–l** below show some of the filters in action. All of these and many more are available on the Bitmaps menu.

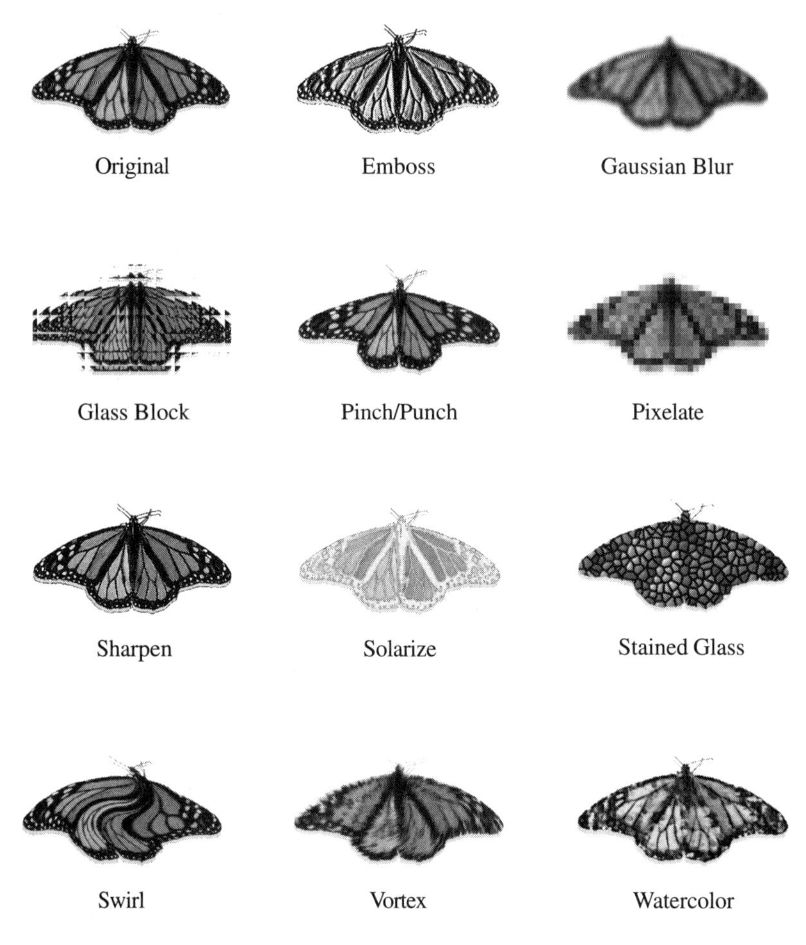

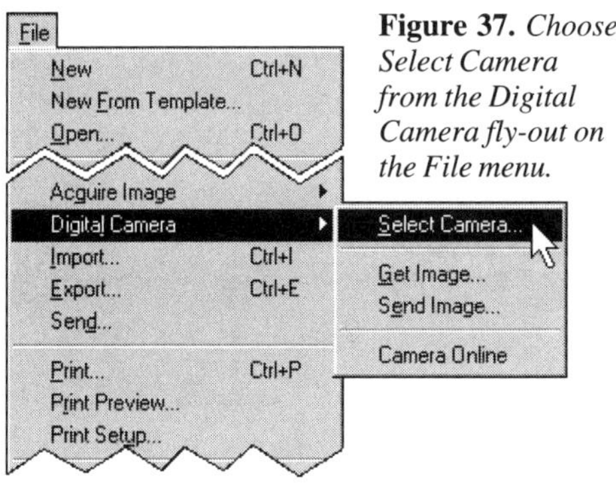

Figure 37. *Choose Select Camera from the Digital Camera fly-out on the File menu.*

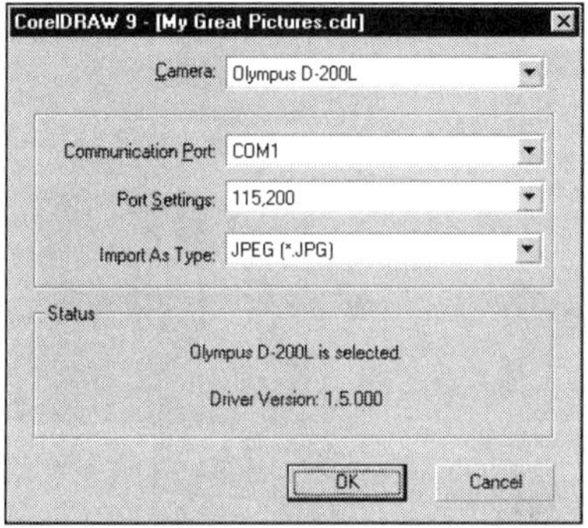

Figure 38. *The Select Camera dialog box is used to set the kind of digital camera you're using, the COM port it's connected to, and how your photos will be imported.*

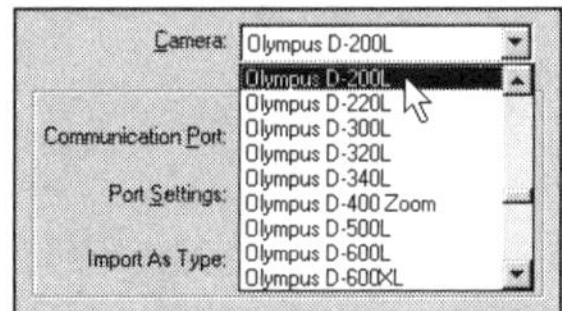

Figure 39. *Use the Camera drop-down list to select the digital camera make and model that you are using.*

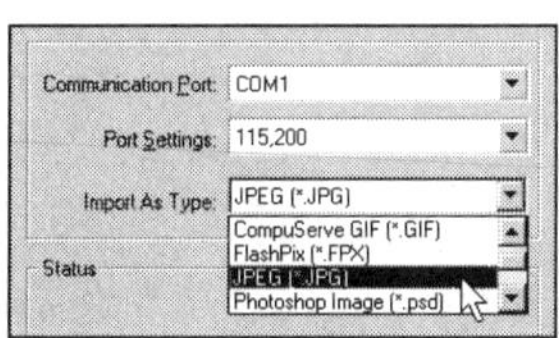

Figure 40. *Select a COM port from the Communication Port drop-down list. Then, select the file type your photos will be imported as using the Import As Type drop-down list.*

Digital cameras are fun, easy to use, and give quick results—a photo is ready as soon as it's taken. CorelDraw 9 includes a new digital camera interface that lets you *download* images from your camera. The interface places the picture onto the drawing window, ready for you to add personal touches and effects. In fact, you could use CorelDraw 9 and your photos to create wonderful flyers, birthday cards, portraits, and much more.

Before you can acquire a photo from your digital camera, you'll need to tell CorelDraw 9 what kind of digital camera you're using. (Make sure you have installed the software that came with your camera, also.)

To tell CorelDraw what kind of digital camera you're using:

1. Turn your camera on. With many digital cameras, this usually involves sliding the lens cover open. Also, be sure the camera is correctly connected to your computer.
2. Choose Select Camera from the Digital Camera fly-out on the File menu (**Figure 37**). The Select Camera dialog box will open (**Figure 38**).
3. Use the Camera drop-down list to select your camera (**Figure 39**).
4. Use the Communication Port drop-down box to set which COM port the camera is connected to (COM 1 is the default) (**Figure 40**).

(continued)

5. Use the Import As Type drop-down list to select what type of file—.Bmp, .Jpg, .Tif, etc.—the photos will be imported as (**Figure 40**).
6. Click OK. The dialog box will close and the camera type will be selected.

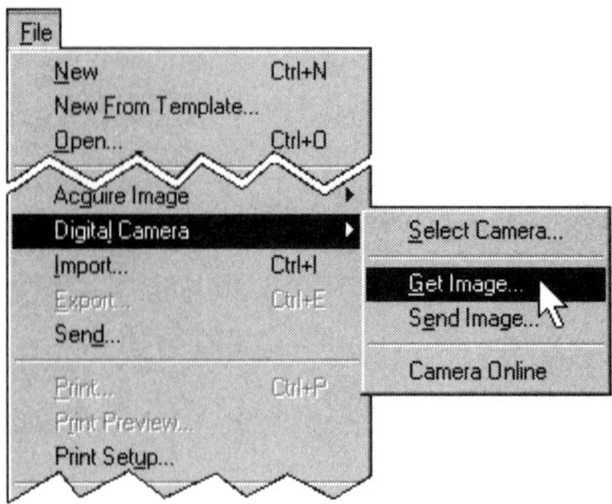

Figure 41. *Choose Get Image from the Digital Camera fly-out on the File menu.*

To download a photo from your digital camera:

1. Turn your camera on. With many digital cameras, this usually involves sliding the lens cover open. Also, be sure the camera is correctly connected to your computer.
2. Choose Get Image from the Digital Camera fly-out on the File menu (**Figure 41**). The Download Photo dialog box will open (**Figure 42**). This dialog box displays *thumbnails*—tiny images—of the photos saved on your camera.
3. Click the thumbnail you would like to download to select it.
4. Click OK. The dialog box will close and the picture will appear selected in the drawing window. The Status Bar will read something such as "Color Bitmap on Layer 1." You can now export the image for use in any type of program or for the Web, or add special touches, using bitmap filters and your other drawing skills (**Figure 43**).

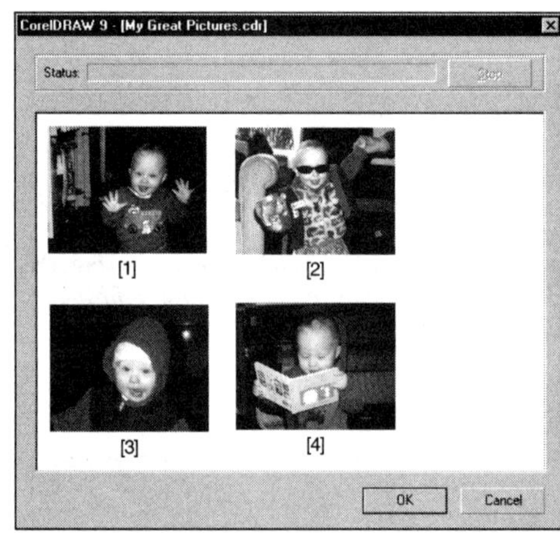

Figure 42. *The Download Photo dialog box is used to select the photo you want to import into CorelDraw.*

Figure 43. *You can add special touches and effects to your photographs. A posterize effect and frame filter have been applied to this photo.*

Download a Digital Camera Photo

Figure 44. *Select the photo you want to adjust.*

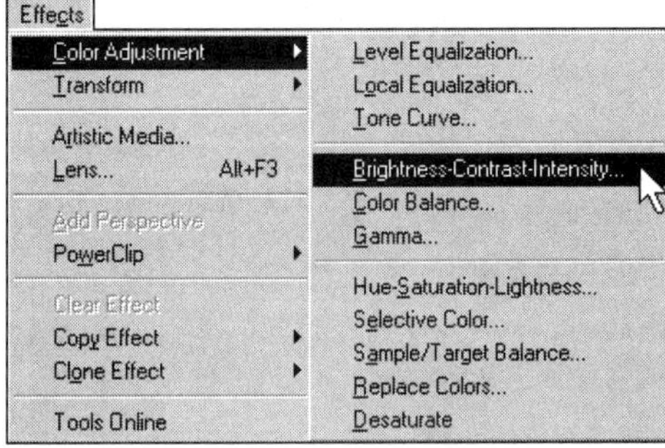

Figure 45. *Choose Brightness-Contrast-Intensity from the Color Adjustment fly-out on the Effects menu.*

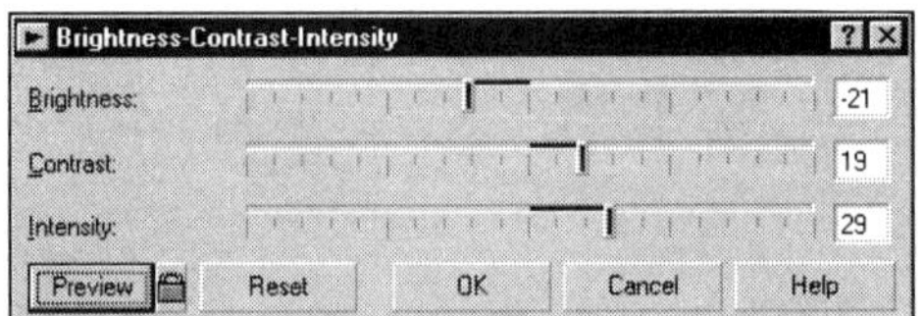

Figure 46. *Use the Brightness, Contrast, and Intensity slider bars to adjust the photo. Click Preview to see the changes you have made.*

Figure 47. *When you click the Preview button, the photo redraws with the settings you have selected.*

Once a photograph has been imported into CorelDraw 9, you can touch it up by adjusting its *brightness*, and *contrast*, and *hue* and *saturation*. Here's what these terms mean:

- Brightness determines how light or dark a photo is.
- Contrast sets the amount of difference between the light and dark areas of a photo.
- A hue is a color in a photo such as red, green, or blue.
- The saturation sets how strong or pure a hue is. For instance, the color red lightly saturated appears pink, whereas full saturation appears red.

To adjust the brightness and contrast of a photo:

1. Use the Pick Tool to select the photo you want to adjust (**Figure 44**).
2. Choose Brightness-Contrast-Intensity from the Color Adjustment fly-out on the Effects menu (**Figure 45**). The Brightness-Contrast-Intensity dialog box will open (**Figure 46**).
3. Use the Brightness, Contrast, and Intensity slider bars to change the settings. Sliding a bar to the left decreases the setting. Sliding a bar to the right increases the setting.
4. Click Preview to see the changes you have made (**Figure 47**).
5. When you are finished adjusting your photo, click OK to close the dialog box.

To adjust the hue and saturation:

1. Use the Pick Tool to select the photo you want to adjust (**Figure 48**).
2. Choose Hue-Saturation-Lightness from the Color Adjustment fly-out on the Effects menu (**Figure 49**). The Hue/Saturation/Lightness dialog box will open (**Figure 50**).
3. In the Channels area, click the option button next to the color you want to adjust. If you want to adjust all the colors at the same time, click the Master option button.
4. Use the Hue, Saturation, and Lightness slider bars to change the settings. Sliding a bar to the left decreases the setting. Sliding a bar to the right increases the setting.
5. Click Preview to see the changes you have made.
6. When you are finished adjusting your photo, click OK to close the dialog box.

Figure 48. *Select the photo you want to adjust.*

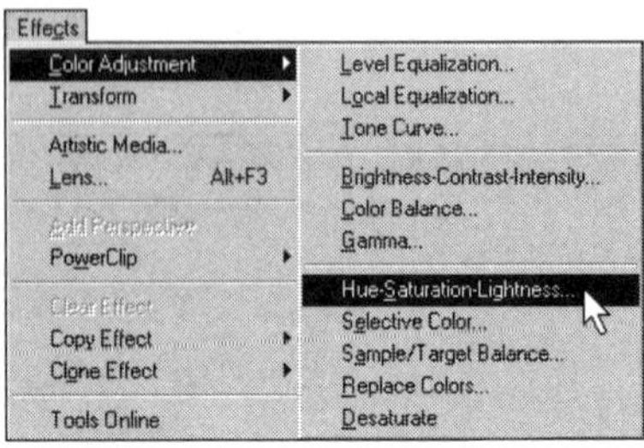

Figure 49. *Choose Hue-Saturation-Lightness from the Color Adjustment fly-out on the Effects menu.*

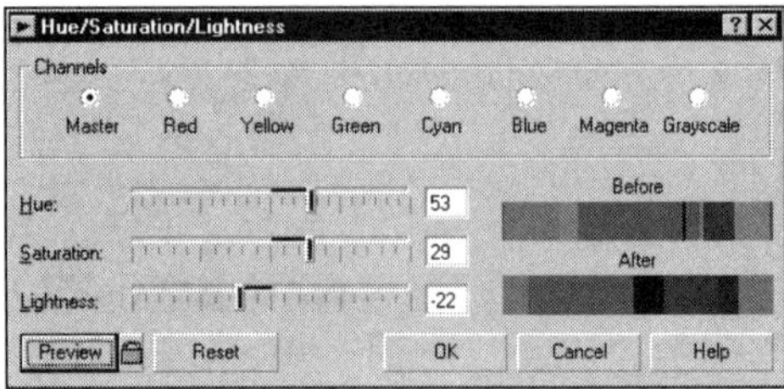

Figure 50. *Select the color you want to adjust in the Channels area, then use the Hue, Saturation, and Lightness slider bars to change the settings.*

SUMMARY

In this chapter you learned how to:

- Add symbols to a document
- Create custom symbols
- Import clipart using the Scrapbook docker
- Import bitmaps
- Convert a vector graphic to a bitmap image
- Make a bitmap look like an impressionist painting
- Create a vignette
- Import photos from your digital camera
- Touch up your photos using the Effects menu

CorelDraw 9 and the Web

The World Wide Web is a train with stops at every house that has a phone line and a modem. More and more people catch that Internet express every day, surfing and creating Web pages. With CorelDraw 9 and its Internet tools, you can jump on board and create your own Web site right in CorelDraw. There's no need for another Web design program.

This chapter will take you through everything you need to know to create a Web page. You'll learn how to change the default ruler and resolution settings and load browser color palettes in preparation for creating your Web page. Then you'll add some text and graphics to the page and discover how to add *bookmarks* and *hyperlinks*. Finally, you'll find out how to publish your page for the Web using CorelDraw 9's *Publish to Internet wizard.*

World Wide Web Terms

- **Alternate text**—text that appears in the position where the graphic will be while the graphic loads.
- **Browser**—the program that decodes the information coming across the phone lines, turning it into the World Wide Web pages you see on your computer monitor. The predominant browsers are Microsoft's Internet Explorer and Netscape's Navigator.
- **Links**—highlighted and usually underlined words on a Web page that transport you to a different Web site or Web page when clicked.
- **Map**—assign a URL to a graphic or text, creating a link to another site or Web page.
- **URL**—*Uniform Resource Locator*. A URL is an address for a Web site. An example of a URL is http://www.bearhome.com.
- **Web server**—a computer connected to the Web that contains Web pages.

Since the Web is a visual medium, CorelDraw's settings should be based on what will work for a computer monitor, not a printed page. A monitor uses pixels as its unit of measure and a screen resolution of 72 *dots per inch* (dpi). (A dot equals a pixel.)

To change the rulers to pixels and set resolution:

1. Right click on a ruler and choose Ruler Setup from the pop-up menu (**Figure 1**). The Options dialog box will open with Rulers selected in the tree view window (**Figure 2**).
2. In the Units area, use the drop-down list next to Horizontal to select pixels.
3. Make sure there's a check mark in the Same units for Horizontal and Vertical rulers check box.
4. Click the Resolution button. The Edit Pixel Resolution dialog box will appear (**Figure 3**).
5. Set the Horizontal resolution to 72.
6. Put a check mark in the Identical values check box, then click OK to return to the Options dialog box.
7. Click OK. The rulers will change to pixels.

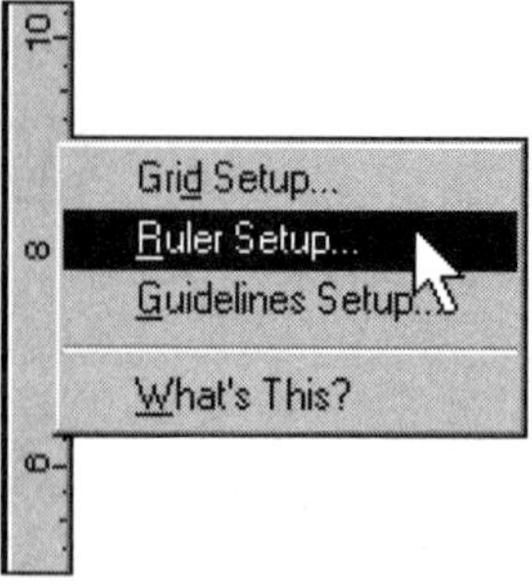

Figure 1. *Right click on a ruler and choose Ruler Setup from the pop-up menu.*

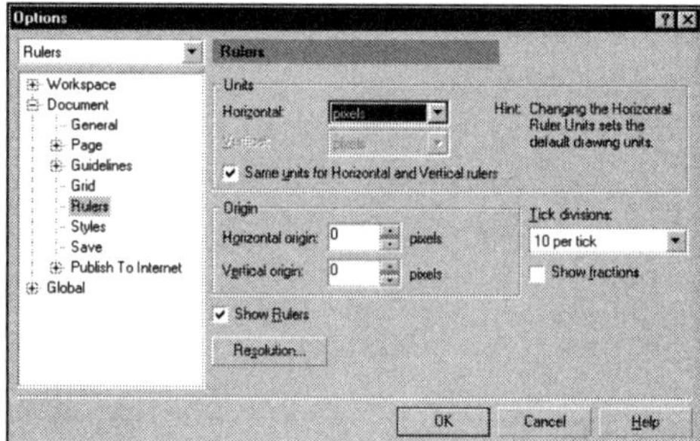

Figure 2. *Set the Horizontal drop-down list to pixels and put a check in the check box next to Same units for Horizontal and Vertical rulers.*

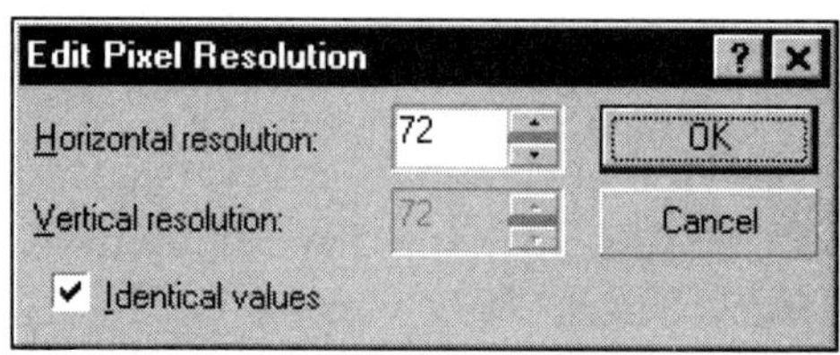

Figure 3. *Set the Horizontal resolution to 72, put a check in the Identical values check box, then click OK.*

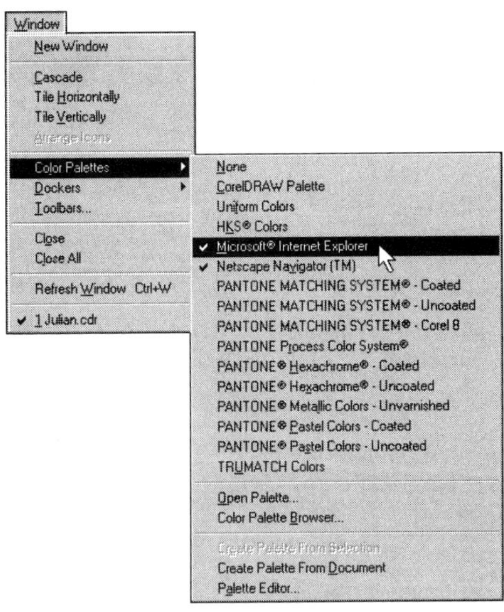

Figure 4. *Select one of the browser palettes from the Color Palettes fly-out on the Window menu. A new CorelDraw 9 feature lets you display both palettes in the drawing window at the same time.*

When you design graphics for the Web, you should use the colors that the Web browsers display well. CorelDraw 9 comes with two color palettes, designed especially for use with Microsoft Internet Explorer and Netscape Navigator. You can load either of these palettes into the Color Palette for easy access.

To load browser colors into the Color Palette:

1. Choose Color Palettes on the Window menu to access the fly-out (**Figure 4**).
2. Select either Netscape Navigator or Microsoft Internet Explorer from the fly-out. You're now ready to create graphics for the Web.

Help with Web Design

The best source for advice on the Web is the Web itself. There are many sites on the Web that offer advice on Web page design and style. Page design isn't just about pretty pictures, it includes creating user-friendly sites that make it easy for visitors to find the information they need. A few sites that offer interesting advice and tools for Web design are:

Sun Microsystem Inc.'s Guide to Web Style:
http://www.sun.com/styleguide

Web Designer's Paradise:
http://desktoppublishing.com/webparadise.html

Web design links available at Yahoo:
http://www.yahoo.com/Computers_and_Internet/Internet/World_Wide_Web/Page_Creation/

A good place to start when designing a Web page is to add a background color or image. Images used as backgrounds on a Web page are usually *tiled*, meaning that an image is repeated seamlessly across and down the page.

To add a background color or tiled image:

1. Choose Options from the Tools menu (**Figure 5**) or press Ctrl+J on the keyboard. The Options dialog box will open with Workspace selected in the tree view window (**Figure 6**).
2. In the tree view window, click the plus sign next to Document, then click the plus sign next to Page (**Figure 7**).
3. Under the Page category, click Background. The Background panel will appear in the dialog box (**Figure 8**).

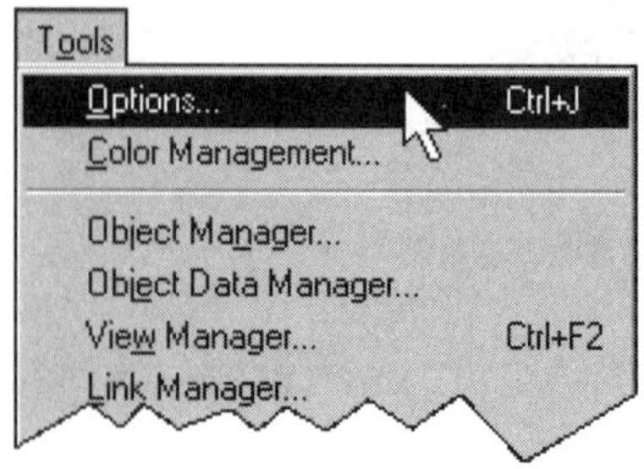

Figure 5. *Choose Options from the Tools menu or press Ctrl+J on the keyboard.*

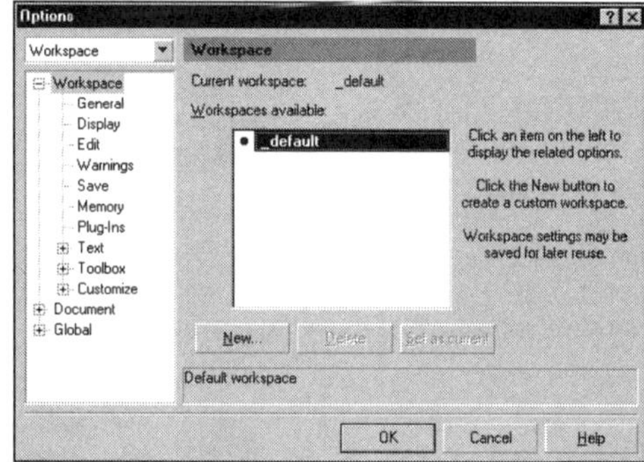

Figure 6. *The Options dialog box opens with Workspace selected in the tree view window.*

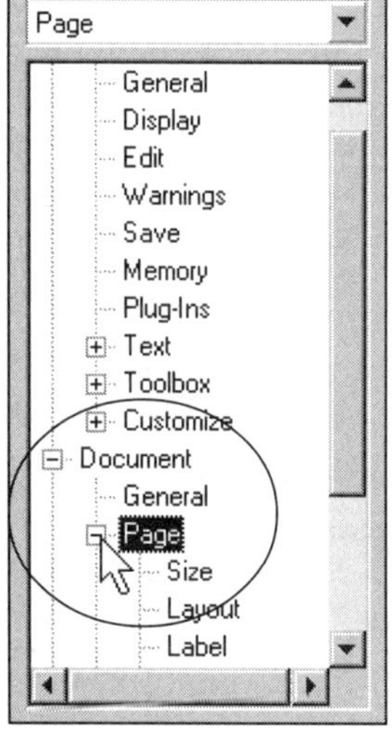

Figure 7. *Expand the tree view by clicking the plus sign next to Document, then clicking the plus sign next to Page.*

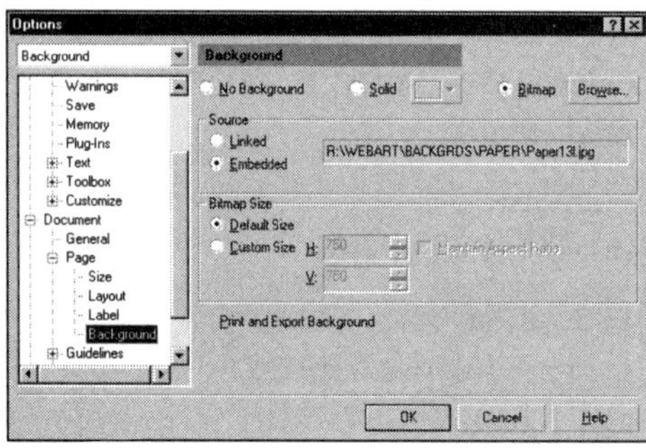

Figure 8. *The Background panel is used to select a solid color or image for the page background.*

Figure 9. *Select the Solid option button, then use the drop-down color palette to select a color.*

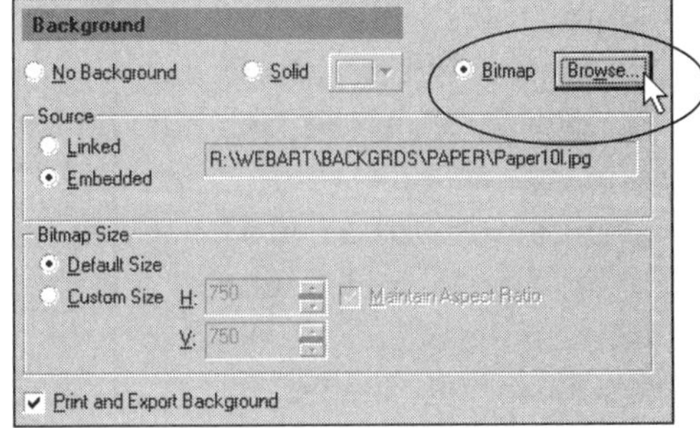

Figure 10. *Select the Bitmap option button, then click the Browse button to open the Import dialog box.*

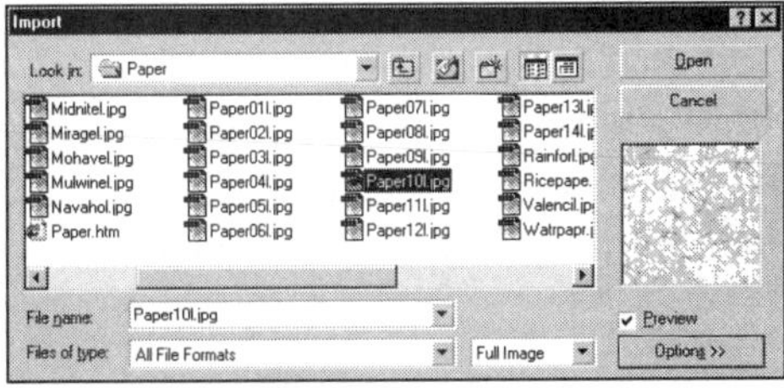

Figure 11. *The Import dialog box is used to select a background image.*

4. Make sure there's a check mark in the Print and Export Background check box found near the bottom of the Background panel.
5. To select a solid color:

   Select the Solid option button and use the drop-down palette to select a color (**Figure 9**).

   To choose a tiled image:

   a. Select the Bitmap option button, then click the Browse button (**Figure 10**). The Import dialog box will appear (**Figure 11**).
   b. Move to the folder that contains the image you want to import. CorelDraw 9 ships with many Web-ready background images. You can find them on CD-ROM #3 in the Webart folder.
   c. In the Source area, select the Embedded option button.
   d. Click OK to close the Import dialog box.
6. Click OK to close the Options dialog box. The solid color or tiled image you chose will appear on the page (**Figure 12**).

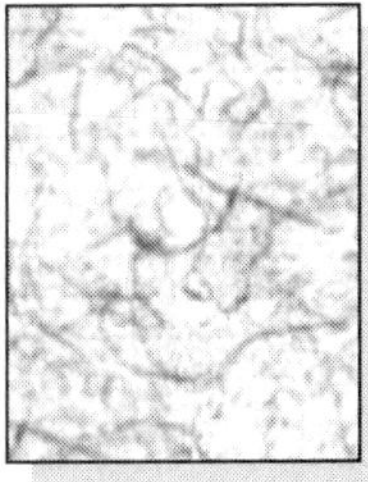

Figure 12. *The page will redraw with the solid color or tiled image as the background.*

GOOD WEB SITE AND PAGE DESIGN

Before you begin designing your Web pages in CorelDraw 9, there are several things you should consider:

Less is more. When you design your Web pages, they should present the information you want to convey in an easy-to-comprehend fashion. Users should be able to move through a site without confusion and easily find what they are looking for. With Web page design, as with good architecture, form should follow function. In other words, there should be a relationship between a Web page's appearance and what it is supposed to do.

Plan Web site flow. Web site flow is the way users will move around your site and its pages. Often, this involves navigation through information displayed in a hierarchical fashion. For instance, if part of your site were used to show dessert recipes, there might be a link to the dessert page from your site's main page. (The main page is also called a *home page*.) One way to plan a Web site is to draw a diagram similar to a flow chart showing every connection between the pages. Many folks use low tech materials, a pencil and piece of paper, to do this.

Maintain a consistent look. Use the same design elements across related pages of a Web site. This will give your site a consistent look and feel, and give the site visual cohesion. In order to maintain visual consistency between the pages in a Web site, you should establish standardized fonts, colors, graphic styles, and site navigation tools, such as buttons.

Use clipart and background colors. Since the Web is a very visual medium, it's important to add art to your pages. CorelDraw 9 makes this easy with its extensive clipart collection. In addition, CorelDraw 9 ships with Web-ready backgrounds and graphics that you can use to dress up your Web pages. Be careful, though: dark or busy backgrounds can make text difficult to read.

Figure 13. *A Web page's title appears in the browser's title bar.*

Besides the file name a Web page is saved with, it should also have a title. When the page is viewed in a browser, the title appears in the title bar of the browser (**Figure 13**). Because these titles are so prominent, they are important and should be carefully given.

To give a page a title:

1. Move to the page to which you want to give the title.
2. Right click on the page and select Properties from the pop-up menu (**Figure 14**). The Object Properties dialog box will open.
3. Click the Page tab to move to that tab page (**Figure 15**).
4. Type the title in the Page Title text box.
5. Click Apply.
6. Click the Close button in the upper-right corner to close the dialog box.

or

1. Move to the page to which you want to give the title.
2. Choose Rename Page from the Layout menu (**Figure 16**). The Rename Page dialog box will appear (**Figure 17**).
3. Type the new title in the Page name text box.
4. Click OK to close the dialog box.

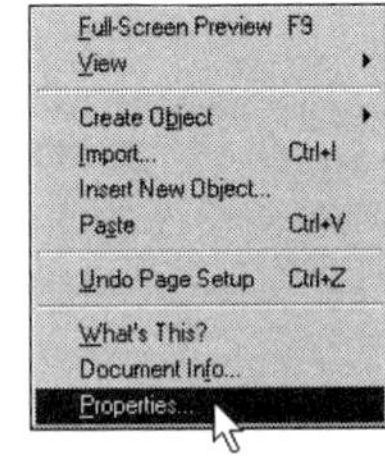

Figure 14. *Choose Properties from the pop-up menu.*

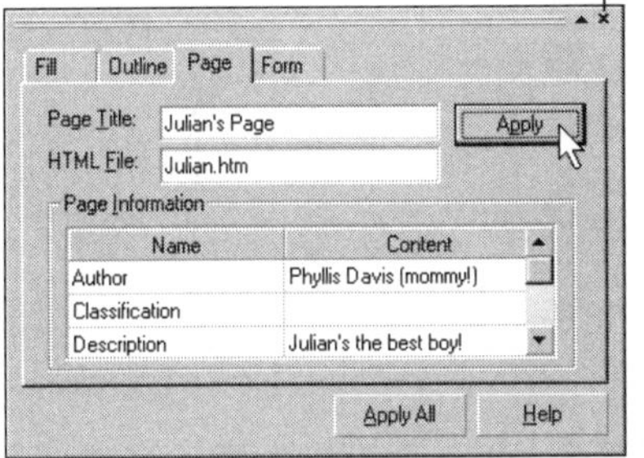

Figure 15. *On the Page tab page, type the page name in the Page Title text box.*

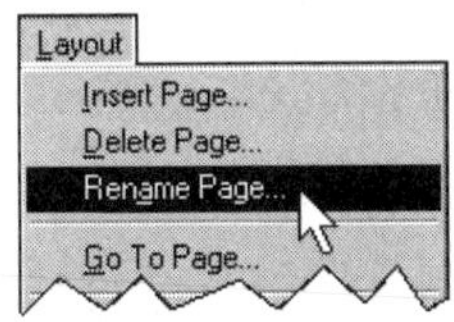

Figure 16. *Choose Rename Page from the Layout menu.*

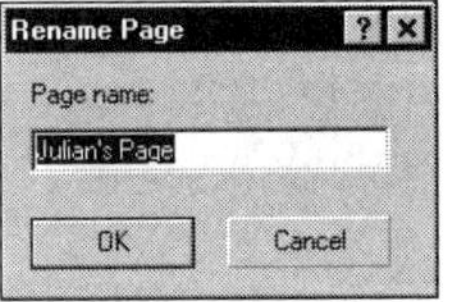

Figure 17. *Type the new title in the Page name text box.*

Give a Page a Title

Adding text to your Web page created in CorelDraw 9 is easy. All you have to do is select the Text Tool, drag a paragraph text frame, then type your text. (Creating paragraph text is discussed on page 157.) In order for text to export for the Web correctly, it must be paragraph text and it must be HTML compatible.

To make text HTML compatible:

1. Select the paragraph text frame with the Pick Tool.
2. Choose Make Text HTML Compatible from the Text menu (**Figure 18**).

or

Right click on the paragraph text frame and select Make Text HTML Compatible from the pop-up menu (**Figure 19**).

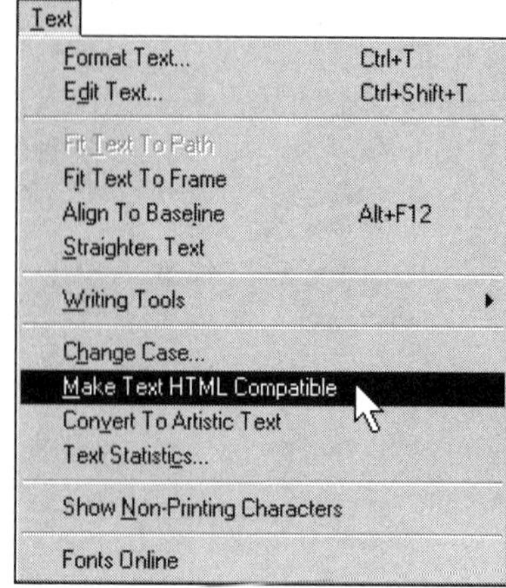

Figure 18. *Choose Make Text HTML Compatible from the Text menu.*

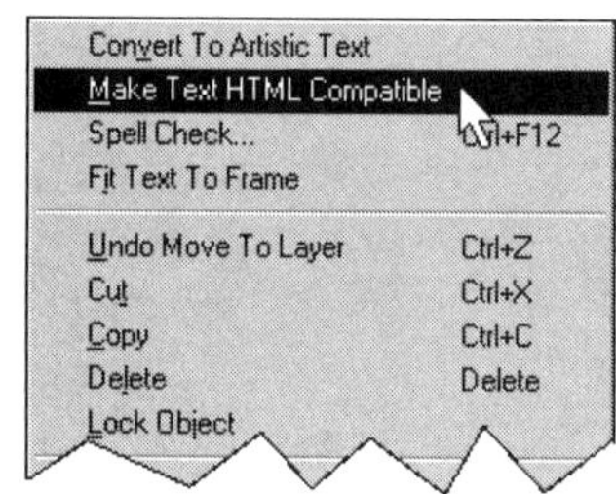

Figure 19. *Choose Make Text HTML Compatible from the pop-up menu.*

Special Fonts and Your Web Pages

Back in *ye olde* days of the World Wide Web (not too long ago!), the only fonts most browsers would display were Times and Courier. These days, you can use any font that you have to design your Web pages. (Since CorelDraw 9 comes with more than 1,400 fonts, you have a lot from which to choose!)

However, if you do use a special font, the people browsing your Web pages must have that font loaded on their computers. Otherwise, the text will appear in the browser's default which, most likely, would be Times. CorelDraw 9 comes with a special feature that lets you download special fonts to users' computers. You'll see how to do this when you export your pages for the Web using the Publish to Internet wizard (see pages 286–288).

Graphics make Web pages visually interesting while helping to bring across the message you are trying to convey. With CorelDraw 9, you can create images, use the vast clipart library that comes with the program, or import images from other sources.

Normally, graphics inserted into Web pages have to be saved in either the .Gif or .Jpg format. CorelDraw 9 takes care of converting images to these formats for you when you export your pages for the Web using the Publish to Internet Wizard. So, go ahead and add any image you want to your Web pages!

If you want to use CorelDraw 9 to create graphics for the Web for use in other Web page generating programs, you can do so by exporting the images as either file format. (For directions on exporting a file see pages 30–31.)

What are the .Jpg and .Gif File Formats?

The .Jpg file format is ideal for photographs and images with depth and small color changes, such as lighting effects. When you export a graphic as a .Jpg, you can set the graphic's Quality Factor. The higher the quality the larger the file size. Keep the quality as low as possible (without sacrificing too much of the image's quality) to minimize file size.

The .Gif file format is typically used for black and white art, line drawings, and images that are less than 256 colors. When you export a graphic as a .Gif in CorelDraw, you will need to specify whether the .Gif should be 87a Format or 89a Format. Here's what those formats do:

- 87a Format (developed in 1987) is the standard .Gif format. This is a good format to use for small images that will load quickly on a Web page. A special feature of this format is that you can create *interlaced* images. An interlaced .Gif file appears on the Web screen in chunks, starting at a low resolution, and progressing after several seconds to its final form.
- 89a Format (guess when it was developed…you got it—1989) is a descendant of the original .Gif format. As with its predecessor, the 87a format, 89a format offers the ability to create interlaced images. You can also create *transparent* images, where sections of the image (usually the background) are invisible. This is handy when a Web page has a special background pattern. You don't have to try to match the graphic's background to the background on the Web page (an impossible task!); instead, the image's invisible background lets the Web page background shine through.

Bookmarks, also called *anchors*, and hyperlinks (or links) let the user jump from one part of a Web site to another. In addition, hyperlinks also let the user jump to other Web sites. Bookmarks and hyperlinks can be assigned to either text or images. When they are assigned to an image, the area that the user clicks is called a *hotspot*.

You can create bookmarks, hyperlinks, and hotspots using either the Internet Objects Toolbar (**Figure 20**) or the Object Properties dialog box (**Figure 21**).

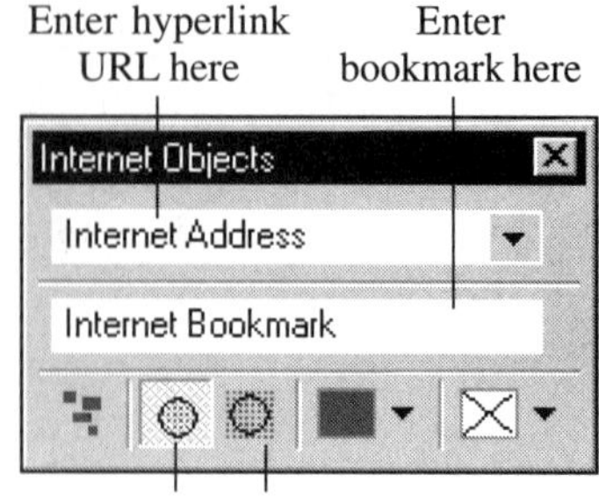

Figure 20. *The Internet Objects Toolbar.*

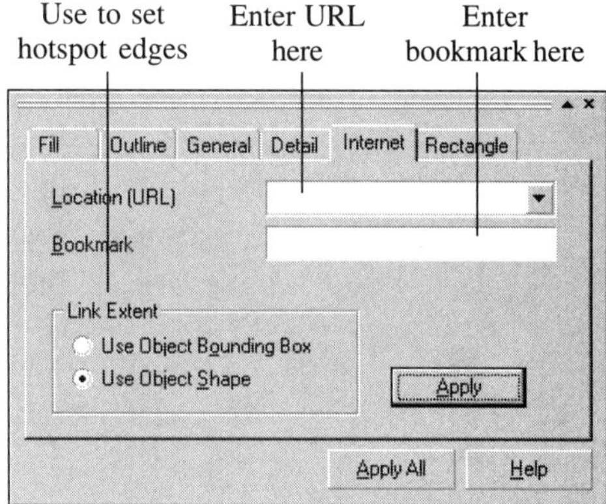

Figure 21. *The Object Properties dialog box with the Internet tab page in front.*

To display the Internet Objects Toolbar:

1. Choose Toolbars from the Window menu (**Figure 22**). The Options dialog box will open with Customize selected in the tree view window (**Figure 23**).
2. In the Toolbars list box, put a check mark next to Internet Objects.
3. Click OK to close the dialog box. The Internet Objects Toolbar will appear in the drawing window.

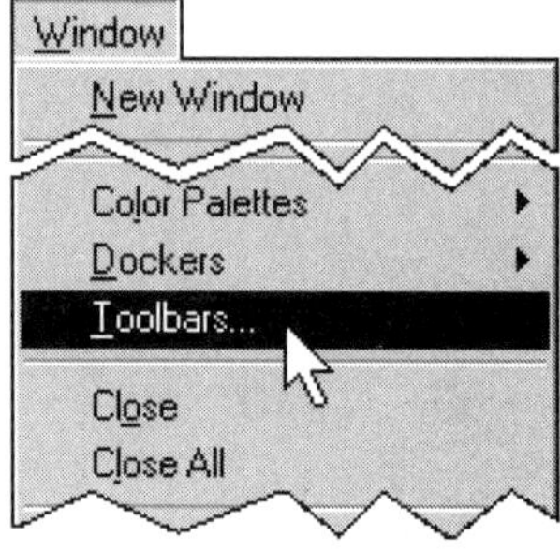

Figure 22. *Choose Toolbars from the Window menu.*

To access the Object Properties dialog box:

1. With the Pick Tool, right click on an image or paragraph text object.
2. Choose Properties from the bottom of the pop-up menu (**Figure 24**). The Object Properties dialog box will open (**Figure 21**).

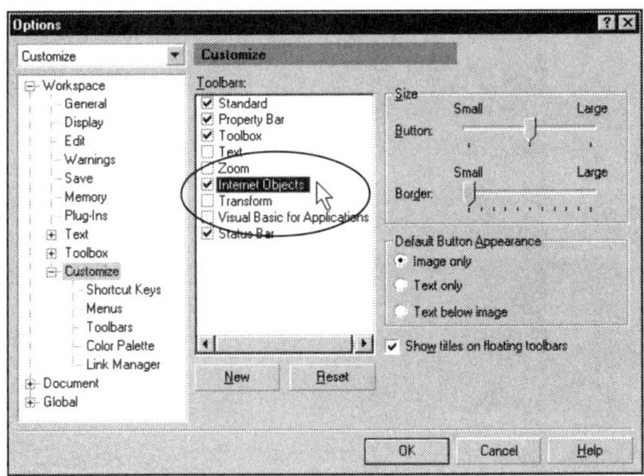

Figure 23. *Put a check mark in the check box next to Internet Objects.*

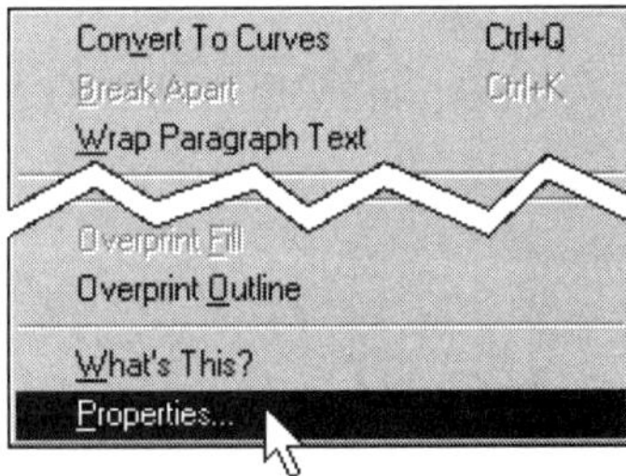

Figure 24. *Choose Properties from the bottom of the pop-up menu.*

Downloading the Latest Browsers

You can download the most recent versions of Internet Explorer and Navigator using the Web. Just enter the following URLs and follow the directions you find there.

To download Microsoft Internet Explorer, go to:
http://www.microsoft.com/windows/ie/download/windows.htm

To download Netscape Navigator, go to:
http://www.netscape.com/download/

For More Information on Creating Web Pages

There are many books about the Web, and designing and programming Web sites. A few helpful ones with interesting, provocative ideas include:

- *HTML 4 for the World Wide Web: Visual QuickStart Guide* by Elizabeth Castro (Peachpit Press)
- *The Non-Designer's Web Book: An Easy Guide to Creating, Designing, and Posting Your Own Web Site* by Robin Williams and John Tollett (Peachpit Press)
- *Web Style Guide: Basic Design Principles for Creating Web Sites* by Patrick J. Lynch and Sarah Horton (Yale University Press)
- *Web Design in a Nutshell: A Desktop Quick Reference* by Jennifer Niederst (O'Reilly & Associates)

Here's how bookmarks and links work: first, a bookmark is assigned to the text object or graphical object to which you want the user to jump. Then, you select and link the text object or graphical object that the user will click to perform the jump to the bookmarked object.

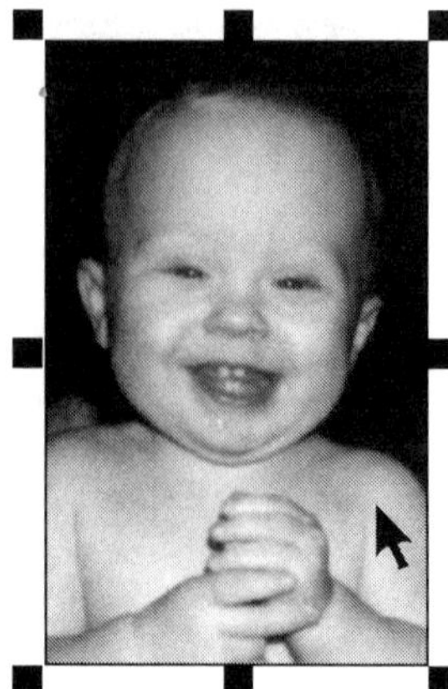

Figure 25. *Select the object to which you want to assign the bookmark.*

To assign a bookmark:

1. Display the Internet Objects Toolbar (see page 280).
2. Select the text object or image you want to assign the bookmark to with the Pick Tool (**Figure 25**).
3. Type the name you want to assign to the object in the bookmark text box on the Internet Objects Toolbar (**Figure 26**).
4. Press Enter on the keyboard. The bookmark is assigned to the object. Every time that object is selected, the assigned bookmark name will appear in the bookmark text box in the Internet Objects Toolbar.

Bookmark text box

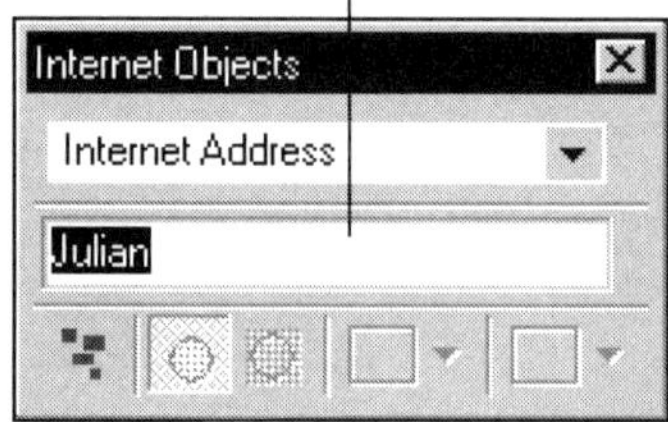

Figure 26. *Type the bookmark name in the bookmark text box, then press Enter on the keyboard.*

or

1. Right click on the object and select Properties from the pop-up menu (**Figure 24**). The Object Properties dialog box will open (**Figure 21**).
2. On the Internet tab page, type the bookmark name in the text box, then click Apply (**Figure 27**).
3. Click the Close button to close the dialog box.

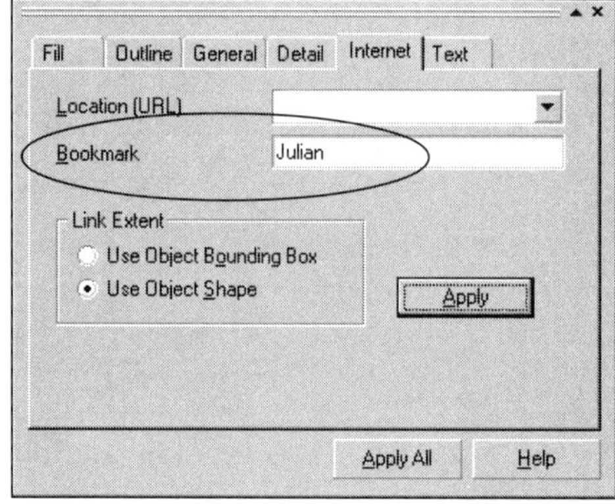

Figure 27. *Type the bookmark name in the Bookmark text box, then click Apply.*

Assign a Bookmark

Figure 28. *Select the object you want to link to the bookmarked object.*

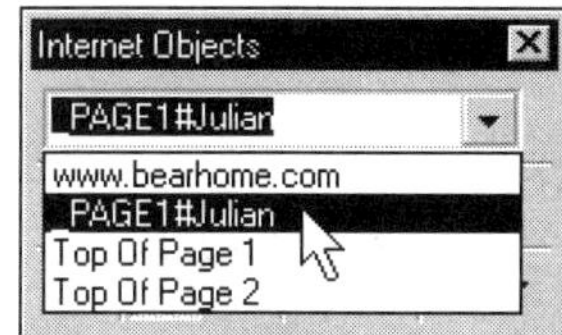

Figure 29. *Select the bookmark from the Internet Address drop-down list.*

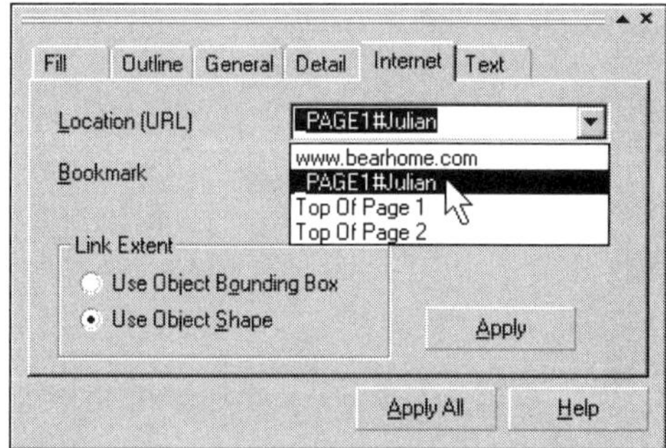

Figure 30. *Select the bookmark from the Location (URL) drop-down list.*

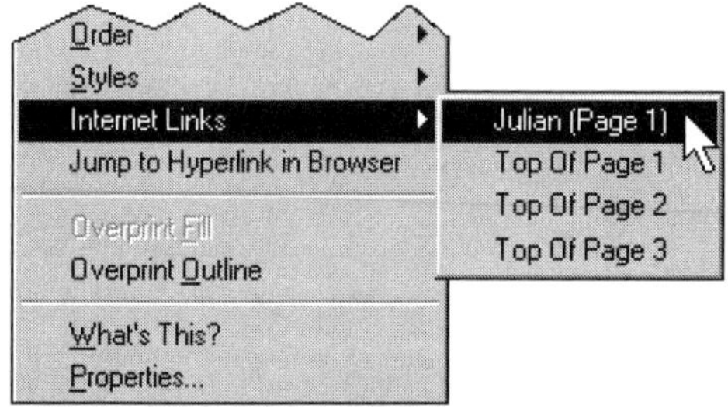

Figure 31. *Select the bookmark from the Internet Links fly-out.*

To link to a bookmarked object:

1. Select the object you want to link to the bookmarked object with the Pick Tool (**Figure 28**). (This is the object the user will click to jump to the bookmarked object.)
2. On the Internet Objects Toolbar, use the Internet Address drop-down list to select the bookmark (**Figure 29**).

or

1. Right click on the object you want to link to the bookmarked object and choose Properties from the pop-up menu (**Figure 24**). The Object Properties dialog box will open.
2. On the Internet tab page, use the Location (URL) drop-down list to select the bookmark (**Figure 30**).
3. Click Apply, then click the Close button to close the dialog box.

or

1. Right click on the object you want to link to the bookmarked object.
2. Choose the bookmark from the Internet Links fly-out (**Figure 31**).

Tip:

- The page where the bookmarked item resides is listed next to the bookmark.

To create a hyperlink:

1. Select a text or graphical object with the Pick Tool (**Figure 32**).
2. Type the URL in the Internet Address text box on the Internet Objects Toolbar (**Figure 33**).

   or

   Select a URL from the Internet Address drop-down list on the Internet Objects Toolbar (**Figure 34**).

Tip:

- If you want to create a hyperlink using only specific words, make sure the text is contained in a paragraph text box and that Make Text HTML Compatible is checked on the Text menu. Select the words with the Text Tool (**Figure 35**), then type in or select the URL from the Internet Address list box in the Internet Objects Toolbar. The selected text will become underlined (**Figure 36**). The underline indicates to folks who browse your Web page that the text is a hyperlink.

Figure 32. *Select the text or graphical object with the Pick Tool.*

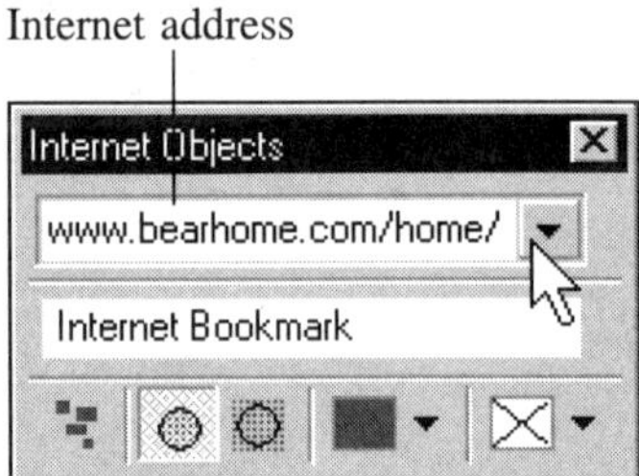

Figure 33. *Type the URL in the Internet Address text box.*

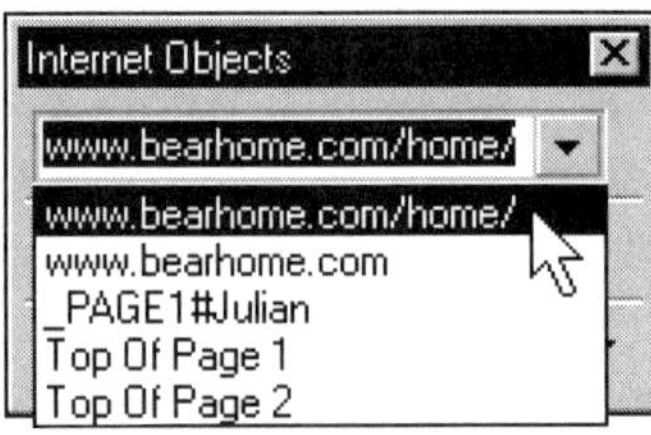

Figure 34. *Select the URL from the Internet Address drop-down list.*

Figure 35. *Select the HTML compatible paragraph text with the Text Tool.*

Figure 36. *The hyperlinked text appears underlined.*

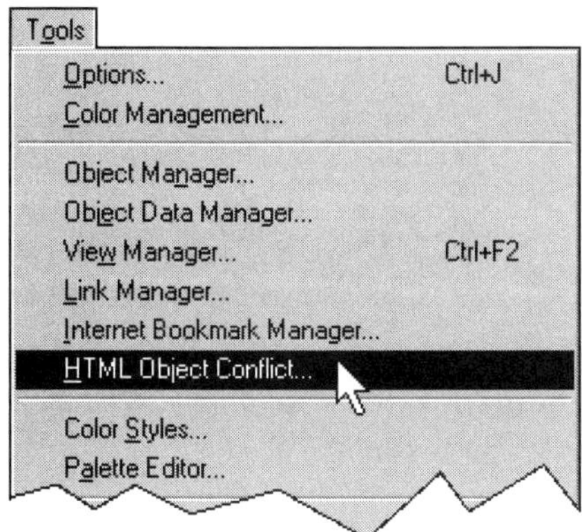

Figure 37. *Choose HTML Object Conflict from the Tools menu.*

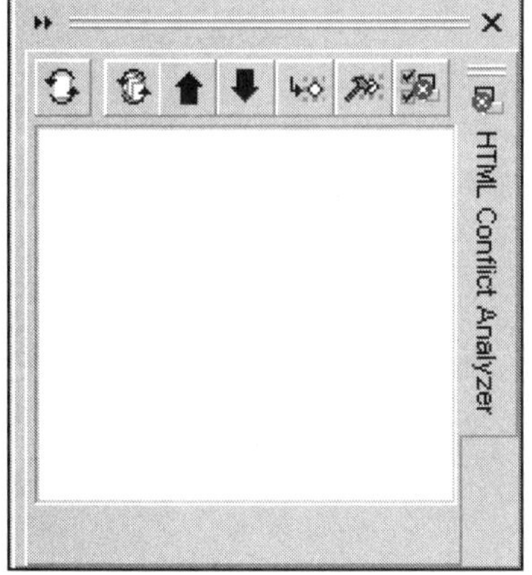

Figure 38. *The HTML Conflict Analyzer finds problems and helps fix them.*

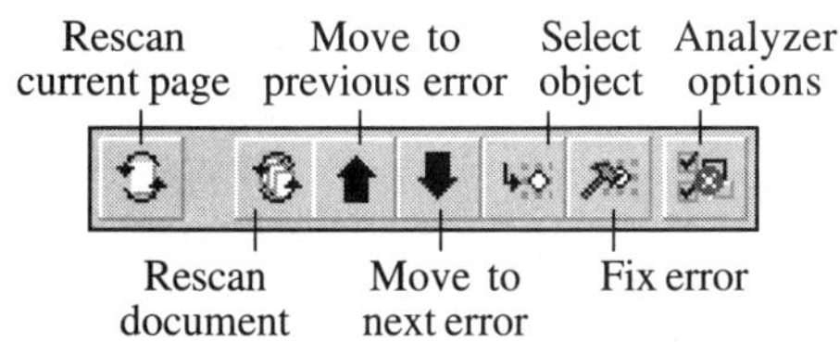

Figure 39. *The HTML Conflict Analyzer buttons.*

Before you export your pages for the Web, it's a good idea to check them to see if there are any conflicts, meaning CorelDraw objects that are not suitable for the Web.

To check for HTML conflicts:

1. Choose HTML Object Conflict from the Tools menu (**Figure 37**). The HTML Conflict Analyzer docker will open (**Figure 38**).
2. Click either the Rescan Current Page or Rescan Document button to check for errors (**Figure 39**). If there are any, they will appear in the docker window (**Figure 40**).
3. Click the Select Object button to move to a conflict.
4. Click the Fix Error button. Usually, CorelDraw will be able to automatically fix the problem. If not, read the description of the conflict in the docker window and manually edit the object to correct it.

Figure 40. *The HTML Conflict Analyzer tells you where the problems are and what is wrong.*

Once you've finished designing your Web pages and checking for conflicts, it's time to export the pages, changing them into HTML files that can be read by Web browsers.

To export your CorelDraw 9 Web pages:

1. Make sure your document is saved.
2. Choose Publish To Internet from the File menu (**Figure 41**). The Publish to Internet wizard will appear (**Figure 42**). This panel lets you specify a location to save the exported files.
3. Click the Browse button near the upper right of the panel to open the Select Directory dialog box (**Figure 43**). Use this dialog box to move to the location where you want to save the exported pages.
4. Click OK to close the dialog box and return to the wizard.
5. Click Next to move to the next panel where you will select how images will be exported (**Figure 44**).
6. Select either the JPEG or GIF option buttons, depending on how you want the images exported (for a discussion of the difference between the two file formats, see page 279).

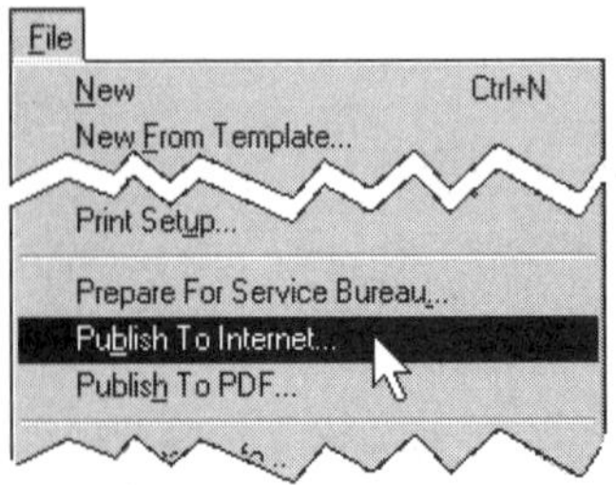

Figure 41. *Choose Publish To Internet from the File menu.*

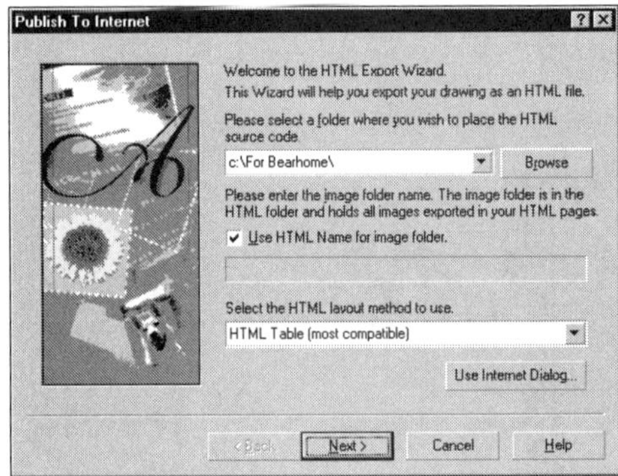

Figure 42. *The first panel lets you specify where the files are saved.*

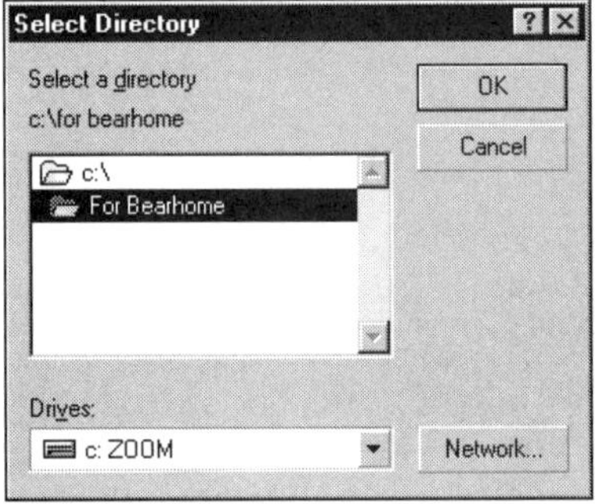

Figure 43. *Use the Select Directory dialog box to specify where the files will be saved.*

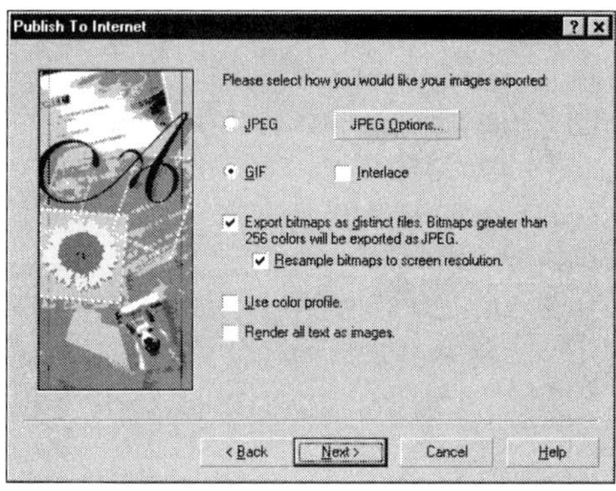

Figure 44. *The second panel of the wizard lets you specify the format in which images are exported.*

Figure 45. *Put a check mark in the Render all text as images check box to export the text on your page as a .gif image file.*

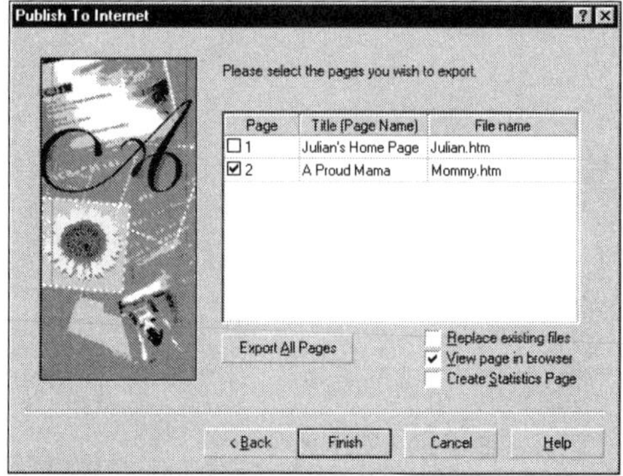

Figure 46. *The third panel of the wizard lets you set page titles and file names, and specify which pages are exported.*

7. Make sure there are check marks in the Export bitmaps as distinct files and the Resample bitmaps to screen resolution check boxes.
8. If you used a non-standard font and want to make sure that it will display correctly in any user's browser, put a check mark in the Render all text as images check box (**Figure 45**).
9. Click Next to move to the next panel where you will select the pages you want to export (**Figure 46**).

(continued)

Be Careful When You Export Text as an Image instead of HTML

It's nice to be able to create a Web page with any font you want, then export that text as an image. Anyone who browses your page on the Internet will see it with that font.

A word of warning, however. If you use a non-standard font (anything besides Times or Courier) for lots of text on your Web page, then export that text as an image, the file size of your page will become quite large. As file sizes get bigger, download times get longer. Many folks browsing the Web might not want to wait for the page to load in their browsers.

10. Use the list box with the Page, Title (Page Name), and File name headers to select the pages that are going to be exported (**Figure 47**).
    - ◆ Put check marks in the check boxes in the Page category to specify which pages to export.
    - ◆ If you want to change the title of a page, click in the Title (Page Name) column and type in a new name.
    - ◆ If you want to change the page's file name, click in the File name column and type in a new file name.
11. Click Finish to export the Web pages and close the wizard. Your pages are ready for the World Wide Web (**Figure 48**)!

Page	Title (Page Name)	File name
☐ 1	Julian's Home Page	Julian.htm
☑ 2	A Proud Mama	Mommy.htm

Figure 47. *Use the list box to select which pages are exported, and change the titles and file names of pages.*

Figure 48. *CorelDraw 9 lets you create fabulous Web pages!*

SUMMARY

In this chapter you learned how to:

- ◆ Change the ruler units to pixels
- ◆ Set the pixel resolution
- ◆ Load browser specific colors into the Color Palette
- ◆ Add text and make it HTML compatible
- ◆ Assign bookmarks and link objects to them
- ◆ Create hyperlinks
- ◆ Check for HTML conflicts
- ◆ Export your pages for the World Wide Web

Printing

CorelDraw 9 stores drawings as mathematical equations and bitmap images as pixels, but both types of graphic are rendered as dots when they are printed. The printed page depends upon the resolution of the output device. The higher the resolution, the finer and sharper the output will be.

For every document you print, you'll need to use the Print dialog box (**Figure 1**). This dialog gives you access to all the print services you need. The new Mini Preview lets you quickly see what will be printed.

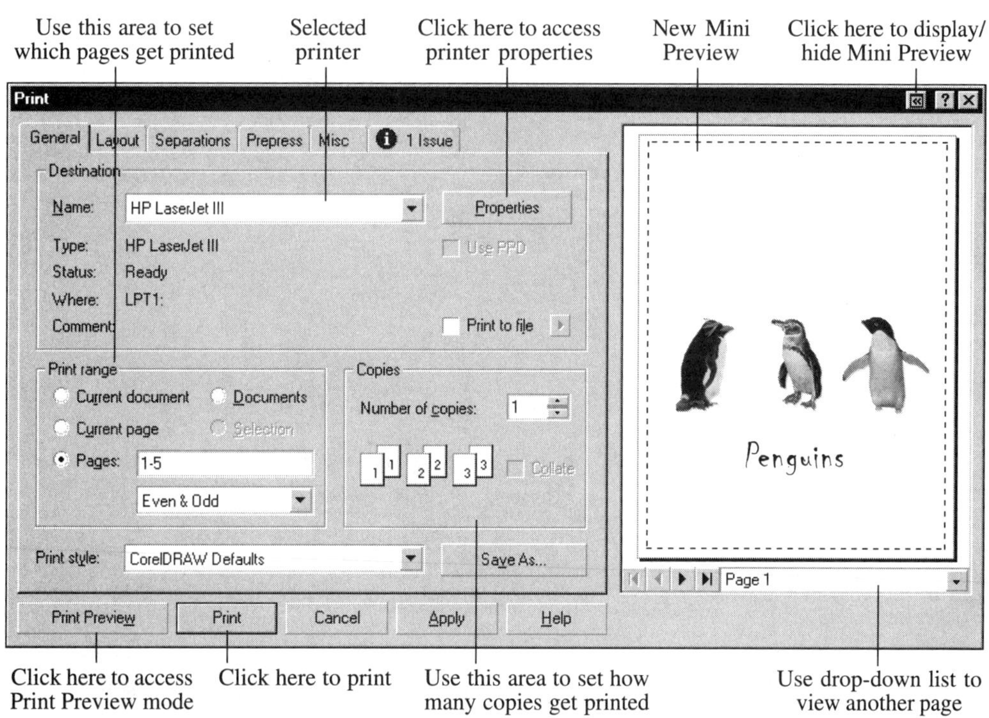

Figure 1. *The Print dialog box and new Mini Preview.*

Printing

To print a document:

1. Choose Print from the File menu (**Figure 2**) or press Ctrl+P on the keyboard. The Print dialog box will open with your default printer selected (**Figure 1**).
2. Click Print.

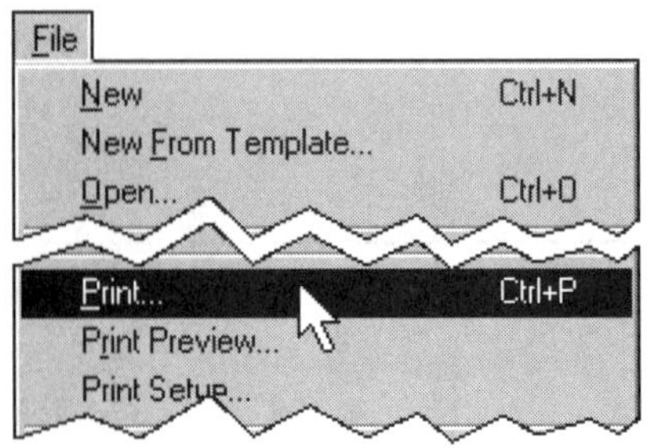

Figure 2. *Choose Print from the File menu.*

Tip:

- Always save your document before you print.

To print more than one copy of a document:

1. Choose Print from the File menu (**Figure 2**) or press Ctrl+P on the keyboard.
2. In the Copies area on the right side of the dialog box, type a number in the Number of copies text box or click the little up arrow to increase the number (**Figure 3**).
3. Click Print.

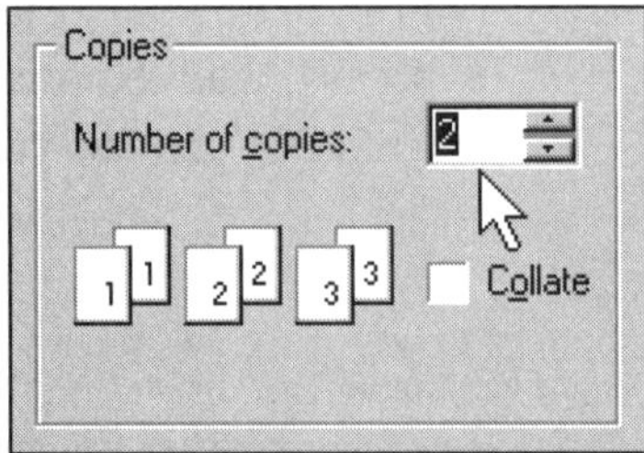

Figure 3. *Use the Number of copies text box to set how many copies of a document will print.*

Tip:

- If your document contains more than one page, the Collate check box will be available. Put a check mark in this box to collate multiple copies of a document.

Setting Page Ranges

If you use the Pages option in the Print range area, you can print specific pages and a page range by specifying page numbers like this: 2, 5, 7–10, 22. If you enter a number followed by a hyphen, for example, 3–, the document will be printed from the specified page to its end.

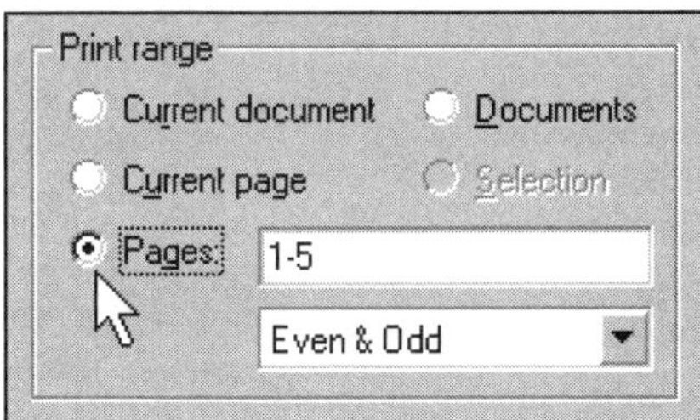

Figure 4. *In the Print range area of the Print dialog box, you can set which pages to print.*

To print specific pages or objects:

1. Open the Print dialog box by choosing Print from the File menu or by pressing Ctrl+P on the keyboard.
2. Select one of the following option buttons in the Print range area (**Figure 4**):
   - **Current document**—this option will print the entire document that is displayed on the screen.
   - **Documents**—if you have several documents open at once, this option lets you select which ones will be printed.
   - **Current page**—this option will print the page that is currently viewed on the screen.
   - **Selection**—if you selected objects before you opened the Print dialog box, selecting this option will print only those objects.
   - **Pages**—you can use the text box next to this option to set the page numbers that will print. Using the drop-down list below this option, you can set whether Even & Odd pages will print or just Even or just Odd.
3. Click Print.

Viewing the Area that Will Print

While working on a document, you can display the area of the page that will print by selecting Printable Area from the View menu.

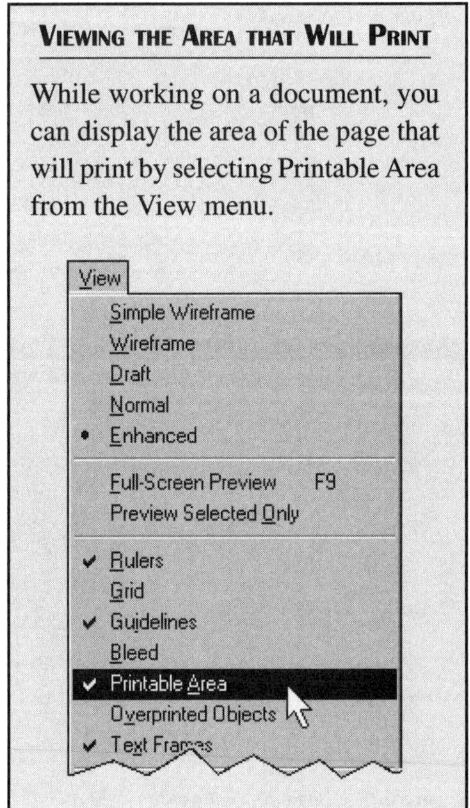

If you create a drawing that is larger than the printer can handle, you can use the Layout tab page to scale the drawing down to fit the printed page, or you can *tile* the printout. You'll know your page is too large for the printer if you view the printable area and see that the printable area's dashed outline is well within the page boundary (for directions on viewing the printable area see the sidebar on page 291). Tiling splits the drawing onto several pages with overlap areas built in. After printing, you can put the pages together to view the entire drawing at its true size.

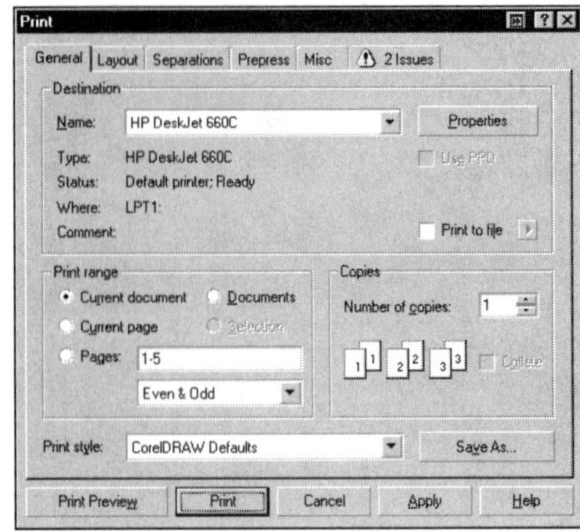

Figure 5. *The Print dialog box with the General tab page in front.*

To scale a printout:

1. Choose Print from the File menu or press Ctrl+P on the keyboard. The Print dialog box will open (**Figure 5**).
2. Click the Layout tab to bring that tab page to the front (**Figure 6**).
3. In the Image position and size area, you can scale the drawing to a percentage by selecting the Reposition images to option button, then using the Scale factor text box and spin buttons (**Figure 7**). If the tiny padlock button is pressed and the padlock appears locked, the printed image will be scaled proportionately.
4. Choose more printing options or click Print.

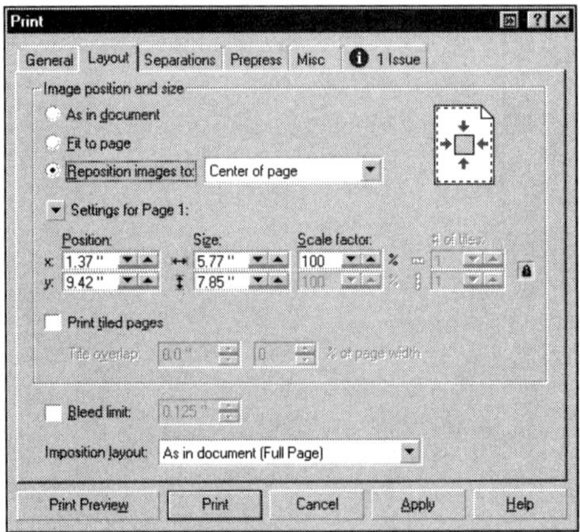

Figure 6. *The Print dialog box with the Layout tab page in front.*

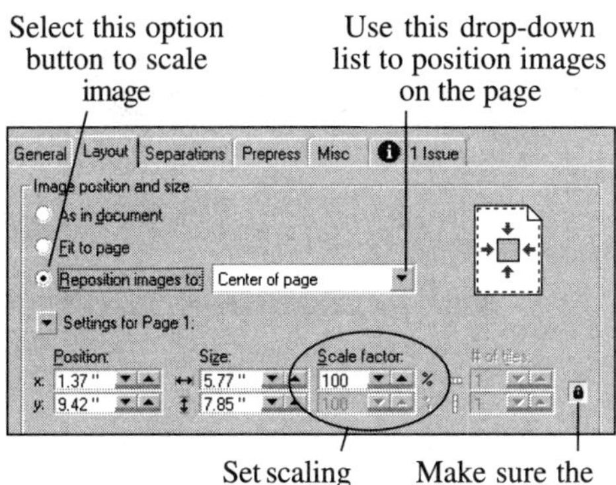

Figure 7. *Use the Image position and size area to scale the printed drawing.*

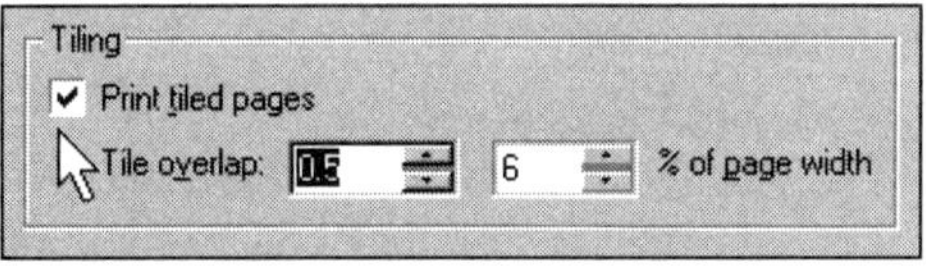

Figure 8. *Enter the amount that you want the tiled pages to overlap.*

To tile a printout:

1. Choose Print from the File menu or press Ctrl+P on the keyboard to open the Print dialog box (**Figure 5**).
2. Click the Layout tab to move to that tab page (**Figure 6**).
3. Put a check mark in the check box next to Print tiled pages in the Tiling area (**Figure 8**). Two text boxes will become available below the check box.
4. Enter a precise measurement for the Tile overlap (0.5 inch is a good setting) or enter a percentage number in the text box to the left of % of page width.
5. Choose more printing options or click Print.
6. When you print the tiled pages, you can piece them together to view the drawing as a whole.

Another Layout Printing Option

There is another option button you can select in the Image position and size area when setting printing layout options: Fit to page. If you select the Fit to page option button, your drawing will automatically resize to fit the printed page.

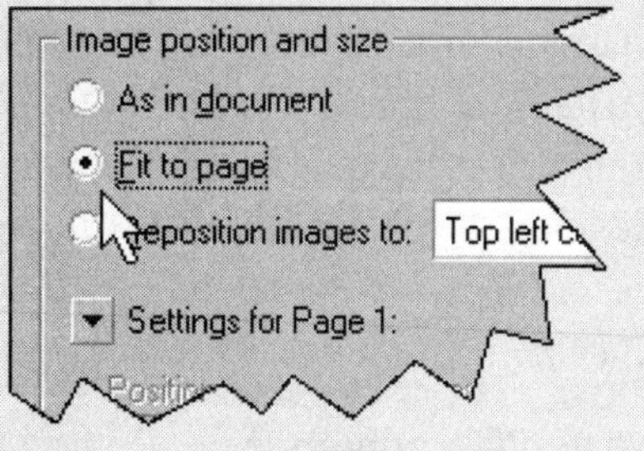

Tile a Printout

Some folks have access to more than one printer. Using the Print dialog box, you can select the specific printer you want to use and set its properties. Some of the properties that you can set include the size and orientation of the paper, the resolution the printer will use, and whether the printer will print pages in color or black only (if it's a color printer).

To select a different printer:

1. Choose Print from the File menu or press Ctrl+P on the keyboard to open the Print dialog box. Near the top of the dialog box in the Destination area is a drop-down list next to Name.
2. Click the small arrow at the right to view the drop-down list (**Figure 9**).
3. Select the printer you want to use.
4. Choose more printing options or click Print.

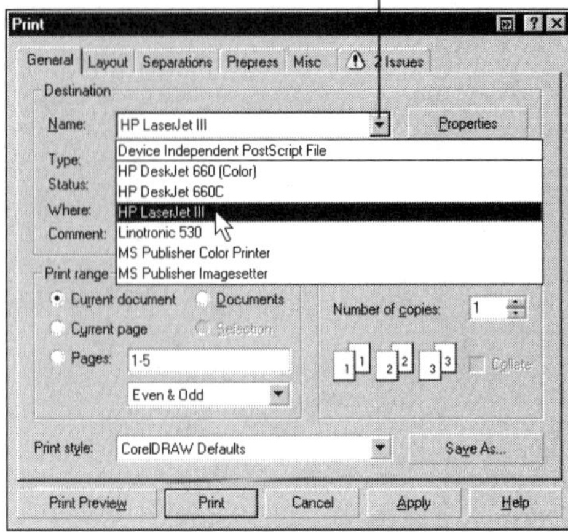

Figure 9. *Use the Name drop-down list in the Print dialog box to select another printer.*

NOT ALL PRINTERS ARE CREATED EQUAL

There are many brands of printers and imagesetters out there in the marketplace, but most of them use only two languages to process printing commands, *PCL* or *PostScript*. Printer Command Language (PCL), developed by Hewlett-Packard, is a printer-dependent language that operates only at the printer level. PostScript, developed by Adobe, is a fully programmable language that can be used to *encapsulate*—completely contain—all the necessary information for printing a document.

Some PCL printers include the DeskJet series by Hewlett-Packard, dot matrix printers, and the Canon BubbleJet series. Some PostScript output devices include the Linotronic and Varityper imagesetters, and the Apple LaserWriter series printers.

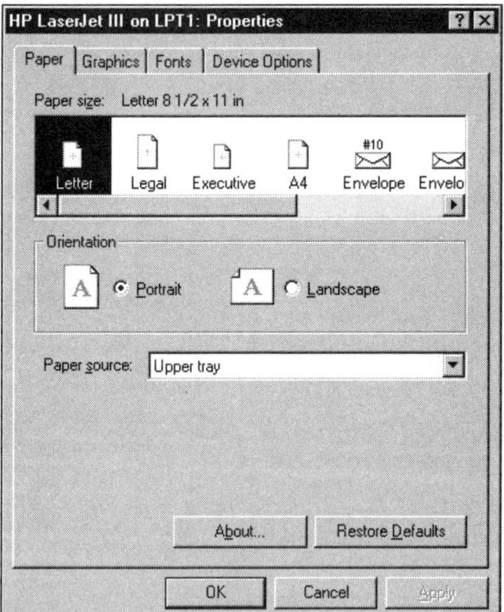

Figure 10. *The Properties dialog box for each printer will be different depending on the printer's capabilities.*

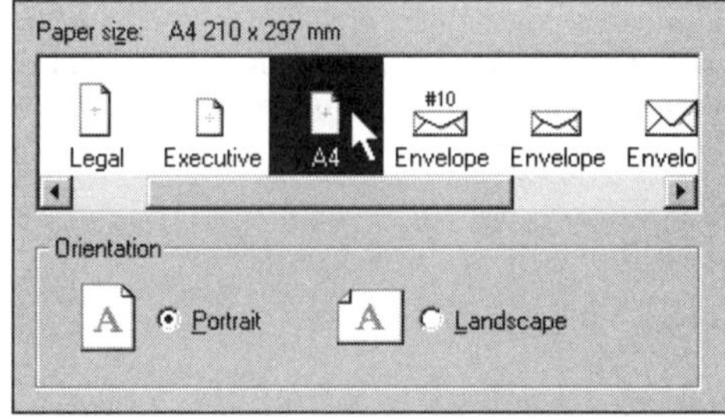

Figure 11. *Click on the paper icon for the size you want. The dimensions of the chosen paper size appear at the top left of the area. To select a page orientation, click either the Portrait or Landscape option buttons.*

To set a different page size and orientation for a printer:

1. Open the Print dialog box by choosing Print from the File menu or pressing Ctrl+P on the keyboard.
2. Use the Name drop-down list to select a printer (**Figure 9**).
3. Click the Properties button to the right of the Name drop-down list. The Properties dialog box for that printer will open (**Figure 10**). This dialog box will contain different options for different printers depending on the printers' capabilities.
4. If the Paper tab page is not already in front, click the Paper tab.
5. Use the scrolling window under Paper size to select a new size, and use the Orientation area to set whether the page will be printed in a portrait or landscape orientation (**Figure 11**).
6. Click OK to close the Properties dialog box.
7. Choose more printing options or click Print.

When preparing files for a service bureau or print shop, you will probably need to generate PostScript (.Ps) or Encapsulated PostScript (.Eps) files, and include crop marks, and information about the project and how you want it printed. If your project is in color, you will need to prepare *color separations*—creating one sheet for each process and spot color—with registration marks (see page 141 for a discussion about color).

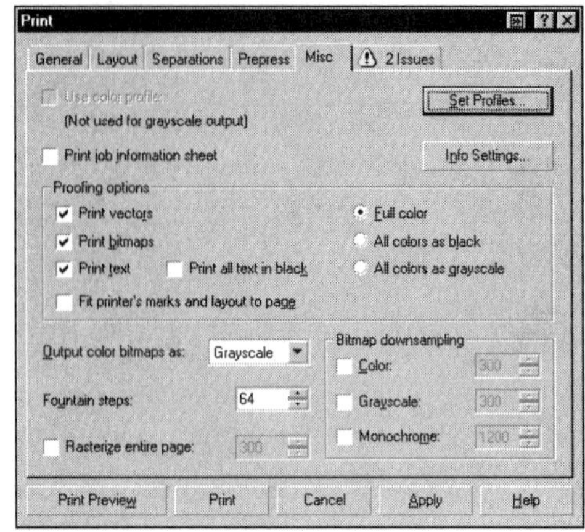

Figure 12. *The Print dialog box with the Misc tab page in front.*

To add crop and registration marks and file information:

1. Open the Print dialog box by pressing Ctrl+P on the keyboard or choosing Print from the File menu.
2. Click the Misc tab to bring that tab page to the front (**Figure 12**).
3. In the Proofing options area, put a check mark in the box next to Fit printer's marks and layout to page (**Figure 13**).
4. To print an information sheet for the printer, put a check in the box next to Print job information sheet.
5. Click the Prepress tab to bring that tab page to the front (**Figure 14**).
6. Put check marks in the check boxes next to the items you want to select as shown in **Figure 14**.
7. Print the document or save it as a file, or continue choosing printing options.

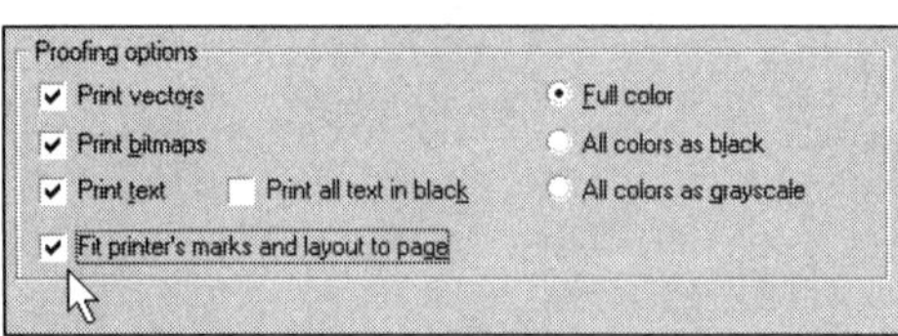

Figure 13. *Put a check in the Fit printer's marks and layout to page, otherwise the printer's marks won't print because they will be outside the printable page boundary.*

CALL YOUR SERVICE BUREAU

Before preparing files for a service bureau or print shop, contact them to find out what file format and printer settings to use.

PROOFING OPTIONS

In the Proofing options area shown in Figure 13, you can set various options that help you proof a project. These options include:

- Print vectors: if checked, your vector drawings will print
- Print bitmaps: if checked, any bitmap images will print
- Print text: if checked, any text in your project will print
- Print all text in black: if checked, any colored text will print in black

These options can come in handy if you have a complex document and only want to print proofs of certain elements at one time.

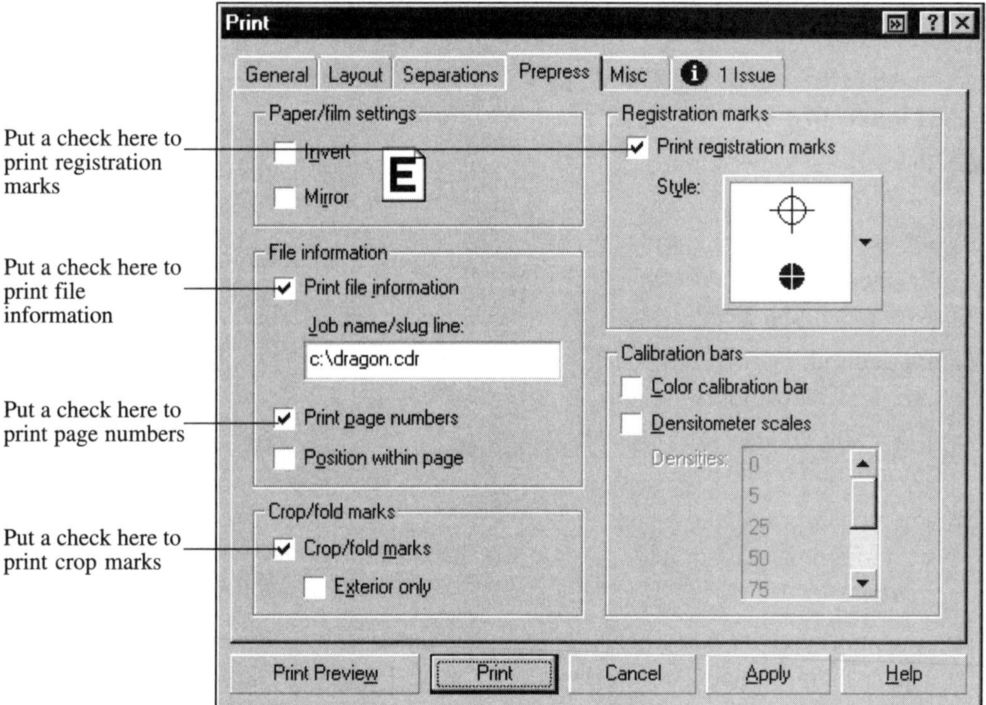

Figure 14. *Use the File information, Crop/fold marks, and Registration marks areas to add file information, page numbers, crop marks, and registration marks to your output.*

To create color separations:

1. Choose Print from the File menu or press Ctrl+P on the keyboard to open the Print dialog box.
2. Click the Separations tab to bring that tab page to the front (**Figure 15**).
3. Put a check mark in the check box next to Print separations.
4. Select the colors that you want printed as separations by putting a check mark in the check box before the color name (**Figure 16**).
5. Click the Prepress tab to move to that tab page (**Figure 14**).
6. Put a check mark in the check box next to Print file information. This will print the name of each color on its separation page.
7. Put a check mark in the check box next to Position within page. This will print the file information on the page.
8. Put a check mark in the box next to Print registration marks.
9. You may continue choosing other printing options or click Print to print the separations or save the print job to file for output at a service bureau or print shop.

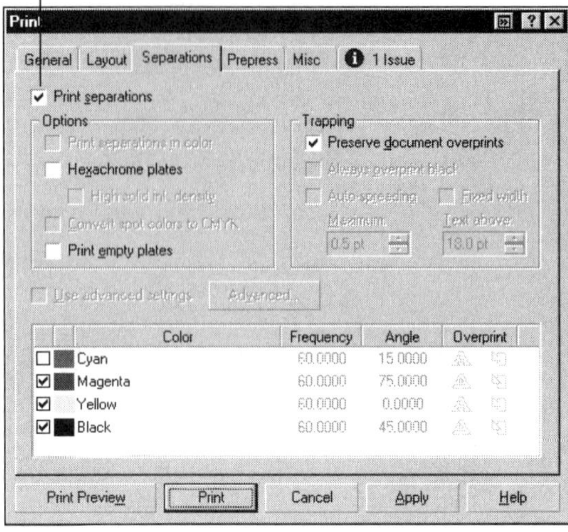

Figure 15. *Use the Separations tab page in the Print dialog box to select separations settings.*

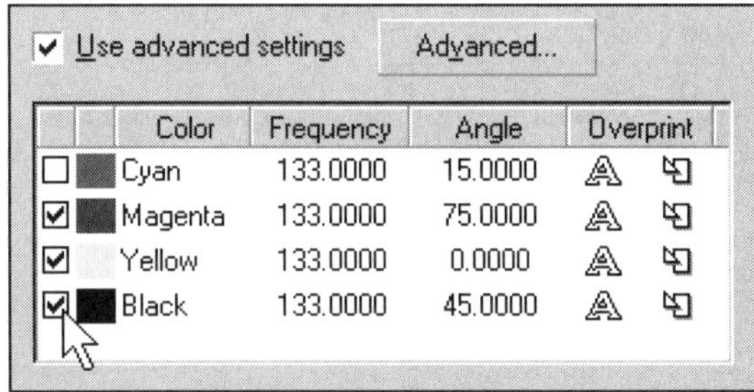

Figure 16. *Click on the color names to select which color separations will be printed.*

HOW DOES OFFSET PRINTING WORK?

When you prepare a project—a brochure, newsletter, poster, etc.—for commercial printing, you will deal with a print shop and possibly a service bureau.

Traditionally, a service bureau takes your prepared CorelDraw 9 files and either prints them using a high-resolution printer, giving you *camera-ready* output, or images the files onto film. If you get camera-ready output, the print shop will use a camera to shoot pictures of the output to create film.

With the advent of computers and transportable large storage media such as DAT tapes, and ZIP and JAZ drives, many graphic artists skip the service bureau, cutting out the intermediate step of film or camera-ready output, and go straight to the print shop with disks containing their project files. Some service bureaus and print shops prefer to use the actual CorelDraw .Cdr files, while others prefer PostScript (.Ps) or encapsulated PostScript (.Eps) files.

The print shop takes any of these media—camera-ready output, film, or computer files—and uses them to make printing plates. The plates are then put on large rollers on a printing press by the *pressman*. If your project contains more than one color, the pressman uses *registration marks* to make sure all the plates are exactly aligned. He or she then runs the printing press. As the plates rotate on the rollers, they pick up a very thin coating of ink and an ink impression is transferred to the paper.

After the ink dries, the paper is trimmed and folded using *crop marks* as a guide. The *print job* is then packed and shipped to you.

To generate a PostScript (.Ps) file:

1. Save your project by choosing Save from the File menu or pressing Ctrl+S on the keyboard.
2. Choose Print from the File menu or press Ctrl+P. The Print dialog box will open (**Figure 1**).
3. Select the printer that you want to use (**Figure 9**). (This must be a PostScript printer.)
4. Place a check mark in the Print to file box (**Figure 17**).
5. Click Print. The Print To File dialog box will appear (**Figure 18**).
6. Move to the folder where you want to save the file.
7. Use the Save as type drop-down list to select PostScript File (*.ps) (**Figure 19**).
8. Type a name in the File name text box.
9. Click Save.

To generate an Encapsulated PostScript (.Eps) file:

1. Save your project by choosing Save from the File menu or pressing Ctrl+S.
2. Choose Print from the File menu or press Ctrl+P. The Print dialog box will open (**Figure 1**).
3. Select the printer that you want to use (**Figure 9**). (This must be a PostScript printer.)
4. Place a check mark in the Print to file box (**Figure 17**).

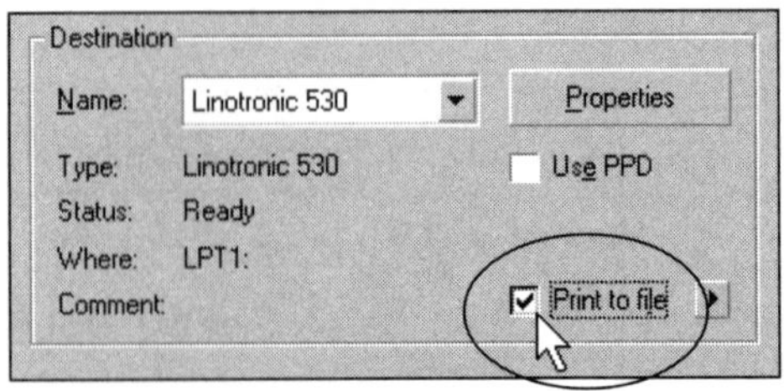

Figure 17. *In the Destination area of the Print dialog box, put a check mark in the box next to Print to file.*

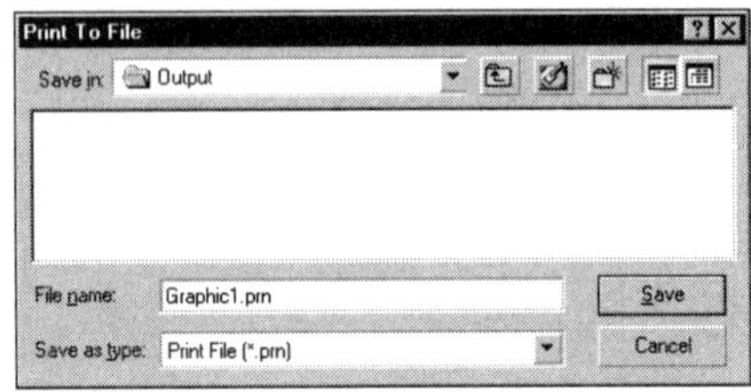

Figure 18. *Use the Print To File dialog box to set where the file will be saved, and the file's name and format extension.*

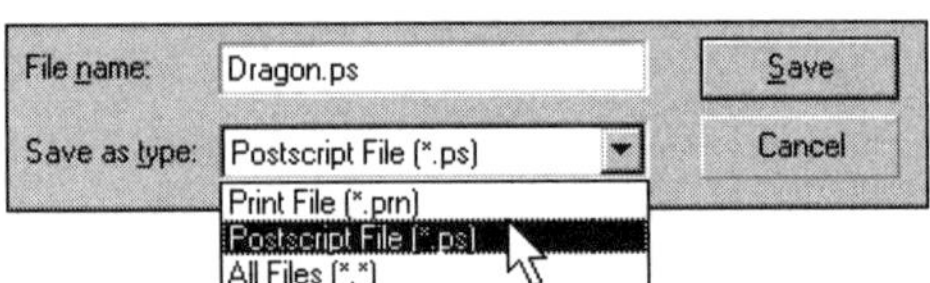

Figure 19. *Use the Save as type drop-down list to select PostScript File (*.ps), then type a name in the File name text box.*

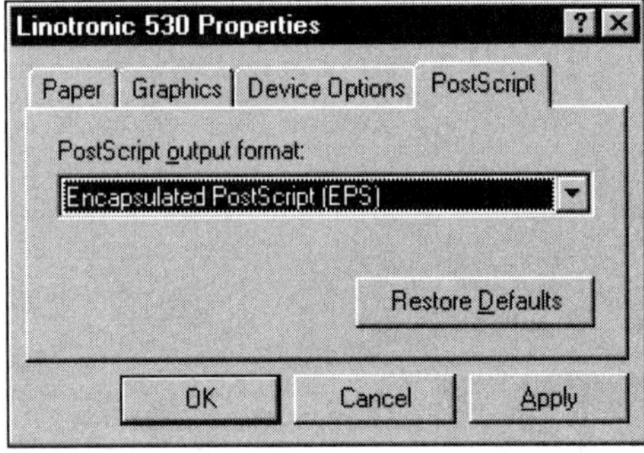

Figure 20. *Use the PostScript tab page to select the output format.*

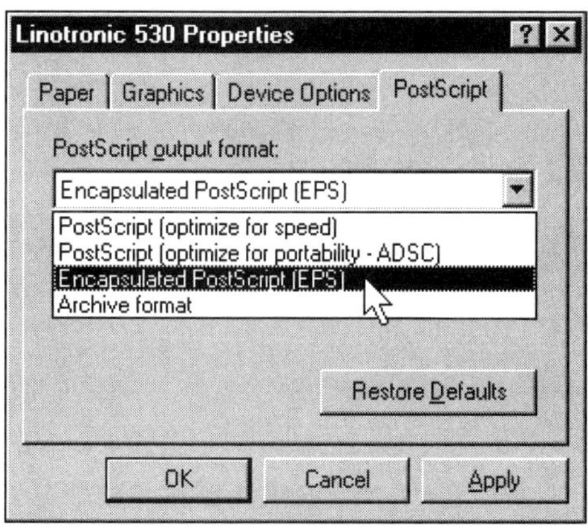

Figure 21. *Select Encapsulated PostScript (EPS) from the PostScript output format drop-down list.*

Figure 22. *Click OK in the Warning dialog box.*

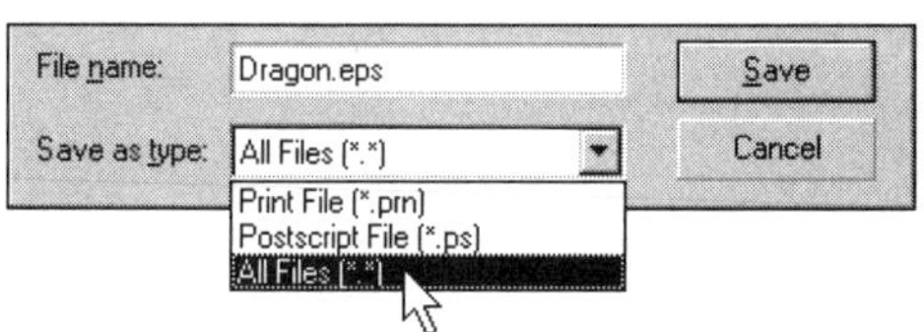

Figure 23. *In the Print To File dialog box, use the Save as type drop-down list to select All Files (*.*). In the File name text box, type a name followed by .Eps.*

5. Click the Properties button. This will open the Properties dialog box for the PostScript printer you have chosen.
6. Click the PostScript tab to bring that tab page to the front (**Figure 20**). (If you don't see a PostScript tab, then you haven't selected a PostScript printer.)
7. Use the PostScript output format drop-down list to select Encapsulated PostScript (EPS) (**Figure 21**). A warning dialog box will appear telling you that Encapsulated PostScript should only be output to a file (**Figure 22**). Don't worry about this "warning." Click OK to close the dialog box.
8. Click OK to close the printer's Properties dialog box.
9. Click Print in the Print dialog box. The Print To File dialog box will open (**Figure 18**).
10. Move to the folder where you want to save the file.
11. Use the Save as type drop-down list to select All Files (*.*) (**Figure 23**).
12. In the File name text box, type the file name *followed by* .Eps (for example, MyFile.Eps). If you don't type this file extension, the file will not be saved correctly.
13. Click Save.

The new Preflight tab in the Print dialog box (**Figure 24**) lets you know if there are any possible problems before you print. When you open the Print dialog box, the Preflight tab will dynamically change to display whether there is a problem (**Figure 25a**), some information that may be helpful to you (**Figure 25b**), or no problems whatsoever (**Figure 25c**).

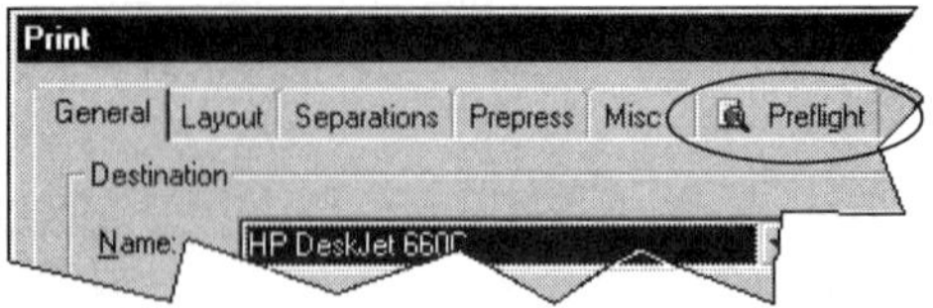

Figure 24. *The Preflight tab and panel give a quick overview of what could be wrong with a print job.*

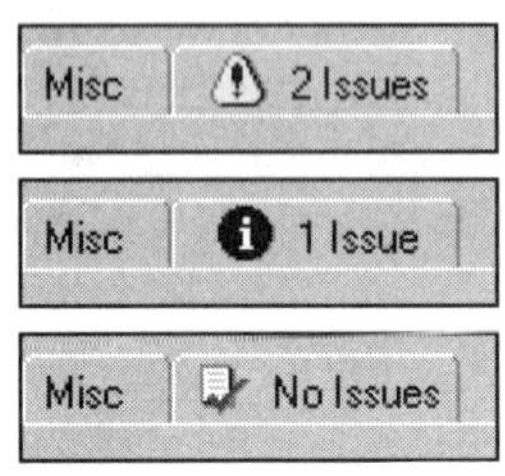

Figures 25a–c. *The Preflight tab changes dynamically to let you know there might be a problem.*

To display the Preflight panel:

1. Open the Print dialog box by choosing Print on the File menu or pressing Ctrl+P on the keyboard.
2. Click the Preflight tab to display the panel's contents (**Figure 26**).

Tip:

- To change the issues that the Preflight tab page looks for, click the Preflight Settings button. The Preflight Settings dialog box will open (**Figure 27**). Use the check boxes to select which issues you want to scan for.

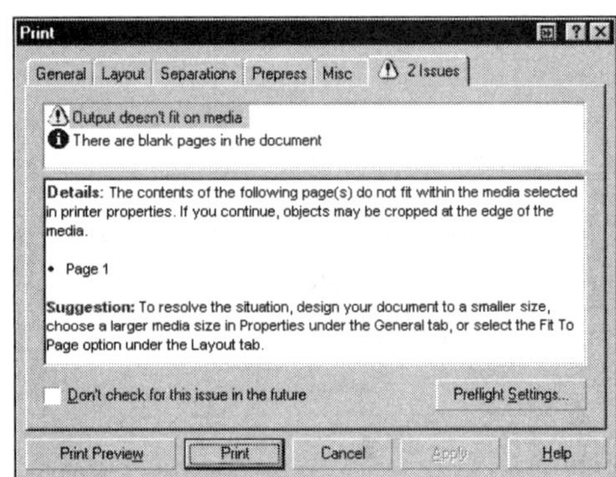

Figure 26. *The information displayed on the Preflight panel can save time by letting you know what's wrong before you print.*

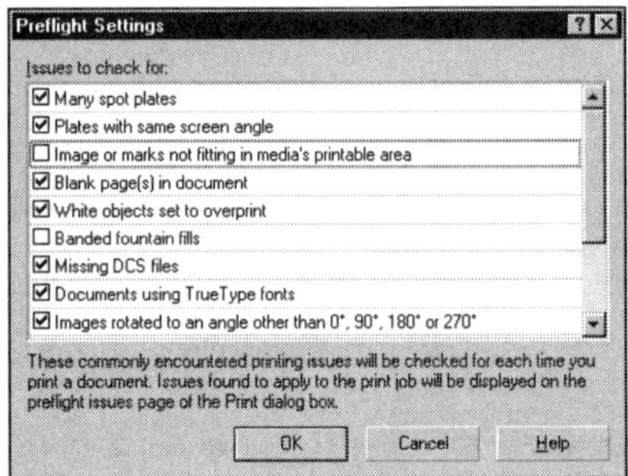

Figure 27. *Use the Preflight Settings dialog box to select which issues are scanned for.*

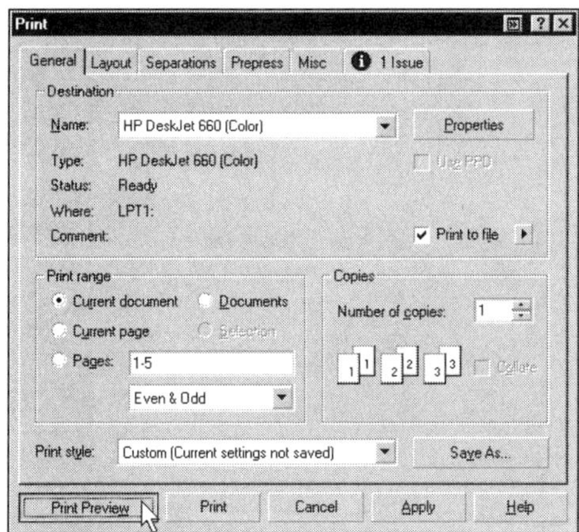

Figure 28. *Click the Print Preview button in the Print dialog box.*

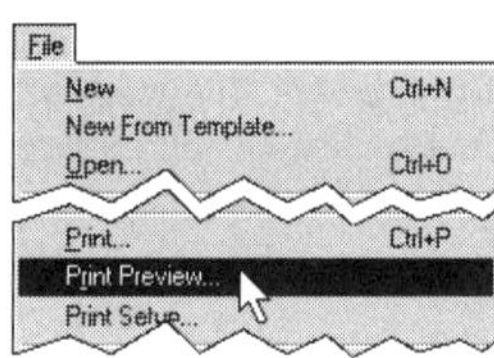

Figure 29. *Choose Print Preview from the File menu.*

The Print Preview window is very helpful in that it shows you the exact area of the page that will print and gives access to all the printing options discussed in this chapter.

To open Print Preview:

If you have the Print dialog box open, click Print Preview (**Figure 28**).

or

Choose Print Preview from the File menu (**Figure 29**). The Print Preview window will open (**Figure 30**).

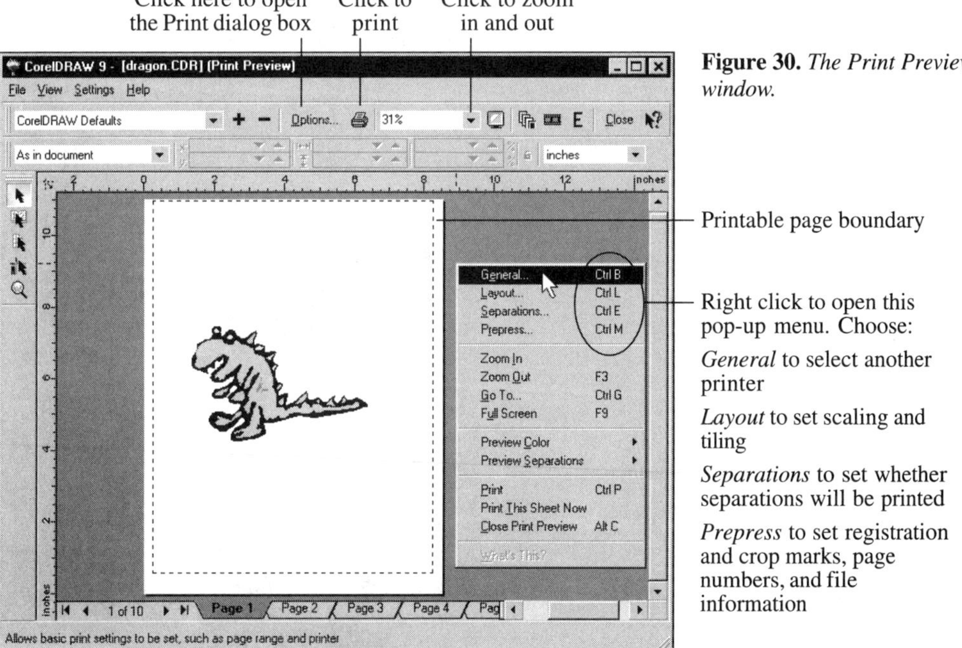

Figure 30. *The Print Preview window.*

If your drawing is too large for the page or so small that it's very difficult to see and you want to print a hard copy proof, you can use the Print Preview window to dynamically scale the drawing.

To scale a drawing in Print Preview:

1. Open the Print Preview window by clicking Print Preview in the Print dialog box or by choosing Print Preview from the File Menu.
2. Click on the drawing. Eight black—very familiar!—handles will appear around the drawing (**Figure 31**).
3. Position the mouse over a handle, press the left mouse button, and drag the handle until the drawing is sized as you want it (**Figure 32**). The mouse pointer will change to a double-headed arrow shaped like an X. In addition, a dashed rectangle will appear around the drawing as you drag.
4. When you release the mouse, the graphic will redraw to its new scaled size.

Tip:

- Scaling the drawing in Print Preview mode won't scale the actual drawing in your document, it will only change the size of the drawing when it's printed.

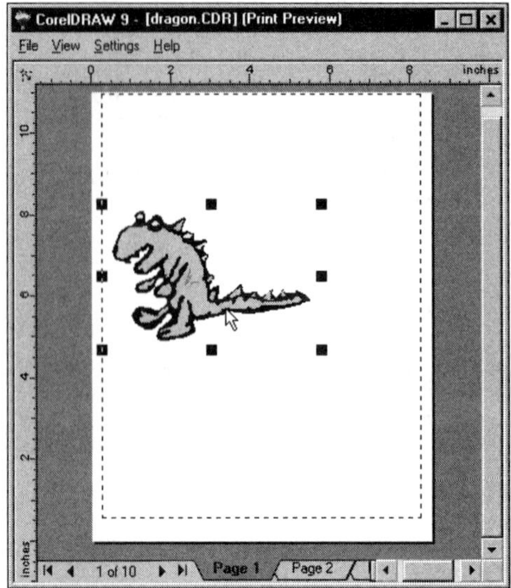

Figure 31. *Click on the drawing to select it. Eight black handles will appear around the drawing.*

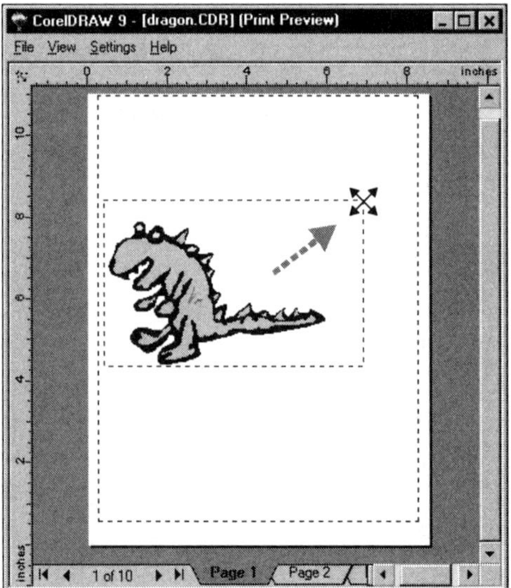

Figure 32. *As you drag, the handles will disappear and be replaced with a dashed rectangle that will grow or shrink as you drag.*

Scale the Printed Page

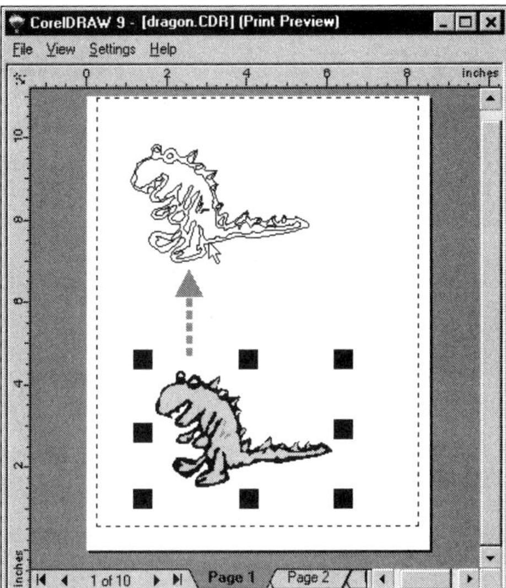

Figure 33. *Drag the drawing to position it on the printed page.*

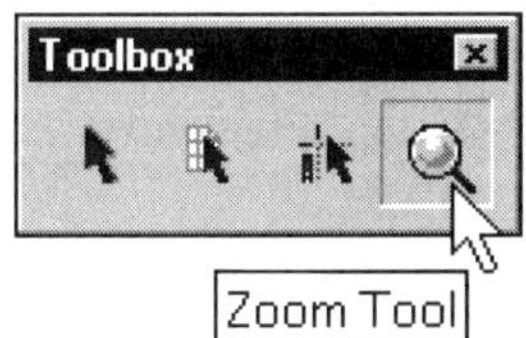

Figure 34. *Select the Zoom Tool from the Toolbox in the Print Preview window.*

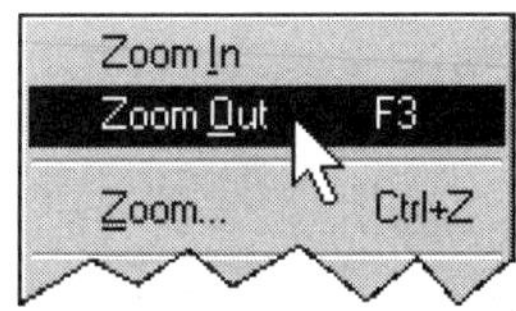

Figure 35. *Choose Zoom Out from the pop-up menu or press F3 on the keyboard.*

To position the drawing on the printed page:

1. Open the Print Preview window by clicking Print Preview in the Print dialog box or by choosing Print Preview from the File Menu.
2. Position the mouse over the drawing, press the left mouse button and drag to the new position on the printed page (**Figure 33**).

Tips:

- Positioning a drawing on the printed page can come in handy if your graphic is partially outside the page boundary.
- Repositioning the drawing on the printed page will not move the actual drawing in your document, it will only affect the position of the drawing on the printed page.

If a drawing element is so small that it's hard to see, you can zoom in to make changes.

To zoom in or out:

1. Select the Zoom Tool from the Print Preview Toolbox (**Figure 34**).
2. To zoom in:
   - Click in the Preview window
   - Marquee select an area

   To zoom out:
   - Right click and choose Zoom Out from the pop-up menu (**Figure 35**).

The new Mini Preview (**Figures 1 and 36**) lets you quickly view what will be printed and where it is positioned on the page. Unlike the Print Preview window discussed on pages 304–305 which lets you scale and move objects on the page to be printed, the Mini Preview just lets you see what will be printed. If you do want to make changes, you can go back to the drawing window by clicking Cancel in the Print dialog box or by opening the Print Preview window by clicking thc Print Preview button.

Figure 36. *The new Mini Preview gives you a quick look at what the printed page will look like.*

To display the Mini preview:

With the Print dialog box open, click the small double-arrow button at the upper right (**Figure 37**).

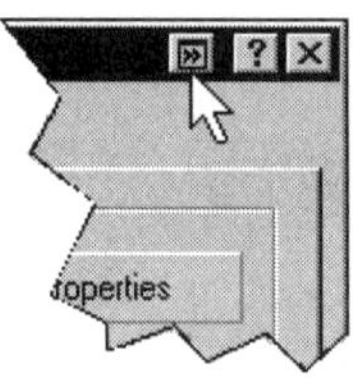

Figure 37. *Click the small double-arrow button at the upper right of the Print dialog box to open the Mini Preview.*

Tip:

- To hide Mini Preview, just click the button again.

SUMMARY

In this chapter you learned how to:

- Print documents
- Print specific pages
- Scale and tile a printout
- Select different printers
- Add crop and registration marks to a printout
- Create color separations
- Generate PostScript and EPS files
- Check the Preflight tab page for possible problems
- Use the Print Preview screen
- Scale and position a drawing on the printed page
- Display the new Mini Preview

Fonts & Clipart in This Book

Below is a list, divided by chapter, of the location for every font and piece of clipart used in this book. The fonts are located on CorelDraw 9 CD-ROM disk #1. The clipart that ships with CorelDraw 9 can be found on either CorelDraw 9 CD-ROM disks #2 or #3.

To add a piece of CorelDraw clipart to your document, use the dockers on the Scrapbook fly-out on the Tools menu or the Symbols and Special Characters docker also on the Tools menu. Adding clipart to a project is discussed in Chapter 16 on pages 256–259.

Chapter 1

Drop cap font: Pablo LET

Balloons: Clipart\Borders\Leisure\Fun00022.Cdr

Chapter 2

Drop cap font: Hollyweird

Chapter 3

Drop cap font: Galleria

Train: Clipart\Borders\Misc\Trainbdr.Cdr

Chapter 4

Drop cap font: MandarinD

Apple: Clipart\Food\Fruits\Applea.Cdr

Car: Symbols and Special Characters docker, Transportation, #74

Crown: Clipart\Spec_occ\Misc\Crown.Cdr

Football: Symbols and Special Characters docker, Sports & Hobbies, #33

Iris: Clipart\Flowers\Flowiris.Cdr

Lion: Clipart\Horoscpe\Set09\Leo9.Cdr

Man with top hat: Symbols and Special Characters docker, People, #53

Rabbits: Symbols and Special Characters docker, Animals2, #53; Clipart\Borders\Animals\Bunnies.Cdr

Sailing Ship: Clipart\Borders\Misc\Shipbord.Cdr

Snowman: Symbols and Special Characters docker, Festive, #42

Star: Symbols and Special Characters docker, Stars1, #41

T-Rex: Clipart\Prehist\Dinosaur\Tyran002.Cdr

Turtles: Clipart\Borders\Animals\Turtle.Cdr

Chapter 5

Drop cap font: VictorianD

Dragons: Clipart\Fantasy\Dragoff.Cdr

Flag: Symbols and Special Characters docker, Festive, #134

Pow!: Clipart\Spec_occ\Misc\Pow_.Cdr

Starfish border: Clipart\Borders\Animals\Sea_life.Cdr

Chapter 6

Drop cap font: Algerian

Clown: Clipart\Spec_occ\Valentin\Valentin.Cdr

Faceted Heart: Clipart\Designs\Icon072.Cdr

Hearts with Arrow: Clipart\Designs\Hearts1.Cdr

Town: Clipart\Borders\Misc\Steep.Cdr

Waves: Photos\Images\Cartoons\Seastorm.Tif

Chapter 7

Drop cap font: Amazone BT

Basketball: Symbols and Special Characters docker, Sports & Hobbies, #34

Flags: Clipart\Flags\Flying\
As they appear from left to right: Skorea.Cdr, Canada.Cdr, Usa.Cdr, France.Cdr, Austral2.Cdr, Austria.Cdr, Japan.Cdr, Norway.Cdr

Footprints: Symbols and Special Characters docker, Tracks, #1

Pot of gold: Clipart\Money\Coins\Potogold.cdr

Seahorse: Symbols and Special Characters docker, Animals 1, #93

Chapter 8

Drop cap font: Jazz LET

Chapter 9

Drop cap font: CaslonOpnface BT

Jets: Clipart\Aircraft\Jets\C141t.Cdr; C141f.Cdr; C141c.Cdr; Airplne1.Cdr; Airplne2.Cdr

Planes: Clipart\Aircraft\Proplane\Ov10bf.Cdr; Ov10bt.Cdr

Chapter 10

Drop cap font: Bertram LET

Bear: Symbols and Special Characters docker, Animals1, #40

Butterfly: Symbols and Special Characters docker, Animals2, #57

Camel: Symbols and Special Characters docker, Animals1, #55

Elephant: Symbols and Special Characters docker, Animals1, #52

Frog: Symbols and Special Characters docker, Animals1, #78

Lightbulb: Clipart\Home\Misc\Litebulb.cdr

Mouse: Symbols and Special Characters docker, Animals1, #74

Orcas: Clipart\Borders\Animals\Whales.Cdr

Rose: Symbols and Special Characters docker, Plants, #72

Shirt: Clipart\Fashion\Clothing\Nwage914.Cdr

Chapter 11

Drop cap font: ShelleyAllegro BT

Chapter 12

Drop cap font: Crazy Creatures

1, 2, 3: Clipart\Numbers\Set101\Elevator.Cdr

Bang: Clipart\Spec_occ\Misc\Bang_.Cdr

California: Clipart\Travel\Misc\Trav0009.Cdr

Cyclone Crest: Clipart\Crests\Army\38infdv1.Cdr

K: Clipart\Letters\Fun\K.Cdr

Ribbon: Clipart\Awards\Ribbons\Ribb0002.Cdr

Chapter 13

Drop cap font: Hazel LET

Black and White Design: Clipart\Designs\Icon032.Cdr

Cake: Clipart\Food\Desserts\Cake01.Cdr

Cat: Clipart\Animals\Pets\Cat01.Cdr

Chicken: Clipart\Birds\Landbrds\Land0009.Cdr

Daffodil: Clipart\Flowers\Flowr006.Cdr

Finch: Clipart\Birds\Songbrds\Finch2.Cdr

Japanese Crest: Clipart\Japan\Signs\Crest4.Cdr

Plaque: Clipart\Awards\Plaques\Award02.Cdr

Tulip: Clipart\Flowers\Flowr041.Cdr

Chapter 14

Drop cap font: Westwood LET

Blouse: Clipart\Fashion\Clothing\Nwage918.Cdr

Boot: Clipart\Fashion\Clothing\Boot.Cdr

Camel: Clipart\Africa\Art\Camel2.Cdr

Coffee Cup: Clipart\Food\Drinks\Cofemug.Cdr

Cowboy Hat: Clipart\Fashion\Acesries\Acses015.Cdr

Crown: Clipart\Fashion\Acesries\Acses004.Cdr

Fish border: Clipart\Borders\Animals\Dancfish.Cdr

Ladybug: Clipart\Insects\Flying\Flyin011.Cdr

Lightbulb: Clipart\Home\Misc\Litebulb2.Cdr

Party Hat: Clipart\Fashion\Acesries\Nwage932.Cdr

Steer Head: Symbols and Special Characters docker, Animals1, #61

TV: Clipart\Home\Electron\Tv_i.Cdr

Venus: Clipart\Fantasy\Venus.Cdr

Chapter 15

Drop cap font: Slipstream LET Plain

Bear: Clipart\Home\Kids\Teddy.Cdr

Bobcat: Clipart\Animals\Wild\Bobcat.Cdr

Camera: Clipart\Leisure\Hobbies\Camera2.Cdr

Cloud: Clipart\Weather\Kkkchld89.Cdr

Crab: Symbols and Special Characters docker, Animals1, #92

Dog: Clipart\Animals\Pets\Pooch.Cdr

Dollar: Clipart\Money\Bills\Dollar.Cdr

Galaxy: Clipart\Borders\Frames\Milky.Cdr

Heart: Clipart\Spec_Occ\Valentin.Cdr

Lizard: Clipart\Australia\Austrail.Cdr

Man: Clipart\People\Misc\Face22.Cdr

Rabbit: Symbols and Special Characters docker, Animals2, #53

Rocket: Clipart\Space\Rockets\Rocket8.Cdr

Sun: Clipart\WeatherKkchld88.Cdr

Turtle: Symbols and Special Characters docker, Animals1, #72

Woman: Clipart\Fashion\People\Model_1.Cdr

Chapter 16

Drop cap font: Scruff

Butterfly: Objects\Animals\Monarch.Cpt

Dancer: Clipart\Color_me\Ballerina.Cdr

Raleigh: Objects\Stamps\Stamp09.Cpt

Shakespeare: Clipart\Carictre\Historic\Shakspre.Cdr

Sunflowers: Photos\Objctvii\764012.Wi

Turtle: Objects\Animals\Turtle.Cpt

Chapter 17

Drop cap font: Arriba Arriba LET

Bear: Clipart\Animals\Icons\Plr_bear.Cdr

Chapter 18

Drop cap font: Charlesworth

Dragon: Clipart\Fantasy\Kkchlf11.Cdr

Electronics border: Clipart\Borders\Bars\Hm_elect.Cdr

Penguins: Photos\Imglsts\Animals\Anim005.Cpt

Appendix A

Drop cap font: ShelleyVolante BT

Fish: Clipart\Borders\Animals\Anim0005.Cdr

Flowers: Clipart\Borders\Plants\Bushbrd.Cdr

Appendix B

Drop cap font: Zinjaro LET

Boats: Clipart\Borders\Leisure\Fun00034.Cdr

Castle: Clipart\Borders\Leisure\Fun00035.Cdr

The CorelDraw 9 Graphics Suite

The CorelDraw 9 Graphics Suite ships with three CD-ROM disks. On these disks are many things—from CorelDraw itself to a photo retouching and image editing studio to fonts, photographs, and clipart.

Disk 1: Programs and Fonts

In addition to CorelDraw 9, there are ten other programs you can choose to install:

- Adobe Acrobat Reader 4—working with the new CorelDraw Publish to PDF feature, Acrobat Reader lets you view .Pdf files. These files are cross-platform and keep the original appearance of your documents.
- Bitstream Font Navigator 3—this program helps you manage fonts. It lets you organize fonts into groups, view and print samples of fonts, and quickly install fonts onto your computer.
- Canto Cumulus Desktop 4—using this program, you can set up indexed catalogs to help you organize your drawings and clipart.
- Corel Capture 9—a screen capture program that lets you take "pictures" of what's on your screen.

- Corel Photo-Paint 9—this bitmap-based program takes over where the bitmap capabilities of CorelDraw 9 leave off. You can use Photo-Paint to add super effects to your graphics and any bitmap image.
- CorelTrace 9—a program that helps you trace bitmap artwork and scanned images and convert them into editable CorelDraw images.
- Corel Script Editor—a macro-type language that lets you create mini-programs that automate many tasks in CorelDraw and Photo-Paint.
- Corel Texture—this program helps you create interesting textures, including marble, stone, wood, and metal. You can use these custom textures as fills and backgrounds for your drawings and Web pages.
- Microsoft Visual Basic for Applications 6—a macro language with the familiar Visual Basic interface that is used to customize and automate your CorelDraw tasks.
- Quick Time 3.0.2—this program is used to play multimedia files such as movies.
- Over 1,000 TrueType and Type 1 fonts alphabetically arranged in folders by name.

Disk 2: Clipart

Over 25,000 pieces of clipart and symbols that range from cars and plants to holiday and medical graphics, arranged in folders by category.

Disk 3: Photos, templates, tiles, and Web graphics

- Hundreds of brush textures and tiles that are good for backgrounds and fills in CorelDraw documents, as well as custom designed Web pages.
- Over 1,000 photographs and floating objects saved as bitmaps and organized by category in folders. You can import them into your CorelDraw 9 projects using the Photos docker found on the Scrapbook fly-out on the Tools menu (see page 259).
- Hundreds of backgrounds and buttons that are ready for use in Web pages. With CorelDraw 9's Web tools and Web-ready art, including the Internet Bookmark Manager, HTML Conflict Analyzer docker, and Publish to Internet wizard, you can design and create documents, export them as HTML files, and get them up on the Web fast! (Turn to Chapter 17 to learn more about CorelDraw 9's Web features.)

Index

P

Index

T

What else would you like to see?

If I write a sequel to this book, what topics and features would you like me to cover? Send an e-mail to: CorelDraw9@bearhome.com